From Thought to Theme

A Rhetoric and Reader for College English

FOURTH EDITION

From Thought to Theme

A Rhetoric and Reader
for College English

FOURTH EDITION

William F. Smith
FULLERTON COLLEGE

Raymond D. Liedlich
CONTRA COSTA COLLEGE

HARCOURT BRACE JOVANOVICH, INC.

New York   Chicago   San Francisco   Atlanta

ISBN: 0-15-529211-0

Library of Congress Catalog Card Number: 73-17753

Printed in the United States of America

Preface

The purpose and plan of this fourth edition remain the same as those of its predecessors: to guide the student from thought to theme — to show through both precept and practice just how the raw materials of experience, ideas, and opinions can be shaped into clear and convincing expository or argumentative prose.

Part One, the Rhetoric, focuses initially on the paragraph, viewing it as a theme in miniature, and providing explicit and detailed discussions of unity, development, and coherence. The principles of sound thinking are then treated in clear and simple terms and applied to the writing process. The rhetoric section concludes with step-by-step instruction in composing the complete theme. More than seventy examples of paragraphs are used throughout Part One to illustrate each rhetorical principle as it is discussed. Most of these paragraphs have an intrinsic interest and are sufficiently self-contained to provide opportunities for discussion and writing. In addition to the examples, more than seventy-five exercises on tear-out sheets encourage immediate application of the material as it is studied.

Part Two, the Reader, contains thirty-two complete selections thematically and rhetorically arranged in eight groups. These essays may be used as sources for discussion, as subjects for rhetorical analysis, and as either points of departure or models for student writing. Most of the selections are brief, many of them short enough to be read and discussed in a single class meeting, and each of the eight sections offers varied points of view on a single subject.

The first three essays in each section are accompanied by introductory notes that point out rhetorical devices and techniques the student should look for in reading; related questions on language and rhetoric follow these selections. The questions and exercises for discussion and writing suggest numerous topics for student themes. The three indexes — Reading Selections by Rhetorical Type, Methods of Development, and Questions on Language and Rhetoric — permit a closer integration of the study of rhetorical principles with the reading of the selections.

Both the Rhetoric and the Reader concentrate on exposition and argumentation, since these are the forms of writing that are most essential to success in college and most commonly used thereafter. We have, however, given greater attention to personal narrative and description in the opening sections of the Reader, as these are usually more accessible modes for beginning college students.

The most significant change in this edition is an attempt to reconcile our usual thematic arrangement of readings with a rhetorical grouping as well. We have in a few instances obviously imposed some rather arbitrary classifications in order to do so, but we hope that such choices will be justified by the functional value of this new arrangement. One-third of the paragraphs in Part One are new to this edition; many of the exercises have been revised and approximately one-half include new material. Two-thirds of the essays in the Reader are new to this edition, and most of these have never before been anthologized. We now have a section on language and one on the media, more selections by women, and new discussions of problems and experiences of blacks and Native Americans.

Although it has become increasingly difficult to single out, and express our gratitude to, individuals, we are no less grateful to the many colleagues and students who have contributed in some way to this fourth edition — particularly those at Fullerton College, De Anza College, and Portland Community College. Over the years Merton Rapp of our publisher's staff has become a friend as well as an editor, and Dorothy Mott of the New York editorial office has given us invaluable assistance. Once again our appreciation goes to our wives, Dorothy and Martha, for their help in many ways, and our thanks to Anne and Steve, Terri and Bobbi.

We hope that instructors and students alike will find this fourth edition to be a useful and stimulating aid in the study of composition.

William F. Smith

Raymond D. Liedlich

Contents

PART TWO | Reader

PART ONE | **Rhetoric**

CHAPTER ONE | Unity

An essential quality of all good writing is *unity,* or singleness of purpose. The paragraph is a unit of thought concerned with the exposition of a single idea, and if it is to communicate that idea clearly and concisely, it must possess oneness. That is, all the detail—the reasons, illustrations, facts—used to develop it must pertain to one controlling idea. Consider, for example, the following paragraph:

One of the generalities most often noted about Americans is that we are a restless, a dissatisfied, a searching people. We bridle and buck under failure, and we go mad with dissatisfaction in the face of success. We spend our time searching for security, and hate it when we get it. For the most part we are an intemperate people: we eat too much when we can, drink too much, indulge our senses too much. Even in our so-called virtues we are intemperate: a teetotaler is not content not to drink—he must stop all the drinking in the world; a vegetarian among us would outlaw the eating of meat. We work too hard, and many die under the strain; and then to make up for that we play with a violence as suicidal. [From John Steinbeck, "Paradox and Dream," from *America and Americans,* The Viking Press, Inc., 1966.]

The controlling idea of this paragraph is contained in the first sentence, "One of the generalities most often noted about Americans is that we are a restless, a dissatisfied, a searching people," and the following sentences provide supporting detail. To illustrate his point, Steinbeck mentions several American traits. Americans fear failure, but are bored with success. They eat and drink too much, but the vegetarian wants to outlaw meat eating and the teetotaler the drinking of alcohol. To compensate for the strain of hard work, which kills many, they resort to play that is similarly destructive.

3

THE TOPIC SENTENCE

The sentence that expresses the controlling idea of a paragraph is called the *topic sentence*. In the paragraph above, it is the first sentence, the sentence on which the unity of the paragraph is based. An important first step in achieving paragraph unity is to express your thought in a topic sentence and place that sentence at the beginning of your paragraph. A beginning topic sentence provides an organizational focus, a guideline that will help you to stick to your subject. It will not guarantee paragraph unity, however. In the following paragraph, for example, the writer begins with a topic sentence, but it does not prevent his wandering off the subject.

Racial discrimination should be abolished in the United States. To discriminate against members of a minority racial group by denying them the right to vote, to attend nonsegregated schools, to live and work free of restrictions based on race alone is to make a mockery of the American ideal that all men are created equal. Furthermore, by continually fomenting social strife and tensions, such discrimination divides Americans at a time when solutions to pressing domestic and international problems demand their concerted efforts. One can understand the black's frustrations when he contemplates his second-class citizenship one hundred years after the Emancipation Proclamation. Nevertheless, the actions of some of the more militant black organizations, which advocate force and intimidation as the means to secure justice and equality, will hinder rather than advance their cause. Finally, racial discrimination in the United States impairs American efforts to lead the free world, a world containing hundreds of millions of people with colored skins.

In the first three sentences of this paragraph the writer stays on the subject. The second sentence presents a reason for abolishing racial discrimination: it makes a mockery of an American ideal. The third sentence adds another reason: domestic strife and social tensions prevent consideration of larger issues. But beginning with the fourth sentence, the writer strays from his controlling idea. From a consideration of the evils of racial discrimination, he turns to a particular type of racial discrimination, discrimination against blacks, and then to Negroes' tactics in the battle against prejudice. In the last sentence he returns to his main point: racial discrimination should be abolished at home because it hampers American foreign policy.

What has happened in this paragraph often happens in students' paragraphs. Although students place the topic sentence first and use it as a guide for supporting sentences, they may nevertheless insert irrelevant ideas. Why? One important reason is that they have not focused sharply enough on a controlling idea in the topic sentence. The topic sentence of the paragraph above seemed sufficiently broad to the writer to justify his comments on Negro tactics in the fight against discrimination. Had he narrowed the topic in his topic sentence and stressed a controlling idea, he would have been less likely to introduce extraneous ideas into the paragraph. Consider this revised version:

Racial discrimination in the United States should be abolished if this country is to live up to its expressed ideals and maintain its leadership of the free world. To discriminate against members of a minority racial group by denying them the right to vote, to attend nonsegregated schools, and to live and work free of restrictions based on race alone is to make a mockery of the traditional American ideal that all men are created equal. It is to flout a basic Christian doctrine—the brotherhood of man—in a nation that prides itself on its Christian heritage. Moreover, racial discrimination foments continual social and civil strife that divides Americans at a time when solutions to pressing domestic and international problems demand their concerted efforts. Such problems as stimulating the American economy, improving the quality of education, and maintaining adequate public services for an expanding population cannot be solved in a nation divided against itself. More important, however, when the attention of Americans is absorbed by internal problems, they cannot attend to larger issues—peace and survival in a world threatened by thermonuclear destruction. The assumption by the United States of the leadership of the free world in the struggle against an aggressive communism carries with it grave responsibilities, responsibilities it cannot hope to meet if the United States cannot prove its moral right to that leadership. And it will be difficult indeed to prove this right to hundreds of millions of Asians, Africans, and Latin Americans if the United States cannot eliminate racial discrimination within its own borders. To fulfill its promises to its own citizens and to its allies and friends in the world community, the United States should eliminate racial discrimination.

The topic sentence of this revised version is more pointed. To the original topic sentence, "Racial discrimination should be abolished in the United States," the clause "if this country is to live up to its expressed ideals and maintain its leadership of the free world" has been added. This new topic sentence stresses a controlling idea. It signals reader and writer alike that the paragraph will discuss why, in terms of the American democratic philosophy and present world conditions, racial discrimination in the United States should be abolished. The writer has now more tightly defined his subject, and he is therefore less likely to be tempted to introduce irrelevant matter.

THE CONTROLLING IDEA

Make certain, then, that your topic sentence contains a key word or group of words that expresses a controlling idea. Occasionally the entire topic sentence will be needed to express this idea, but more frequently it will be expressed in a word or phrase. A controlling idea will help you to limit your subject to one that you can deal with more completely in a paragraph and to avoid the kind of broad, general topic sentence that tempts students to include a variety of detail only loosely related to their central idea. Here are some examples of broad, general topic sentences with suggested revisions of them. Each revision sharpens the focus of the original sentence by stressing a controlling idea.

ORIGINAL	REVISED
To the Moon by J. Chapman is an interesting book.	*To the Moon* by J. Chapman presents an interesting account of the problems of landing a man on the moon.
Professional ice hockey is exciting.	Professional ice hockey is fiercely competitive.
Communism is evil.	Communism threatens man's individuality by restricting his freedom of expression.
Theodore Roosevelt was a good president.	Theodore Roosevelt did much to preserve the natural beauty of America.

The topic sentence of a paragraph may include more than one idea, as in the following sentence:

The study of psychology is *interesting* and *useful*.

The two ideas in this topic sentence could be developed, although briefly of course, in a single paragraph. The controlling idea in this next sentence, however, is too comprehensive for development in one paragraph:

America is a *democratic society* based on a system of *free enterprise*, which emphasizes *individual initiative*.

Adequate development of the ideas in this sentence would require several paragraphs, for each of the italicized terms would have to be explained and illustrated. To attempt such a discussion in a single paragraph would create serious problems in unity, especially for an inexperienced writer.

EXERCISE 1

Underline the topic sentence in each of the following paragraphs.

1. Women, in short, are fundamentally more resistant than men. With the exception of the organ systems subserving the functions of reproduction women suffer much less frequently than men from the serious disorders which affect mankind. With the exception of India women everywhere live longer than men. For example, the expectation of life of the female child of white parentage in the United States at the present time is over seventy-one years, whereas for the male it is only sixty-five and a half years. Women are both biologically stronger and emotionally better shock absorbers than men. The myth of masculine superiority once played such havoc with the facts that in the nineteenth century it was frequently denied by psychiatrists that the superior male could ever suffer from hysteria. Today it is fairly well known that males suffer from hysteria and hysteriform conditions with a preponderance over the female of seven to one! Epilepsy is much more frequent in males, and stuttering has an incidence of eight males to one female. [From Ashley Montagu, "The Natural Superiority of Women," *Saturday Review,* March 1, 1952, p. 28. Copyright 1952 The Saturday Review Associates, Inc.]

2. Those who get disturbed about slang as something "modern" that is "corrupting" the language ought to know that it is as old as language itself. Indeed, it *is* language, and one of the minor pleasures of reading is to come across it in the literature of the past. Chaucer, for instance, uses *gab* exactly as we use it today. A desirable woman was a *piece* in the 14th century, and a *broad* or a *frail* in the 16th. Bishop Latimer, in a sermon before Edward VI (1547), said that those who had defrauded the king of money ought to "make restitution . . . *cough up.*" John Adams, in a morning-after letter (1774), said, "We drank sentiments until 11 o'clock. Lee and Harrison were very *high.*" Charlotte Brontë referred to a foolish person as a *sap*—as others had been doing for 200 years before her. [From Bergen Evans, "Now Everyone Is Hip About Slang," *The New York Times,* March 22, 1964, p. 22. © 1964 by The New York Times Company. Reprinted by permission.]

3. This racial struggle of ours in America has so many intricate and amusing angles that nobody taking an active part in it can ever be bored. Its very variety from North to South—from Boston where New England Negroes side with New England whites in opposing black southern migration, to Mobile on the Gulf where a Negro dare not oppose anybody—keeps the contest exciting. In the far West a Negro can sometimes eat in a Mexican restaurant but he cannot eat in a Chinese restaurant—so it is fun figuring out just where you can eat. In some towns a colored man can sit in the balcony of a theatre, but in others he has to sit in the last three rows on the left downstairs because the balcony is for whites who smoke. So, trying to see a movie in the United States can be for a Negro as intriguing as working a crossword puzzle. [From Langston Hughes, "The Fun of Being Black," *The Langston Hughes Reader,* George Braziller, Inc., 1958. Reprinted by permission of Harold Ober Associates, Inc.]

4. The meat was eaten fresh, or dried in the sun, pounded, and mixed with berries to make pemmican. The tanned hides were fashioned into moccasins and leggings, dresses and shirts, and summer coverings for beds. The thick robes made snug blankets for winter, and the scraped hides were stitched together to cover tepees. Rawhide was used in trunks and containers, cooking pots, ropes, quivers, and saddles. Warriors took the thick, tough hide from a bull's neck to make shields. Hoofs were boiled to obtain glue; horns provided spoons and ladles. Rib bones formed sled runners; other bones served as tools; sinew made bowstrings. Thick woolly bison hair stuffed medicine balls, and the beard decorated bows and lances. Nothing was wasted—even the tail found use as a whip or fly swatter. [From Robert M. McClung, "Bison, Monarch of the Plains," *Wild Animals of North America,* National Geographic Society, 1960, pp. 98–99.]

5. Man is but a reed, the weakest thing in nature, but he is a reed that thinks. It is not necessary that the whole universe should arm itself to crush him. A vapor, a drop of water, is enough to kill him. But if the universe should crush him, man would still be nobler than that which slays him, for he knows that he dies; but of the advantage which it has over him the universe knows nothing. Our dignity consists, then, wholly in thought. Our elevation must come from this, not from space and time, which we cannot fill. Let us, then, labor to think well: this is the fundamental principle of morals. [From Blaise Pascal, *Pensées.*]

EXERCISE 2

A. The controlling idea of a topic sentence is the key word or group of words that expresses its basic idea. In the following topic sentences circle the word or words that contain the controlling idea.

EXAMPLE   A dictionary is a (useful) book for a college student.

1. At least three easily distinguishable kinds of college professors can be found on American campuses today.

2. The practice of civil disobedience to effect political and social changes involves serious consequences both for the practitioner and the larger society.

3. Young people can be of great help to a political campaigner.

4. Good English is clear, appropriate, and vivid.

5. Filling out a federal income tax form is a bewildering and frustrating experience.

6. Richard Wagner, the great composer, was in many ways an unscrupulous man.

7. The modern whaling ship is more elaborate than its predecessor in the nineteenth century.

8. Sociologists point to a number of causes for student protest in the 1960s.

9. The value of a person in contemporary America is frequently a matter of economic rather than moral considerations.

10. The word *classic* has a variety of meanings.

B. Revise the following topic sentences to narrow the focus and stress a dominant idea.

EXAMPLE

ORIGINAL   The new Carter automobile is a fine car.
REVISION   Superior workmanship, beautiful design, and economic operation make the new Carter a fine automobile.

1. Some students have an easy time in college.

_____

_____

2. The proposal to abolish traditional marriage ties for a short-term renewable contract is foolish.

_____

_____

3. Advertising often has a bad influence on people.

_____

_____

4. A primary cause for the so-called generation gap in many families is a teen-ager's language.

_____

_____

5. Foreign travel is good for Americans.

_____

_____

6. If the American economy is to continue to function well, both labor and management will have to be controlled.

_____

_____

7. The new X-109 Martin roadster is a fantastic car.

_____

_____

8. Governmental attempts to force journalists to reveal their sources should be resisted.

_____

_____

9. Professor Daugherty's latest book, _Inside Australia's Outback,_ is an interesting study.

_____

_____

10. The transportation system in this country will have to be redesigned.

_____

_____

PRIMARY AND SECONDARY SUPPORTING DETAIL

When your topic sentence is somewhat complicated, you will often have to develop your paragraph more extensively than when your topic sentence is simple. In this case, some of your sentences will contain more important ideas than others. That is, the detail in some sentences will directly support the controlling idea, whereas the detail in other sentences will explain and clarify these direct supporting statements. We can thus conveniently distinguish between *primary* support—detail that relates directly to the main idea of the paragraph —and *secondary* support—detail that explains and clarifies primary support. In the following paragraph the topic idea is supported by a number of primary statements, each of which relates directly to the controlling idea of the topic sentence—the benefits to wild animals of forest fires.

Countless animals and plants rely upon fire to maintain habitats in a healthy state. Deer rest and feed in the open spaces cleared by fire in and around forests. Elk once wintered in valleys kept clear by fire. Many shore birds, waterfowl, and songbirds need treeless spaces to feed and nest; cattail marshes, if unburned, become impenetrable for the herons and rails that live there. Muskrat catches in the productive areas of Louisiana and Maryland fell dramatically after Smokey the Bear prevented the trappers' customary burning of decadent vegetation after each season. Woodcocks and quail cannot forage on a forest floor that accumulates more than about six inches of litter, and their numbers are dropping in fire-free areas. [From Richard J. Vogl, "Smokey's Mid-Career Crisis." Copyright 1973 by Saturday Review Co. First appeared in *Saturday Review*, March 1973, p. 27. Used with permission.]

In this next paragraph the topic sentence is supported by two primary statements and three secondary statements.

I have come to marvel at the instinct of animals to make use of natural laws for healing themselves. They know unerringly which herbs will cure what ills. Wild creatures first seek solitude and absolute relaxation, then they rely on the complete remedies of Nature—the medicine in plants and pure air. A bear grubbing for fern roots; a wild turkey compelling her babies in a rainy spell to eat leaves of the spice bush; an animal, bitten by a poisonous snake, confidently chewing snakeroot—all these are typical examples. An animal with fever quickly hunts up an airy, shady place near water, there remaining quiet, eating nothing but drinking often until its health is recovered. On the other hand, an animal bedeviled by rheumatism finds a spot of hot sunlight and lies in it until the misery bakes out. [From D. C. Jarvis, *Folk Medicine*, p. 10. Holt, Rinehart and Winston, Inc.]

An analysis of each of these two paragraphs illuminates this difference between primary and secondary supporting statements.

CONTROLLING IDEA
Countless animals and plants rely upon fire to maintain habitats in a healthy state.

Primary Support
1. Deer rest and feed in spaces cleared by fire.
2. Elk spent the winters in valleys kept clear by fire.
3. Birds need treeless spaces to feed and nest and herons and rails need to be able to penetrate cattail marshes for a living place.
4. The muskrat population in Louisiana and Maryland declined because fire had not burned off decadent vegetation.
5. Woodcocks and quail need [clean] forest floors [floors that are] kept clean of litter by fire.

CONTROLLING IDEA
Animals have an instinct for using natural laws to heal themselves.

Primary Support
1. Animals know unerringly which herbs will cure what ills.
2. They first seek solitude and absolute relaxation and then rely on natural remedies—the medicine in plants and pure air.

   Secondary Support
   A bear grubbing for fern roots; a wild turkey compelling her babies in a rainly spell to eat leaves of the spice bush; an animal, bitten by a poisonous snake, chewing snakeroot—all are typical examples.
   An animal with fever quickly hunts up an airy, shady place near water where it remains quiet, eating nothing but drinking often until its health is recovered.
   An animal troubled by rheumatism lies in hot sunlight to bake out its misery.

When you have decided on a topic sentence, then, examine its controlling idea carefully. If it is fairly complex, you will probably need both primary and secondary support to develop it adequately. The writer of the following paragraph uses both primary and secondary support to develop his controlling idea.

The most dangerous members of our society are those grown-ups whose powers of influence are adult but whose motives and responses are infantile. The adult has certain kinds of power denied to the infant. He has physical strength. If he still hits out at life with the anger of a frustrated infant, he can work more destruction and inflict more pain than would be possible to the person physically immature. In the second place, he has authority over someone: he is parent, teacher, employer, foreman, officer of a club, public official, or perhaps simply a member of a majority group that is permitted to keep members of a minority group "in their place." Few adults are without authority over anyone. The adult, therefore, whose emotional linkages with life are still undeveloped has a greater power to make other people miserable than has the child. In the third place, the adult has a vastly increased opportunity to add artificial to natural power through such devices as ownership and membership. He can drive a car and use its strength as his own; he can join an organization and use the influence of numerous others to press a cause he could not effectively press alone. If his linkages of knowledge and feeling are still as few and tenuous as those that fit the power-status of a five-year-old or even a ten-year-old, he can do harm beyond measure. [Reprinted from *The Mature Mind* by H. A. Overstreet. By permission of W. W. Norton & Company, Inc. Copyright 1949 © 1959 by W. W. Norton & Company, Inc.]

The controlling idea of this paragraph is contained in the first two sentences: adults whose motives and responses are infantile are dangerous to society because they possess certain kinds of power denied to the infant. Three primary supporting statements are used to support the topic idea. What are they? Which sentences provide illustration and clarification of these primary statements? A clear understanding of the way this paragraph is assembled should provide practical guidance when you find that you have to supply more than primary support to develop an idea in a paragraph.

This discussion of primary and secondary detail is intended to clarify a basic characteristic of the structure of the expository or argumentative paragraph. As you will discover in your reading and writing, however, this distinction is not precisely applicable to every paragraph of this type. Every sentence of such a paragraph does not necessarily add a new primary or secondary supporting detail. Some sentences, particularly those at the beginning of a paragraph that is part of a longer composition, may refer to an idea developed in a preceding paragraph. Other sentences may simply repeat, as a means of emphasis, an idea in a preceding sentence of the same paragraph.

In the following excerpt from T. S. Matthews' "What Makes News," for example, the first three sentences of the second paragraph deal with one idea—the putative power of the press to influence public opinion. The first sentence, "In what way is the press supposed to be so powerful?" iterates the thought of the topic sentence of the preceding paragraph and thus serves to link these two paragraphs together. The next sentence, "The general notion is that the press can form, control, or at least strongly influence public opinion," expands upon the idea of the preceding sentence by elucidating the "way" in which the press is thought to exert its power. And the third sentence, "Can it really do any of these things?" contains the controlling idea that the following sentences develop.

Topic Sentence

The biggest piece of claptrap about the press is that it deals exclusively, or even mainly, with news. *And the next biggest piece of claptrap is that the press has enormous power.* This delusion is persistent and widespread. It is taken for granted by the public-at-large, who are apt to be impressed by anything that is said three times; it is continually advertised by the press itself; and it is cherished by press lords, some of whom, at least, should know better.

Linking Sentence

Topic Sentence

(1) In what way is the press supposed to be so powerful? (2) The general notion is that the press can form, control, or at least strongly influence public opinion. (3) *Can it really do any of these things?* Hugh Cudlipp, editorial director of the London *Daily Mirror,* and a man who should know something about the effect of newspapers on public opinion, doesn't share this general notion about their power. He thinks newspapers can echo and stimulate a wave of popular feeling, but that's all: "A newspaper may successfully accelerate but never reverse the popular attitude, which common sense has commended to the public." In short, it can jump aboard the bandwagon, once the bandwagon is under way, but it can't start the bandwagon rolling or change its direction once it has started. [From T. S. Matthews, "What Makes News," *The Atlantic Monthly,* December, 1957, p. 82. Copyright © 1957 by T. S. Matthews. Reprinted by permission of the author.]

EXERCISE 3

A. In the following exercise a topic sentence and three sentences containing primary support are supplied as material for a paragraph. Supply the necessary secondary support in the blanks provided.

TOPIC SENTENCE The rapid growth in world population will create serious problems for mankind.

Primary Support
1. A larger population will hamper efforts to control pollution of the air and water.

   Secondary Support

   a. _____

   _____

   b. _____

   _____

Primary Support
2. The economies of several underdeveloped nations will be adversely affected by an expanding population.

   Secondary Support

   a. _____

   _____

   b. _____

   _____

Primary Support
3. An increase in population will lead to a decrease in living and recreational space.

   Secondary Support

   a. _____

   _____

   b. _____

   _____

B. Read the following paragraph carefully and analyze it, following the examples of paragraph analysis presented on page 14. That is, write out its controlling idea and the primary and secondary supporting sentences.

Families who like to go camping can now choose from a variety of recreation vehicles, each one designed to meet a specific need. For the family that regularly takes long vacations every summer, in addition to monthly treks to the mountains or seashore, and wants a good deal of comfort and convenience, the motor home is a good choice. Prices range from approximately $7,000 to $20,000 — the higher the cost, the greater the luxury. The basic advantage of the motor home is that it is self-contained and comfortable. All the fuss and inconvenience usually connected with setting up and taking down camping gear is eliminated. Families that take an occasional outing in the woods on a weekend, of course, would not need the fancy motor home. For them the converted van or the pickup camper would suffice. Like the motor home, the van provides self-contained eating and sleeping — but not bathing — facilities. It would, however, be a bit crowded for a large family. The pickup camper has similar facilities, but it is usually roomier. And the smaller size camper, because it has a more durable suspension system, is more suitable for rough terrain. The camper-trailer opens up to form a tent-like covering for shelter. It fits the needs of hardy campers, those who do not demand so much comfort but who do want more than a ground-level tent between them and the elements. The variety of recreation vehicles now available makes it possible for most camping families to choose a vehicle that fits their camping needs and their budget.

CONTROLLING IDEA _____

_____

Primary Support and *Secondary Support*

_____

_____

_____

_____

_____

_____

PLACEMENT OF THE TOPIC SENTENCE

We have suggested that you place the topic sentence first. This advice is especially valid for inexperienced writers, for a beginning topic sentence provides the best guideline and the most effective check against irrelevant matter. However, as you gain skill and experience in writing lucid, well-developed paragraphs, you may occasionally wish to place the topic sentence elsewhere. For example, you may use it not to announce your topic but to summarize it. In this case you would place it at the end of the paragraph, as the writer of the following paragraph does:

Within the past thirty years, Americans have become increasingly more mobile, increasingly more addicted to moving around. According to a recent study, an American family changes its residence on the average of once every five years. Approximately forty million Americans change their address every year. The number of American living in mobile homes has also grown dramatically. Each year more and more people are lured by the prospect of being able to move their homes to other neighborhoods, cities, or states with a minimum of fuss. The effect of this heavy internal migration, however, has been to disrupt and uproot family life and to make personal loyalties and commitments to community organizations and affairs more tenuous. Frequent movement breeds anonymity and indifference to others. It increases personal isolation and loss of identity. Some observers, in fact, attribute the increase in crime, divorce rates, alcoholism, drug addiction, loss of interest in local politics and community affairs, and a general voter disenchantment with and distrust of political and social institutions to the loss of personal and community contacts caused by this shifting population. American mobility, consequently, needs to be reexamined. By contributing to an alienation and weakening of social values, it is creating a serious problem for the health and stability of American life.

Another method is to begin and close with a topic sentence.

Clearly, there is no need of bringing on wars in order to breed heroes. Civilized life affords plenty of opportunities for heroes, and for a better kind than war or any other savagery has ever produced. Moreover, none but lunatics would set a city on fire in order to give opportunities for heroism to firemen, or introduce the cholera or yellow fever to give physicians and nurses opportunities for practicing disinterested devotion, or condemn thousands of people to extreme poverty in order that some well-to-do persons might practice a beautiful charity. It is equally crazy to advocate war on the ground that it is a school for heroes. [From Charles W. Eliot, "Five American Contributions to Civilization," *The Oxford Book of American Essays,* ed. Brander Mathews, The Century Company, 1914.]

In some paragraphs you may need two sentences to express your central idea. In the following paragraph the first two sentences convey the main idea, that memorizing rules of punctuation will not automatically ensure good writing.

Many rules have been formulated for the use of the various marks of punctuation, and people have thought that by simply memorizing these rules they might find a key to good writing. Unfortunately, as teachers of punctuation will be among the first to point out, this is not the case. By acting as a visual aid, punctuation can help one to comprehend a carefully thought piece of writing, but it cannot supply meaning. If a written composition, be it a letter, set of directions, or a critical essay, seems to lack precision and directness, the writer will do well to consider first of all whether it is properly organized, not whether it is properly punctuated. Ordinarily, meaningful and well-organized writing is not hard to punctuate. One's style of punctuation is generally determined by the type and purpose of the writing. Compared to a sports story in the daily paper, a treatise on physics will be marked by more complex constructions, and, accordingly, a greater amount of punctuation. This does not mean that one kind or style of punctuation is better than another. It simply indicates that the precise distinctions in thought and meaning which concern the scholar and scientist require more detailed, complex statement, and hence more detailed and complex punctuation, than the factual, comparatively simple story of a baseball game. The former type of writing is designed to compress a maximum amount of exact and complicated information within a limited space. The purpose of the latter is to provide a simple, easily readable account which will entertain and inform its readers. In both instances, the punctuation has the same function: to aid the writer in conveying his particular message to his readers. Punctuation that performs this function is "good" punctuation; when punctuation fails to realize this aim it is faulty. [From the *Thorndike-Barnhart Comprehensive Desk Dictionary* by E. L. Thorndike and Clarence L. Barnhart. Copyright © 1965 by Scott, Foresman and Company. Reprinted by permission of the publisher.]

The topic sentence of this next paragraph is the fourth sentence, "But this does not go down to the roots of American society. . . ." The first three sentences lead into this sentence, and the sentences following it develop its controlling idea, the masculine nature of American society.

   During the last 50 years American women, chiefly through inheritance, have come to possess a formidable amount of economic power. This is a country of rich widows. The extent of their influence has helped to create this legend that women are in charge. But this does not go down to the roots of American society, does not change its fundamental character: It is still dominated by the masculine and not the feminine principle. How do I know? Well, here is a quite simple test. At the present time America possesses sufficient instruments of destruction to kill every man, woman and child on earth. This macabre achievement, which has demanded an astonishing amount of technical skill and superb organization and the expenditure of billions and billions of dollars, not only represents the masculine principle triumphantly asserting itself but also suggests the male mind coming to the end of its tether. Where is the feminine principle, where is Woman, in this madness? Where is the feminine emphasis here upon love, on the happiness of persons? Is this how women want their money spent? We have only to ask the question to know the answer. Here is a society shaped and colored by male values. It is about as much like a matriarchy as the Marine Corps. [From J. B. Priestley, "Women Don't Run the Country," *The Saturday Evening Post,* December 12, 1964. Reprinted with permission from *The Saturday Evening Post* © 1964 The Curtis Publishing Company.]

In some paragraphs, particularly narrative and descriptive paragraphs, the topic idea may be implied rather than explicitly stated. The implied topic idea of the paragraph below is a description of a storm. Notice how carefully Samuel Clemens, through the character of Huck Finn, selects and groups his visual and audio details to render a unified impression of the storm:

   We spread the blankets inside for a carpet, and eat our dinner in there. We put all the other things handy at the back of the cavern. Pretty soon it darkened up and begun to thunder and lighten; so the birds was right about it. Directly it begun to rain, and it rained like all fury, too, and I never see the wind blow so. It was one of these regular summer storms. It would get so dark that it looked all blue-black outside, and lovely; and the rain would thrash along by so thick that the trees off a little ways looked dim and spider-webby; and here would come a blast of wind that would bend the trees down and turn up the pale underside of the leaves; and then a perfect ripper of a gust would follow along and set the branches to tossing their arms as if they was just wild; and next, when it was just about the bluest and blackest—fst! It was as bright as glory and you'd have a little glimpse of tree-tops a-plunging about, away off yonder in the storm, hundreds of yards further than you could see before; dark as sin again in a second, and how you'd hear the thunder let go with an awful crash and then go rumbling, grumbling, tumbling down the sky towards the underside of the world, like rolling empty barrels down stairs, where it's long stairs and they bounce a good deal, you know. [From Samuel L. Clemens, *The Adventures of Huckleberry Finn*, Chapter 9.]

THE CONCLUDING SENTENCE

Be careful not to introduce a new idea or point of view at the end of your paragraph. Under pressure to develop an idea fully, students occasionally add in the final sentence an idea that is only loosely related to the controlling idea and so dissipate the unified impression they have labored to effect. Consider, for example, the following paragraph:

A number of methods for combating juvenile delinquency are currently in use. Some cities punish the parents or guardians of juvenile delinquents by fining or arresting them. The potential delinquent, presumably, would think twice before breaking the law if he knew his mother would be jailed for his crime. In other cities a curfew forbids youths under eighteen to be on the streets after 11 P.M. The National Recreation Association recommends organized leisure-time activities for youths as the best preventative against delinquency. Providing attractive recreational facilities and interesting programs, it is hoped, will keep youngsters off the streets and divert their energies into more constructive channels. A fourth method, the most common, places the juvenile offender in a correctional institution, a reformatory, where an attempt is made to rehabilitate him. All these methods of treating juvenile delinquency have one thing in common—they have all failed. Perhaps the best solution to the problem would be to reestablish a program like the Civilian Conservation Corps that operated in the 1930s.

The writer's purpose in this paragraph, explained in the first sentence, is to discuss various methods for dealing with juvenile delinquency; and in fulfillment of this purpose he describes four methods. In the last sentence, however, he disrupts the unity of this paragraph and weakens his effect by proposing his own solution to juvenile delinquency, the reestablishment of a program similar to the CCC of the depression years. This solution is, clearly, not among the methods currently used to combat juvenile delinquency, and it therefore does not belong in this paragraph. The writer should have reserved it for treatment in another paragraph.

One final suggestion: if you are writing a single paragraph, especially one that is rather long or complex, you can improve its unity by reinforcing the controlling idea in your concluding sentence, as does the writer of the following paragraph:

What have the American intellectuals done to acquire in their country the position of authority and respect which they say the intellectual enjoys in Europe? They are serious in their own professions. If they are novelists or playwrights, they write good novels and plays. Physicists and chemists do excellent work in the world's finest laboratories. The jurists define the law. And so it goes. But are they truly aware of the additional responsibility which may lead them to questions which require answers on a universal level — that is, the level of intelligence itself? In general, I do not think so. Recently I dared to suggest mildly that American novelists ought to feel a somewhat deeper responsibility to their country for the false picture which the world has of her. I was answered by a whole concert of indignant replies — as if I had set fire to the temple of Minerva with my own hand. Well, let me repeat the offense. It is my conviction that the American intellectuals have an immense sin of omission on their conscience, and that it has poisoned their whole lives. [From Raymond-Leopold Bruckberger, "An Assignment for Intellectuals," *Harper's Magazine*, February, 1956. Copyright 1956 by Raymond-Leopold Bruckberger. Reprinted by permission of Harold Matson Co.]

EXERCISE 4

A. In the following exercise there are three topic sentences, accompanied by a number of supporting sentences. Some of the accompanying sentences directly support the controlling idea of the topic sentence; others are irrelevant. Eliminate the irrelevant sentences and organize the remainder into a paragraph, adding whatever detail may be necessary.

1. Living abroad is becoming increasingly popular with Americans today.

   a. Some seek escape from the hurry and worry of contemporary American life, the rat race for material rewards.
   b. They seek the more leisurely, culturally richer life; they hope to find this in such cities as Paris, Rome, Vienna, and Brussels.
   c. The rapid growth in American business interests abroad has dramatically increased the size of American "colonies" in foreign countries in recent years.
   d. In fact, American businessmen and their families comprise the largest single group of Americans living abroad.
   e. The influx of American products and institutions has not been universally welcomed by the people of the host countries.
   f. European critics complain that this new American "invasion" is corrupting European life.
   g. The current American businessman or tourist, however, is a great improvement over his predecessor of a generation ago.
   h. A third group consists of United States government employees, technical experts, researchers, and so forth, those sent abroad to administer foreign aid programs and to provide technical assistance to underdeveloped nations.
   i. And, finally, college-age youths travel abroad to study, to loaf or relax before getting a job, or simply to enjoy the fun of travel.

2. Conventional standards governing sexual behavior in the United States have been liberalized in recent years.

   a. Evidence of a new sexual permissiveness is evident in the entertainment world.
   b. Former sexual taboos in the motion picture industry have been relaxed to the point that the sex act itself is displayed on the screen.
   c. Sexual references and racy language are much more common in television movies today than they were a few years ago.
   d. Film critics disagree about the artistic value of explicit sex in motion pictures.
   e. Some critics believe explicit sex in films is a sign of health and maturity.
   f. Some critics see the presentation of explicit sex as harmful to the public and damaging to the motion picture as an art form.
   g. A few years ago bars and cocktail lounges created a stir by offering topless waitresses and dancers; today they provide bottomless dancers, as well.
   h. It is not unusual to read about motion-picture actresses who have given

birth to children out of wedlock and who, moreover, reject the idea of formal marriage ties to legitimize the birth.

    i. Traditional attitudes about marriage have been affected; premarital and extramarital sex are more common.

    j. The percentage of illegitimate births has risen.

    k. A more casual attitude toward sex is evident among the young on college campuses.

    l. College infirmaries and clinics now dispense birth control pills to coeds as a regular service.

    m. This liberalizing of sexual mores in the United States may be a healthy sign, a sign that Americans are finally throwing off a repressive attitude toward sex inherited from the Puritans; but it may also be a sign of sickness and decadence.

3. The teacher performs a vital function in our culture today.

    a. He performs an essential socializing task by helping the child move from the self-contained world of his family to the wider world of his school and community.

    b. The child must learn to work and play harmoniously in the larger group, adjusting to the environment of a wider social activity, if he is to acquire the foundation for a happy, useful life in a democracy.

    c. As the child matures, his teacher helps him to develop a receptive attitude toward intellectual pursuits as well as social activities, to respect and respond to the life of the mind.

    d. He is largely responsible for transmitting the cultural heritage, the essential knowledge about the political, social, and cultural institutions of his country and of the world.

    e. He teaches each student to discover and develop his own special talents, to acquire vocational skills.

    f. When he is dedicated to his task, he can strongly influence the moral life of his students.

    g. He can help them develop a sound philosophy of life.

    h. Yet, in spite of the admitted importance of the teacher in our society, his calling is not always valued.

    i. He earns considerably less than other professionals—lawyers, doctors, dentists, engineers—and in many states, no more than skilled tradesmen or factory workers.

    j. The future of this nation, its place in the community of nations as well as the happiness and well-being of its citizens, is in no small way dependent on how well the teacher performs his function.

B. In the following paragraphs the beginning topic sentences have been omitted. Read each paragraph carefully, and then construct a sentence that conveys the main idea of the paragraph.

1. One of the most serious problems affecting these programs is inflation: rising costs of medicine, depreciation of funds available for construction of facilities, increase in doctors' fees. In Sweden, for example, a free, compre-

hensive dental service enacted by the government had to be revised and the patient forced to pay 50 percent of the bill. Costs for health care have risen sharply in Denmark, Holland, and France as well. Holland even had to suspend medical education temporarily because of lack of money. Another problem is the inevitable bureaucratic ineptness. European critics contend that too much of the doctor's time is spent in filling out forms rather than in administering to the sick, and, as a result, patients must wait longer to see a doctor. Free or inexpensive medicines have resulted in an increase in their use, and the cost of processing prescriptions has risen. Government-backed health programs are not about to collapse in Europe, but they are beset with serious problems that demand attention if the high quality of European medical care is to be maintained.

2. First, violence is self-defeating and counterproductive. It creates a mood of repressiveness in Congress, in state legislatures, and in the majority of people, a mood that makes more peaceful, enduring solutions to social problems more difficult to achieve. True, violence may produce some temporary benefits as a result of heightened public awareness of the plight of the poor and the dispossessed, yet in the long run it engenders a backlash, a stiffening of resistance to needed changes in many persons' attitudes toward the rights of minority groups. Second, violence could destroy the whole social fabric of America, and with it, of course, any hope for progress. Any group that justifies violence in support of its own "sincere," "unselfish" aims either ignores or forgets that other groups can do the same. Violence in support of "freedom" will also be used in defense of "order" with tragic consequences.

3. Even the flimsiest compact or sports auto has a wall of sheet metal and a heavy engine and frame to cushion or absorb glancing blows and head-on collisions. The cyclist swaps this armor for speed and maneuverability, and an overwhelming enjoyment of road feel and wind-in-the-face motion — wheeling out just for the hell of it. A motorist rides inside his machine, a cyclist sits astride his. You're closer to the road on a bike and, consequently, closer to its hazards. Sand, gravel, wind, rain, and other drivers are not just annoyances or discomforts, they're physical enemies; in the wrong circumstances they can effectively cause you no end of grief and a long insurance settlement. [From "How to Avoid Killing Yourself" by the Editors of *Esquire*, November, 1965.]

4. What would a society without language be like? It would of course have no writing or other means of communication by words, for all these are ultimately dependent on spoken speech. Our means of learning would therefore be greatly restricted. We should be obliged, like the animals, to learn by doing or by observing the actions of others. All of history would disappear, for without language there would be no way of re-creating past experiences and communicating them to others. We should have no means of expressing our thoughts and ideas to others or of sharing in the mental processes of our fellow-men. Indeed, it is very likely that we should not think at all. Many psychologists maintain that thought itself requires the use of language, that the process of thinking is really talking things over with ourselves. [From Harry Hoijer, "Language in Culture," from *Man, Culture, and Society,* ed. Harry L. Shapiro. Copyright © 1956 by Oxford University Press, Inc. Reprinted by permission.]

C. Examine the following paragraphs for unity and be prepared to point out the specific weakness of those that lack unity and to explain how they might be improved. Check to see that each sentence in the paragraph supports a controlling idea in a topic sentence. As an aid here, enclose the topic sentence of each paragraph in brackets and underline its controlling idea. In those paragraphs that contain primary and secondary support, make certain that each primary statement directly develops the controlling idea and that each secondary statement provides a relevant explanation or clarification of each primary statement. As an aid here, place a capital P before each primary statement and a capital S before each secondary statement.

1. _____Professional boxing should be banned because it is brutal and unsportsmanlike. _____Boxing is the art of attack and defense, with the fists protected by padded gloves. _____It is the art of hitting an opponent without getting hit yourself. _____Good boxing takes control and coordination. _____Pugilism was the first form of boxing. _____It differs from modern boxing because the fist was not padded. _____Boxing in its modern form began in 1866, when the public became disgusted with the brutality of pugilism.

2. _____I decided to attend Banning College for three reasons. _____I

had spent hours talking with my parents and my high-school counselor before making up my mind. _____These hours were not wasted because I am now certain Banning College is the ideal school for me. _____First, it has fine facilities. __5__I plan to study chemical engineering, and Banning's new science and engineering buildings have the latest and best equipment. __P__Second, it has a distinguished faculty. __5__My father is a mechanical engineer, and he says that I will be studying under recognized leaders in the field. __P__Finally, Banning is less expensive than comparable colleges I have investigated. __5__And expense is an important consideration today. __5__Even with the help my parents can provide, I will have to earn part of my tuition by waiting on tables. __1__Working one's way through college, however, is not a disadvantage. __1__Students who have to support themselves while in college get more out of their education. __2__They learn self-reliance and independence. __P__For these reasons, then—facilities, faculty, and expense—I have made up my mind to attend Banning College.

3. _____The college freshman faces a number of problems as he begins college work. _____If he is not able to solve them, the results can be disastrous. _____The most serious problem he faces concerns his studies. _____If he has not learned good study habits in high school, he will be in serious trouble in college, for the range and intensity of college-level subjects make great demands on a student's capacity for concentration. _____Every college student should have a place to study that has adequate lighting and that is in a quiet environment. _____He should not try to study while the radio is blaring or the television set is on. _____The college freshman must also learn to budget his time wisely, or he is likely to find that he has concentrated on one or two subjects to the detriment of others. _____Another problem the freshman faces concerns extracurricular activities. _____An incoming student sometimes finds himself tempted to attend a dance, a football rally, or a fraternity party when he should be studying. _____Yet, unless

29

he achieves self-discipline, he may find himself on probation after his first semester. _____Some students, however, seem to need the threat of expulsion to succeed. _____Finally, the freshman must learn to adjust to the rigors of college competition. _____Students who have excelled in their high-school studies become frustrated and depressed when they do not achieve on a similar level in college. _____This keener competition that the freshman faces can, if he adapts himself to it calmly, lead him to a mature understanding of his abilities and limitations. _____Unhappily, it may also lead to serious emotional upset if he sets unrealistically high academic goals for himself.

4. *1. 5.* The serious depletion of oil and natural gas reserves in the United States has prompted investigation of a number of new sources of energy. *P*_____One of the most promising of these is the fast breeder nuclear reactor. _____*S* The conventional nuclear power plant taps only 1 percent of the energy produced by the splitting (fission) of uranium atoms; and uranium 235, the fuel used, is scarce. ____*S* The fast breeder reactor, however, by a process of transforming uranium into plutonium, produces more fuel than it consumes and therefore virtually eliminates the problem of the scarcity of nuclear fuel. _____*P* An even more fantastic machine now being experimented with is the fusion reactor. ____*S* It combines heavy hydrogen atoms to produce helium atoms, releasing nuclear energy that can be converted into electricity. *S*_____ Because the fusion reactor uses for fuel an element contained in sea water, the successful development of this device would solve man's energy problems for a long, long time. *P*_____Other promising sources of energy are contained in sunlight, subsurface heat, ocean tides, and everyday trash. _____*S* Various experiments are under way to trap sunlight to create heat energy that can be used in boiler turbines to produce electric current. ____*S* Geothermal power is produced by drilling holes into the earth and forcing cold water into one hole. ____*S* As it comes into contact with hot rock four or five miles below the surface, the water is heated and fractures the rock. _____*S* The hot water then rises to the surface in another hole and is used to drive a turbine to produce electricity. ____*S* In several regions of the world,

the ebb and flow of the tides could be harnessed to produce electrical power, as they are on the Rance River estuary in France. _____And, finally, the lowly trash Americans accumulate in ever-increasing quantities, about two and one-half billion tons a year, should not be overlooked. _____Experts estimate that if it were burned in power plants, enough electricity could be generated to take care of 50 percent of this country's current energy needs.

5. _____Critics of America's space exploration program have often described it as an irresponsible, expensive operation that soaks up public funds that could be put to better use, but this view overlooks many substantial achievements of the program. _____Communications satellites have, for example, greatly improved international communication. _____On-the-spot television broadcasting of the 1972 Olympics in West Germany dramatically increased interest in the games throughout the world. _____Space satellites are also being used to discover mineral resources, to monitor air and water pollution, and to provide better understanding and prediction of the weather. _____The space program has vastly increased man's knowledge. _____The Apollo Program, in particular, has provided much information about the history and formation of the moon, and other programs have provided similar information about other planets. _____Space technology has made possible the development and manufacture of many useful products. _____Miniature calculators, improved X-ray machines, better computers, and thousands of other products have been part of the spinoff of the space venture. _____But perhaps its most significant contribution has been its impetus to the maintenance of America's technological leadership. _____Fifteen years ago the Soviet Union gained world recognition for its scientific achievement in putting *Sputnik* in orbit, and communism appeared to be the wave of the future. _____Since that time, however, consistent American successes in space have reestablished this country's preeminence in this field and prodded the Russians into cooperative space ventures with the Americans. _____American and Soviet cooperation in space exploration could lead to greater cooperation in other fields and thus enhance chances for world peace. _____The

31

American investment in space has been expensive, but it has not been irresponsible. _____In fact, it could prove to have been the wisest investment this country has ever made.

D. In the following short theme the writer describes a high school teacher he liked. Read the two paragraphs carefully at least twice, making certain you understand the dominant impression conveyed by the writer. Then read the material once more, this time noting specific details of appearance and action that communicate this impression.

Mr. Turner

I liked most of my high-school teachers. They were for the most part friendly and competent, willing to help any student who showed the faintest flicker of interest in their subjects. I liked them—but I do not remember them very distinctly, except for Mr. Turner, my physiology teacher. He was a lively, eccentric little man, five feet five inches in his bare feet, with a freckled, bald head. When he smiled, his mouth stretched from ear to ear, and his eyes sparkled brightly. If a student went to Mr. Turner after class and asked a question that pleased him, he would grasp the student firmly by the elbow, knit his brows in furious concentration as he formulated an answer, and relax into a grin as his questioner nodded his head in understanding. He spoke with a slight lisp, which became pronounced whenever he was upset, as he was whenever he had to speak somewhat harshly to discipline a student. Once during an examination, Ben Sanders, who played right tackle on our football team, crept stealthily across the classroom floor to give a fellow athlete a "hot foot." Mr. Turner spotted him and, with a glint of determination in his eyes, tiptoed behind him and tapped him on the shoulder. As Ben rather sheepishly straightened up, Mr. Turner eyed him intensely. "Mr. Thanders," he said, spraying Ben with a saliva mist, "pleath thee me after clath." We all laughed, not disrespectfully, but because of the incongruity of our diminutive teacher disciplining a student who towered fourteen inches over him (and weighed 100 pounds more).

That year Mr. Turner turned sixty-five, and he retired from teaching in June. The day before the final examination, his last day of teaching after forty-three years, he spoke to us briefly, his lisp slightly more noticeable than usual because of the emotion of the moment. He praised our attentiveness—he nodded slightly in the direction of Ben Sanders—and our progress. He said he had finally decided what he wanted to do in life, and he looked forward to retirement so he could get on with it. As I recall, he said he had always wanted to work in a dental laboratory, and he had gotten a job helping to make false teeth in a dentist friend's laboratory. As he finished speaking, we all clapped and stood up. As we walked out, he grasped each of us by the hand and elbow and wished us well. I can still see him, beaming and nodding his head as I wished him good luck.

The central impression here is that of a "lively, eccentric little man." This controlling idea is explicitly expressed in the fourth sentence. The preceding three sentences provide background information. Succeeding sentences contain the pictorial details that convey the picture of a likable and energetic, though eccentric, teacher—his size, smile, firm grasp, and lisp. Two incidents are included, one involving Ben Sanders and the other concerning Mr. Turner's retirement plans, that provide further concrete illustration of the controlling idea. Think back over your own experiences, and select a person who has made a strong impression on you—a relative, a friend, a teacher, an employer. Write a brief paper of one or two paragraphs in which you present a unified impression of that individual. Select your details carefully, using only those that directly relate to the impression you wish to convey.

E. Read the following poem carefully, at least twice. It is carefully constructed to present a dominant impression of a man, Richard Cory. Though he is shown to have several admirable qualities, they are all related to one overriding quality. What is that quality? What adjective best describes him? Bear in mind that you are not asked to relate the message of the poem, its central idea, but only the dominant quality of Richard Cory. Is the name Richard Cory well chosen? Why? How does it reinforce his dominant quality?

Richard Cory*

Whenever Richard Cory went down town,
We people on the pavement looked at him:
He was a gentleman from sole to crown,
Clean favored, and imperially slim.

And he was always quietly arrayed,
And he was always human when he talked;
But still he fluttered pulses when he said,
"Good-morning," and he glittered when he walked.

And he was rich—yes, richer than a king—
And admirably schooled in every grace:
In fine, we thought that he was everything
To make us wish that we were in his place.

So on we worked, and waited for the light,
And went without the meat, and cursed the bread;
And Richard Cory, one calm summer night,
Went home and put a bullet through his head.

*By Edwin Arlington Robinson

SUMMARY

The most important quality of good writing is clarity. To achieve clarity and conciseness in your paragraphs, you must make sure they are unified. The following suggestions will help you write unified paragraphs:

1. Be sure that each paragraph has a controlling idea expressed in a topic sentence. As a check against irrelevancy, it is helpful to place this sentence at the beginning of a paragraph, but occasionally it may be placed elsewhere—at the end of a paragraph, for example, to summarize rather than to announce a topic.

2. Make certain that primary supporting detail focuses clearly on the controlling idea.

3. If the central idea requires more than primary support, make certain that secondary supporting detail explains and clarifies the primary detail.

4. Be especially careful to avoid inserting a new idea in the last sentence of the paragraph.

CHAPTER TWO | Development

A second important quality of an effective paragraph is completeness. A major weakness in student writing is the underdevelopment of paragraphs, the failure to supply sufficient detail to clarify, illustrate, or support the controlling idea. Because the paragraph is an organic entity—a group of related sentences that develop a single idea—it must be reasonably complete if it is to communicate this idea satisfactorily. Consider, for example, the following paragraph:

The notion that the only valuable knowledge to be acquired in college is that which can be put to some practical use is mistaken. Students who limit their choice of subjects to those emphasizing the acquisition of technical skill restrict their opportunities for intellectual growth and stimulation. College students should therefore not avoid the liberal arts in their choice of subjects.

This paragraph begins with a clear, concise topic sentence, but the paragraph is incomplete, for the topic sentence has not been fully developed. The only argument offered to support the idea that a concentration on practical subjects is mistaken is that such a focus inhibits intellectual growth and stimulation. Moreover, the writer does not substantiate this argument. He should have explained how or why intellectual growth is inhibited, and he should have offered other arguments as well. The writer of this paragraph has simply not said enough about his controlling idea. By adding clarifying detail and supporting arguments, he could have developed his controlling idea more fully and made his thesis more persuasive. Here is a revised version:

The notion that the only valuable knowledge to be acquired in college is that which can be put to some practical use is mistaken.

Students who limit their choice of subjects to those emphasizing the acquisition of technical skill restrict their opportunities for intellectual growth and stimulation. Courses that train students to build a computer, manage a business, or design a turbine engine are of course useful. Modern civilization would not be possible without them. But an exclusive concentration on utilitarian subjects narrows a student's range of interests and produces inward-looking individuals. Liberal studies—philosophy, art, literature, history, law—however, lead outward to the great network of ideas that have stimulated men's minds for centuries. They expose the student to fundamental questions about the nature of man and society, about the ends of human life. They help him learn to see himself in his proper perspective apart from purely personal concerns. The liberal studies thus provide a balance to the technical studies. They also open avenues and outlets that a student can pursue in later life apart from his work. The increasing productivity of machines promises a future of abundant leisure, but added leisure time will be tedious for those without a range of intelligent interests and activities.

This second version is more convincing because its controlling idea has been more fully developed. The original argument that a concentration on technical subjects inhibits intellectual growth has been clarified by contrasting the direction of liberal studies with that of technical studies. And a second argument has been added: nontechnical subjects stimulate interests that a student can pursue later on in life in his leisure time.

The more fully developed the paragraph, the longer it will be, as in the example above; but there is no set length for a paragraph. In expository writing the majority of paragraphs consist of clusters of sentences that develop one idea. The writer, having finished with one aspect of his subject, moves on to another aspect in a new paragraph. Occasionally, however, factors other than thought movement influence paragraph length. Newspaper paragraphs, for example, often consist of only one sentence. The narrow-column format makes it necessary to reduce paragraph length to make it easier for the reader to digest information. Considerations of rhythm and emphasis may also dictate shorter paragraphs, particularly in the longer essay or article. A short paragraph sandwiched between longer ones may provide a change of pace, a chance for the reader to pause slightly and assimilate what he has read before continuing; or it may underscore an important point, the contrast in paragraph size focusing the reader's attention. And introductory or concluding paragraphs may also be short for similar reasons. The kinds of expository paragraphs you will be required to write, however, usually demand 100 to 150 words (six to ten sentences) for adequate development. But regardless of paragraph length, your main concern will be to include sufficient detail so that your reader can comprehend your meaning without having to supply his own information.

The ability to write well-developed paragraphs requires a good deal of practice in thought development. The quality of your paragraphs will depend largely on your ability to think of effective ways to illustrate and support your ideas. A ready supply of ideas is therefore a basic asset to any writer. However, this supply is seldom available to the average college freshman. You are certainly not abnormal, therefore, if you have had trouble finding material to support your ideas in a written assignment. But you can do something about it. You can increase your stock of ideas and your fund of information and thereby facilitate your thinking and your writing.

One way of doing this is through reading—newspapers, weekly news magazines, books. Your studies will provide ample opportunity for improving your reading skills, but you will find that the news and editorial sections of first-rate newspapers and news magazines are especially valuable sources of ideas and information. When you need information on a specific subject, consult the *Readers' Guide to Periodical Literature,* a library reference work that alphabetically lists magazine articles by subject and by authors' last names. Listening to radio and television news commentators and conversing with persons knowledgeable in particular subjects will also provide information and insight.

What you learn through reading, listening, and conversing will increase your stock of ideas. But what you learn in these ways needs to be related to what you know firsthand—what you have learned from your own experience, your own feelings, impressions, and reflections—if it is to become a permanent part of your intellect. To record their impressions and reactions to what they have read and observed, professional writers frequently keep a journal. By writing down their thoughts and impressions, they can retain what might otherwise be forgotten. As a young writer you will also find it useful to keep a journal and to record your responses to events; for it can serve as the seedbed in which ideas for future paragraphs and essays will germinate.

Your journal need not be a formal one. A simple notebook in which you jot down phrases, sentences, or more extended ideas will suffice. Your entries might look something like these:

1/15/74   Lincoln wrote that progress is brought about by unreasonable men. This is probably true. Those who fought for free public schooling a hundred years ago were probably considered "kooks." On the other hand, not all unreasonable men improve things. Hitler, Mussolini, Stalin were unreasonable.

1/22/74 "The future," as one politician once put it, "lies ahead." It may not, after all; for ecologists tell us that the highly industrialized American economy has created serious problems for our survival by using so many of the world's exhaustible resources and polluting the atmosphere. Yet economists argue that the only way underdeveloped nations can improve the lot of their people is through greater industrialization of their economies, which means that these countries will steadily devour more natural resources and pollute the environment, too.

1/25/74 It is ironic that those who would destroy the American "Establishment" with fire or bombs frequently speak of the need for love and brotherhood in the world. Santayana wrote, "Fanaticism consists in redoubling your effort when you have forgotten your aim."

Keeping a journal will obviously not transform you in one semester into a thoughtful, prolific writer. It will not immediately solve the problem of gathering ideas for interesting paragraphs, but it will, if seriously undertaken, force you to think more clearly and to become more sensitive and responsive to your experience. It will force you to express those vague, half-formed notions in writing and thus clarify and fix them in your mind. In the discussion that follows you will see examples of well-written paragraphs. By studying and imitating these common patterns of paragraph development, you will learn some simple techniques for expanding an idea into a fully formed paragraph.

Your choice of method in developing a paragraph will usually be determined by your topic sentence. That is, a well-written topic sentence generally implies a method of development. Consider the following topic sentence:

The farmer's income increased dramatically between 1940 and 1946.

This statement obviously calls for factual detail to support it. Now consider the following sentence:

Slang is frequently vivid and expressive.

Here one certainly needs illustrative detail. Consider this sentence:

The political labels "conservative" and "reactionary" are frequently confused in political discussions today.

This statement clearly requires a combination of definition, comparison, and contrast to develop it adequately.

In the following pages several patterns or ways of developing expository paragraphs are discussed and illustrated: (1) illustration, (2) factual detail, (3) comparison and contrast, (4) analysis, (5) definition, and (6) combination of methods. The first two—illustration and factual detail—are, together with reasons or judgments, the basic materials of which most expository paragraphs are constructed. The others represent common methods of organizing facts, judgments, and illustrations to construct a paragraph. (Developing a paragraph by the use of reasons will be considered later in a discussion of the argumentative paragraph.) This list does not include all the possible methods of developing paragraphs, but it does offer a variety of frequently used patterns that should give you some guidance.

1. ILLUSTRATION

An easy and effective way to support an idea is to use examples. The writer makes a statement and then clarifies it through illustrative detail: he points to a specific occurrence, condition, or fact that concretely illustrates his idea. In your paragraphs you may decide to use only one carefully sustained example to support your controlling idea, as the writer of the following paragraph does:

It will surprise nobody to learn that sex plays an enormously important part in selling. But how it works is frequently surprising. Sex images have, of course, long been cherished by admakers, but in the depth approach sex takes on some extraordinary ramifications and subtleties. A classic example is the study of automobiles made by Dr. Dichter which became known as "Mistress Versus Wife"—a study responsible for the invention of the most successful new car style introduced to the American market for several years. Dealers had long been aware that a convertible in the window drew the male customer into the showroom. They also knew that he usually ended by choosing a four-door sedan. The convertible, said Dr. Dichter, had associations of youth and adventure — it was symbolic of the mistress. But the sedan was the girl one married because she would make a good wife and mother. How could an automobile symbolically combine the appeals of mistress and wife? The answer was the celebrated hardtop, which Dr. Dichter's organization takes full credit for inspiring. [From Vance Packard, "The Ad and the Id," *Harper's Bazaar*, August, 1957, p. 164. Copyright 1960 by Vance Packard.]

Or you may use several examples:

How does a woman communicate interest in a man? In addition to such familiar gambits as smiling at him, she may glance shyly at him, blush and then look away. Or she may give him a real come-on look and move in very close when he approaches. She may touch his arm and ask for a light. As she leans forward to light her cigarette, she may brush him lightly, enveloping him in her perfume. She'll probably continue to smile at him and she may use what ethologists call preening gestures — touching the back of her hair, thrusting her breasts forward, tilting her hips as she stands or crossing her legs if she's seated, perhaps even exposing one thigh or putting a hand on her thigh and stroking it. She may also stroke her wrists as she converses or show the palm of her hand as a way of gaining his attention. Her skin may be unusually flushed or quite pale, her eyes brighter, the pupils larger. [From Edward and Mildred Hall, "The Sounds of Silence," *Playboy*, June, 1971.]

In general, several examples are more convincing than one. But a carefully chosen example, one that clearly illustrates and is honestly representative, is preferable to a series of superficial, atypical ones. If your controlling idea is fairly complex, it is probably better to use one extended example so that you have ample opportunity to develop your idea fully. In either case, the important point is that your examples be clear, relevant, and as specific as possible.

A pattern of development similar to illustration is the use of an anecdote — a short narrative of some incident, frequently personal or biographical — to illustrate an idea. In the following paragraph William H. Whyte, Jr., uses an anecdote to illustrate his belief that executives of modern companies value the genial, cooperative employee more than the man of genius.

Even when companies recognize that they are making a choice between brilliance and mediocrity, it is remarkable how excruciating they find the choice. Several years ago my colleagues and I listened to the management of an electronics company hold a postmortem on a difficult decision they had just made. The company had been infiltrated by genius. Into their laboratory three years before had come a very young, brilliant man. He did magnificent work and the company looked for even greater things in the future. But, though he was a likable fellow, he was imaginative and he had begun to chafe at the supervision of the research director. The director, the management said, was a rather run-of-the-mill sort, though he had worked loyally and congenially for the company. Who would have to be sacrificed? Reluctantly, the company made its decision. The brilliant man would have to go. The management was unhappy about the decision but they argued that harmonious group thinking (this was the actual word they used) was the company's prime aim, and if they had promoted the brilliant man it would have upset the whole chain of company interpersonal relationships. What else, they asked plaintively, could they have done? [From William H. Whyte, Jr., "The Fight Against Genius," *The Organization Man*, Simon and Schuster, Inc., pp. 213–14. Copyright © 1956 by William H. Whyte, Jr.]

When you use an anecdote to illustrate your controlling idea, make certain that it is concise and to the point. Do not develop it to such length that the reader forgets the point it was intended to support.

The following paragraphs all use some form of illustration to develop a thought. In the first paragraph the writer illustrates the attitude of a "lowbrow" consumer toward fashion and taste.

The lowbrow consumer, whether he is an engineer of bridges or a bus driver, wants to be comfortable and to enjoy himself without having to worry about whether he has good taste or not. It doesn't make any difference to him that a chair is a bad Grand Rapids copy of an eighteenth-century *fauteuil* as long as he's happy when he sits down in it. He doesn't care whether the movies are art, or the radio improving, so long as he has fun while he is giving them his attention and getting a fair return of pleasure from his investment. It wouldn't occur to him to tell a novelist what kind of book he should write, or a movie director what kind of movie to make. If he doesn't like a book he ignores it; if he doesn't like a movie he says so, whether it is a "Blondie" show or *Henry V*. If he likes jive or square-dancing, he doesn't worry about whether they are fashionable or not. If other people like the ballet, that's all right with him, so long as he doesn't have to go himself. In general the lowbrow attitude toward the arts is live and let live. Lowbrows are not Philistines. One has to know enough about the arts to argue about them with highbrows to be a Philistine. [From Russell Lynes, "High-brow, Lowbrow, Middlebrow," *The Tastemakers,* pp. 319–20. Copyright 1949 by Russell Lynes. Reprinted by permission of Harper & Row, Publishers, Inc.]

In the next paragraph the writer uses several examples.

But Pidgin's seemingly imprecise vocabulary can be almost poetic at times. There could hardly be, in any language, a friendlier definition of a friend than the Australian aborigine's "him brother belong me." Or consider his description of the sun: "lamp belong Jesus." Pidgin can be forthright, too. An Aussie policeman is "gubmint catchum-fella." An elbow is "screw belong arm." Whiskers are "grass belong face." When a man gets old there, he is "no more too much strong." When he's thirsty, "him belly allatime burn." Even the English language is a little spicier today for the inclusion of a good many expressions borrowed from Pidgin, though few who use them are aware of their origin. Among them: chow, make-do, savvy, can do (and no can do), pickaninny, joss, and look-see. [Copyright © 1963 by Gary Jennings. First published in *Harper's Magazine* in an article entitled "Pidgin: No Laughing Matter."]

Gloria Steinem, a leader in the Women's Liberation movement in the United States, uses illustration to support her contention that in an ideal society men and women would choose rather than simply accept their roles.

Men will have to give up ruling-class privileges, but in return they will no longer be the only ones to support the family, get drafted, bear the strain of power and responsibility. Freud to the contrary, anatomy is not destiny, at least not for more than nine months at a time. In Israel, women are drafted, and some have gone to war. In England, more men type and run switchboards. In India and Israel, a woman rules. In Sweden, both parents take care of the children. In this country, come Utopia, men and women won't reverse roles: they will be free to choose according to individual talents and preferences. [From Gloria Steinem, "What It Would Be Like If Women Win," *Time,* August 31, 1970, p. 22. Reprinted by permission from *Time, The Weekly Newsmagazine.* Copyright Time Inc., 1970.]

EXERCISE 5

A. Write a paragraph of 100 to 150 words on one of the topics listed below, and use examples to develop it. As you plan your paragraph, transform the topic into a sharply defined, specific idea and express it as your topic sentence. Then list all the examples you can remember from your own experience or reading—consult your journal here—that might be used to develop your controlling idea. As you consider your supporting detail, you may wish to modify your original topic sentence. Do not hesitate to do so. Formulating a topic sentence at the beginning is simply a way of ensuring unity. After you have eliminated irrelevancies from your list, write your paragraph and make certain that the illustrations you present in support of your controlling idea are clear, concrete, and interesting. (Use this procedure in planning your paragraphs for the exercises that follow each section of this chapter.)

1. expressive slang terms
2. strengths (or weaknesses) of the American character
3. a friend with an unusual trait
4. sense and nonsense in American education
5. a common characteristic of modern youth
6. fallacies in old sayings (Use an anecdote.)
7. conformity or eccentricity in American life
8. permissive or restrictive aspects of American life
9. famous persons who have excelled in more than one field
10. life in a commune

B. The following quotations contain interesting subjects for paragraphs. Select one, explain its meaning, and provide illustrations to support your interpretation.

1. What we call "Progress" is the exchange of one nuisance for another.—Havelock Ellis
2. It is foolish to fear the thorns when one beholds the rose.—Arabic proverb
3. He who would speak the truth must have one foot in the stirrup.—Turkish proverb
4. It seems to me that the only law which there is any merit in obeying is the one you do not agree with. . . .—Lord Hailsham, Britain's Lord High Chancellor
5. Wisdom, in short, whose lessons have been represented as so hard to learn by those who were never at her school, only teaches us to extend a simple maxim universally known and followed. . . . And this is, not to buy at too dear a price.—Henry Fielding

2. FACTUAL DETAIL

Factual detail is often used to support an idea. The writer may begin his paragraph with a topic statement and then support that statement with facts and statistics. Or he may present his details first and place his topic sentence at the end as the logical conclusion to be drawn from his evidence. The following paragraph is arranged with the topic idea at the beginning.

Of some 200 million tons of waste poured into the air each year, automotive vehicles contribute 94.6 million tons. What flows out of an automobile exhaust pipe is a mixture of five principal gases and chemicals, none of them good: carbon monoxide, sulphur oxide, hydrocarbons, various oxides of nitrogen and tiny particles of lead. When the exhaust products of 4 million cars are trapped in a basin such as Los Angeles and acted upon by strong sunlight, the result is photochemical oxidant, better known as smog. Arie Hagen-Smit, a Caltech biochemist, identified in 1950 the most harmful ingredients in the whisky-brown air as ozone, PAN (peroxyacl nitrate) and nitrogen dioxide. Ozone, a form of oxygen, is very reactive chemically, bleaching anything it touches, causing dead spots on leaves, cracking rubber and deteriorating cotton fabrics. PAN causes the eye irritation without which no smog would be complete, as well as the acrid odor; nitrogen dioxide provides the color—and damage to lung tissue. [From "The Ravaged Environment," *Newsweek*, January 26, 1970, p. 37. Copyright Newsweek, Inc., January, 1970.]

Because both facts and judgments are useful in supporting topic sentences, and because confusion between the two sometimes weakens student writing, a brief explanation of their differences should be instructive. A fact is a report, a statement of what has actually happened or of what actually exists. It can be verified: one can test the accuracy of the report through his own observation or computation or by consulting a reliable source. For example, the following statement is factual:

Richard Nixon defeated George McGovern in the 1972 presidential election.

A judgment, on the other hand, records a personal opinion. It indicates approval or disapproval. Unlike a factual statement, it cannot be proven true or false. The following statement is judgmental:

Lyndon Johnson was an effective president.

Many statements, however, cannot be so precisely differentiated as these two examples. The following statement involves both fact and judgment:

Mountain climbing is an arduous activity.

It can be verified to an extent, and yet it clearly includes judgment.

In your writing make certain that your paragraphs do not consist solely of judgments unsupported by facts. Judgments can serve both as topic sentences and as supporting detail, but they need to be grounded in and illustrated by facts if they are to be convincing. The student who wrote the following paragraph, for example, relied too heavily on judgment unsupported by fact to prove his point.

The New Left radicals in the United States seek to disrupt and discredit the American political system. Its supporters rage against the "Establishment" for having enslaved the poor and minority groups, yet they offer no program of their own to correct these social ills. They condemn American foreign policy as imperialistic, yet they extoll the "wars of liberation" urged by Mao and Castro. If the political atmosphere in this country becomes increasingly polluted, the radicals must bear a good share of the blame.

Such words and phrases as "disrupt and discredit," "rage against the 'Establishment,'" "condemn American foreign policy," and "must bear a good share of the blame" express the writer's judgment. But he has not supported this judgment with facts. A revised version, with factual statements added, is more persuasive.

I do not believe that the New Left movement in the United States is likely to transform this country radically. Although most leaders of the New Left protest against the "Establishment" for enslaving the poor and minority groups, a close study of their speeches reveals that they have offered no concrete programs to correct the ills they deplore. Nor does there seem to be any evidence that they wish to do so. For example, the long-range goal of the "revolution," according to Abbie Hoffman (and other members of the Chicago Seven), is "eternal life and free toilets." Such leaders prefer to make their audiences laugh while they discredit our existing society or advocate its destruction. But I have yet to read of any practical proposals put forth by these radicals for constructing a new or better society. The avoidance of serious, constructive proposals can be demonstrated by the adamant refusal of some of these leaders to cooperate with other, less radical men or groups that have historically been associated with reform movements in this country. An example is the New Left's rejection and ridicule of liberal Democrats and nonmilitant civil rights leaders. American foreign policy also comes under fire. Yet here again, many speeches by New Left radicals indicate that they have chosen to concentrate on a crude, unreflective anti-Americanism rather than to make positive proposals for peace. In their view, the United States today is simply an imperialistic, materialistic society. Rather than drawing parallels between United States involvement in Vietnam and communist aggression in Hungary, Czechoslovakia, or East Germany, some radical leaders prefer to consider America as the *primary* obstacle to world peace. Whatever influence the New Left might have had in forcing apathetic Americans to rethink their values and to reconsider their government's domestic and foreign policies is being vitiated by the mindless, emotional negativism of the most radical New Left leaders.

The central proposition is more soundly argued in this revision, for several facts have been supplied to bolster the judgments of the original. Although the reader may still reject the proposition, he is aware of the evidence that led the writer to his conclusion.

The following paragraphs provide further illustration of the use of factual detail as supporting material.

Such a drastic shift in U.S. policy in the Middle East is hardly on the horizon today. Still, the potential clout of the Arab oil nations is nothing short of awesome. "If nothing changes," observes Walter Levy, a New York-based oil consultant, "by 1980 the U.S. will be dependent on the Mideast for up to 55 percent of its oil imports, and Western Europe and Japan will be dependent on the same area for some 75 to 80 percent of theirs." Such a lock on the market would make the treasuries of many Arab states almost as supersaturated with hard currency reserves as their deserts are with oil. Saudi Arabia alone would have $30 billion in gold and hard currency by 1983 (by contrast, the U.S. today has only $13 billion in monetary reserves), and Libya, with only 2 million people, is now sitting on $3 billion in reserves. Notes Levy: "They are converting a liquid Fort Knox underground to a solid Fort Knox aboveground." [From "Liquid Gold = Fluid Politics," *Newsweek*, February 19, 1973, p. 49. Copyright Newsweek, Inc. 1973, reprinted by permission.]

Americans today are spread around the world in an omnipresence that has no parallel in history. At this moment, 2.5 million Americans (including a million servicemen) are living abroad in 130 countries and three dozen non-countries. There are more Amis in West Germany (515,000) than in five states of the Union, more gringos in Mexico City (25,000) than in Mexico, Mo.—more Yanks in London, England, (18,000) than in London, Ohio, or London, Ky. And nearly everywhere the population of Americans abroad is exploding. Forty years ago, the entire American colony in Thailand —all thirteen of them—sat down to Thanksgiving dinner together; this week, anyone who tries to provide a proper holiday feast for the U.S. civilian population of Bangkok will have to come up with enough turkey and cranberry sauce for 6,000 people. Similarly, the number of Americans living in Lebanon has doubled in the past ten years—while in Denmark it has tripled. And the American influx into Iran, according to one longtime U.S. resident of Teheran, is comparable to the Mongol invasion. [From "The Everywhere Generation," *Newsweek*, November 28, 1966, p. 43. Copyright Newsweek, Inc. 1966, reprinted by permission.]

EXERCISE 6

A. The controlling idea in each of the following sentences could be developed into a paragraph with supporting factual detail. Consult reference works in the library and supply several facts in support of each idea. List your data in the spaces provided.

1. Throughout history earthquakes have been among the most destructive natural calamities plaguing mankind.

_____

_____

_____

_____

2. Top-flight professional athletes in the United States are handsomely paid.

_____

_____

_____

_____

3. Japan's industrial recovery following the Second World War has been phenomenal.

_____

_____

_____

_____

4. Strip mining for coal seriously damages the land.

_____

_____

_____

_____

B. Select one of the four topic sentences given in A and, using the factual information you have listed, write a paragraph of 100 words or more.

3. COMPARISON AND CONTRAST

In a paragraph of *comparison* the writer points out similarities between two or more things. In a paragraph of *contrast* he points out their differences. As a student you will frequently be asked to compare or contrast philosophical ideas, historical figures, characters in a novel, or political parties. By studying these two patterns carefully and by practicing the techniques involved, you can improve your ability to develop and communicate your thought clearly.

The supporting material for comparison or contrast frequently consists of factual details, judgments, or examples. In the following paragraph the writer points up the resemblance in the character of the American Southerner and the Afrikaner (an inhabitant of South Africa born of white—usually Dutch—parents) and supports his comparison by a series of factual statements:

Quite apart from the color problem, there are strong resemblances in the character of the American Southerner and the Afrikaner in South Africa; they were molded by the same kind of history and sociology. Both societies have developed from the isolation of the frontier, with the gun, the Bible, and the ox-cart as their powerful symbols. Both have a stern Calvinist tradition, a lingering belief that they are a "chosen race," and a sense of guilt augmented by the habit of miscegenation. In both continents, the richer whites have a slow patriarchal charm, fostered by heat and leisure; while the poor whites have a violent roughness, alternating between hatred for the Negro and real sympathy and understanding for him. [From Anthony Sampson, "Little Rock & Johannesburg," *Nation,* January 10, 1959, pp. 23–24.]

The writer of the next paragraph finds a parallel between the situations and temperaments of Abraham Lincoln and Hamlet. Factual details support the central idea that is contained in the last sentence.

It may not be an accident that the two Broadway plays which have met this season with the highest praise from the critics are *Hamlet* and *Abe Lincoln in Illinois.* Shakespeare's creation and America's native son were both puzzled liberals. Both were deeply affected by the injustices of the world and by their own seeming inability to right them. Lincoln came close to insanity at one stage in his young life. Hamlet feigned insanity for a purpose, and the commentators have written volumes trying to decide whether the deception did not in the end become grim reality. Lincoln struggled out of his despairing mood, put the ghost of little Ann Rutledge in the back of his mind with the equally lovely ghost of universal righteousness, married Mary Todd, compromised with many expediences, composed the Gettysburg Address and the Second Inaugural, and saved the Union. Hamlet went down in the muck of circumstances. The mood of Hamlet and the mood of Lincoln, the predicament of Hamlet and the predicament of Lincoln, are as modern as television, as old as the hills. [From "Great Individuals," an editorial in *The New York Times*, October 22, 1938. © 1938 by The New York Times Company. Reprinted by permission.]

The distinction between popular songs and jazz is the subject of the next paragraph. Supporting material consists largely of the writer's judgments.

First, let me clarify the distinction between popular songs and jazz. In "true" jazz, as the jazz connoisseur understands the term, the basic interest on the part of both musician and listener is in the music as music. Originality and inventiveness in improvisation are highly prized, as are the qualities of instrumentation and of rhythm. Popular music, on the other hand, stands in about the same relationship to jazz as the so-called "semi-classics" stand in relation to Bach, Beethoven, and Brahms. Just as the musical ideas of the classics are diluted, often to a point of inanity, in the "semi-classics," so are the ideas of jazz (and of semi-classics) diluted in popular music—diluted, sweetened, sentimentalized, and trivialized. [From S. I. Hayakawa, "Popular Songs versus the Facts of Life," ETC, Vol. 12, 1955, p. 83.]

The pattern of development of the following paragraph includes both comparison and contrast. The writer discusses the similarities and differences in appearance and temperament between Roger Baldwin, the founder of the American Civil Liberties Union, and Norman Thomas, a Socialist and a former candidate for the Presidency.

In many ways, Baldwin and his friend Norman Thomas are alike. They wear the same baggy clothes, address public gatherings with the same high-pitched vehemence, and have the same look of worn rectitude. For thirty-six years, they have been crusading together for the rights of the underdog. But there is a difference. An acquaintance of both puts it this way: "When Norman hears about some injustice, he fires up, gets red in the face, bangs his fist on the table, and says, 'That's an outrage!' But I've never seen Roger get sore. He leans back, smooths his hair over his bald spot, and says, 'Let's see. What's the angle here?' Roger's reactions are entirely professional, clinical. He'd no more think of getting angry or upset about a violation of civil liberty than a surgeon would about a case of cancer." [From Dwight Macdonald, "The Defense of Everybody," *The New Yorker,* July 11, 1953, p. 31.]

Arrangement of Supporting Material

You may arrange the supporting material for a paragraph based on comparison or contrast in a variety of ways. If you are comparing two persons, for example, you may present the information about the first person in the first four or five sentences and the information about the second person in the remaining sentences. The paragraph below illustrates this method. Masculine and feminine body behavior are contrasted; each is described in a block of sentences:

Such patterns of masculine and feminine body behavior vary widely from one culture to another. In America, for example, women stand with their thighs together. Many walk with their pelvis tipped slightly forward and their upper arms close to their body. When they sit, they cross their legs at the knee or, if they are well past middle age, they may cross their ankles. American men hold their arms away from their body, often swinging them as they walk. They stand with their legs apart (an extreme example is the cowboy, with legs apart and thumbs tucked into the belt). When they sit, they put their feet on the floor with legs apart and, in some parts of the country, they cross their legs by putting one ankle on the other knee. [From Edward and Mildred Hall, "The Sounds of Silence," *Playboy,* June, 1971.]

Another method is to alternate between subjects in successive sentences, as does the writer of the paragraph who compares Hamlet and Lincoln:

Lincoln came close to insanity at one stage in his young life. Hamlet feigned insanity for a purpose. . . . Lincoln struggled out of his despairing mood. . . . Hamlet went down in the muck of circumstances.

A third way is to deal with the objects in the same sentence, as

Anthony Sampson does in comparing the American Southerner with the Afrikaner:

> Both societies have developed from the isolation of the frontier, with the gun, the Bible, and the ox-cart as their powerful symbols. Both have a stern Calvinist tradition. . . .

And, of course, it is possible to combine these various methods, as Dwight Macdonald does in the paragraph above to compare and contrast Roger Baldwin with Norman Thomas. In the second and third sentences of that paragraph, the author deals with both subjects in the same sentence:

> They wear the same baggy clothes, address public gatherings with the same high-pitched vehemence, and have the same look of worn rectitude. For thirty-six years, they have been crusading together for the rights of the underdog.

However, beginning with the fourth sentence, "But there is a difference," he treats each subject in separate sentences:

> An acquaintance of both puts it this way: "When Norman hears about some injustice, he fires up, gets red in the face, bangs his fist on the table, and says, 'That's an outrage!' But I've never seen Roger get sore."

In a composition of several paragraphs you will have a similar choice in arranging detail. For example, if you were contrasting Los Angeles with Milwaukee on the basis of educational opportunities, recreational facilities, and variety of industries, you could focus on Los Angeles in the first few paragraphs, each paragraph dealing with one of these three points, and then consider Milwaukee in the remaining paragraphs; or you could discuss educational opportunities, recreational facilities, and variety of industries in this order, shifting your focus between Los Angeles and Milwaukee as you progressed. In compositions of several pages, it is probably more effective to use this alternating focus. The steady comparison or contrast of detail keeps the purpose of the paper more clearly and forcefully in the reader's mind.

Analogy

A special kind of comparison is the *analogy*, a comparison of two things that are unlike but that have similar attributes. The paragraph that developed the likeness between Hamlet and Lincoln is a straight comparison: both objects belong to the same class. There is a resemblance between the things themselves. However, a comparison of death and sleep is an analogy: they are not similar states, but they have similar attributes—the cessation of activity and the appearance of repose.

Carefully used, the analogy can be instructive. Alexander Pope, an eighteenth-century English poet known for his wit, uses a brief analogy to emphasize a truth about human egoism:

> 'Tis with our judgments as our watches, none
> Go just alike, yet each believes his own.

The analogy is especially helpful in explaining the unfamiliar in terms of the familiar. For example, a lecturer in physiology in a class of teen-age boys might compare the heart with an automobile engine. Or a historian might compare the rise and fall of great civilizations with the life cycle of a human being. Thomas Huxley, a famous British biologist and defender of Charles Darwin's theory of evolution, uses analogy to enliven and clarify his idea that man needs to study the laws of nature in order to survive.

> Yet it is a very plain and elementary truth, that the life, the fortune, and the happiness of every one of us, and, more or less, of those who are connected with us, do depend upon our knowing something of the rules of a game infinitely more difficult and complicated than chess. It is a game which has been played for untold ages, every man and woman of us being one of the two players in a game of his or her own. The chessboard is the world, the pieces are the phenomena of the universe, the rules of the game are what we call the laws of Nature. The player on the other side is hidden from us. We know that his play is always fair, just, and patient. But also we know, to our cost, that he never overlooks a mistake, or makes the smallest allowance for ignorance. To the man who plays well, the highest stakes are paid, with that sort of overflowing generosity with which the strong shows delight in strength. And one who plays ill is checkmated—without haste, but without remorse. [From Thomas Henry Huxley, "A Liberal Education," *Macmillan's Magazine*, 1868.]

In the following paragraph a British astronomer, Fred Hoyle, uses analogy to illustrate the theory of an expanding universe:

Observations indicate that the different clusters of galaxies are constantly moving apart from each other. To illustrate by a homely analogy, think of a raisin cake baking in an oven. Suppose the cake swells uniformly as it cooks, but the raisins themselves remain of the same size. Let each raisin represent a cluster of galaxies, and imagine yourself inside one of them. As the cake swells, you will observe that all the other raisins move away from you. Moreover, the farther away the raisin, the faster it will seem to move. When the cake has swollen to twice its initial dimensions, the distance between all the raisins will have doubled itself—two raisins that were initially an inch apart will now be two inches apart; two raisins that were a foot apart will have moved two feet apart. Since the entire action takes place within the same time interval, obviously the more distant raisins must move apart faster than those close at hand. So it happens with the clusters of galaxies. [From Fred Hoyle, "When Time Began," *The Saturday Evening Post*, February 21, 1950, p. 96. Reprinted by special permission of *The Saturday Evening Post*. © 1950 by The Curtis Publishing Company.]

EXERCISE 7

Write a paragraph of 100 to 150 words on one of the topics listed below, and develop it by means of comparison or contrast. Decide on the bases of your comparison or contrast before you begin to write, and keep these bases in mind as you write. For example, if you plan to contrast two political leaders, you might contrast their origins, personalities, and political and philosophical attitudes. If you plan to compare two automobiles, you might want to compare their design, performance, economy, and comfort.

1. a comparison or contrast of two current political leaders (Study carefully the two paragraphs above that compare Hamlet with Lincoln, and Baldwin with Thomas.)
2. a comparison or contrast between the attitudes of today's college-age generation and those of a preceding college-age generation on education, sexual behavior, race, dress, or money
3. a contrast of the teaching styles of two instructors
4. a contrast of two views on capital punishment, welfare, space exploration, rearing children, college athletics, or building the Alaskan pipeline
5. a comparison or contrast of two American automobiles or of two styles of driving an automobile
6. an analogy between shopping in a supermarket and selecting courses of study
7. a contrast of an idealized conception of a national holiday—Christmas, Easter, Mother's Day, or others—with your own firsthand experience of a particular celebration of it
8. an explanation of how Plato uses comparison, or more precisely analogy,

in his description of the nature of reality (This information can be found in the first few pages of Book VII of the *Republic*.)
9. a comparison or contrast of two friends, of a conservative and a liberal, a liberal and a radical, a conservative and a reactionary, or a socialist and a communist
10. a contrast of two qualities—wit and humor, wisdom and intelligence, training and education, courage and rashness, ignorance and prejudice

4. ANALYSIS (DIVISION AND CLASSIFICATION)

Analysis is the process of dividing a subject into its component parts. It is an effective way of organizing material when the subject is rather complex. In using this process, the writer splits his subject into smaller parts in the topic sentence and then develops each part in turn, using any suitable method of development. In the following paragraph the writer uses both definition and example to support his subordinate points.

Students of language generally recognize two levels of English usage: standard and substandard. Standard English is typically found in books, magazines, newspapers, or in the conversation of educated persons. Substandard English, as its name suggests, is used by persons of limited education. It is mainly spoken, for those who use it do not generally have occasion to write other than personal letters; and it is usually confined to small geographical areas. Such constructions as "Him and me was real scairt," "She ain't gwine to do it," and "He did it hisself," marked by localisms and double negatives, are representative of the kinds of words and phrases classified as substandard English usage.

Topics that are easily separated into chronological, spatial, or structural components are especially suitable for analytic treatment. A chronological analysis divides on the basis of time. You would use this method if you were going to explain a process (tell how to make or do something) or analyze a historical event by dividing it into periods. In the following passage Norman Lewis, an expert on reading, explains how to read Hendrik van Loon's *The Arts* to illustrate the process of learning to read a difficult book.

Start the book at a time when you will be able to lose yourself in it daily for a period of about two weeks. First read the front pages —the dedication, the table of contents, the list of illustrations, the foreword, and the prologue—in order to get into the mood, to get a motivating taste of the flavor of the book. Then turn to the end pages and read the suggestions under the caption "On How to Use This Book." Next, riffle through the pages and examine the multitude of delightful black-and-white and water-color drawings and read the scintillating captions under each. These mood-inducing activities — which, incidentally, should be your habitual way of preparing to read any books as long, as deep, and as inclusive as this one — will prepare you for the actual reading of the text.

Now divide the book into as many approximately equal parts as the number of days you expect to devote to it. To get the most enjoyment and value out of a book of this nature, plan on ten to twenty consecutive days' reading. Develop the discipline of returning religiously to the book every day, or nearly every day, until you have finished it. After the first few days, this will not be a hard discipline to enforce. [From Norman Lewis, *How to Read Better and Faster*, rev. ed., Thomas Y. Crowell Company, 1951, p. 311.]

The student who wrote the following paragraph analyzed Germany's military progress in the first year of the Second World War into three phases: the eastward thrust, the northern thrust, and the westward thrust.

During the first year of the Second World War, German military forces thrust first to the east, then to the north, and finally to the west. Successful in his attempt to regain the Sudetenland from Czechoslovakia, Hitler demanded that Poland give up the Polish Corridor and Danzig. When it became evident that Poland would not submit to his demand, German troops invaded Poland in September of 1939. German aircraft bombed and strafed Polish military formations and defenseless cities as well. Then mobile armored divisions drove through, encircled, and cut off enemy ground forces. After twenty-seven days Poland capitulated. In April of the following year, the German army occupied Denmark and Norway on the pretext that Britain and France were preparing to attack Russia, Germany's new ally, through the Scandinavian countries. On May 10, 1940, Germany's military juggernaut invaded the Netherlands and Belgium in its drive to conquer France. French defenses proved no match for Hitler's blitzkrieg tactics either, and on June 22, 1940, France was forced to sign an armistice with Germany.

The writer of the next two paragraphs analyzes a geographical area, the American West. In the second paragraph, particularly, the writer divides his subject into its geographical subdivisions. This type of analysis is sometimes called spatial analysis.

Fortunately the West is no longer a shifting frontier, but a region that can be marked off on a map, traveled to, and seen. Everybody knows when he gets there. It starts in the second tier of states west of the Big River. A line drawn from the southern tip of Texas to the farthest boundary of central North Dakota marks roughly its eastern boundary. It starts almost in the tropics; it reaches almost to the northern limits of the Temperate Zone. Hemmed in by Canada on the north and Mexico on the south, it runs with the sun to the Pacific. It comprises more than half of the nation's area—all or part of seventeen very large states. The airline distance around it is one-fifth the distance around the earth. This is the West, as distinguished from the other two great regions, the North and the South. Internally the West is divided into three strips, laid one beside the other on a north-south axis—a mountain strip in the center flanked by a Great Plains strip to the east and the Pacific slope strip to the west. These gigantic natural features give variety and part of the character to the country; but they do not explain it, either separately or in combination. One can never understand the West—all of it—in terms of the rolling plains, the craggy mountains, or the slope to the sea, for none is common to the entire region. They divide rather than unify; they do not bind the West to its inevitable destiny. [From Walter Prescott Webb, "The American West, Perpetual Mirage," *Harper's Magazine*, May, 1957, p. 25. Reprinted by permission of Mrs. Walter Prescott Webb.]

A structural analysis divides a subject into its parts, types, elements, and shows how these subdivisions are related to each other to form a whole. The paragraph on page 57 that analyzes English usage is of this type. In the following paragraph, the writer analyzes the structure of an atom. (Note the use of analogy here also.)

The structure of atoms is like that of a minuscule solar system, with a heavy nucleus in the center as the sun, and much smaller bodies revolving around it as the planets. The nucleus is made up of two types of particles: protons, carrying a positive charge of electricity, and neutrons, electrically neutral. The planets revolving about the nucleus are electrons, units of negative electricity, which have a mass about one two-thousandths the mass of the proton or the neutron. The number of protons in the nucleus determines the chemical nature of the element, and also the number of planetary electrons, each proton being electrically balanced by an electron in the atom's outer shells. The total number of protons and neutrons in the nucleus is known as the mass number, which is very close to the atomic weight of the element, but not quite equal. Protons and neutrons are known under the common name "nucleons." [From William L. Laurence, *The Hell Bomb*, Alfred A. Knopf, 1951.]

These categories of analysis—chronological, spatial, and structural —are somewhat arbitrary. They overlap. The paragraph describing Germany's military moves in the Second World War, for example, contains a spatial as well as a chronological analysis; and the paragraphs on the American West could be considered a structural as well as a spatial analysis. Labels are not important here. What is important is that, whatever type of analysis you use, you make certain to show how the parts relate to each other and to the whole. Otherwise your analysis is apt to degenerate into a collection of facts without a central focus.

Here are some additional examples of paragraphs developed by analysis. In the first the writer uses definition and illustration to support his analysis.

The common varieties of bores are well known to everyone. Ambrose Bierce said that a bore is "a person who talks when you want him to listen," but as apt as the definition is, the species is a good deal more complicated than that. There are, for example, many gradations of boredom, such as the Crashing Bore whose conversation weighs on you like an actual physical burden that you want to throw off because it is stifling you, and quite a different kind, the Tinkling Bore whose conversation bothers you in the way that an insistent fly does, annoying but not dangerous. There are such types as the Still Waters Run Deep variety who defy you to say anything that will change the expression on their faces much less elicit an encouraging word from them. There you are on the sofa with them, their intense eyes peering at you with something between hopelessness and scorn, impressing on you the deep reservoir of their self-sufficiency and challenging you to ruffle the waters that lurk there. I cite this merely as an example of the passive as opposed to the militant type (both the Crashing and the Tinkling are militant), for it is those who make you feel like a bore who are the most boring of all. [From Russell Lynes, "Bores," in *Guests: Or How To Survive Hospitality*, p. 16. Copyright, 1951 by Harper & Row, Publishers, Inc. Reprinted by permission of Harper & Row, Publishers, Inc.]

In this next paragraph the writer uses examples to support his analysis.

Broadly speaking, invasions of privacy are of two sorts, both on

the increase. There are those, like wiretapping, bugging and dis-
closure of supposedly confidential documents, that could conceivably be dealt with by changes in law or public policy. Then there
are those that appear to be exercises of other rights—for example,
freedom of speech, of the press, of inquiry. A newspaper reporter
asks an impertinent personal question; the prospective employer
of a friend wishes to know whether the friend has a happy sex life;
a motivational researcher wishes to know what we have against
Brand X deodorant; a magazine wishing to lure more advertisers
asks us to fill out a questionnaire on our social, financial and intellectual status. Brandeis' "right to be let alone" is unique in that
it can be denied us by the powerless as well as by the powerful—
by a teen-ager with a portable radio as well as by a servant of the
law armed with a subpoena. [From Richard H. Rovere, "Privacy
and the Claims of Community," *The American Establishment and
Other Reports, Opinions and Speculations.* © 1958, 1962 Harcourt Brace Jovanovich, Inc. By permission of author and publisher.

EXERCISE 8

Write a paragraph of 100 to 150 words developing by analysis one of the
following topics.

1. varieties of sports fans, cigarette smokers, salesmen, automobile drivers,
   women's libbers, comic strips, dogs of a certain breed
2. the operation of a solar power plant that generates electricity, a fast breeder
   nuclear power plant, a sea water desalting plant
3. teacher types
4. the rotary internal-combustion engine, a steam turbine, a diesel engine
5. a manufacturing process—the making of aluminum, steel, glass
6. classify students on one of the following bases: attitude toward studies,
   politics, the opposite sex, success, athletics
7. a limited geographical area—a stretch of beach, a desert scene, a camp-
   site by a lake, a boulevard scene
8. an important battle of the Second World War—El Alamein, Guadalcanal,
   Bastogne

5. DEFINITION

Students are frequently asked to define terms from a variety of
disciplines: *capitalism, naturalism, symbolism, atomic fission, os-
mosis, plasticity,* and so forth. Learning to write clear definitions
will therefore be of practical value to you. But more important, good
definition promotes clear thinking and writing. Many disagreements
would never have occurred if the disputants had taken care to define
their terms adequately.

There are several ways to define. One is to use *examples*, illustrative instances:

An example of a *Bildungsroman* is *David Copperfield.*

This method is useful when a writer can assume that his readers know something of the meaning of the term: the examples simply provide further clarification. But when the reader lacks this knowledge, this method is rather confusing.

A second method defines by means of a *synonym*, a word with a similar meaning:

To denigrate means to defame, to sully, to disparage.
A roué is a rake, a debauchee.

This method is helpful if the synonym clarifies the original term, but not if the synonym is likely to be more abstract or general than the original term, as, for example:

Equivocal means ambiguous.

A third method, the *historical* or *etymological* method of definition, clarifies the meaning of a word by revealing its origin and the changes in meaning it has undergone. The following extract from *Webster's Third New International Dictionary* illustrates this type of definition.

Sinister . . . [Middle English *sinistre,* from the Latin *sinister* left, on the left side (whence Latin *sinistrum* evil, unlucky, inauspicious); from the fact that omens observed from one's left were considered unlucky] . . . (2) *obsolete:* conveying misleading or detrimental opinion or advice (the sinister application of the malicious, ignorant, and base interpreter—Ben Jonson) . . . (4) evil or productive of evil: BAD, CORRUPTIVE (the sinister character of the early factory system—Walter Lippmann) . . . (5) . . . b. of ill omen by reason of being on the left side (the victor eagle, whose sinister flight retards our host—Alexander Pope) . . . [By permission. From *Webster's Third New International Dictionary.* Copyright 1966 by G. & C. Merriam Company, publishers of the Merriam-Webster Dictionaries.]

Another method, the *formal* definition, defines a term by placing it in a general class and then differentiating it from other members of the same class:

Term		*Class*	*Differentiating Detail*
A monarchy	*is*	a form of government	in which power resides in the hands of one person.
Induction	*is*	a method of reasoning	in which one proceeds from the examination of specific facts to the formulation of a generalization to account for them.
A palisade	*is*	a defensive contrivance	usually of stakes, which are formed as a fence.

Defining analytically is an exacting process. You must observe several precautions to avoid inadequate and fallacious definitions:

1. The term to be defined should be specifically placed in a class. Statements that appear to be analytic definitions are sometimes simply descriptions of the object:

A steel mill is a noisy, smoky place with tall chimneys;

and sometimes they are interpretations of it:

Home is where the heart is.

In classifying an object, avoid using "is where" or "is when." *Where* signifies location, *when* signifies time, and neither represents a class of things:

ORIGINAL   Democracy is when the people rule themselves.
REVISION   Democracy is a form of government in which the people rule themselves.

2. The general class into which the term is placed should not be too extensive. Defining a telescope as something that helps the eye to see distant objects is not very helpful: the class of things is simply too broad. It could include, for example, binoculars, eyeglasses, magnifying glasses, and many others. In general, the narrower the classification, the clearer the definition. A telescope would thus be more precisely defined as an optical instrument, consisting of parts that fit and slide one within another, that enlarges the image of a distant object.

3. The definition should not repeat the name of the thing to be defined or a derivative of it:

Certified mail is mail that has been certified.

This definition still leaves the reader uninformed as to what "certi-fied mail" means. Definitions that repeat the term to be defined, as in the example above, are called *circular* definitions, for they lead the reader back to where he started. A better definition would be:

Certified mail is first class mail for which proof of delivery is se-cured but for which no indemnity value is claimed.

4. The differentiation should be sufficient to distinguish the term clearly from other members of the class:

Buddhism is a religion of Asia.

This definition does not supply enough information to distinguish Buddhism from Mohammedanism, Hinduism, or Christianity, all religions of Asia. With the necessary information added, the meaning is clearer:

Buddhism is a religion of central and eastern Asia derived from the teachings of Gautama Buddha, who taught that suffering is in-herent in life and that one can escape from it into *nirvana*—a state of spiritual peace—through mental and moral self-purification.

5. The definition should not be expressed in highly technical, obscure language. Dr. Samuel Johnson's definition of *network* as "anything reticulated or decussated, at equal distances with inter-stices between the intersections" is accurate but complex. The defini-tion of *network* as a fabric or structure of threads, cords, or wires that cross each other at regular intervals and are knotted or secured at the crossings, as defined in *Webster's Third New International Dictionary*, is much simpler and clearer.

Observing these precautions will improve the clarity and precision of your formal definitions. There are times, however, when you will have to write more than a single sentence, a minimum definition, to define a term adequately. An explanation of Mohammedanism, freedom, or liberalism would obviously require more than one sen-tence. In developing a paragraph by means of definition, it is a good idea to start with a minimum definition as a basis and then use ex-amples, comparisons, contrasts, historical information, and so forth, to support and extend your definition. Definitions that are developed in one or more paragraphs are called *extended* definitions.

In the following paragraph James Fenimore Cooper defines a
gentleman.

The word "gentleman" has a positive and limited signification.
It means one elevated above the mass of society by his birth, manners, attainments, character, and social condition. "Gentleman" is
derived from the French *gentilhomme,* which originally signified
one of noble birth. This was at a time when the characteristics of the
condition were never found beyond a caste. As society advanced,
ordinary men attained the qualifications of nobility, without that
of birth, and the meaning of the word was extended. It is now possible to be a gentleman without birth, though, even in America,
where such distinctions are purely conditional, they who have
birth, except in extraordinary instances, are classed with gentlemen.
To call a laborer, one who has neither education, manners, accomplishments, tastes, associations, nor any one of the ordinary requisites, a gentleman, is just as absurd as to call one who is thus qualified, a fellow. The word must have some especial significance, or
it would be synonymous with man. One may have gentlemanlike
feelings, principles and appearance, without possessing the liberal
attainments that distinguish the gentleman. Least of all does money
alone make a gentleman, though, as it becomes a means of obtaining
the other requisites, it is usual to give it a place in the claims of the
class. Men may be, and often are, very rich, without having the
smallest title to be deemed gentlemen. A man may be a distinguished gentleman and not possess as much money as his own
footman. [Reprinted from *The American Democrat* by James Fenimore Cooper, 1838. Copyright © 1969 by Funk & Wagnalls, A
Division of Reader's Digest Books, Inc. All Rights Reserved.]

Historian Arthur M. Schlesinger defines the terms *radical* and
conservative in the paragraph below:

It should be clear, then, that the radical is a person who, in contrast to the conservative, favors a large participation of the people
in the control of government and society and in the benefits ac-
cruing from such control. To attain his ideal the radical may become
a protagonist of change; he usually has been one, as a matter of
history, but this fact is a mere incident to, and not the touchstone
of, his radicalism. The temperament of the radical is sanguine.
He can say with Jefferson: "I steer my bark with Hope in the
head, leaving fear astern. My hopes, indeed, sometimes fail; but
not oftener than the forebodings of the gloomy." The conservative, on the other hand, is skeptical of the capacity of the mass of

the people to protect their own interests intelligently; and believing that social progress in the past has always come from the leadership of wealth and ability, he is the consistent opponent of the unsettling plans of the radical. If the old saw is true that a pessimist is the wife of an optimist, perhaps the cynicism of the conservative is amply accounted for by his enforced association with the radical. The radical regards himself as a man of vision; but the conservative sees him only as a visionary. The radical as a type is likely to be broad-minded and shallow-minded; the disinterested conservative is inclined to be high-minded and narrow-minded. ["What Do the Terms Mean?" Reprinted with the permission of The Macmillan Company from *New Viewpoints in American History* by Arthur M. Schlesinger. Copyright 1922 by The Macmillan Company. Renewed 1950 by Arthur M. Schlesinger.]

In this paragraph Winston Churchill defines *civilization*. A minimum definition of the term is contained in the third sentence.

There are few words which are used more loosely than the word "Civilization." What does it mean? It means a society based upon the opinion of civilians. It means that violence, the rule of warriors and despotic chiefs, the conditions of camps and warfare, of riot and tyranny, give place to parliaments where laws are made, and independent courts of justice in which over long periods those laws are maintained. That is Civilization—and in its soil grow continually freedom, comfort and culture. When Civilization reigns in any country, a wider and less harassed life is afforded to the masses of people. The traditions of the past are cherished, and the inheritance bequeathed to us by former wise or valiant men becomes a rich estate to be enjoyed and used by all. [From Winston Churchill, *Blood, Sweat, and Tears,* G. P. Putnam's Sons, p. 45. Copyright 1941 by Winston S. Churchill.]

In the following definition of an intellectual, the second sentence contains a minimum definition, and the writer extends his definition in the remaining sentences by means of a process analysis and a comparison.

What is an intellectual? I shall define him as properly an individual who has elected as his primary duty and pleasure in life the activity of thinking in a Socratic way about moral problems, whether these be social or individual. He explores such problems consciously, articulately, and candidly, first by asking factual questions, then by asking moral questions, finally by suggesting action which seems appropriate in the light of the factual and moral information which he has elicited. His function is analogous to that of a judge, who must first ascertain the facts, then the law, and in the end must accept the obligation of revealing in as obvious a manner as possible the course of reasoning which led him to his decision. [From Morton Cronin, "The American Intellectual," *AAUP Bulletin,* June, 1958.]

EXERCISE 9

A. In the blanks below indicate which of the following methods is used to define: (1) example, (2) synonym, or (3) formal. Write the number of your answer in the blank to the right of the sentence.

1. The lobster, shrimp, crab, and barnacle are examples of *crustaceans*. _____

2. A *mountebank* is a charlatan. _____

3. Fielding's *Jonathan Wild* is an example of prose satire. _____

4. A *ballad* is a narrative poem, usually of folk origin and meant to be sung, consisting of simple stanzas and a recurrent refrain. _____

5. A *minnesinger* is a troubadour. _____

B. Some of the definitions given below violate the conditions necessary for a minimum formal definition. Mark the definitions as follows: (1) if the term has not been specifically placed in a class, (2) if the class into which the term has been placed is too large, (3) if the term is not sufficiently differentiated from other members of the same class, (4) if the term to be defined, or a derivative of it, is repeated in the definition, (5) if the definition is expressed in highly technical language, (6) if the definition seems clear and sound.

1. An *oligarchy* is a form of government in which the ruling power and influence is exercised by oligarchs. _____

2. *Pidgin* is the name of a mixed language, or jargon, developed by natives in the Orient and South Pacific for purposes of trade and incorporating the vocabulary of one or more languages with a simplified form of the grammatical system of one of these. _____

3. A *barometer* is a gadget for predicting the weather. _____

4. A *palisade* is a defensive barrier or fortification. _____

5. *Golf* is a game played with a small ball. _____

6. A *cynic* is a person who knows the price of everything and the value of nothing. _____

7. A *dictatorship* is rule by a dictator. _____

8. An *idealist* is one who believes in and follows a set of ideals. _____

9. A *blurb* is a brief description, usually enthusiastic, that appears on the dust jacket of a book and that recommends it to prospective readers. _____

10. A *raphe* is the part of the funiculus of an anatropous ovule adnate to the integument, forming a ridge along the body of the ovule that provides a diagnostic character in the various seeds. _____

C. Rewrite each of the following formal definitions in one sentence making them more precise or more informative. Be prepared to explain why the original version is inadequate.

1. Deduction is a method of reasoning.

_____

_____

_____

2. Athena is one of the gods of Greek mythology.

_____

_____

_____

3. A radical does not believe in the American way of life.

_____

_____

_____

D. Reread the three paragraphs dealing with the terms *gentleman, radical* and *conservative,* and *intellectual* (pp. 65–67). List for each definition (1) the *general class* into which the term has been placed and (2) the *differentiating detail* that distinguishes the term from other members of the class.

Term	Class	Differentiating Detail
1. A gentleman *is*	_____	_____
	_____	_____
2. A radical *is*	_____	_____
	_____	_____
3. An intellectual *is*	_____	_____
	_____	_____

E. Write an extended definition of any of the following terms. Use illustration, comparison, contrast, or any other method of supporting topic sentences to develop your definition. Consult a dictionary, an encyclopedia, or any other reference work that will aid you, but write the definition in your own words.

1. a hypochondriac
2. a hypocrite
3. a neurotic or a psychotic
4. a bore or a boor
5. an idealist, a realist, or a fatalist
6. a liberal, a conservative, or a reactionary
7. a radical, a rebel, a racist, or a martyr
8. a connoisseur or a dilettante
9. a demagogue
10. a patriot or a chauvinist
11. a humanist or a scientist
12. an alcoholic
13. a communist or a socialist
14. a pacifist or a militarist
15. an amateur or a professional

6. COMBINATION OF METHODS

A good many, if not most, of the paragraphs you write will use a combination of the methods of paragraph development that were explained and illustrated in this chapter. If you are developing a paragraph by means of examples, then statistics and other factual detail may strengthen your point. If your controlling idea requires definition for support, you will probably find comparison and contrast useful in providing additional clarification.

Here are two paragraphs that combine a variety of methods in their development. In the first, Albert Jay Nock discusses the meaning of education and training. He argues that education, unlike training, promotes dissatisfaction with the material rewards of life. In developing his point, he uses contrast, illustration, and judgmental observations.

Education, in a word, leads a person on to ask a great deal more from life than life, as at present organized, is willing to give him; and it begets dissatisfaction with the rewards that life holds out. Training tends to satisfy him with very moderate and simple returns. A good income, a home and family, the usual run of comforts and conveniences, diversions addressed only to the competitive or sporting spirit or else to raw sensation—training not only makes directly for getting these, but also for an inert and comfortable contentment with them. Well, these are all that our present society has to offer; so it is undeniably the best thing all round to keep people satisfied with them, which training does, and not to inject a subversive influence, like education, into this easy complacency. Politicians understand this—it is their business to understand it—and hence they hold up "a chicken in every pot and two cars in every garage" as a satisfying social ideal. But the mischief of education is its exorbitance. The educated lad may like stewed chicken and motor cars as well as anybody, but his education has bred a liking for other things too, things that the society around him does not care for and will not countenance. It has bred tastes which society resents as culpably luxurious and will not connive at gratifying. Paraphrasing the old saying, education sends him out to shift for himself with a champagne appetite amid a gin-guzzling society. [From Albert Jay Nock, "The Disadvantages of Being Educated," in *Free Speech and Plain Language* by Albert Jay Nock. Copyright 1937, William Morrow and Co., Inc.]

In the following paragraph the writer uses illustration, contrast, judgments, and analogy to develop his controlling idea:

On the most superficial level, the roles of male and female are increasingly merged in the American household. The American man is found as never before as a substitute for wife and mother — changing diapers, washing dishes, cooking meals and performing a whole series of what once were considered female duties. The American woman meanwhile takes over more and more of the big decisions, controlling them indirectly when she cannot do so directly. Outside the home, one sees a similar blurring of function. While men design dresses and brew up cosmetics, women become doctors, lawyers, bank cashiers and executives. "Women now fill many 'masculine' roles," writes the psychologist Dr. Bruno Bettelheim, "and expect their husbands to assume many of the tasks once reserved for their own sex." They seem an expanding, aggressive force, seizing new domains like a conquering army, while men, more and more on the defensive, are hardly able to hold their own and gratefully accept assignments from their new rulers. A recent book bears the stark and melancholy title *The Decline of the American Male*. [From Arthur Schlesinger, Jr., "The Crisis of American Masculinity," *The Politics of Hope*, Houghton Mifflin, 1962.]

EXERCISE 10

A. In the space provided indicate a suitable method of paragraph development for each of the following topic sentences:

1. Germany's military strategy during the first year of the Second World War included three phases: an eastward thrust, a northern thrust, and a westward thrust. _____

2. The purchasing power of the dollar has declined markedly since 1939. _____

3. One who obtains a college education secures several advantages in life. _____

4. Wit is not the same thing as humor. _____

5. The Bearcat is an economical car to drive. _____

6. Alcoholism has increased dramatically in the United States during the past ten years. _____

7. Patriotism should be distinguished from chauvinism. _____

8. At times my father can be very stubborn. _____

9. Four types of standard English usage can be identified: formal, informal, literary, and technical. _____

10. Subversion means various things to various people. _____

11. Building a hot rod is a painstaking process. _____

12. Hunting is an abominable (or fascinating) sport. _____

13. Television advertising is sometimes misleading. _____

14. Students use the library in a variety of ways. _____

15. A successful salesman must be sociable. _____

16. Honesty is not always the best policy. _____

17. Annual per capita income in the United States greatly exceeds that in Latin America. _____

18. A political campaign manager is like a general. _____

_____

19. Radical political groups in this country often exhibit a rigid attitude in

their demands for solutions to world problems. _____

_____

20. A free press is not always a responsible press. _____

_____

B. For each of the six topics listed below, write five topic sentences that
could be used as the basis of a paragraph.

1. the population explosion

_____

_____

_____

_____

_____

2. the automobile and air pollution

_____

_____

_____

_____

_____

3. the coming energy crisis in the United States

_____

_____

_____

_____

_____

4. medical care in the United States

_____

_____

_____

_____

_____

5. the institution of marriage in modern times

_____

_____

_____

_____

6. truth in advertising

_____

_____

_____

_____

C. Use the following sentences (and others you may wish to add) as supporting material for a paragraph on environmental pollution. Compose an appropriate topic sentence, and place it at the beginning of your paragraph.

1. Hundreds of millions of years have been required to produce the plant and animal life now existing on the earth.
2. Man's pollution of the air, water, and soil threatens life on earth.
3. Chemicals in particular do serious damage to the ecological balance.
4. If the insecticide DDT is sprayed on plants, it will enter the bodies of animals and humans eating these plants.
5. Because of its durability, DDT retains its power to poison soil and bring about harmful changes in living tissue.

6. Rain washes DDT off plants and into the soil, rivers, lakes, and oceans, polluting water and killing fish.
7. Strontium 90 is a dangerous chemical.
8. Strontium 90 is released into the air by nuclear explosions; it settles on plants and is absorbed into the earth.
9. Strontium 90 can cause death in human beings by lodging in the bones and producing cancer.
10. Man must change his attitude toward nature: he is a part of nature, and to survive he must not destroy his environment.

D. Analyze the following paragraphs for completeness. Explain how those paragraphs you believe to be undeveloped could be improved.

1. *Huckleberry Finn* is a great American novel. Probably no other novel written by an American has had such an appeal for children and adults as this one. Although Samuel Clemens did not himself think it was his best work, in the judgment of millions of readers, including many fine critics, *Huckleberry Finn* is a great American novel.

2. Before buying a used car, you should inspect it carefully. Examine the engine first, for engine repairs can be costly and inconvenient. In checking the engine, look at the exhaust smoke. If it is blue, it may mean worn piston rings. Check the dip stick also. Heavy oil is sometimes used to make a mechanically defective engine run more smoothly. After examining the engine, inspect the body. Look for dents, scrapes, and rusted metal. Any body-repair cost should be added to the selling price. Open and close the doors to determine if the body is aligned. The frame of a car that has been in a serious accident may be bent out of shape; if this is the case, the doors may not hang or shut properly. A close scrutiny of the interior may also reveal evidence of the kind of care the car has received. Inexpensive seat covers may hide torn upholstery and broken springs. Next, consider the make and model of the car. Popular makes and models have a higher resale value. One more word of advice: if you know little about automobiles, take along a friend or a mechanic to advise you. Buying used cars involves some risk. If you want to get the most for your money in a used car, be alert and cautious.

3. The government should supervise the television industry more carefully. There are so many commercials on television today, the viewer can hardly concentrate on the program he is watching. And many of these commercials are misleading. Advertising money may keep television networks solvent, but it destroys the quality of entertainment they present.

4. It is more important for a man to have a college education than for a woman to have one. If a man lacks a college education, he cannot get a good job, and statistics reveal that a college graduate can earn about $100,000 more than the nongraduate. This is ample proof that if a man wants to provide for his family, he will need a diploma. Furthermore, women who go to college usually get married, and then their education is wasted.

5. Those who say that punishment is for the purpose of reforming the

prisoner are not familiar with human psychology. The prison almost invariably tends to brutalize men and breeds bitterness and blank despair. The life of the ordinary prisoner is given over to criticism and resentment against existing things, especially to settled hatred of those who are responsible for his punishment. Only a few, and these are the weakest, ever blame themselves for their situation. Every man of intelligence can trace the various steps that led him to the prison door, and he can feel, if he does not understand, how inevitable each step was. The number of "repeaters" in prison shows the effect of this kind of a living death upon the inmates. To be branded as a criminal and turned out in the world again leaves one weakened in the struggle of life and handicapped in a race that is hard enough for most men at the best. In prison and after leaving prison, the man lives in a world of his own; a world where all moral values are different from those professed by the jailer and society in general. The great influence that helps to keep many men from committing crime—the judgment of his fellows—no longer deters him in his conduct. In fact, every person who understands penal institutions—no matter how well such places are managed—knows that a thousand are injured or utterly destroyed by service in prison, where one is helped. [From Clarence Darrow, *Crime: Its Cause and Treatment*. Thomas Y. Crowell Company, 1922.]

E. As a preliminary suggestion to help you develop a paragraph by means of examples (pp. 42–43), you were advised to work up a brief outline, transforming the topic into a specific topic sentence, jotting down details as they entered your mind, eliminating irrelevant items, and so forth. This procedure is helpful, for it demands that you think about your subject and get your thoughts in order before you begin to write, thus ensuring a more unified paragraph. Another useful technique, one proposed by Robert Louis Stevenson, involves imitation. Stevenson urged the young writer to imitate a variety of writing styles. Through such imitation, he argued, the writer would gradually begin to develop a richer style of his own. One advantage of this method is that it offers the writer a model, a standard for comparison—a decided asset to an inexperienced writer, who, though he may have a fairly good idea of what he wants to say, begins to flounder because he cannot find the right words, phrases, or sentences in which to express it.

After selecting a passage to imitate, Stevenson read the selection carefully, concentrating on its rhythm and structure. When he had fixed this movement and pattern in his mind, he selected an appropriate subject and tried to express his own thoughts in a similar style. Apply this procedure in this exercise. Read the model paragraph carefully, noting the placement of the topic sentence, the kinds of detail used to support the controlling idea, and the wording and sentence structure. Then choose one of the topics listed and compose your own paragraph, imitating the general pattern and style of the model.

The topic sentence in this paragraph is the first sentence. The second sentence comments on the controlling idea in the topic sentence—capital punishment should be abolished—and informs the reader that the primary detail will consist of reasons. Sentences 3, 7, 9, and 10 supply these reasons. Sentences 4, 5, 6, 8, 11, 12, and 13 provide secondary support. You need not try to imitate the exact structure or wording of each sentence, but copy the general plan of the paragraph and use expressions such as "in recent years," "for one thing," "another argument," "it is also argued," and "but perhaps the most appealing argument" to introduce your reasons. Round off your paragraph with an appropriate quotation.

(1) *In recent years* an increasing number of Americans have become convinced that capital punishment should be abolished. (2) This conviction may appear to be a sentimental evasion of the harsh reality of increasing criminal violence in this country, but reasons for this attitude are not hard to find. (3) *For one thing,* executing a murderer does not deter others from committing murder. (4) States that have prohibited the death penalty — Michigan, Maine, Iowa, Minnesota, to name a few — have not experienced a significant increase in their murder rate. (5) Nor was this the case in eighteenth-century England when many crimes, including pickpocketing, were punishable by death; and public hangings were held to emphasize the point. (6) People gathered to witness the hanging often had their pockets picked by skilled thieves undeterred by the threat of the noose tightening around their own necks. (7) *Another argument* frequently raised against capital punishment is that it involves an appalling risk. (8) Since judges, juries, and prosecuting attorneys are not infallible, an innocent person may be executed. (9) *It is also argued* that legal execution is a primitive, discredited idea rooted in revenge and retribution. (10) *But perhaps the most appealing argument* is that it violates the sanctity of human life. (11) It is a negative, life-denying symbol of man's inhumanity to man. (12) Albert Camus, the French Nobel Laureate, writes, "The man of today wants laws and institutions suitable to a convalescent, which will curb him and lead him without crushing him. . . . The death penalty," he adds, ". . . is a revolting butchery, an outrage inflicted on the person and body of man." [From "Reflections on the Guillotine," Albert Camus.]

TOPICS
1. the values of a college education
2. a person you most admire in contemporary America
3. the pass-fail grading system for college students
4. the increasingly permissive attitude toward sex among modern college students
5. a favorite recreational activity — car racing, surfing, skiing, scuba diving, and so on
6. offshore oil drilling
7. hunting as a sport
8. developing wilderness areas for recreational purposes
9. popularity of sports cars, vans, motorcycles, bicycles, campers, or mobile homes
10. better treatment for blacks, Spanish-speaking people, or Indians in the United States

SUMMARY

Good paragraphs must be adequately developed. You should there-fore take special care to see that your paragraphs contain sufficient supporting material to explain clearly and fully your topic state-ment. There are a number of ways to do this: (1) use *illustrative detail*—examples, illustrations, anecdotes—when you can clarify by pointing to a particular incident, a concrete phenomenon; (2) use *facts* and *statistics* when verifiable detail is required to substantiate your point; (3) use *comparison* and *contrast* if you can explain your subject best by noting how it is similar to or different from another object or situation; (4) use *analysis* if your subject lends itself natu-rally to subdivision; (5) use *definition* when your purpose requires the establishment of the meaning of a term; and (6) use a *combina-tion* of any of these methods whenever you need or desire a variety of supporting material.

CHAPTER THREE | Coherence

Clear, readable paragraphs must be coherent as well as unified and well developed. Their sentences must not only adequately develop a controlling idea but they also must link together smoothly. Each sentence should lead into the next so that the reader can easily follow the progression of thought. To achieve this orderly progression, you must arrange your material in some logical sequence and provide connecting links between sentences.

To help your reader understand your meaning quickly and easily, you must take special care with this first task, the proper ordering of ideas. In the following paragraph, for example, the lack of an orderly grouping of the sentences disrupts the continuity.

(1) The yes man had no place in the pioneer tradition. (2) The pioneer had his faults and his virtues. (3) The virtues included a sturdy independence, and the compulsion, if need arose, to look every man level in the eye and tell him to go to hell. (4) Reasonably secure in the fruits of his own labor and thus economically independent, he could express in any company his honest opinion as forcibly as he pleased, and, subject to the local *mores*—the base line from which all human behavior must stem—he could translate his beliefs into tangible performance. (5) The faults included a prodigal wastefulness, a disposition to befoul one nest and move on to the next, a certain laxity in respect to the social amenities. (6) His opinions may have been frequently deplorable, his acts often crude and peremptory, but he was free to be true to the bent that he knew—and so, by the Eternal! a man, and not a rubber stamp. (7) He could vote for candidates he respected, agitate for reforms he believed in, refuse to do jobs which galled his sense of decency or craftsmanship, come and go as the seasons dictated, but not at the bidding of any overlord.

This paragraph contains enough detail to support its controlling idea, but it lacks an orderly progression. The first two sentences convey its controlling idea: although the pioneer had faults to balance his virtues, he was no yes man. The second sentence, by mentioning faults first, leads the reader to expect the writer to deal first with them. The third sentence, however, begins with his virtues. The fourth sentence continues the discussion of virtues. In the fifth sentence the focus shifts to the pioneer's faults. But in the sixth and seventh sentences the focus shifts back to virtues. The paragraph would have been more coherent and hence less confusing if all the details concerning faults had been presented first and those concerning virtues second. The intention of the paragraph is clearly to emphasize the virtues of the pioneer (four sentences concern virtues; only one concerns faults), yet the fifth sentence confuses the organization of the detail and so diffuses the force of the paragraph. The sixth sentence, furthermore, should conclude the paragraph, for it summarizes the dominant idea, and it contains the strongest emotional force of any sentence.

Notice how much more coherent the paragraph becomes when the same sentences are grouped more logically. The paragraph now appears as Stuart Chase composed it.

The yes man had no place in the pioneer tradition. The pioneer had his faults and his virtues. The faults included a prodigal wastefulness, a disposition to befoul one nest and move on to the next, a certain laxity in respect to the social amenities. The virtues included a sturdy independence, and the compulsion, if need arose, to look every man in the eye and tell him to go to hell. Reasonably secure in the fruits of his own labor and thus economically independent, he could express in any company his honest opinions as forcibly as he pleased, and, subject to the local *mores*— the base line from which all human behavior must stem—he could translate his beliefs into tangible performance. He could vote for candidates he respected, agitate for reforms he believed in, refuse to do jobs which galled his sense of decency or craftsmanship, come and go as the seasons dictated, but not at the bidding of any overlord. His opinions may have been frequently deplorable, his acts often crude and peremptory, but he was free to be true to the best that he knew—and so, by the Eternal! a man, and not a rubber stamp. [From Stuart Chase, "The Luxury of Integrity," *The Nemesis of American Business*, The Macmillan Co. Copyright 1931, p. 30.]

ORDERING IDEAS

If your paragraphs are to be coherent, then, you must first arrange your materials in a logical order. The kind of order you use will depend on your purpose and the nature of your materials. When you wish to narrate a sequence of events or present the steps of a process, you should use a *narrative order,* arranging the detail on the basis of time. When you wish to describe something—a landscape, a person, the structure of an atom—you should use a *descriptive order,* organizing the detail in terms of spatial relationships. And when you wish to explain an idea, you should use an *expository order,* grouping the detail in the most effective sequence to support and clarify your idea. These three categories are somewhat arbitrary—the controlling idea of an expository paragraph, for example, may be developed by means of a spatial or process analysis—but they do provide a convenient illustration of common patterns of ordering sentences in a paragraph. In the discussion that follows we shall explain and illustrate these three methods in greater detail.

Narrative Order

Arranging the detail of a paragraph in chronological order is a natural and effective method of describing a historical event. The writer of the following paragraph groups his detail in this manner as he briefly reconstructs Grant's attack on Vicksburg during the Civil War.

Meanwhile the fighting resumed. In the west Grant began an investment of Vicksburg. He moved south from Memphis, made camp on the west bank of the river, and felt out possible approaches through the swampy jungle athwart the mouth of the Yazoo. Its impracticability turned him to the more audacious strategy of a sweep around the Confederate rear to attack Vicksburg's weaker exposure on the south and east. Preparatory to this move he sent a cavalry force on a still wider encirclement to burn bridges and tear up tracks leading toward Vicksburg. Then with some twenty thousand men he marched south, rendezvoused with the Union flotilla for a recrossing of the Mississippi, and swung east, north, and west toward his target. En route he had to fight five pitched battles with Pemberton's men from Vicksburg and Johnston's from

Chattanooga. In these engagements he took ten thousand prisoners and drove the remainder of Pemberton's men back into Vicksburg. Two attempts to carry the fortification by assault failed, but siege and bombardment succeeded. On July 4 Pemberton and his command of some thirty thousand men surrendered. Capture of Fort Hudson soon followed and the Mississippi was securely in Union hands. The strategy of driving a wedge through the Confederacy along the all-important Mississippi had been achieved. [From John W. Caughey and Ernest R. May, *A History of the United States*, © 1964 by Rand McNally and Company, Chicago, p. 253. Reprinted by permission of Rand McNally College Publishing Company.]

Descriptive Order

The details in a descriptive paragraph are arranged to give the reader a clear picture of the object described. In the following paragraph Richard Rovere describes the physical appearance of a former classmate. He has skillfully organized the detail around two prominent features of his subject — his mouth and his pockets. He deals first with his mouth and then with his pockets. He does not shift confusedly back and forth between them and so blur the image.

The two most impressive things about him were his mouth and the pockets of his jacket. By looking at his mouth, one could tell whether he was plotting evil or had recently accomplished it. If he was bent upon malevolence, his lips were all puckered up, like those of a billiard player about to make a difficult shot. After the deed was done, the pucker was replaced by a delicate, unearthly smile. How a teacher who knew anything about boys could miss the fact that both expressions were masks of Satan I'm sure I don't know. Wallace's pockets were less interesting than his mouth, perhaps, but more spectacular in a way. The side pockets of his jacket bulged out over his pudgy haunches like burro hampers. They were filled with tools — screwdrivers, pliers, files, wrenches, wire cutters, nail sets, and I don't know what else. In addition to all this, one pocket always contained a rolled-up copy of *Popular Mechanics*, while from the top of the other protruded *Scientific American* or some other such magazine. His breast pocket contained, besides a large collection of fountain pens and mechanical pencils, a picket fence of drill bits, gimlets, kitchen knives, and other pointed instruments. When he walked, he clinked and jangled and pealed. [From Richard Rovere, "Wallace," *The New Yorker*, February 4, 1950, p. 28.]

Expository Order

Expository order includes a number of grouping patterns. The most frequently used are the *inductive,* the *deductive,* and the *climactic.* Induction is a process of reasoning in which one proceeds from an examination of particular facts to the formulation of a conclusion that accounts for these facts. An inductive paragraph often ends with its topic sentence. When a writer thinks his reader may resist the point he wishes to make, he often uses an inductive order to present his facts, illustrations, and definitions before his conclusion.

In the paragraph below Bernard DeVoto reserves his main point — that man cannot escape the fate of his fellows by trying to isolate himself from them — for the last sentence, after he has presented the concrete detail that illustrates it.

At the beginning of the recent depression, a man I knew suddenly became rich. He bought a large estate in a remote but fertile farming country and set out to make it self-sufficient. It was to provide everything necessary for life, flour from his own wheat, meat from his own herds, fish from his own ponds, electricity from his own power plant. All this was because the revolution (the paralyzing but never specifically defined terror of those days) might break out any moment. His plan was entirely unworkable. His power plant would stop operating as soon as the gasoline trucks stopped making deliveries. The mobs he envisioned would overrun his place like locusts. And so on. It was a panic dream, a nightmare. But I wondered, even if his dream of safety could be realized, what his life would be worth to him. Just beyond his high fences his fellow countrymen would be meeting their destiny, warring horribly perhaps, and dying by the thousands — but grappling with the problems of the real world and working out some way of going on. They would be alive. My friend, digesting his dinner in safety, would have no part in their experience. He would be withdrawn from human destiny, and so, while he walked his peaceful fields, he would be dead. [From Bernard DeVoto, "Homily For a Troubled Time," *Woman's Day,* January, 1951. Reprinted by permission of Mrs. Bernard DeVoto.]

Deduction is a process of reasoning that proceeds from a generalization to a conclusion derived from that generalization. A paragraph in which the materials have been arranged deductively thus begins with the topic statement followed by the detail in support of this statement. The following paragraph illustrates the deductive order of development:

Expressing one's thoughts is one skill that the school can really teach, especially to people born without natural writing or speaking talent. Many other skills can be learned later — in this country there are literally thousands of places that offer training to adult people at work. But the foundations for skill in expression have to be laid early: an interest in and an ear for language; experience in organizing ideas and data, in brushing aside the irrelevant, in wedding outward form and inner content into one structure; and above all, the habit of verbal expression. If you do not lay these foundations during your school years, you may never have an opportunity again. [From Peter Drucker, "How to Be an Employee," *Fortune*, May, 1952, p. 127. Reprinted courtesy of *Fortune.*]

A reader is apt to remember best what he reads last. Therefore, writers frequently organize their detail in an order of climax, beginning with the least important detail and closing with the most important. This pattern is effective when one of the facts, examples, or judgments used to develop a paragraph is especially relevant and impressive. In the following sentences the ideas are arranged in an order of climax:

1. In 1923 Henry Merritt became a full professor, published his first book, and won a Pulitzer Prize.
2. Last Thursday I had a frustrating day: I slept through my eight o'clock class, failed a test in biology, and smashed my car against a telephone pole.
3. The cashmere sport coat was well-tailored and good looking, but far too expensive for me.

The paragraph below is arranged in an order of climax:

A work of literature may be studied in relation to its author, to the culture from which it springs, and to the text itself. One may study a writer's work for the information it gives about the character of the writer or about his world view. A reader must be careful, however, in drawing inferences about a man from his writings: the attitudes and values of the hero of a novel do not necessarily reflect those of the author. Because a literary work is a product of an age, a knowledge of the political and economic conditions and the philosophic and religious ideas of that age is useful. A knowledge of Dante's theological views, for example, helps the student to better understand the *Divine Comedy.* But however interesting and helpful, concern for the author or his background is essentially secondary. The study of the work itself is primary. If one is to get at the heart of a novel, a play, or a poem, he must focus on its content and structure. He must concern himself with the experience—the ideas and attitudes—the author communicates and the form in which he communicates it.

Three other possibilities for the ordering of detail in an expository paragraph are the orders of *familiarity, complexity,* and *cause and effect.* A writer attempting to explain a difficult subject frequently arranges his detail in an order of familiarity, proceeding from the known to the unknown. For example, if he were explaining the principle of jet propulsion, he might begin with a reference to the flight of a balloon from which the air had suddenly been released. In the order of complexity simpler details are presented first and are followed by more complicated ones. And in the order of cause and effect, the writer organizes his material to trace the relationship between a cause and its resulting effect. The cause-and-effect order is quite similar to the narrative order, but it has a causal rather than a chronological emphasis.

EXERCISE 11

A. The sentences in the following paragraphs have been scrambled so that they are improperly ordered. Rearrange the sentences to form a more coherent paragraph, and indicate this order by writing the numbers of the sentences in their proper sequence in the blanks following each paragraph. Indicate also the type of order each writer has used: *narrative, descriptive,* or *expository.*

1. (1) In their search for the button, some go to the psychoanalyst, some go to church, and some read "self-help" books. (2) He becomes increasingly attracted to that which is man-made and mechanical, rather than to that which is natural and organic. (3) The man whose life is centered around producing, selling, and consuming commodities transforms himself into a commodity. (4) But while it is impossible to find the button for happiness, the majority are satisfied with pushing the buttons of cameras, radios, television sets, and watching science fiction becoming reality. (5) Many men today are more interested in sports cars than in women; or they experience women as a car which one can cause to race by pushing the right button. (6) Altogether they expect happiness is a matter of finding the right button, not the result of a productive, rich life, a life which requires making an effort and taking risks. [From Eric Fromm, "Our Way of Life Makes Us Miserable," *The Saturday Evening Post,* July 25–August 1, 1964. Reprinted with permission from *The Saturday Evening Post* © 1964 The Curtis Publishing Company.]

Proper Sequence _____

Type of Order _____

2. (1) Another non-racing vehicle, however, proved to be one of the most popular entries in the show. (2) But the classics of the 30's hold little appeal for the young drivers of the 70's, and during the day the yellow roadster often seemed forlorn and ignored by the crowds of students. (3) From the carpeted floor, grained plywood panels rose to an acoustical ceiling of suspended cork tiles, and eight speakers filled the interior with stereo sound from a tape recorder mounted under the dash and equipped with remote controls. (4) It was a bright orange 1969 Dodge van, and all day clusters of observers peered into the dark cavern between its rear doors. (5) Inside they found a pillow-and-stereo-finished pad, completely equipped for rocking out. (6) Another tape deck stood in the van itself; it wasn't clear whether it was an integral part of the system or just an auxiliary. (7) A psychedelic sound light flashed and throbbed with the pulse of the music, and for really solid comfort there was a small portable liquor cabinet—the bottles all empty, however, in deference to campus rules. (8) One could lie back on the huge pillows concealing the engine housing, tune, turn, and drop off to sleep—after switching on the ultraviolet light for a last look at the psychedelic posters. [From James Armstrong, "Class and Comfort at the Auto Show," *The Faculty Focus,* Vol. 8, Issue 4, Fullerton Junior College, May, 1969.]

Proper Sequence _____

Type of Order _____

3. (1) If the venture were successful, the profits remaining after expenses had been paid would be distributed periodically among the stockholders or the owners. (2) The sale and distribution of goods and services in the United States are, for the most part, controlled by private citizens. (3) After they had obtained the use of a building, purchased clothing, and employed a manager, they would be ready to open. (4) For example, if a group of clothing salesmen wished to start their own clothing store, they would first have to think about capital. (5) They might raise it by borrowing it from a bank or by selling shares of stock. (6) When private citizens wish to start a business, they follow a sequence of steps.

Proper Sequence _____

Type of Order _____

B. Leaf through a magazine, newspaper, or book to find an example of a paragraph organized in each of the following patterns: (1) narrative, (2) descriptive, and (3) expository. Be prepared to explain which of the various types of expository order is used in the paragraph illustrating the expository order.

C. Using a climatic order, write a paragraph of 100 to 125 words on one of the following subjects:

1. masculine man—a vanishing breed?
2. the unrestricted sale of firearms
3. the transition from high school to college life
4. the relaxation of restrictions regarding the portrayal of sexual behavior in motion pictures
5. lowering the voting age to eighteen
6. birth control to limit population growth
7. the growing problem of waste disposal in the United States
8. insurance costs

D. Select an interesting object, scene, or person and write a paragraph of 100 to 125 words describing your subject. Focus on one or two prominent features. Select effective detail. Do not attempt a complete rendering.

DEVICES FOR ENSURING COHERENCE

·Coherence in a paragraph depends basically on an orderly arrangement of ideas. If the reader cannot follow the direction of thought,
he is apt to become confused and puzzled, to feel that the parts of
the paragraph do not cohere. But incoherence is not solely a matter
of logical sequence. It depends also on the use of explicit connecting
links between sentences. Consider, for example, the following adap-
tation of a paragraph about one of the most successful creations of
the motion picture industry—the Western hero.

> The Western hero is a figure of repose. He resembles the gangster
> in being lonely and to some degree melancholy. His melancholy
> comes from the "simple" recognition that life is unavoidably se-
> rious, not from the disproportions of his own temperament. His
> loneliness is organic, not imposed on him by his situation but be-
> longing to him intimately and testifying to his completeness. The
> gangster must reject others violently or draw them violently to
> him. The Westerner is not compelled to seek love; he is prepared
> to accept it. He never asks of it more than it can give. We see him
> constantly in situations where love is at best an irrelevance. If
> there is a woman he loves, she is usually unable to understand his
> motives; she is against killing and being killed; he finds it impos-
> sible to explain to her that there is no point in being "against"
> these things: they belong to his world.

The continuity of thought in this paragraph is obstructed by the
lack of explicit connecting links between sentences. As a result, the
writer's thought does not flow as smoothly from sentence to sentence.
When the links are provided, notice how much more coherent the
paragraph becomes, how much clearer the contrast between the
gangster and the Westerner.

> The Western hero, *by contrast,* is a figure of repose. He resembles
> the gangster in being lonely and to some degree melancholy. *But*
> his melancholy comes from the "simple" recognition that life is
> unavoidably serious, not from the disproportions of his own tem-
> perament. *And* his loneliness is organic, not imposed on him by
> his situation but belonging to him intimately and testifying to his
> completeness. The gangster must reject others violently or draw

them violently to him. The Westerner is not *thus* compelled to seek love; he is prepared to accept it, *perhaps, but* he never asks of it more than it can give, *and* we see him constantly in situations where love is at best an irrelevance. If there is a woman he loves, she is usually unable to understand his motives; she is against killing and being killed, *and* he finds it impossible to explain to her that there is no point in being "against" these things: they belong to his world. [From Robert Warshow, "The Westerner," *The Immediate Experience,* Doubleday & Co., 1954.]

Transitional Words and Phrases

The words and phrases italicized in the paragraph above act as bridges between the sentences. *By contrast, but, thus,* and similar expressions provide transitions between sentences to make it easier for the reader to follow the writer's thought. Although overuse of such expressions as *therefore, however,* and *in the last analysis* can make writing awkward and mechanical, used moderately and with variety they can improve paragraph coherence. Beginning writers should try to develop skill in the use of these expressions.

Some words and phrases commonly used to provide continuity between sentences, or within the sentence itself, are listed below.

Relationship	*Expression*
addition, continuation	and, also, in addition, moreover, furthermore, first, second, again
contrast	but, however, nevertheless, notwithstanding, on the other hand, yet, still
exemplification, illustration	for example, as an illustration, for instance, in other words, that is, in particular
similarity	similarly, likewise, in a like manner, in the same way, in a similar case
conclusion, result	therefore, consequently, thus, as a consequence, then, hence
concession	though, although, even though, granted that, it may be true that
summation, conclusion	to sum up, in conclusion, finally, in summary, in short, in sum
emphasis	indeed, in fact, I repeat, certainly, truly, admittedly

Repetition of Key Terms

The repetition of key words and phrases provides another way to connect sentences within a paragraph. The deliberate repetition of words that carry the basic meaning emphasizes them in the reader's mind and thus serves to weave together the sentences that contain them. Students are frequently advised to avoid repeating words, and such advice is often valid. The frequent recurrence of unimportant words can make writing mechanical and monotonous, thus dulling reader interest. But do not be afraid to repeat important words to explain your thought clearly. A haphazard use of synonyms for the sake of variety may simply confuse your reader and defeat your purpose.

The paragraph below provides a pattern of linkage through the repetition of such words as *Japanese, company, employee.*

As a result, the *Japanese* worker usually feels a deep loyalty to his firm, which almost always employs him until he retires or dies. Working for the advancement of the *company* is elevated into a life goal for the worker. *Japanese* society encourages this by identifying a man not by his profession, but by the *company* he works for. "If you ask a man what he does," says one *Japanese* businessman, "he will say he is with Mitsubishi regardless of whether he is a driver or vice president." Often a *Japanese employee's* life revolves more around his *company* than his family. A 1971 government poll revealed that almost one-third of *Japanese employees* felt that work was the most meaningful part of their lives. [From "The Japanese Yen for Work," *Newsweek*, March 26, 1973, p. 82. Copyright Newsweek, Inc. 1973, reprinted by permission.]

In the following paragraph the writer ties his sentences together through a repetition of the words *thinking, thought, writing,* and *words.*

It is surely no accident that greater lucidity and accuracy in *thinking* should result from the study of clarity and precision in *writing.* For *writing* necessarily uses *words,* and almost all *thinking* is done with *words.* One cannot even decide what to have for dinner, or whether to cross town by bus or taxi, without expressing the alternatives to oneself in *words.* My experience is, and the point of my whole course is, that the discipline of marshaling *words* into formal sentences, *writing* them down, and examining the written statement is bound to clarify *thought.* Once ideas have been written down, they can be analyzed critically and dispassionately; they can be examined at another time, in another mood, by another expert. *Thoughts* can therefore be developed, and if they are not precise at the first written formulation, they can be made so at a second attempt. [From F. Peter Woodford, "Sounder Thinking Through Clearer Writing," *Science,* Vol 156, May 12, 1967, pp. 743–45. Copyright 1967 by the American Association for the Advancement of Science.]

Parallelism

A third way to ensure continuity within a paragraph is to phrase important ideas in the same grammatical structures. The recurrence of similar grammatical forms and the consequent repetition of rhythmic patterns tends to make writing concise, emphatic, and easy to follow. Recurring patterns of expression are effective in speech as well as writing, as the first example below illustrates. The parallel repetitions in each passage have been italicized.

1. "that this nation, under God, shall have a new birth of freedom; and that government *of the people, by the people, for the people,* shall not perish from the earth." [From Abraham Lincoln's "Gettysburg Address."]

2. "Reading maketh *a full man;* conference *a ready man;* and writing *an exact man.* And therefore, *if* a man *write little, he had need have a great memory; if he confer little, he had need have a present wit;* and *if he read little, he had need have much cunning.*" [From Francis Bacon, "Of Studies."]

3. "We hold these truths to be self-evident, *that* all men *are created* equal, *that* they *are endowed* by their Creator with certain unalienable rights, *that* among these *are life, liberty* and the *pursuit* of happiness." [From the Declaration of Independence.]

Observe how skillfully the writer of the next paragraph uses parallel repetition to structure his thought and give balance and coherence to his ideas.

The undergraduate in the American college or university is simultaneously the center of our hopes and our exasperations. Some people look upon *his attitudes, his antics,* and *his activities with amusement;* others, almost *with horror. To some he is the essence of frivolity, the acme of irresponsibility, the representation of* flouted *traditions* and crumbling *standards; to others he is* one of a generation of youth like all previous generations, with all their characteristics merely repeated. *To some* the student *is the source of statistics* on juvenile delinquency; *to others he is the* eternal and essential *champion of challenge. To some* his blunders are inexcusable; *to others* they are inevitable. The only thing certain is that nothing he does goes unnoticed or uncommented upon. [From Samuel B. Gould, "September Undergraduate: Hope vs. Exasperation," *Saturday Review*, September 15, 1962, p. 52. Copyright 1962 Saturday Review, Inc.]

The first sentence of this paragraph contains the controlling idea — that the undergraduate of American colleges and universities is, paradoxically, both a promising and an exasperating creature — and the sentences that follow develop this contrast. In the second sentence, for instance, this contrast is italicized in the parallel prepositional phrases *with amusement* and *with horror*. In the third sentence the writer uses the clause *to some he is*, which he repeats throughout the remainder of the paragraph to link his sentences together and to emphasize his controlling idea.

In the next paragraph the writer uses parallel repetition to stress her point that "untutored teen-age consumers bear a large share of responsibility in elevating the punk."

Some say that religion no longer plays a vital role in setting standards, that we may pay it lip service but no heed. *Some say that parents no longer* pass on to their children a clear code of ethics. *Some blame* the school for not providing what the home neglects, and here I think a legitimate question can be raised concerning one particular aspect of education: the standards of craftsmanship. If the young were taught the basic requirements of a good job, they would be more critical of *the singer without a voice, the star without talent.* Untutored teen-age consumers bear a large share of responsibility in elevating the punk. It is *their money that buys the records* of the bad singer, *their ecstatic squeals that sustain* him, *their tastes that too many of the mass media cater to.* [From Marya Mannes, "Let's Stop Exalting Punks." Reprinted with permission from the January 1963 *Reader's Digest*, p. 47. Copyright 1962 by The Reader's Digest Association, Inc. Condensed from *The Saturday Evening Post.*]

Pronoun Reference

Another way to establish continuity between sentences is through the use of pronouns. Using a pronoun in one sentence to repeat a noun in a previous sentence provides an effective link between these sentences. In the following paragraph, lines have been drawn connecting pronouns with their antecedents to indicate graphically how the reader's attention is naturally directed back to the antecedent

of a pronoun. This repetition of key words through the use of pronouns ties these sentences together.

The individual in today's world, therefore, can no longer look
to the nation as the main source of his security. It is able no longer
to protect him against invasion of assault from other nations. It is
able no longer to furnish the main conditions of his growth or to
safeguard his values or institutions or culture or property. No matter
how wide the oceans that surround the nation, no matter how
bristling its defenses, its people are totally vulnerable to shattering
attack. The nation possesses retaliatory power, true, but even in
the exercise of that power, it engages in a form of self-assault, for
power in today's world is directed against the delicate and precari-
ous conditions that make existence possible, and indeed, against
the mainstream of life itself. [From Norman Cousins, "Triumph
of the Bully," *Saturday Review,* May 14, 1960, p. 24. Copyright
1960 Saturday Review, Inc.]

In the next example the writer repeats *he* and *his* to carry his
thought throughout the paragraph.

Just under three hundred years ago, the Lucasian Professor of
Mathematics at Cambridge did a distinctly unusual thing. *He*
decided that one of *his* pupils was a much better mathematician
than *he* was, and in all respects more fitted for *his* job. *He* wasn't
content with this exercise in self-criticism. *He* promptly resigned
his Chair, on condition that *his* pupil be immediately appointed.
In the light of history, no one can say that *his* judgment was wrong.
For the Professor's name was Barrow, and *he* was a very good
mathematician by seventeeth-century standards; but *his* pupil
was Isaac Newton. [From C. P. Snow, "On Magnanimity," *Harper's Magazine,* July, 1962, p. 37.]

Beginning writers frequently have trouble in using the demonstra-
tive pronouns *this* and *that* as a means of transition. When *this* or
that is placed at the beginning of one sentence to refer to something
in a previous sentence, ambiguity can result if the pronoun is not followed by a noun. Consider, for example, the following sentence:

Father could get angry, all right, but he had a sense of humor, too. This used to upset Mother, however, for . . . .

It is not clear from reading this sentence whether *this* refers to Father's anger or to his sense of humor. This ambiguity is easily avoided by placing a noun immediately after *this*, specifying to what it refers.

Father could get angry, all right, but he had a sense of humor, too. This sense of humor (or this anger) used to upset Mother, however, for . . . .

Ambiguity does not, however, always result when *this* appears by itself at the beginning of a sentence. So long as the writer's meaning is clear—an important "if"—there is no reason *this* or *that* may not refer to a larger element than a single antecedent, to a clause or even to the general idea of a preceding sentence.

Occasionally, of course, a senator or a congressman becomes involved in a dishonest business affair. This does not mean that politicians are crooks. On the contrary . . . .

EXERCISE 12

A. Underline the transitional expressions in the following paragraphs and indicate in the blanks at the end of each paragraph the relationship that each expression shows.

1. The cult of the average man means conformity to the standards of the current majority. To de Tocqueville this was "enfeeblement of the individual." A more recent observer, Fromm, who also looked at the American scene from a European viewpoint, likewise finds this conformity repressive to self-expression. But he fails to see that the American is not a passive automaton submitting to cultural compulsives like European provincials. The American voluntarily and consciously seeks to be like others of his age and sex — without in any way becoming an anonymous atom in the social molecule. On the contrary, all the devices of the society are mobilized to glamorize the individual woman and to dramatize every achievement of men and women that is unusual — but still within the range of approved aspirations of the conforming majority. "Miss America" and the "typical American mother" are widely publicized each year, but an announced atheist (no matter of what brilliance and accomplishment) cannot be elected President. [From Clyde Kluckhohn, *Mirror for Man*, p. 236. Copyright 1949. Used with permission of McGraw-Hill Book Company.]

_____

_____

_____

2. Fortunately, this first-name business for parents is as yet limited. But manners generally are primitive enough in American homes, as anyone knows who accepts invitations from his friends to dine *en famille*. It is undemocratic to set up a children's table. It is also undemocratic to encourage children to listen to adult conversation. During intervals — when little mouths happen simultaneously to be stuffed up with food, for instance — the parents inevitably discuss the subject of children. Children, they tell you, are *people*. The children express themselves. The parents preen themselves. The only person who does not get a piece of this democracy is the guest. This lopsided egalitarianism even favors dogs and cats, with whom a guest must often cope with no assistance whatever from his host. They too, it seems, are *people*. [From Morton J. Cronin, "The Tyranny of Democratic Manners," *The New Republic*, January 20, 1958, p. 14. Reprinted by permission of *The New Republic*, © 1958, Harrison-Blaine of New Jersey, Inc.]

_____

_____

_____

3. The questions about which you should have an open mind depend upon

your age and your occupation. It is no use perpetually reconsidering the decisions that have determined the framework of your life. A young man, let us say, is in doubt as to whether he shall become a doctor or a lawyer, and until the moment when a decision becomes necessary he does well to weigh the pros and cons carefully. But when he has decided, no purpose whatever is served by asking himself once a day, or once a month, or once a year, whether the opposite decision would not have been wiser. Even this, however, cannot be said absolutely. He might be a lawyer in a country that became totalitarian, and he might find that, if he remained in the profession, he would have to help in securing the condemnation of innocent men. In that case he might decide to throw up his profession. [From Bertrand Russell, "Can We Afford to Keep Open Minds?" *The New York Times Magazine,* June 11, 1950, p. 9. © 1950 by The New York Times Company. Reprinted by permission.]

_____

_____

_____

B. What device or devices does the writer of each of the following paragraphs use to provide coherence? Write your answers in the blanks following each paragraph.

1. No, the upsurge of left-wing sentiment and left-wing opinion on the American campus today is not the sort of thing progressive parents and educators had in mind ten years ago when they benevolently urged students to become "socially committed" and "more idealistic." They naively wished them to have intelligent discussions of Vietnam, not to hurl insults and epithets at Averell Harriman (as happened at Cornell), or tear up their draft cards, or laud the Viet Cong. They wished them to be urbane and tolerant about sex, not to carry placards with dirty words, or demand the sale of contraceptives in the college bookstore. They wished them to be concerned for civic and social equality for the Negro, not to denounce "white America" as a pious fraud, whose "integration" did not differ essentially from South Africa's apartheid, or express sympathy with a mindless (if occasionally eloquent) black nationalism. They wished — they wished, in short, that their children be just like them, only a wee bit bolder and more enlightened. Instead, these children are making it very clear that being just like their parents, progressive or not, is the fate they wish most desperately to avoid. [From Irving Kristol, "What's Bugging the Students," *The Atlantic Monthly,* November, 1965, p. 109.]

_____

_____

_____

2. Intrinsically, however, marihuana is less dangerous and less harmful to the human body than is alcohol. It is, for example, not habit-forming, whereas

alcohol is. While the alcoholic commonly substitutes alcohol for food, marihuana sharply stimulates the appetite. Chronic alcoholism is associated with
various psychotic conditions and diseases such as Korsakoff's psychosis and
cirrhosis of the liver. In comparison, the smoking of marihuana produces
relatively trivial physical effects, although it does appear that immoderate
use of the more concentrated products of the hemp plant also produce del-
eterious bodily effects. Such effects, however, are not conspicuous among
American reefer smokers, probably because of the relatively small quantities
of the essential drug that are ingested from the poor quality marihuana
ordinarily consumed in this country. The American marihuana smoker who
inadvertently uses too much when he switches, let us say, to the more potent
ganja plant raised in Mexico and the West Indies is likely to experience
nothing more alarming than going to sleep and waking up hungry. [From
Alfred R. Lindesmith, "The Marihuana Problem—Myth or Reality," *The
Addict and the Law,* Indiana University Press, 1965, p. 223.]

3. Kitsch is everywhere and surrounds us all. Kitsch is hideous hordes of
plaster reindeer and bow-tied footmen defiling the front lawns of Middle
America. It is the Rose Bowl Parade, the Eiffel Tower, the Nuremberg sta-
dium, Disneyland, wax museums, heroic statuary, miniature castles, musical
wedding cakes, cuckoo clocks and artificial flowers. It is a well coiffed
Charlton Heston leading the people of Israel through a huge vat of quivering
Jell-O on the way to the promised land, or a dainty coffee cup emblazoned
with a swastika. Kitsch, in brief, is bad taste in every conceivable form—and
the modern world is its most prolific creator. [From "The World of Bad Taste,"
Newsweek, January 19, 1970, p. 86. Copyright Newsweek, Inc., January,
1970.]

C. The transitional expressions in the paragraphs below have been omitted.
Supply an appropriate word or phrase for each omission.

1. The ability to follow an argument, or to construct one for ourselves, is
what people are usually talking about when they say that the purpose of a
liberal education is to teach you to think. _____ "to
teach you to think" has a silly sound, because, _____,
everybody thinks without being taught. We all put two and two together

103

_____, by some sort of mental chemistry, come out with something new and different, _____ we may be helpless when we try to give an account of the process to ourselves or to explain to someone else the reasons why we should be justified in drawing the conclusions that we believe are sound. _____, we cannot think in the full sense of the word until we can think self-consciously and explicitly — _____, until we can, through argument, lay out the bases, as well as the results, of our thinking and communicate them to other people for their judgment, criticism, and perhaps acceptance. [From Warner A. Wick, "The Argument in Philosophy," *The Journal of General Education*, VII, 1953, p. 82.]

2. Soviet propagandists have long boasted that scientific socialism has created an ideal society in Russia, _____ life in the Soviet Union today, after fifty-six years of communist rule, is hardly utopian. _____, food shortages have periodically plagued the Russians, although more than half the people work the land, as contrasted with about 2 percent in the United States. The Soviet system has, _____ _____, made great strides in transforming a backward, agrarian society into a modern industrial power, _____ it has stifled freedom of thought and expression in the process. Soviet youth, _____, have been given a distorted view of world history and taught to question nothing and to put their faith in communism and the Communist party. Those few who have publicly protested governmental restrictions on artistic expression and free speech have often been denounced and jailed, and sometimes placed in insane asylums. The government has _____ prevented its citizens from reading Western magazines and newspapers. Officials argue that Soviet citizens are not interested in the decadent bourgeois world, _____ these same officials go to great lengths to curb that interest by preventing Soviet citizens from traveling outside Russia. The Soviet system has not created the workers' paradise its propagandists depict, _____

it has made some progress. Political dissidents and artists out of favor are no longer shot. They are simply put in labor camps or committed to mental hospitals.

D. In the following pairs of sentences the flow of thought between sentences is somewhat obstructed. Rewrite the sentences to make this connection smoother, using the specific devices indicated in the parentheses.

1. A good teacher needs to be fair and friendly. He needs to be firm as well. (transition word)

_____

_____

_____

2. The beginning sentence of a composition should accomplish two things. First, it should introduce the topic, and second, the writer must arouse the reader's interest. (parallel repetition)

_____

_____

_____

3. Polite society still has not accepted the union leader. The union leader has yet to be considered of sufficient social importance to be included in the society pages of newspapers. (pronoun reference)

_____

_____

_____

_____

4. Some current critics of public education in the United States argue that progressive education has destroyed what was once a flourishing public school system. A study of the public schools of a generation or two ago does not support this claim. (transition word)

_____

_____

_____

_____

5. Traveling salesmen who saw Arthur Miller's play *Death of a Salesman* praised it highly. The play is a savage indictment of business ethics. (transition word)

_____

_____

_____

_____

6. As our population grows and our cities become more crowded, we will have to build better systems of mass transportation. It is also imperative that we provide more public recreation facilities. (parallel repetition)

_____

_____

_____

_____

7. Jean Monnet, the principal architect of the European Common Market, was a Frenchman with vision. Some historians consider him to be one of the greatest statesmen twentieth-century France has produced. (transition word)

_____

_____

_____

_____

8. The radius of the moon is slightly more than a thousand miles. The moon has an area one-sixteenth the size of the earth's. (pronoun reference)

_____

_____

_____

9. Teen-age marriages create many problems. Young married couples frequently lack the emotional maturity to adjust to each other's temperament. (repetition of key term — try *problem*)

_____

_____

_____

10. Communist propaganda includes a great many myths about America. One of these false notions is that Americans are warmongers. (repetition of key term)

_____

_____

_____

E. Construct a coherent paragraph using the following notes and any pertinent information you wish to add. Use at least two of the devices for ensuring continuity discussed in this chapter: transitional words, pronoun references, parallelism, and repetition of word and phrase. The notes are not arranged in a logical order in their present listing.

1. massive school integration not easily achieved
2. white resistance serious, black community divided
3. busing a reasonable choice in a small community
4. busing conflicts with concept of neighborhood school
5. added expense of busing a burden to school funds
6. voter resistance to extra taxes needed for busing
7. interferes with participation in after-school activities
8. in large metropolitan areas, busing much more difficult
9. disillusioned blacks believe black control and extra money for ghetto schools a more immediate answer
10. large-scale busing could provoke white flight to distant suburbs

POINT OF VIEW

Point of view defines the position, the point of focus, a writer assumes in relation to his subject. It embraces matters of tone, person, tense, number, and voice. Maintaining a consistent point of view is essential to paragraph coherence. If, for example, you are discussing a subject in the third person, you should stay in the third person unless you have good reason for shifting to first or second person. The same principle applies to tense, number, tone, and voice. A reader is likely to become confused if you change from the past to the present tense, from a singular to a plural noun, from an objective, matter-of-fact tone to a subjective one, or from the active to the passive voice of the verb.

Tone

Tone refers to the attitude a writer takes toward his subject and reader. It can vary widely, depending on his purpose, subject, audience, and interests. A student writing about his roommate might assume an informal, personal, even whimsical tone. If he were discussing the advisability of tax reform, however, his tone would probably be more serious and objective.

The problem of tone is complex, but a knowledge of the distinctive qualities of the formal and the informal tone should be helpful. Formal writing uses a more extensive and exact vocabulary; it frequently alludes to historical and literary events; its sentences are usually longer and more carefully structured than those used in general conversation; and it follows the traditional conventions of

English grammar carefully, avoiding contractions, omissions, and abbreviations. Informal writing permits the use of colloquial words and phrases. Its vocabulary is less extensive and its sentences less elaborate, with more of a conversational rhythm. Informal writing also permits the use of first- and second-person personal pronouns (*I, you, we*) and contractions (*I'm, you're, he's*)

The writing demanded of a college student frequently involves the discussion of serious issues and thus requires the more formal, impersonal approach. But whatever tone you adopt, be careful not to shift from an impersonal, serious treatment of your subject to a breezy, colloquial tone, and vice versa, unless there is good reason for doing so and your reader has been adequately prepared for the shift.

INCONSISTENT	CONSISTENT
In the treatment of serious psychological disorders, the therapist seeks to establish rapport with his patient so that he can be induced to take it easy and discuss his problems freely.	In the treatment of serious psychological disorders, the therapist seeks to establish rapport with his patient so that he can be induced to relieve his tensions and discuss his problems freely.
Rocko McNally was a gutty fighter. He could take it as well as dish it out. His capacity for absorbing punishment was, however, exceeded during a match with Kid McGuff. In that contest, he was rendered unconscious in the sixth round by his opponent's right fist.	Rocko McNally was a gutty fighter. He could take it as well as dish it out. His ability to take a punch was, however, exceeded in his match with Kid McGuff, who flattened him with a right in the sixth round.

Person

Pronouns and verbs can be classified according to person, a form whose change indicates whether a person is speaking (first person), is being spoken to (second person), or is being spoken about (third person). A shift in person, as indicated earlier, disrupts continuity. Be careful, therefore, not to change person carelessly from sentence to sentence as you develop your paragraph. Whether you decide to use the informal first or second person (*I, we, you*) or the more formal third person (*he, they*), maintain a consistent point of view throughout.

INCONSISTENT

To get the most from a lecture, a student should listen carefully and take notes. You should not, however, try to record everything your instructor says. Limit your notes to the important points of the discussion.

CONSISTENT

To get the most from a lecture, listen carefully and take notes. Don't try to record everything your instructor says, however. Limit your notes to the important points of the discussion.

Tense

A verb undergoes changes in form to show the time of its action or state of being—the past, present, or future. These changes in verb forms are called tenses. Once you have determined the tense you will use in developing your topic, avoid shifting this tense unless you have prepared your reader for the change.

INCONSISTENT

After a delay of thirty minutes, the curtain came down, and the orchestra begins to play. Then the house lights dim, and the audience grows quiet.

CONSISTENT

After a delay of thirty minutes, the curtain came down, and the orchestra began to play. Then the house lights dimmed, and the audience grew quiet.

As noted above, if tense changes occur, the reader must be prepared for them. When he is, they do not violate the principle of consistency. In the following passage the writer maintains a consistent point of view with regard to time even though he changes tense.

The original settlement of Paris *was founded* by a Gallic tribe in the first century B.C. Paris *is* thus about 2000 years old. During these years it *has become* perhaps the most beautiful and cultured city in Europe. In fact, in the opinion of many travelers, it *is* the most beautiful city in the world.

The writer begins in the past tense to establish a point of reference for his remarks. In the second sentence he moves into the present tense to state a fact about Paris at the present time. In the third sentence he shifts to the present perfect tense with *has become,* but this shift does not violate consistency of tense either, for the verb reports a condition—the beauty and sophistication of Paris—that began in the past and continues into the present. And in the last sentence the writer returns to the present tense, again to express a current opinion about his subject.

Number

Number refers to the changes in a word that indicate whether its meaning is singular or plural. As you read over your writing, make certain that you have not shifted number needlessly. If the meaning of a word is singular in one sentence, do not make it plural in subsequent sentences.

INCONSISTENT	CONSISTENT
The student who wants to improve his writing can, in the majority of cases, do so if he puts his mind seriously to it. If they are not willing to make this effort, however, the results will be minimal.	The student who wants to improve his writing can, in the majority of cases, do so if he puts his mind seriously to it. If he is not willing to make this effort, however, the results will be minimal.

Voice

Voice refers to the form of the verb that indicates whether its subject acts or is acted upon. If the subject of the verb acts, the verb is said to be in the *active* voice:

Larry won the election.

If the subject is acted upon, the verb is said to be in the *passive* voice:

The election was won by Larry.

The active voice is used more often than the passive voice, the latter being reserved for occasions when the doer of the action is either unknown or unimportant or when the writer wishes to stress the importance of the receiver of the action. Examine your sentences carefully to make certain that you have used the appropriate voice.

INCONSISTENT

In September of his freshman year, Harvey decided to work thirty hours a week in order to buy a car. After conferring with his counselor about his program, however, the plan was abandoned by him.

CONSISTENT

In September of his freshman year, Harvey decided to work thirty hours a week in order to buy a car. After conferring with his counselor about his program, however, he abandoned the plan.

EXERCISE 13

A. Underline the words and phrases in the following paragraphs that reveal an inconsistency in point of view. In the blanks following the paragraph, identify the error more specifically as one of inconsistency of person, tense, number, or tone; and then correct the error.

1. In a newspaper column in the *Los Angeles Times*, March 2, 1973, Roy Wilkins criticizes the quota system as a means of achieving racial equality for minority groups. Mr. Wilkins argued that it is ridiculous for a member of a minority group to claim that "because they are 40% of the population, they should have 40% of the jobs, 40% of the elected offices, etc." No person of ability, according to Mr. Wilkins, wants his horizon limited by an arbitrary quota or wants to see people promoted or placed in positions for which they are not qualified because of a numerical racial quota. A black-tilted system, Mr. Wilkins adds, does no favor for Negroes. He blasts whitey for discriminating against Negroes over the years, but insists there must not be a lowering of standards. "Guidelines are in order. . . . Persuasion and pressure are in order," he says, but not a quota system that must be crammed down the throats of American citizens.

_____

_____

_____

2. A hot rod is a stock automobile that has been rather severely altered to increase its speed potential. The builder of a rod, or iron, as it is sometimes called, concentrates on the engine, the body, and the wheels to transform the original automobile into a low-slung, shiny, beautifully finished "bomb." The engine is the heart of a rod. To increase its power, the builder usually adds two, and sometimes three, extra carburetors, enlarges the cylinder walls, and replaces the old pistons with shorter ones. You can get greater compression and hence more power from a motor when you do this. Next, they will "channel," or cut down the body and weld it to the frame, shaping the body line to a smooth contour with lead and body putty. To increase traction at the rear wheels (and thus increase acceleration when he wishes to "dig out" from an intersection light), he replaces the original rear tires with oversized tires and the front wheels with smaller wheels. As a final touch you cover the body with a dazzling lacquer finish, chromeplate the engine, and paint the under parts green or white. The result of all these labors, in the opinion of the builder, is a poetically beautiful hunk of machinery, a thing of beauty and a joy forever.

_____

_____

_____

B. Revise the following sentences to make the point of view consistent.

1. No matter how hard one tries, you can never please some persons.

    _____

    _____

2. The accident had been serious. A new Buick had caromed off a stalled truck and, after it had left the road, smashed into a fire hydrant. The driver of the Buick was bleeding profusely from cuts on his face and neck. His left hand had been severed by the front window. Man, what a mess! Finally, I couldn't take it any longer, and I beat it.

    _____

    _____

    _____

    _____

3. One usually feels depressed after taking one of Professor Bradley's exams. You wonder why he considers details, rather than concepts, so important.

    _____

    _____

    _____

4. In the 1930s radicals of the far left advocated extreme measures to solve the problems caused by the depression. In the nineteen seventies the kooks of the far right also suggested radical solutions to national and international problems.

    _____

    _____

    _____

    _____

5. In the summer he enjoyed surfing at the beach; in the winter skiing at Squaw Valley was enjoyed by him.

    _____

    _____

6. The successful politician must know the difference between a skirmish and a battle. That is, they must know when to settle for less than what they want in a piece of legislation and when to fight hard for an important principle.

    _____

    _____

_____

_____

7. When Henry Martin calls the assembly to order, the students stopped talking and gave him their attention.

_____

_____

8. Spade the soil thoroughly and rake it smooth. Then the manure should be spread evenly, one bag to a hundred square feet.

_____

_____

9. Whenever I arose to speak, a heckler in the back row begins to interrupt me.

_____

_____

10. Congress is the legislative body of the government of the United States. Some critics maintain, however, that they spend too little time legislating and too much time procrastinating.

_____

_____

_____

_____

SUMMARY

Coherence is a third quality of good writing. To make your writing coherent, be sure that your material is organized in some logical order, that your sentences are tied together smoothly, and that your point of view is consistent throughout. The most important quality is the first, for if your thought is developed in an orderly way, you have the basis of a coherent paragraph. Continuity between sentences and point of view are then less of a problem. If your thought lacks logical progression, the addition of transitional expressions and the maintenance of a consistent point of view cannot by themselves supply coherence.

Coherence is the result of careful planning and organization. Therefore, think through what you want to say before you begin to write, and keep your reader in mind as you write. If you build your paragraph as a unit of thought and help your reader to move smoothly from sentence to sentence as you develop that thought, your reader will have no trouble grasping the meaning of your paragraph.

CHAPTER FOUR | Argumentation

The preceding chapters have dealt largely with exposition, the kind of writing that explains. When you wish to convince others of the soundness of your opinions, you will need also the skills of *argumentation*. The characteristics of good exposition — unity, adequate development, coherence — apply as well to argumentation. But persuasive argument requires, in addition, specific knowledge of the processes of logical reasoning and facility in the art of persuasion.

Simply defined, argumentation is a process of reasoning in which a coherent series of facts and judgments is arranged to establish a conclusion. A discussion of argumentation can be complex, for there are many ways of arranging these facts and judgments. However, the discussion that follows will be a simple one, for what is important here is not that you gain a precise knowledge of the variety and complexity of argumentation, but rather that you understand the basic pattern of all arguments and, more important, that you learn to use sound, logical arguments in your own writing.

Any argument, however complex, expresses a relationship between one assertion and another. The first assertion serves as the reason for the second. For example, if you say "Professor Sanderson's exams are difficult. Therefore, I'll have to study hard this weekend," you are making an argument. The second statement is a conclusion based on the first statement.

The first part of an argument may consist of a series of statements:

In the presidential election of 1960, 63.8 percent of the Americans eligible to vote actually voted. In the election of 1964, the percentage was 62. And in 1968 it was 61. As these statistics reveal, a sizable segment of the American electorate does not take its voting privilege seriously.

In this example the *conclusion,* the last sentence, follows a series of factual statements. This kind of argument, which proceeds from a study of particulars to the making of a generalization based on those particulars, is called an *inductive* argument; and the supporting particulars that precede the conclusion are called the *evidence*.

A *deductive* argument, another popular type, begins with a general statement and closes with a particular statement. The supporting reasons in this type of argument are called the *premises*. In the following deductive argument, the first two statements provide the premises from which the conclusion is derived.

PREMISES   All Americans are freedom-loving.
            George is an American.
CONCLUSION George is freedom-loving.

In the following pages we will discuss in greater detail the nature, uses, and limitations of these two kinds of arguments.

In induction, as explained above, we proceed from a study of particulars to the making of a generalization to account for them. Dr. George Gallup uses an inductive approach in his public opinion polls. He may poll members of a group, farmers for example, and then make a generalization, based on his findings, of the political sentiment of farmers. In deduction we begin with a generalization and use this generalization to deal with a particular case. For example, assume that Dr. Gallup concludes that farmers will vote for candidate X in a forthcoming election. If we begin with this generalization and infer that since North Dakota is a farming area, its residents will vote for candidate X, we are arguing deductively.

THE INDUCTIVE ARGUMENT

Let us consider first the relationship between induction and writing. The conclusion that any researcher draws from his study of specific cases is necessarily tentative. As you would expect, a generalization based on many samples is more reliable than one based on few. A large sampling, however, does not guarantee a sound generalization. The sampling must be representative as well. To ensure the reliability of his conclusions regarding the popularity of political figures, Dr. Gallup makes certain to poll a sufficient number of voters from a broad cross section of American life.

Convincing Evidence

If your own conclusions are to be accurate and persuasive, you must, like Dr. Gallup, support them with an *adequate* and *repre-*

sentative sampling of detail that relates to the subject. If this *evidence consists of factual statements, such statements should be verifiable.* In the paragraph below, the writer fails to provide the necessary evidence, the concrete facts, to justify his conclusion.

> Over the past three decades American liberals have been advocating policies and programs that have brought on the ruin of this country. These liberals have continually urged vast federal work projects that obstruct the operation of our free enterprise system, and they have accepted deficit financing as a method of paying for these programs. Deficit financing is never in the public interest, for it produces inflation that destroys the purchasing power of the dollar. Liberals have also sought to hamstring and dictate to American business and industry by urging the creation of regulative agencies such as the SEC, the FCC, and the NLRB. Fortunately, however, Americans are beginning to realize the insidious influence of liberal programs and policies; and with the rebirth of conservatism that is sweeping the country, we will once again achieve our freedom and independence.

This paragraph is a collection of generalizations; it has several topic ideas — government work projects, deficit spending, federal regulative agencies. To revise it satisfactorily, the writer would have to limit himself to one topic and supply the evidence to justify any generalization he makes about it.

The following paragraph also lacks adequate supporting evidence:

> Americans need not worry about the gloomy predictions of pessimists that disaster awaits us because of population growth and pollution. For example, reports indicate that city air is getting cleaner, not dirtier. One hundred years ago the air over large eastern cities was filled with smoke so thick it could be cut with a knife. Yet today coal smoke has been largely eliminated. Our rivers, lakes, and oceans may not be as pure as they once were, but the amount of water pollution has been grossly exaggerated. Alarmists point to mercury contamination of fish caused by industrial wastes as proof of contamination; yet, as scientists know, the amount of mercury in the oceans today is not significantly higher than it was fifty years ago. Doom sayers predict that world population growth represents a time bomb that will explode and destroy us if population is not curtailed. But according to government reports, the birth rate in the United States has been dropping since 1955. Moreover, demographic experts believe that if the trend is not reversed, the United States will be faced with a serious shortage of people. An objective assessment of these facts invalidates the assumption

that pollution and population growth pose a serious threat to the American people.

This paragraph appears to contain a good deal of factual information to support its thesis, but a careful reading reveals that the evidence is tenuous and vague, incapable of justifying the assertion made in the first sentence. Such phrases as "reports indicate," "as scientists know," "according to government reports," and "demographic experts believe" purport to introduce concrete, factual detail. But what specific reports contain information of the quality of city air? What scientists say that mercury contamination of the oceans has not increased? And what demographic experts believe that population growth is not a serious problem? Unless such particulars are supplied, a thoughtful reader is justified in withholding his assent to the writer's conclusion.

The following paragraph is interesting and lively. In this case the writer has supplied specific evidence, but the instances he cites are not sufficiently representative to justify the sweeping generalization in his opening statement.

Women make poor automobile drivers. Whenever Mother relieves Father behind the wheel on a long automobile trip, I tremble. She clutches the wheel tightly in her hands, stares anxiously at the road ahead, and invariably drives off the road onto the shoulder to avoid colliding with oncoming cars. My Aunt Phoebe, although more relaxed, is no better. She keeps up a steady conversation with all her passengers while gazing out the window to take in the beauty of the passing landscape. She is serenely indifferent to traffic signs; and if it were not for her friendly treatment of policemen who stop her, Uncle Art would have paid a small fortune in traffic tickets. But my sister is the worst of the three. . . .

An inexperienced writer who bases his conclusions on atypical evidence frequently does so through ignorance of the complexity of his subject. However, a well-informed, experienced writer who selects only those facts that support his position and ignores others that do not is guilty of stacking the cards. A writer who stacks the cards may cite an impressive body of facts and maintain a fairly objective tone, yet create a false impression of his subject in the reader's mind because of the facts that he has omitted. Consider, for instance, this appraisal of the strength of communism today:

International communism is a worldwide failure. In Western Europe, Asia, Africa, and Latin America, communism is looking less like the wave of the future and more like the ebbing tide of the past.

After the Second World War, Western Europe was ripe for communism—its economy was shattered, its political institutions were weakened, and the Communist party had increased its strength. Yet today Western Europe is a bastion of strength against communist penetration. Its economy, stimulated by the creation of the Common Market agreements, has achieved one of the highest growth rates in the world. And the Communist party, far from dominating the political scene, has steadily declined. Contrast this progress with Soviet failures in agriculture and with the increasing concern and envy of the satellite countries of the industrial revival of Western Europe, and the conclusion is obvious: communism has simply failed in Western Europe.

Nor is the picture much brighter for the Communists in Asia and Africa. Communist China's industrial and agricultural growth has leveled off as a result of its own ineptness and its disputes with Russia. In Africa both the Russian and the Chinese Communists have tried to spread their brand of revolution in the newly emerging nations, but none has attached itself to the Russian or Chinese orbit. In fact, they are turning gradually to the West for aid and assistance. In South America the efforts of the former Marxist government to transform Chile into a model communist state, an example of what revolutionary socialism can achieve, were also unsuccessful. We in the West, fearful of the communist threat to dominate the world, are too prone to accept the Communists' assessment of their success. For all their boasting that they will bury us, it is likely that they will be the ones to be buried.

Although the writer presents several facts and judgments to bolster his contention that international communism is a conspicuous failure—such as the Communists' inability to penetrate Western Europe, Soviet failures in agriculture, Red China's industrial problems, the unsuccessful attempts of the Communists to subvert the emerging nations of Africa—his presentation is distinctly one-sided. He does not mention, for example, the growth of Soviet influence in Eastern Europe during the past twenty years, the increasing prominence of Red China in Asia, the existence of communist Cuba in the Caribbean, nor the fact that, in spite of the overthrow of the Allende government in Chile, the threat of communist revolution in South America has not been eradicated! A more reliable estimate of the strength of communism would include facts from both sides of the question. In your own attempts at persuasive writing, be sure that you have not omitted important facts that do not support your argument. If you have, revise your paper to present a more balanced view. A balanced view may not be as bold or dramatic as a one-sided view, but it is more effective with informed readers.

Evidence that consists of *the opinions or the testimony of others also needs to be carefully examined* to ascertain that opinions are those of a qualified observer—one who is competent in his field and able to report his observations accurately and objectively. It is a natural human tendency to believe in those who share our opinions and to seek out evidence that confirms these opinions, but it is a tendency that can be fatal to persuasive writing—and to truth. The president of a tobacco company is hardly an unbiased source of information on the health hazards of cigarettes. A chief of police may not be qualified to determine satisfactorily the difference between pornography and literary art. And a retired physicist, however famous for research done in the past, may not be able to speak authoritatively on recent scientific developments.

In the preceding paragraphs we have emphasized the need to supply adequate evidence for generalizations. We have said that the evidence must not be one-sided, that it should be grounded in fact, and that if an "expert" is quoted, he must be a legitimate authority. When evidence supporting generalizations meets these tests, a thoughtful reader is likely to consider a writer's arguments carefully. Occasionally, however, a writer defeats his purpose by the wording of his generalization or by drawing an unsound conclusion from his evidence. In the discussion that follows we will examine briefly a few common types of faulty inductions.

Common Inductive Fallacies

A writer who makes a *hasty generalization* fails to supply enough evidence to support his generalization. The writer of the paragraph on women drivers (p. 122) is guilty of this error. The solution to this problem is not to avoid generalizations for fear they might be exaggerated (you would have a very difficult time communicating with anyone if you were limited to absolutely unquestioned generalizations) but to make certain your generalizations are justified by the supporting evidence. Reread your papers carefully, therefore, and revise any extravagant unsupported statements.

UNSUPPORTED

Segregation of the races has been a part of Southern life for decades. Therefore integration will not work. You can't change human nature.

IMPROVED

Segregation of the races has been a part of Southern life for decades. Successful integration will therefore take time. Southern attitudes and behavior patterns must be changed, and such changes are not made quickly.

Generalizations drawn from *statistical data* need to be examined carefully because statistics can be manipulated to yield a variety of interpretations. For example, if a man increases his contribution to a charitable organization from five dollars to ten dollars a year, he can legitimately claim to have increased his contribution 100 percent, an impressive figure to one not aware of the actual amount involved. Or suppose that a report of the income of individuals working in a small business firm indicates that the average annual salary of the employees is $10,000. This information by itself might lead you to the conclusion that these employees were well paid and that the owners of the firm were justified in refusing to consider salary increases. Upon closer examination, however, you discover that, of the ten persons working in the firm, five earn $5,000 annually, three $6,000, one $7,000, and one $50,000. The average annual salary of this group is in fact $10,000, but for most people *average* connotes *typical;* yet only one of the ten persons actually earns $10,000 or more in a year. The typical salary in this case would be closer to $6,000 than $10,000. Be careful, then, when you use statistics to establish or reinforce a generalization. If one figure of a set of figures is considerably larger or smaller than the others (for example, the $50,000 salary in the case cited above), taking an average of them will distort their relationship. In such cases it would be more informative to report the *median* value (the middle figure in an odd number of figures) or the *mode* value (the figure that appears most frequently). In short, use statistics as honestly and informatively as you can, lest your reader suspect that you have manipulated them to suit your purpose.

Thus far we have discussed the hasty generalization and the generalization based on deceptive statistics. A third type of faulty induction is the *post hoc fallacy,* which occurs when we assert that one event caused another because it preceded it. If one thing occurs before another, it does not *necessarily* cause the latter. This kind of inference is known technically as the *post hoc, ergo propter hoc* fallacy ("after this, therefore because of this"), or, more simply, the *post hoc* fallacy. That one political administration was in office when war broke out, for example, does not mean that that administration brought on the war. The fact that the number of capital crimes committed in a state decreased the year after capital punishment was abolished does not prove that the change in punishment caused this decrease.

It frequently happens, of course, that one event *is* the cause of another. When a person collapses after being struck a blow on the head, it is fairly clear that the first event, the blow, caused the second, the collapse. But establishing a causal relation between two events is often more difficult. It is especially difficult in the field of economics. Here is an example:

> The recent tax cut passed by Congress was obviously warranted. The American economy was given the shot in the arm it needed. Retail sales and business profits have gone up, the rate of unemployment has gone down, and our foreign trade has expanded.

To prove that the tax cut specifically caused the improvement in retail sales, business profits, and foreign trade would necessitate the examination of a considerable body of facts. An economist, or an experienced reader, would want to know, for example, the effect of seasonal variation in consumer spending, government spending, the business community's confidence in the economy, and the actions of foreign governments in reducing tariffs, before he could accept such an explanation.

One of the methods of paragraph development presented in Chapter Two was the *analogy,* a comparison of two things that are unlike but that have similar attributes. Analogy is frequently used as evidence to support an argument.

> Recently *The New York Times* reported an address by Supreme Court Justice Powell in which he deplored the deterioration of the nation's moral fiber and cited, as an example, the open selling of student themes and term papers to college and university undergraduates.
>
> It seemed to me a rather feeble for instance, and one which a politician (and let's not pretend the Supreme Court isn't a political as well as a judicial body) might well eschew. If it's all right for the President of the United States to hire people to write his speeches on which the fate of nations may rest, why isn't it equally acceptable for a college student to hire someone to write his term papers, on which nobody's fate rests but his own? [From Ed Zern, "Exit Laughing," *Field and Stream,* December, 1972, p. 160.]

This example illustrates an important fact about analogies: they frequently break down by ignoring basic differences in the two things compared. This analogy between the selling of term papers to college students and the President's hiring of speech writers, as an illustration, overlooks an important difference between these two practices. The awesome responsibilities and complex, time-consuming duties that burden a President of the United States make it impossible for him to write every speech he gives and, therefore, justify the employment of speech writers. The public understands and accepts the practice. A college student is not so burdened. Moreover, the obvious fraudulence of falsifying the authorship of term papers and the prohibition against it are clearly understood and accepted by most college students. When you use analogy to buttress an argument, therefore, keep its limitations in mind. It can clarify a point made in an argument, but it cannot settle the argument.

EXERCISE 14

A. Factual information and the testimony of experts could be used to support the following generalizations. In the blanks below each generalization list the kinds of factual information you could use and an authority you might consult.

EXAMPLE Nurses are underpaid.

1. statistics on nurses' income—average salary and general range of income, from beginning to veteran nurses' income
2. comparison of nurses' income with that of other professional persons—doctors, lawyers, and so forth
3. opinions of leaders of American Medical Association; American Nurses Association; Secretary of Health, Education, and Welfare

1. College football is not a dangerous sport.

2. High-school students are more eager to secure a college diploma than their parents were.

3. Television programs are designed to appeal to a mass audience.

4. Young men are the worst automobile drivers on the road.

5. The mass media of communication—newspapers, magazines, radio, television—exploit the violence and sordidness of American life for commercial gain.

6. Working conditions for men and women in the United States have improved significantly over the past fifty years.

_____

_____

_____

7. The prohibition against professional athletes competing in the Olympic Games is not very well enforced.

_____

_____

_____

8. A college education increases one's earning power.

_____

_____

_____

9. The motion picture industry in the United States is not as flourishing today as it was fifteen years ago.

_____

_____

_____

10. Top-flight professional basketball players are well paid.

_____

_____

_____

B. Weaknesses in inductive arguments discussed in the preceding pages include the following:

1. sampling of evidence too selective
2. lack of sufficient evidence
3. authority quoted incompetent or biased
4. generalization based on deceptive statistics
5. hasty generalization
6. *post hoc* fallacy
7. false analogy

Identify the weaknesses in each of the following arguments by placing one of the numbers in this list after it. In some cases more than one criticism might apply.

1. My Uncle Ted says the schools don't teach kids to read any more, and he ought to know what he's talking about. He's a proofreader on the Miltown *Beacon*.

      _____

2. A rise in juvenile delinquency became noticeable immediately after the Second World War. It is clear that war causes juvenile delinquency.

      _____

3. All I said was that the Women's Liberation movement was nothing but another pressure group run by a bunch of frustrated, discontented females, and this dame slugs me. Just goes to show you, Harry, you can't really talk seriously to women. They're too emotional.

      _____

4. Sam Snide must be a Communist. He favors reestablishing friendly relations with Cuba, he opposed the war in Vietnam, and now he says he wants the federal government to set up some kind of national health insurance. The Communists support every one of these ideas.

      _____

5. The Pure Food and Drug Act has prevented the sale of food and drugs harmful to the body. Congress should also investigate ways to eliminate unscrupulous publishers.

      _____

6. Seven students took an examination, and their scores were 98, 65, 62, 61, 59, 58, and 50. The average score was thus 64. Only two of the seven students taking this examination scored above the average. Obviously most of these students hadn't studied very hard for the examination.

      _____

7. Frenchmen are great lovers.

      _____

8. I've been working in the Complaints and Adjustment Department of Stacy's Department Store for fifteen years, and I have learned that women shoppers are surly and ill-tempered.

      _____

9. The fraternity boys at Rowling Hills College are certainly wild. When I visited my sister on the campus last weekend, she arranged a date for me with an Alpha Beta, and I barely escaped with my life.

      _____

10. Heretofore I have placed little faith in the stories of bureaucratic mismanagement in Washington, but lately my eyes have been opened. My friend's uncle has a brother working in the Department of the Interior (fish and game) who claims that the examples of inefficiency and stupidity he has heard about would cause a businessman to explode in anger. Obviously we need a new administration in Washington.

      _____

C. Read the following selections carefully and evaluate the logic used in each. In the space provided after each passage identify the main weaknesses in the arguments advanced. In particular, look for examples of insufficient evidence, false analogy, and a biased source of evidence.

1. The recent conflict between the powerful United Auto Workers Union and the automobile manufacturers over the union's demand for higher wages brought to mind a recent conversation I had with my son. He wanted to earn money to buy a new bicycle and had decided to make and sell wooden address plates to the neighbors. In discussing the project with him, I pointed out that his profit would depend on his efficiency in making the plates and on the number he could sell. To increase his profit, therefore, he would have either to improve his efficiency or sell more plates. These simple economic laws are relevant to the labor-management disputes in the automobile industry. Increased pay for auto workers likewise depends on their efficiency in making automobiles and on the success of management in selling them. Unless workers increase their efficiency—and so reduce operating costs—or unless the manufacturers sell more cars, higher pay for automotive workers is unjustified. It is as simple as that.

---

2. Before my son went away to college last fall, I had a serious talk with him about the importance of studying hard so that he could get into medical school. I was therefore a little worried by his last letter, for he told me that he wanted to join a fraternity next year. I was afraid fraternity life would interfere with his studies and that he might give up his plans to become a doctor. I decided to talk to some of the fellows at the office whose sons had gone to college. Talbot told me that his son had joined a fraternity in his junior year and that it had not affected his studies adversely. On the contrary, joining a fraternity had been good for him: it had taken some of the rough edges off the boy, taught him some manners, and given him some polish. Wortham was similarly enthusiastic. His son had been out of college three years, but the contacts he had made in the fraternity had helped him tremendously in his business career. Like myself, Wortham had been worried about wild fraternity parties and crazy stunts when his son expressed the desire to join a fraternity; but his boy assured him that fraternity life was not like that at all. After thinking it over carefully, I have come to the conclusion that fraternity life is good for young men going to college.

---

3. Conservation groups are planning to battle with power companies over a tract of land in Wyoming, North Dakota, and Montana that may hold as

much as 200 billion tons of coal. What worries environmentalists, as well as ranchers and farmers in the area, is that in the process of strip mining the coal the power companies will despoil and scar the land. Spokesmen for the utility companies, however, discount such fears. They have promised to restore any land that needs it. Moreover, this country needs the coal to produce energy, and the utility companies have paid for the right to mine the coal. To deny them the right to the coal would be to deny citizens the right to use their own property as they see fit. This right is fundamental to the American way of life. The evidence clearly supports the power companies. They should be allowed to strip mine the coal.

_____

_____

_____

THE DEDUCTIVE ARGUMENT

In the preceding pages we have studied the relation between inductive reasoning and writing, but, as we mentioned there, writing uses both induction and deduction. In induction one examines a number of particulars and formulates a generalization and then, by deduction, applies the generalization to a particular case. If you learn through an inductive process that salesmen are extroverts, you can apply this information to the salesman who sits beside you on a train and can anticipate a lively conversation. Your reasoning process could be patterned as follows:

1. Salesmen are extroverts.
   The man sitting opposite me is a salesman.
   Therefore, the man sitting opposite me is an extrovert.

This type of argument is known as a *syllogism,* the basic form of the deductive argument. It has three parts: two premises followed by a conclusion. The *major premise* makes a general statement about something—an object, an idea, a circumstance. In the example above, "Salesmen are extroverts" is the major premise. The *minor premise* contains further information about one of the terms in the major premise. "The man sitting opposite me is a salesman" is the minor premise of the example. And the *conclusion* is a logical inference to be derived from the premises. The last sentence in our syllogism is its conclusion.

Here are two examples of a syllogism, with their premises and conclusions indicated.

2. MAJOR PREMISE All men are mortal.
   MINOR PREMISE Socrates is a man.
   CONCLUSION   Socrates is mortal.

3. MAJOR PREMISE All Communists believe in the eventuality of war between socialist and capitalist states.
   MINOR PREMISE Hensley Cartright is a Communist.
   CONCLUSION   Hensley Cartright believes in the eventuality of war between socialist and capitalist states.

The major premise commonly precedes the minor premise, but it need not. In the following syllogism, for example, the minor premise appears first:

> 4. MINOR PREMISE   Tippy is a cocker spaniel.
>   MAJOR PREMISE   Cocker spaniels are dogs.
>   CONCLUSION   Tippy is a dog.

If the conclusion of a syllogism is a logical extension of the ideas contained in the premises, as it is in each of the four syllogisms presented above, the conclusion is said to be *valid*. But a valid conclusion is not necessarily a *true* conclusion. Consider, for example, the following syllogism:

> 5. MAJOR PREMISE   All Irishmen have fiery tempers.
>   MINOR PREMISE   Timothy Carmody is an Irishman.
>   CONCLUSION   Timothy Carmody has a fiery temper.

The conclusion in this syllogism is valid: it follows necessarily from the premises, but the major premise is inaccurate—all Irishmen do not have fiery tempers—and thus the conclusion is untrue. A syllogism can yield a true conclusion only when both the premises are true and the conclusion is valid. In the following discussion we shall consider the characteristics of the valid conclusion and the true conclusion in greater detail.

The Valid Conclusion

The first rule of a valid syllogism is that it must have only three terms, each of which appears twice in the three statements. A *term* is the subject or predicate of a statement. In the syllogism

> 6. MAJOR PREMISE   All children are curious.
>   MINOR PREMISE   Stephen is a child.
>   CONCLUSION   Stephen is curious.

the two terms in the major premise are *children* and *curious*, and the term *child*, which appears in both the major and minor premises (but not in the conclusion), is called the *middle term*.

Another rule of a valid syllogism is that the middle term must be "distributed" in one of the premises; that is, the middle term must appear in a premise that includes or excludes all the members of a class. The term *chemists,* for example, is distributed in each of these statements:

All chemists are intelligent. No chemists are intelligent.

In syllogism 6 above, the term *children* is distributed in the first premise, "All children are curious." In the following syllogism the middle term, *honorable men,* which appears in both major and minor premises, is distributed in the second premise:

7. MINOR PREMISE　　All writers are honorable men.
   MAJOR PREMISE　　All honorable men are open-minded.
   CONCLUSION　　　All writers are open-minded.

But consider this next syllogism:

8. MAJOR PREMISE　　All Italians are music lovers.
   MINOR PREMISE　　Gilbert is a music lover.
   CONCLUSION　　　Gilbert is an Italian.

The middle term in this syllogism, *music lover,* is not distributed in either premise. Neither premise includes or excludes all those who love music. The term *Italian* is distributed in the major premise, but it is not the middle term. Therefore, the conclusion does not follow, and the syllogism is invalid. A conclusion that does not follow from the premises of a deductive argument is called a *non sequitur.*

A syllogism in which the meaning of the middle term changes from major to minor premise also produces an invalid conclusion. In the following argument the meaning of *democratic* differs in the two premises, and the conclusion is thus a *non sequitur.*

9. MAJOR PREMISE　　All political leaders having democratic sympathies are popular.
   MINOR PREMISE　　Governor Fagin has Democratic sympathies.
   CONCLUSION　　　Governor Fagin is popular.

The pattern of valid and invalid deductions is usually clarified by the use of diagrams. For example, in syllogism 6 the major premise states "All children are curious." If we draw a small circle to represent children and a larger one to represent individuals who are curious and then place the small circle within the larger, we can diagram the relationship between children and curiosity contained in the major premise.

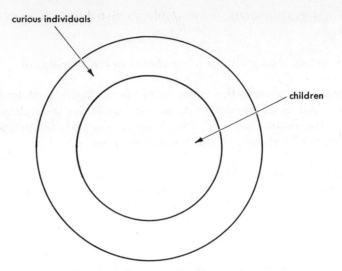

By drawing a still smaller circle to represent Stephen and placing it within the circle marked "children," we can diagram the minor premise, "Stephen is a child."

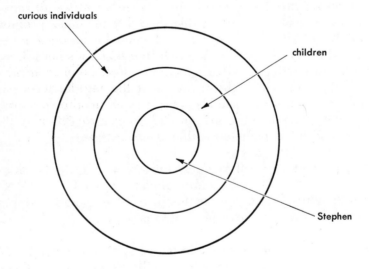

As the diagram now shows, the smallest circle is necessarily included in the largest circle, and the conclusion is thus valid: Stephen *is* curious.

Using the same system of circles to diagram syllogism 8, we can clearly see that its conclusion does not follow. The major premise, "All Italians are music lovers," can be represented thus:

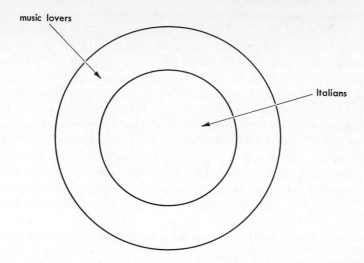

The minor premise, "Gilbert is a music lover," allows us to place the circle representing Gilbert any place within the larger circle: it does not have to be placed within the circle marked "Italians."

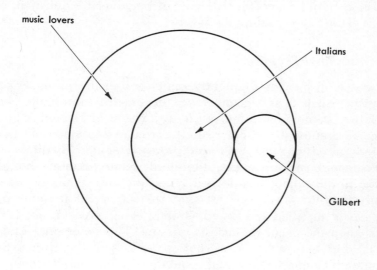

Therefore, the conclusion "Gilbert is an Italian" is a *non sequitur*—it does not follow.

The True Conclusion

We said earlier that a valid conclusion is not necessarily a true conclusion. The major premise must also be true before the argument can produce a true conclusion, and true conclusions are essential to convince a careful reader. The more firmly rooted in accurate, verifiable observation the major premise is—the more thorough the process of induction that produced it—the sounder it is. "All men are mortal" is an accurate premise; it is a generalization born of universal human experience. Any syllogism based on it may yield a true conclusion. Few premises, however, are so unquestionably accurate. Arguments based on such premises as "The United Nations is a plot to subvert the United States," "Blondes have more fun," and "Americans are crass materialists" are likely to result in faulty conclusions. In constructing deductive arguments, therefore, make certain that your premises are accurate and your reasoning valid. In other words, make certain that your syllogisms yield true conclusions. A logically deduced conclusion derived from unsound premises is like a well-constructed house built on a poor foundation. Both are likely to collapse.

The criteria for the valid conclusion and the true conclusion mentioned above do not cover all syllogisms, but they are sufficient for our purposes here. Several common problems related to the deductive argument, however, should be considered. These include the concealed premise and the fallacies of begging the question, oversimplification, and evading the issue.

The Concealed Premise

A writer or speaker frequently omits one of the premises of his syllogism. Such a syllogism is not necessarily unreliable, but it presents a problem for an inexperienced writer or listener, who may accept an argument without realizing it is an argument and that its implied premises must be tested. The statement "Realtors make good school-board members; therefore, Henry Babbit should be elected to the school board" is a syllogism with its minor premise, "Henry Babbit is a realtor," missing. In such cases the minor premise is easily supplied and tested. Greater care, however, needs to be taken when the major premise is missing. The statement "The current tax bill before Congress should be passed: the United States Chamber of Commerce favors it" contains the concealed premise that the kind of tax legislation promoted by this organization is good for all Americans and should be enacted. The truth of this assumption is open to serious question—many economists would certainly oppose it—and because it is so central to the argument, the writer cannot ignore it without weakening his case.

Examine your own arguments, then, to see that they are not based on hidden, untenable premises. And when reading or discussing an issue with others, analyze the arguments proposed for the same purpose. If any contain concealed premises, supply the missing premises and test them for accuracy.

Begging the Question

An argument that begs the question assumes as proved the point the argument is trying to establish. This fallacy is also known as the circular argument, for the conclusion of the argument is merely a restatement (in the same words or synonyms) of the basic premises, leaving the reader no wiser at the end of the argument than he was at the beginning. The following arguments illustrate this fallacy:

1. Sam is uncouth; therefore, he is crude and boorish.
2. All Americans believe in freedom because freedom is a basic American belief.
3. Writers are hard-working. Therefore, all writers work hard.

Frequently this kind of argument requires several sentences to complete it.

> Self-reliant citizens do not need federal aid to help them pay for their children's education or their medical bills. People with independence of spirit and initiative can provide these things by themselves. Therefore they do not need federal aid for education or medical bills.

To the careless or uninformed reader this passage may appear to constitute an effective argument against federal aid for education and medical care, when in fact it contains no argument at all. The last sentence, meant to be a conclusion, simply reasserts the idea contained in the two preceding sentences. As this example illustrates, the lack of logic and supporting evidence makes the circular argument a poor risk with careful readers.

Oversimplification

Oversimplification is a common fallacy in argumentation. Persons who are frustrated with the complexity of modern life and who desire simple, direct solutions for its problems commonly indulge in oversimplification. The rabid segregationist who regards civil rights legislation as indicative of the federal government's desire to tyrannize the South, the radical reactionary who believes that abolishing the income tax would solve the unemployment problem, and the military leader who feels that American security can be ensured by simply brandishing nuclear weapons — all these views are oversimplifications of complex problems.

A characteristic tendency of people who oversimplify is to divide people, ideas, and things into two or three sharply contrasting groups. There is a right way and a wrong way to do things, a moral way and an immoral way. Democrats are good, Republicans are bad; the federal government is bad, local government is good; economic systems are socialistic or capitalistic. The weakness of such conclusions is that they omit the possibility of other alternatives: they reject any middle ground between these polar positions. Few economic systems in the world, for example, are either purely capitalistic or purely socialistic. When revising your papers, therefore, reexamine your statements to see that you have not oversimplified issues. An intelligent reader will not be persuaded by simple answers to difficult questions.

Evading the Issue

The evidence used to prove an argument not only must be sufficient and representative, as explained earlier; it must be pertinent as well. When a writer or speaker engaged in a dispute presents evidence that does not relate to the point of his opponent's argument, he commits the error of evading the issue. An arguer who evades the issue often uses one of the following techniques: (1) the "smear" technique, (2) the "transfer" technique, and (3) the "bandwagon" technique. In the first of these, the arguer attacks the man instead of dealing with the issues he introduces. The following arguments illustrate this technique:

1. I'm against Senator Barker's amendment to the Constitution. He's simply a fascist reactionary who would like to see the country run by big businessmen.
2. You can disregard Bill Olson's warning on automation; he's a typical labor boss trying to stop economic progress.
3. I'll never understand what movie critics see in Leslie Windgate. He's irritable, conceited, and immoral. He's been married five times.

In each of these examples, the writer uses abuse rather than relevant evidence to support his argument. Leslie Windgate's unsuccessful married life and his unpleasant disposition, for example, are not relevant considerations in an evaluation of his acting ability.

The transfer technique involves an appeal to authority—to a famous name or universally sanctioned idea—to validate an argument. Advertisers, newspaper editors, and politicians frequently attempt to gain acceptance for a product or a point of view by using this technique.

1. Linebacker Bull McCrunch smokes Crisp cigarettes. He reports . . .
2. Movie actress Ariel Tempest washes her hair regularly with Bubble shampoo.
3. Elvis Presley, discussing recent developments in modern art, said . . .
4. Benjamin Franklin would never have approved of such a huge federal debt.

All these statements illustrate the fallacy of the simple appeal to authority. What Benjamin Franklin said may no longer be relevant in today's world. Nor can one accept Elvis Presley's opinion on art simply because he is widely known. Of course, if these individuals were quoted on subjects within their competence, this fallacy would not apply. Linebacker McCrunch's knowledge might be relevant to a discussion of football and Elvis Presley's to one about contemporary popular music.

Speakers or writers who ignore the issue through an appeal to the passions and prejudices of the crowd use the bandwagon approach. For example, a political campaigner frequently modifies his approach to accommodate his audience. In Harlem he appeals to his listeners as blacks; in Arkansas he appeals to them as farmers. The following passage illustrates this emotional appeal:

I know that the people of this great nation will not reject a man who has throughout his entire public life worked and fought for the good of America. I know that they will not reject a man of the people, a man dedicated to the preservation of American freedoms against the threat of godless communism.

Advertisers also use this device:

Don't be left behind. Join the crowd and switch to Blitz beer.

The weakness of the bandwagon approach is that in its appeal to the emotions of the audience it submits little or no factual or logical evidence for consideration.

EXERCISE 15

A. Place a V after each of the following syllogisms that has a valid conclusion and an I after each one that has an invalid conclusion. (Diagram each syllogism on a piece of scratch paper to help you determine its validity.) Indicate the cause of an invalid argument by writing one of the following numbers next to an I: (1) undistributed middle term, (2) more than three terms used, (3) shift in meaning of middle term.

EXAMPLE   All dogs drool.
Sheila drools.
Sheila is a dog.   _____ I, 1 _____

1. All cats chase mice.
   Fifi is a cat.
   Fifi chases mice.   _____

2. All tourists are considerate.
   Anne is a tourist.
   Anne is considerate.   _____

3. Some Communists are traitors.
   Alexis is a Communist.
   Alexis is a traitor.   _____

4. All newspapers are enlightening.
   The *New York Times* is a newspaper.
   The *New York Times* is enlightening.   _____

5. All rich people are content.
   Barbara is rich.
   Barbara is content.   _____

6. Some novelists are good psychologists.
   All scholars seek the truth.
   All novelists seek the truth.   _____

7. All students who swear are immoral.
   Isaac Bickerstaff is a student who swears.
   Isaac Bickerstaff is immoral.   _____

8. All men are mortal.
   Roberta is not a man.
   Roberta is not mortal.   _____

9. All geniuses are introverts.
   Professor Smedley is an introvert.
   Professor Smedley is a genius.   _____

10. All rats like cheese.
    Robert likes cheese.
    Robert is a rat.   _____

B. In the following syllogisms some conclusions are true, some are valid, and some are invalid. If the conclusion is true, place a T in the blank after it. If it is valid, place a V in the blank, and if it is invalid, place an I in the blank. (Remember that a true conclusion and a valid conclusion follow logically from the premises, but only a true conclusion follows from sound, accurate premises.)

1. All movie stars are wealthy.
   Debbie Torch is a movie star.
   Debbie Torch is wealthy.   _____

2. All successful men enjoy wealth and social position.
   Dr. Schweitzer was a successful man.
   Dr. Schweitzer enjoyed wealth and social position.   _____

3. All scientists who seek to eliminate human diseases are
      praiseworthy.
   Dr. Salk is a scientist who seeks to eliminate human
      diseases.
   Dr. Salk is praiseworthy.   _____

4. All students cheating on examinations are dishonest.
   Frank is dishonest.
   Frank cheats on his examinations.   _____

5. All human beings are fallible.
   English instructors are human beings.
   English instructors are fallible.   _____

6. All college students need to write clearly.
   Joshua is a college student.
   Joshua needs to write clearly.   _____

7. All extroverts are conceited boobs.
   Peter Per Scott is a conceited boob.
   Peter Per Scott is an extrovert.   _____

8. All sorority girls are sophisticated and well-bred.
   Marilyn is a sorority girl.
   Marilyn is sophisticated and well-bred.   _____

9. All superstitious people are ignorant.
   Barbara is wise.
   Barbara is not superstitious.   _____

10. All Americans who serve their country in the Peace
       Corps are to be commended.
   John Franklin is serving his country in the Peace Corps.
   John Franklin is to be commended.   _____

C. The following statements are deductive arguments with hidden major premises. Supply the missing premise of each argument.

EXAMPLE   Of course Clampson dental cream is good; it's advertised in *Peek* magazine.

Missing Premise   Products advertised in *Peek* magazine are good.

1. André Bouton is quite a lover, but then he is a Frenchman.

   Missing Premise _____

   _____

2. William Heckworthy is obviously a successful man. He drives a new car every year.

   Missing Premise _____

   _____

3. This past Christmas was a good one; retail sales were up 10 percent over last year.

   Missing Premise _____

   _____

4. *The Bountiful Boudoir* is obviously a good book; it sold more than 2 million copies the first year of its publication.

   Missing Premise _____

   _____

5. Buy Volkswagen. It never dates you.

   Missing Premise _____

   _____

D. The following statements are deductive arguments with missing minor premises. Supply the missing premise in each argument.

1. Eloquent senators make fine presidents. Therefore, Senator Connors should be elected president.

   Missing Premise _____

   _____

2. Blondes lead exciting lives. Lorraine's life must be very exciting.

   Missing Premise _____

   _____

3. A liberal arts course is a waste of time. Consequently, I'm not going to major in history.

   Missing Premise _____

   _____

4. Football players need to be big and beefy. Therefore, Kerrigan ought not to go out for football.

   Missing Premise _____

   _____

5. People who smoke Puritan cigars have discriminating taste. Larry obviously has discriminating taste.

   Missing Premise _____

   _____

E. Identify the fallacies in the following arguments.

1. This measure, ladies and gentlemen, which will permit the Department of Agriculture to sell surplus American wheat to the Russians, is nonsensical, if not treasonable. The American people are not going to approve of helping to feed their sworn enemies, the Communists. On the contrary, patriotic Americans will protest this measure as an exercise in stupidity.

   _____

2. Senator Wilson's views on the American economy are not worth listening to. He's just a fuzzy-minded, ignorant radical.

   _____

3. I'm tired of all these pussyfooting pacifists. The only thing the Communists respect is force. Instead of sending our boys into the jungles of Asia, we ought to drop the hydrogen bomb on China.

   _____

4. Wayne is shy and introverted because he's afraid to assert himself.

   _____

5. National League baseball players agree. Sheffield razor blades make shaving a sheer delight.

   _____

USING REASONS TO DEVELOP A PARAGRAPH

The information on inductive and deductive reasoning just presented should help you use reasons to develop a paragraph. The persuasiveness of this type of paragraph depends on the soundness of the reasoning that supports the central idea. Make certain, therefore, that your inductions are based on a sufficient number of relevant facts, examples, and judgments. If you quote authorities, make certain they are competent and objective. Be careful, too, that your deductions follow logically from sound premises.

Read the following paragraphs carefully, and note how the writer of each uses reasons to develop and clarify his central idea.

*First
Reason*

*Second
Reason
Third
Reason*

The new creed, with its dismissal of free discussion and its conviction that violence will mystically generate policy and program, represents an assault on rationality in politics — an assault based on the ultimate proposition that rights and wrongs in public affairs are so absolute and so easily ascertainable that opposition can be legitimately destroyed. This assault on the Bill of Rights and on libertarian democracy is in my judgment wrong, because no one is infallible. It is stupid, because the beneficiaries of this view will not be the idealists of the left but the brutalists of the right. It is dangerous, because it represents a reversion to and rationalization of the strain of hatred and violence in our own national tradition: the politics of lynch law against the politics of Lincoln. It is a vote for the worst against the best in our political ethos. [From Arthur Schlesinger, Jr., "America 1968: The Politics of Violence," *Harper's Magazine*, August, 1968, p. 23.]

*First
Reason
Second
Reason*

The phrase "conquest of nature" is certainly one of the most objectionable and misleading expressions of Western languages. It reflects the illusion that all natural forces can be entirely controlled, and it expresses the criminal conceit that nature is to be considered primarily as a source of raw materials and energy for human purposes. This view of man's relationship to nature is philosophically untenable and destructive. A relationship

Third   to the earth based only on its use for economic enrich-
Reason   ment is bound to result not only in its degradation but
            also in the devaluation of human life. This is a perver-
            sion which, if not soon corrected, will become a fatal
            disease of technological societies. [From René Dubos,
            A God Within, p. 40. Charles Scribner's Sons 1972.]

EXERCISE 16

A. The following subjects are often the basis of sharp differences of opinion.
Write a topic sentence expressing such an opinion on one of the subjects
and develop a paragraph for it by the use of reasons.

1. working while attending college
2. installment buying
3. capital punishment
4. religion in the classroom
5. loosening morals and the younger generation
6. student protests and demonstrations
7. the American automobile—madness or magnificence
8. the value of "general education" courses

B. Ben Robinson has been tutoring minority students in his spare time at the
college he attends. His work has brought him into close association with
leaders of a militant faction who, hitherto unsuccessful in their studies,
have shown marked improvement under Ben's guidance. Through hard
work and sympathetic understanding, he has, in fact, gained their trust and
affection. He has also gained the respect and admiration of Dean Olson,
under whose guidance the tutorial program was established. Recently the
militant students have engaged in several confrontations with the dean
because of his opposition to their efforts to gain control of the program.
Now they have asked Ben to join them in their plan to occupy the dean's
office and to use "whatever means are necessary to show him we mean
business." What should Ben do?

Write a paragraph indicating the course of action you think Ben should
take. Think carefully about the consequences of the course you propose,
as well as of those you reject, and develop those thoughts into specific
reasons to support your choice.

PERSUASION

Persuasive writing is not solely a matter of logic: it is also a matter
of language and attitude. To convince your reader, you must attend
to the clarity, honesty, and emotional impact of your arguments as
well as to their logical construction. Much persuasive writing deviates

from the truth to appeal to the prejudices of an audience, but writers who continually engage in emotive, slanted writing ultimately damage whatever cause they serve. This does not mean, of course, that you should never use emotional words in your writing. On the contrary, effective persuasion sanctions — even demands — an emotional plea at times. Moreover, strict objectivity is impossible — no one can completely avoid the influence of his subjective preferences. Nonetheless, your basic purpose in argumentative writing is to elicit from your reader a favorable response to your ideas, and you are not likely to obtain such a response from a thoughtful reader if he thinks your emotions have blurred your objective regard for the truth.

Definition of Terms

The most important element in persuasive writing is clarity, for regardless of how logical your arguments may be or how responsibly you have dealt with the facts, if you have not expressed yourself clearly, you will not convince many readers. Accurate, precise definition of terms is especially important. Be careful, therefore, to define clearly those terms central to your meaning. In particular, such words as *liberty, freedom, truth, justice, liberal, conservative,* and *propaganda* need to be pinned down, for they are subject to a wide range of interpretation. The following illustrates this problem:

> The American people have been deceived about the nature of their government. They have been taught that the United States is a democracy, when actually it is a republic. Consequently, proposals to modify the system of electing a president to make it more democratic are irrelevant.

This passage is vague because of the writer's failure to tell us what he means by *democracy* and *republic*. Since both terms can be used to describe forms of government in which the power resides in the voters who elect representatives to decide public issues, the writer should specify the sense in which he is using these terms if he is to convince rather than confuse us. The revision below eliminates this confusion, although one may still not agree with the conclusion.

> A republic is commonly defined as a form of government in which the voters elect representatives to meet and decide public issues. A pure democracy is a form of government in which the voters themselves assemble in one place to decide these issues. Accepting this distinction, we can describe the United States as a republic rather than a democracy. Hence, proposals to modify the system of electing a president to make it *more* democratic are irrelevant.

VAGUE AND UNCLEAR

It is time Americans recognized the danger of extremist groups. These subversives should be controlled before they do real damage to the American way of life.

IMPROVED

Political groups and organizations that advocate radical measures to meet the problems of our time threaten the stability of American life. What constitutes a "radical" measure is, of course, open to dispute, but most Americans would probably agree that the term could be applied to such proposals as impeaching the Supreme Court justices, establishing local guerrilla "armies," dissolving the United Nations, and the like. Although radical groups have a right to express their opinions and gain adherents to their cause, they should be watched carefully to see that they do not break any laws.

Exaggeration

Exaggeration is a fairly common element in much argumentative writing. Editorial writers, political figures, salesmen, and advertisers use exaggeration to stimulate interest in their ideas or products. The use of the superlative is such a common feature of motion picture advertising, for instance, that the public is almost reluctant to attend a film that has not been described in advance publicity as "stupendous," "breathtaking," "the picture of the decade." Political columnists sometimes indulge in exaggeration to emphasize their opinions, as the following passages illustrate:

Willkie was never a real Republican. . . . He was a socialist Democrat, the tool of Democratic subversives who tried to convince Americans that Soviet Russia was a real ally. He is largely to blame for the United Nations. He was used by Roosevelt to further . . .

Congressman Barnes is one of the loudest of the TVA zealots. He comes from Tennessee, where the TVA is a lush local racket. . . .

Such phrases as "the tool of Democratic subversives," "to blame for the United Nations," "loudest of the TVA zealots," and "lush local racket" tell us much more about the writer's state of mind than about his subject. Here are examples of exaggerated statements with suggested revisions:

EXAGGERATED

The foreign aid program succeeds in doing nothing but pouring money down a rat hole. It is a vast giveaway program that aids no one.

The lessons of history are unmistakable. Either we reduce our tax rate, or the United States faces imminent economic chaos and disaster.

REVISED

Our foreign aid program needs to be examined carefully to see if we cannot eliminate some of the waste and mismanagement in its operation.

Reducing tax rates in the countries of Western Europe after the Second World War provided a needed stimulus to their economies. In all likelihood, lower taxes in the United States would produce a similar expansion.

Emotive Language

A problem related to clarity involves loaded or slanted words, words that reveal the user's feelings and attitudes, his approval or disapproval. Loaded words are rather commonly used in situations in which people's feelings are aroused — political discussions, for example. In the opinion of one person, Senator Jones is intelligent, firm, compassionate in his regard for the underdog. To another he is opinionated, rigid, a maudlin do-gooder. In the course of a conversation between these two persons, people working in Washington, D.C., might be referred to as intellectuals or eggheads, public servants or bureaucrats, faithful employees or time-servers.

The following passage provides further illustration of the use of loaded words. The opinions are those of a Mississippi circuit judge on the subject of Mississippi whiskey.

If when you say whiskey you mean the devil's brew, the poison scourge, the bloody monster, that defiles innocence, dethrones reason, destroys the home, creates misery and poverty, yea, literally takes the bread from the mouths of little children; if you mean the evil drink that topples the Christian man and woman from the pinnacle of righteous, gracious living into the bottomless pit of degradation and despair, and shame, and helplessness, and hopelessness, then certainly I am against it.

But if when you say whiskey you mean the oil of conversation, the philosophic wine, the ale that puts a song in their hearts and laughter on their lips, and the warm glow of contentment in their eyes; if you mean Christmas cheer; if you mean the stimulating drink that puts the spring into the old gentleman's step on a frosty, crispy morning; if you mean the drink which enables a man to magnify his joy, and his happiness, and to forget, if only for a little while, life's great tragedies, and heartaches, and sorrows; if you mean that drink, the sale of which pours into our treasuries untold millions of dollars, which are used to provide tender care for our little crippled children, our blind, our deaf, our dumb, our pitiful aged and infirm; to build highways and hospitals and schools, then certainly I am for it.

This is my stand, I will not retreat from it. I will not compromise. [From Kenneth Vinson, "Prohibition's Last Stand," *The New Republic*, October 16, 1965, p. 11. Reprinted by permission of *The New Republic*, © 1965, Harrison-Blaine of New Jersey, Inc.]

As these differences of opinion about Senator Jones and about whiskey reveal, special feelings and associations attach to words. The person who approves of Senator Jones describes him in words that arouse favorable feelings—*intelligent, fair, compassionate.* The person who disapproves of the senator uses words that arouse unfavorable feelings—*opinionated, rigid, a maudlin do-gooder.* Similarly, one who refers to whiskey as *the oil of conversation, the philosophic wine,* or *Christmas cheer* clearly approves of it; one who regards it as *the devil's brew, the poison scourge,* or *the bloody monster* rather clearly disapproves of it. The suggestions and associations that cluster about a word make up its *connotative* meaning. The connotations of *firm,* for instance, are positive: the word suggests determination, courage, solidity—all attractive qualities. The connotations of *rigid,* however, are negative: it suggests stubbornness, inflexibility, a narrow-minded unwillingness to compromise—all unattractive qualities.

Words have *denotative* meanings as well as connotative meanings. The denotative meaning of a word signifies its literal, explicit meaning—the object or idea it stands for. The denotation of *firm* and *rigid* is the same—unyielding, difficult to move. The distinction, then, between the connotative and denotative meaning of a word is that its connotation includes the feelings and attitudes associated with it; its denotation does not. And, as illustrated, the connotation of a word may be positive or negative.

Emotive words, words with strong connotations, vary in their power to arouse feeling. *Political nonconformist, reactionary, fascist* — all evoke feelings of anger in many people's minds. But *fascist* evokes a stronger reaction than does *political nonconformist.* Because emotive words can powerfully influence people's opinions, some writers employ them frequently to condemn persons and ideas they do not like. By using loaded words such as *traitor, subversive, demagogue,* and the like, they hope to lead their readers into forming unfavorable opinions of their subjects without examining the supporting evidence. As a method of neutralizing the appeal of loaded language, Max Black, a well-known authority on critical thinking, suggests that the reader identify the emotive terms of a passage and then replace the original emotive words with neutral terms (words with little or no emotional charge) or with terms that have contrasting connotations.* As an illustration, the emotive words in the following passage are listed in the first column, and the corresponding neutral words and words with contrasting connotations are listed in the next two columns.

It is time for decent Americans to speak out against an absurd tax system that permits greedy, conniving oil tycoons and assorted "fat cats" to escape paying their fair share of income tax. Legislators, tax lawyers, and other frauds who defend the practice spew the garbage that tax loopholes provide an essential stimulus for the monied class to invest in business and industry to keep the economy healthy. Hogwash and soul butter! Congressmen who utter such drivel selfishly want to protect their sources of campaign contributions; tax lawyers don't want to lose their fat fees for finding such deductions. Until the mass of taxpayers vigorously protest this outrage, they will continue to be the patsies in this annual income tax con game.

*Max Black, *Critical Thinking,* 2nd ed., Prentice-Hall, Inc., 1952, pp. 172–76.

EMOTIVE WORDS	WORDS WITH MORE NEUTRAL CONNOTATIONS	WORDS WITH CONTRASTING CONNOTATIONS
decent	ordinary	conventional
absurd	incongruous	unique
greedy	money-conscious	thrifty
conniving	manipulating	shrewd
fat cats	rich businessmen	wealthy investors
frauds	deceptive individuals	clever individuals
spew the garbage	say	argue with conviction
loopholes	deductions	tax incentives
monied class	persons with money	the financially independent
hogwash and soul butter	not so	I sincerely disagree
drivel	opinions	convictions
selfishly	simply	understandably
fat	large	handsome
outrage	injustice	established custom
patsies	victims	sufferers
con game	collection process	assessment

Substituting more neutral words for the emotive words of the original produces this version:

It is time for ordinary Americans to speak out against an incongruous tax system that permits money-conscious, manipulating oil tycoons and assorted rich businessmen to escape paying their fair share of income tax. Legislators, tax lawyers, and other deceptive individuals who defend the practice say that tax deductions provide an essential stimulus for persons with money to invest in business and industry to keep the economy healthy. Not so! Congressmen who utter such opinions simply want to protect their sources of campaign contributions; tax lawyers don't want to lose their large fees for finding such deductions. Until the mass of taxpayers vigorously protest this injustice, they will continue to be the victims in this annual income tax collection process.

This version communicates the essential meaning of the first version, but its emotional overtones have been dampened so that the reader is less likely to be bulldozed by the implications and innuendos of the original. A second revision, this time using the "purr"

words of the third column in place of the "snarl" words of the first,
yields the following:

It is time for conventional Americans to speak out against a
unique tax system that permits thrifty, shrewd oil tycoons and assorted wealthy investors to escape paying their fair share of income
tax. Legislators, tax lawyers, and other clever individuals who defend the practice argue with conviction that tax incentives provide
an essential stimulus for the financially independent to invest in
business and industry to keep the economy healthy. I sincerely disagree! Congressmen who utter such convictions, understandably,
want to protect their sources of campaign contributions; tax lawyers
don't want to lose their handsome fees for finding such deductions.
Until the mass of taxpayers vigorously protest this established custom, they will continue to be the sufferers in this annual income
tax assessment.

The point of this discussion, it should be stressed, is not that emotive language should be avoided because it is customarily used by
those who distort and exaggerate. On the contrary, persuasive writing
deliberately and legitimately appeals to the emotions of the reader.
Many respected writers and speakers employ emotion successfully to
persuade others of the truth of their ideas. But it must be used with
care. If your reader believes that you are substituting emotion for
credible evidence, that you are trying to browbeat him into agreement, he is apt to dismiss your arguments as biased and unreliable.
In short, deal honestly with your reader. If you use an emotional
appeal, let him see the evidence that justifies it.

EXERCISE 17

A. Read the following passage carefully. Underline the emotive terms, list them in the blanks at the end of the passage, and then supply words with opposite, or nearly opposite, connotations in the second list.

Standard off-the-rack liberals drip tears of compassion for the wife of a convicted murderer facing execution in the gas chamber, but few of these salon socialists put on such a display for the wife of a murdered policeman. The monster who coldbloodedly slays the owner of a liquor store or brutally molests a child invariably evokes sympathy as his case moves through the courts. The victims of these moral outrages are forgotten. Sentimental sociologists and cocktail-hour psychologists spout the nonsense that capital punishment represents "cruel and unusual" punishment and should therefore be ruled unconstitutional. What about the "cruel and unusual" punishment suffered by those criminally assaulted? Do-gooders and other mental midgets maintain the fiction that life imprisonment is a more effective and moral deterrent than capital punishment. The truth is, however, that few killers spend the rest of their lives in prison, a fact conveniently overlooked by those who agonize over violence. The degenerates who murder decent citizens deserve no such concern. They should be brought to justice and executed.

| | WORDS WITH CONTRASTING |
EMOTIVE WORDS	CONNOTATIONS
_____	_____
_____	_____
_____	_____
_____	_____
_____	_____
_____	_____
_____	_____
_____	_____
_____	_____

B. The following appraisal of the threat of international communism is one-sided, for it omits important facts about communist failures. The appraisal presented on pp. 122–23 is also one-sided. Using facts appearing in each of these slanted versions, write a balanced view of the danger of the communist threat.

International communism seriously threatens the survival of Western civilization today. Since the end of the Second World War, it has dramatically extended its influence throughout the world. In Poland, Czechoslovakia, Bulgaria, Rumania, and Hungary the Communist party dominates the lives of the people. In Asia the most populous nation on earth, China, is now communist and exerts a baleful influence on India, Thailand, North Vietnam, and Cambodia along its borders. Nor has the Western Hemisphere remained unpolluted. Cuba has become a communist beachhead in the Caribbean, aiding and fomenting revolutions in Central and South America against democratically elected governments. Constitutional government in Brazil is also threatened by communist agitation, and if Brazil falls, South America cannot be saved. And the military's violent overthrow of the Marxist government in Chile has not hurt the communist cause in South America. A realistic evaluation of the growing power of worldwide communism yields an unavoidable conclusion: unless the West can muster its strength immediately to dam the communist flood, its civilization will be washed away like that of Rome.

C. Rewrite the following sentences to change their emotional tone by substituting for the italicized words and phrases neutral words or words with contrasting connotations. Substitute as directed after each sentence.

EXAMPLE

ORIGINAL   Congressman Robertson is a *stubborn politician.*
(Change to favorable connotation.)
REVISION   Congressman Robertson is a *determined statesman.*

1. Uncle Jim is a *public servant.* (Change to unfavorable connotation.)

    REVISION _____

2. Harry's father is a *shrewd* lawyer. (Change to unfavorable connotation.)

    REVISION _____

3. Labor *leader* George Meany spoke to the president. (Change to unfavorable connotation.)

    REVISION _____

4. In his thirteenth year with the company Hanks was *fired* for *laziness.* (Change to favorable connotation.)

    REVISION _____
    _____

5. Mr. Alger was an *aggressive, determined* businessman, who *gained financial success* by his *clever* real estate *transactions.* (Change to unfavorable connotation.)

REVISION _____

_____

_____

6. Frances has a *dignified, self-confident* air about her. (Change to unfavorable connotation.)

   REVISION _____

   _____

7. Homer's father has a *perverted* sense of humor. (Change to a neutral
term.)

   REVISION _____

   _____

8. Sobelskey was convicted of being a Russian *spy*. (Change to a neutral
term.)

   REVISION _____

   _____

9. On the political platform he is a *demagogue, pandering to the passions of
a mob of rustic ignoramuses.* (Change to favorable connotation.)

   REVISION _____

   _____

10. He *crammed* hard but *flunked* the test. (Change to favorable connotation.)

    REVISION _____

    _____

D. The following two advertisements comment on economic conditions in
the United States. Read them carefully and write a short theme comparing
and contrasting their use of emotive language and the evidence—the
facts, opinions, logic—used to support the points made. Reread pages
51–56 to review comparison and contrast as methods of paragraph development. Support your own statements with specific illustrations from the
two advertisements.

We Mass-Produce Almost Everything in This Country—Except Character

It used to be that when you wanted something, you worked to earn it. Now
you stage a riot to get it given to you at someone else's expense.

If your father or grandfather lost his job, he took whatever work he could
get, and he went (probably walked miles) to where there *was* work—*any*
honest work—being done. Now hordes of relief "clients" refuse a job unless

it is to their liking, and they demand the job be brought to them in their community.

This nation was built by immigrants (beginning in the 1600's and earlier) who struggled here for opportunity, and would have scorned the false idea of "something for nothing." Now it seems to be an almost universal (and all too often the only) ambition.

It used to take a lifetime of gruelling work and scrimping for a family or a country to earn a little surplus, a taste of security. Now mobs of stupid "students" and whole "emerging nations" demand they be given, out of *your* earnings and with no effort on their part.

"Minority groups" all over the earth seem to think the world owes them everything they want. So vicious destructiveness makes necessary higher taxes to pay for more police to protect decent citizens; higher taxes for playgrounds and parks, which hoodlums promptly make unsafe; higher taxes for schooling for gangs who don't seem to want or are unable to be educated. The minority groups whose rights no one seems to consider are the taxpayers and decent citizens—who may have been pampering evil too long. [From an advertisement for the Warner & Swasey Company. *Newsweek*, September 6, 1965, p. 1.]

Unfortunately, College Kids Don't Even Dislike American Business. They Just Ignore It.

That's our biggest problem. Because dislike, at least, would give us a chance for a dialogue. But indifference just closes the door in our face.

So each June, business goes right on losing more bright young people to teaching, public service, government and other non-business fields for the wrong reasons.

Because they think business is dull, money-grubbing, conformist, self-centered—you name it.

And we haven't convinced them otherwise.

Sure, there are still more students who want a career in business than don't. And there are plenty of companies, like Olin, who haven't felt the squeeze.

But that doesn't mean we can ignore the problem, or even settle for half-way measures to solve it.

There are other factors involved.

Last year, business got only two graduates for every three it wanted. (In engineering, it was one for two.)

But this year, with the number of graduates remaining roughly the same, corporation hiring goals jumped 53% higher.

Allow for the effect of the draft, and the fact that more students than ever before are going on to graduate school before settling on a career, and the picture gets even bleaker.

So business just can't afford to lose any graduates unnecessarily.

What's the answer?

Part of it is to recognize that today's student is no longer interested in the old lures of salary, pension and profit sharing alone. He's looking for challenge and responsibility, too.

He wants the opportunity to help solve the great social issues of our time—
ignorance, poverty, race relations, and a dozen others.

And, if he doesn't know that this opportunity does exist in business—probably to an even greater degree than in government or social work—then he
hasn't been reached with the facts.

That's why if any company is having trouble attracting students, it ought to
take a new look at itself.

Has it kept pace with the new goals of our kids? Is it telling them—indeed,
is it in a position to tell them—what they really want to know? Or is it merely
blaming "student attitudes" for its own shortcomings?

Changes based on the answers to these questions won't be easy to make,
of course.

But it's certainly worth trying, whatever the cost. Because if companies
with recruiting problems can succeed in getting their stories across to students, they won't be just helping themselves.

They'll be helping all business. [From an advertisement for Olin Corporation. *Newsweek*, 1967. Reprinted courtesy of Olin Corporation.]

E. The following newspaper editorial comments upon a Chilean election in
which a coalition of socialist and communist political parties led by Salvador Allende retained its control of the government. Read the editorial
carefully and, in a paragraph or two, comment on the soundness of its
reasoning and the persuasiveness of its language. Keep these points in
mind as you formulate your analysis: What opinion of Allende is expressed
in the editorial? Is that judgment supported by evidence? Is the evidence
one-sided? Does the writer frequently resort to emotive language to make
a point? Is the writer fair to Allende?

For 2½ years now, Chile has been run by the world's first freely elected
Marxist government. The Chilean people went to the polls the other day
to pass judgment on its performance. And while the Socialists and Communists by no means won a vote of confidence, the results don't offer much
comfort to those who believe that the Marxist experiment has failed and
should be ended before the country slips into political and economic chaos.

These were off-year congressional elections, so Socialist President Salvador
Allende was not on the ballot. But both sides viewed the election as an important test of public sentiment toward the Marxist government.

When the votes were counted, it was a standoff.

The opposition forces, spearheaded by the Christian Democrats, got 55%
to 43% for candidates representing the Marxist coalition. Thus the anti-
Marxist parties continue to control Congress—but they do not have enough
votes to impeach Allende or roll back the more excessive elements of his
Socialist program.

Because of the way the Chilean election system works, the Allende forces
actually picked up a few seats in the Senate and Chamber of Deputies. But
they still lack the strength to put through legislative or constitutional revisions that would enable them to accelerate the socialization of Chile.

163

Unless the two sides can reach a working arrangement, the situation spells stalemate. And stalemate is something the Chilean people can ill afford.

There are some plus marks on the Allende record. Unemployment is down. The infant-mortality rate has been cut. More housing is being built. It may well be true that Chile's poorest people are better off than before. These gains, however, have been accompanied by incredible mismanagement of the economy.

Prices go up by at least 10% to 15% a month. There are serious shortages of such staples as meat, eggs, milk, butter and bread—and these shortages will almost certainly grow worse in the Chilean winter just ahead.

Meanwhile, thanks in part to massive imports of foodstuffs, the nation's foreign exchange reserves are depleted. And with imported parts no longer available, the country's transportation and industrial facilities are falling apart.

Allende and his Communist partners in the coalition are pragmatists. There is speculation that, with the elections over, they will impose an unpopular but badly needed period of austerity in order to break the back of inflation.

There is talk, too, that Allende will seek a political truce of sorts by bringing nonradical elements, perhaps even Christian Democrats, into his government.

The impression is growing, finally, that the dispute over compensation for seizure of U.S.-owned copper mines will be papered over, opening the way for greater Chilean access to international credits.

None of this will be possible, however, unless Allende is willing to brave the prospect of an open break with his own party's extremists, who would rather see Chile collapse in economic and political chaos than to compromise with the "enemies" of the revolution.

Allende has not shown any great willingness to stand up to the ultraleftists in the past, which is one reason the Chilean economy is in such a mess. It is far from clear that he has the will to do so now. ["The Standoff in Chile," an editorial in the *Los Angeles Times,* March 8, 1973. Copyright, 1973, *Los Angeles Times.* Reprinted by permission.]

SUMMARY

Effective argumentative writing requires the ability to think logi-cally—to reason correctly from the evidence or premises—and to persuade others to accept your reasoning. In this chapter we have briefly investigated the basic processes of reasoning, induction and deduction, and examined some common fallacies in reasoning. We have said that generalizations resulting from induction must be adequately supported; that is, there must be sufficient evidence to justify the generalization, and the evidence must be representative and factual. And if testimony is used, the authority quoted must be qualified and objective. Deduction produces true—and therefore useful—conclusions when the premises are accurate and the conclu-sions valid. To persuade your reader to accept your arguments, you must convince him of your integrity, and the best way to accomplish this is to express yourself clearly and honestly. Choose your words carefully, therefore, and avoid highly charged language.

CHAPTER FIVE | # The Theme

   In your college work you will frequently be asked to write compositions of several hundred words. Research papers, expository essays, book reviews, final examinations—all require more extensive development of an idea than is possible in a single paragraph. The problems you will encounter with the longer paper are not radically different from those of the paragraph. An essay of 500 words demands the same careful attention to unity, development, and coherence as does the paragraph. But, because of the greater length and complexity of such a composition, you will find it necessary to plan it more thoroughly. To make your meaning clear to a reader, you will have to think more carefully about what you want to say and how you want to say it.

   Many students who have trouble with writing assignments seem to think that writing is an inherited talent, that those who write well simply have a facility for it and that if one lacks this facility, there is little to be done about it. However, good writing does not simply result from natural ability: it results from thoughtful planning, intelligently directed effort, and writing and rewriting. Those who write well, as most professional writers would testify, do not reach for a piece of paper and begin to write lucid, polished prose. On the contrary, they must plan and revise their work carefully. In short, good writing requires not genius, but a willingness to learn and a steady application of what has been learned.

   There are no simple, mechanical rules to follow in writing a theme; a system that works well for one writer may not work well for another. But by following a series of steps, you should be able to avoid many of the frustrations and false starts that plague students who begin to write with no plan of procedure. These steps include:

1. selecting a topic
2. narrowing the topic
3. thinking through the topic
4. gathering and organizing material
5. outlining
6. writing the first draft
7. revising the first draft
8. preparing the final copy

As you develop skill in writing themes, you will be able to modify and condense these steps into three or four operations, especially for themes written in class; but until you develop such proficiency, you would be wise to follow each step carefully. We will consider these steps in order.

1. SELECTING A TOPIC

Sometimes you will be allowed to select your own topic; at other times a topic will be assigned. When it is assigned, be certain you know precisely what is required before you begin. Knowing what the subject or question calls for is especially important when you are writing an essay examination or a theme in class, for time limitations do not permit extensive revision if you have misunderstood the subject. For example, if the assignment calls for a discussion of the causes of the French Revolution, concentrate on the causes of the revolution. Do not devote a major portion of your paper to a description of the cruelties perpetrated upon the aristocracy during the Reign of Terror.

When you can select your own subject, choose one from your own experience or one that arouses your interest. Like many students, you may underrate the value of your experiences, but a personal experience that taught you something about life frequently makes an interesting theme topic. It need not be an earth-shaking event, one that illuminated a profound idea, but simply an experience that had meaning for you and that you would like to share with your reader. If you review the events in your life carefully, you will find many such experiences worth relating. Topics of current public interest being discussed in newspapers and magazines and on radio and television also provide excellent material for student writing. If such a topic stirs your interest, investigate it further; your classmates will probably share this interest and would like to know your opinions on the subject.

A procedure you may find helpful when you have difficulty in selecting a subject is simply to sit down and begin writing whatever comes into your head. Experts on creativity say that even if you do not have the vaguest idea for a topic when you begin, the mere act of putting ideas on paper in a free-association process releases creative energy. After you have jotted down as much as you can on paper, look over what you have written. Very likely you will discover a topic there that can be developed into an interesting theme. Of course, much will be confused and incoherent at this point; but as you explore the possibilities of a topic, you can rearrange, reorder, analyze, and classify until what you have written makes sense. You can then eliminate the irrelevant and begin building an outline.

EXERCISE 18

A. Think back over your own experiences, and make a list of ten to fifteen subjects that could be used as theme topics. Select those experiences that provided you with an insight into life.

1. _____
2. _____
3. _____
4. _____
5. _____
6. _____
7. _____
8. _____
9. _____
10. _____
11. _____
12. _____
13. _____
14. _____
15. _____

B. Peruse several newspapers and weekly news magazines for a few days, and make notes of current topics that you would like to write about. List ten of them below.

1. _____
2. _____
3. _____
4. _____
5. _____
6. _____
7. _____
8. _____
9. _____
10. _____

2. NARROWING THE TOPIC

The problem of narrowing your topic is not so crucial if you have been assigned a specific topic. However, if you are allowed to choose your own subject, or if the assigned topic is rather broad, you should restrict it to one you can handle within the length of the paper you intend to write. For example, your instructor may ask you to write an impromptu 300-word theme in class, or he may assign a 700-word paper to be written out of class. This stipulation of length is not designed to make you produce an exact number of words: it is meant rather to define the scope of your subject. The shorter your paper, the more you will have to restrict your topic.

Let us assume that you are assigned a 500-word theme on a subject of your own choice and that you decide to write on college sports. You could write 500 words on college sports by presenting an overview of the subject, moving rapidly from one large aspect to another. In successive paragraphs you might deal with the types of sports offered on a college campus, their respective requirements for participation, the general value of participation to the student, and so on. But this kind of treatment would be too general to arouse much interest. By rejecting such a broad topic in favor of a more limited one, such as "Volleyball: No Game for Sissies" or "The Value of Intramural Sports," you can reduce the scope of your subject to a topic that can be successfully managed in 500 words. Not having so much ground to cover, you could develop each point in greater detail and produce a much more interesting paper.

In selecting your topic, then, consider carefully the proposed length of your paper. You might begin with a broad subject to discover how much you know about it, but as you proceed, you will need to focus on one aspect of it. The character of your intended audience will also affect your choice of subject. You can expect an audience of your fellow English students to understand and respond to a lively discussion of some topic of current public interest or an account of a personal experience. But they are not likely to understand or be interested in a technical explanation of some complicated engineering process. For example, a paper on the importance of desalting ocean water to satisfy the world's growing need for water is more suitable than a detailed, scientific discussion of the desalinization process.

EXERCISE 19

A. Consider these items as possible subjects for a 500-word theme. Some are too broad for such an assignment; after these write *too broad*. Some are too technical; after these write *too technical*. And some are suited for such a theme; after these write *satisfactory*.

1. philosophy _____

2. poverty _____

3. guerrilla warfare _____

4. the used car as a status symbol _____

5. recent improvements in the analog computer _____

6. automatic arc welding _____

7. my favorite boss _____

8. education for citizenship _____

9. shooting underwater pictures _____

10. violence in American life _____

B. These subjects are too general to be covered in a short theme. Select five that interest you and divide each into three subtopics, each to serve as the subject of a 300- to 500-word theme.

1. television

_____

_____

_____

2. prejudices

_____

_____

_____

3. family

_____

_____

_____

4. ecology

_____

_____

_____

5. race relations in the United States

_____

_____

_____

6. college

_____

_____

_____

7. religion

_____

_____

_____

8. architecture

_____

_____

_____

9. sports

_____

_____

_____

10. transportation

_____

_____

_____

3. THINKING THROUGH THE TOPIC

Having chosen your topic and limited it to something you can handle in the space available, you must consider carefully just what you want to say about it. You may have a definite purpose in mind before you begin to organize your thoughts. More often, you may not be able to formulate your aim until you have collected and organized your material in some detail. But whether you establish your purpose early or evolve it as you work out the plan of your paper, you will find it helpful at this stage to spend some time thinking about your general intention, about what you want your reader to get from reading your paper. This preliminary thinking will often give you a framework for your ideas and so minimize the frustrations of getting started.

4. GATHERING AND ORGANIZING MATERIAL

Composing a theme, like composing a paragraph, demands careful attention to supporting detail. Because of its greater length, a theme requires more facts, illustrations, and judgments to support its ideas; and it takes time to accumulate this material. When you are given a week to prepare a paper, therefore, do not wait until the night before the paper is due to begin thinking about supporting materials, but begin gathering them immediately.

Materials for writing come from a variety of sources — from personal experiences, lectures, class discussions, campus bull sessions, books, magazines, newspapers, and so forth. When writing an essay examination, you will depend largely on the experiences and ideas of others — on lecture notes, on notes of your readings, and on your own thoughts about what you have heard and read. When writing a theme on a personal experience, however, you will have to rely on your own feelings and attitudes for ideas.

As many experienced students will tell you, a good way to organize your ideas for an essay to be written in class (under pressure or within a limited time period) is to work up a brief informal outline of your thoughts before you begin to write. Begin with the major ideas, the ideas that will serve as the topic sentences of your paragraphs, and then supply a few supporting details under each main heading. An informal outline of an essay on the disadvantages of a college student's owning an automobile might look something like this:

Parking and traffic problem
   Parking spaces during popular class hours scarce
   Tardiness and absences because of traffic jams
Expense of operation
   Initial cost—financing and depreciation
   Insurance
   Upkeep
Interference with studies
   Part-time job to keep up payments reduces study time
   Maintenance costs cut into educational supplies budget

This kind of scratch outline need not be very elaborate. Its function is simply to help you to organize your thoughts before you begin to write. The short time it takes to prepare is amply justified by the improvement it will make in the coherence and unity of your writing. Having established a framework for your thoughts, you can devote more attention to their lucid and precise expression.

A paper written out of class can be developed in greater detail. For example, if you were given a week to write a paper on the characteristics of good college teachers, you might begin by listing the ideas obtained from your reading as well as those derived from your own experience. Your list would probably contain irrelevant and awkwardly phrased items, but this is not important at this stage. The important thing is to get your ideas down on paper so that you will not forget them before you begin to write. Your preliminary listing of detail might develop in this manner:

1. Praises student achievement
2. Has patience
3. Accepts student limitations and range of abilities
4. Knows subject
5. Sense of humor
6. Love of subject
7. Does not patronize, talk down to students
8. Command of language—expresses himself clearly
9. Keeps abreast of developments in his field
10. Provides interesting, illuminating material in lectures rather than a rehash of text
11. Considerate, tactful—can accept opposing views
12. Does not simply read lectures but asks questions, leads discussion
13. Prepares well, structures course
14. Stimulates student interest in subject by his own enthusiasm
15. Good teachers need more recognition

16. Brings in material of current interest
17. Students differ in their opinions
18. Knows related fields
19. Good teachers are popular
20. Frequently brings in interesting books from his own library to recommend
21. Continues study of subject matter on his own
22. Provides additional help when asked—cheerfully

Grouping related items and discarding irrelevant ones is the next step. The items in the list above might be grouped under the following main headings:

Attitude toward students
    Praises student achievement (1)
    Has patience (2)
    Accepts student limitations and range of abilities (3)
    Does not patronize, talk down to students (7)
    Considerate, tactful—can accept opposing views (11)
Knowledge of subject
    Keeps abreast of developments in his field (9)
    Provides interesting, illuminating material in lectures rather than a rehash of text (10)
    Knows related fields (18)
Love of subject
    Stimulates student interest in subject by his own enthusiasm (14)
    Frequently brings in interesting books from his own library to recommend (20)
    Continues study of subject matter on his own (21)
Class presentation
    Sense of humor (5)
    Command of language—expresses himself clearly (8)
    Does not simply read lectures but asks questions, leads discussion (12)
    Prepares well, structures course (13)

The grouping of detail in this preliminary outline is somewhat arbitrary. A sense of humor (item 5), for example, might illustrate an attitude toward students as well as serve as a device to enliven classroom presentation. Note also that items 15, 16, 17, and 19 have been eliminated. Item 16 repeats number 10; and items 15, 17, and 19—that good teachers deserve more recognition, that students have different ideas on what makes a good teacher, and that good teachers are popular—are not relevant to a discussion of the qualities of a good teacher.

As you look over your groupings, you may discover that one heading contains many more items than any other. If this occurs, you may decide to write on the subject of that heading rather than on your original subject. Shifting your attention to your new subject, you could then supply additional detail and organize it in the same manner as you did the original topic. This possibility illustrates an important fact about an outline: it is not irrevocable. It is only a means to an end; and when you modify your purpose, you can modify your outline accordingly.

After you have completed this grouping, you must arrange your major and minor ideas in some effective order. The order you use will depend on the nature of your materials and on your purpose (see pp. 85–89). For an expository theme such as this one, an order of climax is usually effective. Examining your ideas, you may decide that a teacher's positive attitude is the most important attribute of a good teacher and so place this idea last for emphasis. You may also decide that knowledge of subject is next in importance and place this idea at the beginning to give it secondary emphasis. Arranging the ideas in a climactic order yields the following informal outline:

A. Knowledge of subject
    1. Keeps abreast of developments in his field (9)
    2. Knows related fields (18)
    3. Provides interesting, illuminating material in lectures rather than a rehash of text (10)
B. Love of subject
    1. Continues study of subject matter on his own (21)
    2. Stimulates student interest in subject by his own enthusiasm (14)
    3. Frequently brings in interesting books from his own library to recommend (20)
C. Class presentation
    1. Command of language—expresses himself clearly (8)
    2. Does not simply read lectures but asks questions, leads discussion (12)
    3. Prepares well, structures course (13)
    4. Sense of humor (5)
D. Attitude toward students
    1. Considerate, tactful—can accept opposing views (11)
    2. Has patience (2)
    3. Accepts student limitations and range of abilities (3)
    4. Does not patronize, talk down to students (7)

    5. Praises student achievement (1)
    6. Provides additional help when asked—cheerfully (22)

With this rough outline as a framework for your theme, you can now begin the first draft. You will still have to supply additional clarifying and supporting detail to develop the minor ideas, but this kind of outline provides sufficient direction for a theme of 300 to 500 words. For a longer theme a more fully developed, formal outline is often required.

EXERCISE 20

A. Select one of the specific topics you listed in Exercise 18A, 18B, or 19B, and supply several facts, ideas, and illustrations gathered from your own reflections or from your reading that you might use to develop it.

TOPIC _____

Detail	1.	_____
	2.	_____
	3.	_____
	4.	_____
	5.	_____
	6.	_____
	7.	_____
	8.	_____
	9.	_____
	10.	_____
	11.	_____
	12.	_____

B. In each of the following groups, one idea could serve as a major heading for the other ideas. Identify the major heading and write it in the blanks provided.

1. would not permit opposing student views; continually gazed out the window while he lectured; favored cute coeds in his grading; made sarcastic remarks about student failings; my worst teacher; an inarticulate, stumbling lecturer

   Main Heading _____

2. extensive facilities for professional training; low tuition; excellent dormitories; good athletic teams; why I chose to attend State University

   Main Heading _____

3. variety of job opportunities; accessible recreational areas; free public colleges and universities; pleasant climate; advantages of living in California; lack of urban congestion

   Main Heading _____

4. helps one learn more about his own language; develops ability to read foreign literature in the original language; importance of learning a for-

eign language; provides practical benefits when traveling in foreign countries; broadens one's cultural insights and understanding of world affairs

Main Heading _____

5. study question carefully; make scratch outline of important points; think before you begin to write; useful advice when writing an essay examination; support main ideas with adequate factual detail, illustrations, or reasons; take care with punctuation, spelling, grammatical constructions

Main Heading _____

C. Arrange the following items under three main headings. One of the items will serve as a title, another as a thesis statement.
  1. An educated man should know a little about everything and a lot about something.
  2. A vision of the good life is needed.
  3. He has the ability to recognize specious reasoning, phony arguments.
  4. Reinforcement of moral virtues — courage, integrity, compassion, honor — are provided by a good education.
  5. The qualities of an educated man.
  6. The corruption of personal honor ultimately corrupts society.
  7. A well-educated man is a harmonious blend of intellectual, moral, and emotional capacities.
  8. Mastery of self-expression is basic in speaking and in writing.
  9. When uncontrolled, the emotions can paralyze, disorient, and isolate man.
  10. Knowledge in the major categories of learning is required — humanities, social sciences, natural sciences.
  11. An educated man is not only willing to listen to others, but he is willing to take a stand himself.
  12. He needs to understand the disruptive powers of the emotions.
  13. To think clearly requires the ability to formulate a persuasive argument and to follow one formulated by another.
  14. A good education gives one knowledge about and experience in controlling his emotions.
  15. Intellectual capacity means a well-stocked, flexible mind as well as a mind capable of thinking clearly and expressing itself clearly.
  16. Development of emotional stability is a third requirement.
  17. Well-educated man is less a victim of his own passions.
  18. Man is more an emotional than a rational animal.

Title _____

THESIS STATEMENT _____

_____

a. _____

_____

_____

_____

_____

_____

b. _____

_____

_____

_____

c. _____

_____

_____

_____

_____

D. Select a subject from the following list, narrow it, and write out three or four main ideas that could be used to develop it.

1. American heroes
2. my home town
3. life styles
4. recreational activities
5. marriage in the modern world
6. new sources of energy
7. violence in American life
8. professional sports
9. disappearing wildlife
10. no-fault auto insurance

GENERAL SUBJECT _____

SPECIFIC SUBJECT _____

Main Idea a. _____

b. _____

c. _____

d. _____

5. OUTLINING

The kind of rough outline described in the preceding section is usually sufficient for a theme of 300 to 500 words. For a longer, more complex writing assignment, however, you will find it helpful to make a more detailed, formal outline. The longer paper requires more careful preparation; it requires you to work out the relationships and the development of your thoughts more thoroughly. And a formal outline forces you to do just this. Beginning writers sometimes neglect the outline because of the time required to prepare it. But, as you will discover, the more time you spend in carefully preparing your outline, the less time you will waste when you begin to write. With a clearly detailed plan of your theme before you, you will not have to grope for ideas to clarify and develop your thesis.

An outline has three parts: the *title*, the *thesis statement*, and the *body*. The body consists of the major and minor ideas that develop the main idea of the outline expressed in the thesis statement. The main ideas are represented by Roman numerals, minor ideas by capital letters, Arabic numerals, and lower case letters, as illustrated in the following system:

I.
 A.
  1.
   a.
    (1)
     (a)

Each main heading (I, II, etc.) need not be developed in as much detail as this illustration. An outline for a theme of 300 to 500 words usually does not require subdivision beyond the first Arabic numerals.

I.
 A.
  1.
  2.
 B.
II.

Capitalize the first word of each heading, and if the heading is a sentence place a period at the end. Occasionally the entries on a sentence outline may extend to two or three lines. When they do, make certain that your left-hand margin does not extend to the left of the period after the topic symbol, as illustrated below.

I. _____

   A. _____

      _____

      _____

The thesis statement appears between the title and the first Roman numeral.

Title

THESIS STATEMENT _____

      _____

I. _____

The thesis statement expresses the controlling idea of your paper. Written just above the first entry of the outline, it serves as a visible guide, a reminder of your main idea so that you can prevent irrelevant material from creeping into your outline.

Your thesis statement should be as precise as you can make it. The more sharply focused it is, the more it will help you in clarifying and developing your thought. For example, "There are several advantages in using a checking account" is not as useful a thesis statement as the more precise, "A checking account provides a convenient and safe method of payment." The latter statement forces the writer to consider each idea and thus ensures a fuller, more specific development of the central idea. If you decide to add or delete items in your outline, revise your thesis statement to reflect any change in your main idea. For example, in developing an outline on the advantages of paying by check, if you decide to discuss the disadvantages as well, you can change your thesis statement accordingly.

The most frequently used forms of the outline are the *topic outline* and the *sentence outline*. The entries on a topic outline are made up of short phrases or single words. The following exemplifies a topic outline:

The Advantages of Attending State University

THESIS STATEMENT   Students attending State University benefit from its pleasant surroundings, its social and cultural life, its reasonable costs, and its variety of curricular offerings.

I. Setting
   A. Pleasant valley
   B. Low, rolling foothills
II. Social life
   A. Fraternities and sororities
   B. Other social groups
      1. Eating clubs
      2. Departmental clubs
      3. Study groups
   C. Extracurricular activities
      1. Sporting events
      2. School dances
III. Cultural life
   A. Active student program
      1. Theater arts program
      2. Fine arts exhibitions
      3. Music department presentations
   B. Professional lectures and performances
   C. Nearby city cultural attractions
IV. Expense
   A. Low tuition
   B. Part-time job opportunities
   C. Available scholarships
V. Curriculum
   A. Excellent liberal arts program
   B. Recognized superiority of professional programs

In a sentence outline each entry is a sentence.

Study Suggestions

THESIS STATEMENT   An effective method for absorbing the material of a reading assignment involves four steps: previewing the assignment, reading the assignment, reviewing the assignment, and reciting the main points.

I. Before you begin to read, preview the assignment.
   A. Make certain of the exact pages to be read.
   B. Read the opening and closing paragraphs.
   C. Examine the major and minor divisions of the selection.
   D. Study the pictures, charts, maps, and so forth that illustrate important points.

II. After this preliminary survey, read the assignment carefully.
    A. Underline the important ideas.
    B. Look up the meaning of unfamiliar words.
    C. Place question marks after statements that need further clarification or support.

III. Review the assignment.
    A. Reread introductory and summary passages.
    B. Analyze the structure of the selection.
        1. Distinguish between major and minor ideas and relate each to the central thesis.
        2. Distinguish between the statement of an idea and an illustration of it.
        3. Consider cause and effect relationships.

IV. Fix the main points in your memory.
    A. Make notes of the structure and important ideas of the selection.
    B. Recite the main points to yourself.
    C. Discuss your interpretation of the author's thought with your classmates.
    D. Relate the information presented in the assignment to that presented in a preceding chapter by the same author or to the ideas of another writer on the same subject.

Of the two forms, the topic outline is generally easier to manage, but because the theme itself will be composed of sentences, the sentence outline provides a more convenient basis than the topic outline for the translation of thought from outline to theme.

If you are to do an effective job of outlining, you must know something of the principles that govern the construction of an outline as well as its format. These concern (1) logical subordination of ideas, (2) parallel structure, (3) single subdivisions, and (4) specific, meaningful headings. The most important of these principles is the first, for the main purpose of a writer's outline is to give him a logical, well-organized structure for his composition. Examine your outline first to be sure that your main headings are logical divisions of the subject expressed in the title and thesis statement. Make certain that the subheadings are logical divisions of the headings under which they are listed. Study the following outline for logical organization and subordination of ideas:

The Ecological Importance of Open Space

THESIS STATEMENT   Open space is essential to the maintenance of a healthful, life-supporting environment.

I. Open space plays a vital role in maintaining breathable air.
  A. Open space vegetation filters particles from the air.
  B. It produces oxygen through the process of photosynthesis.
II. Urban areas produce the elements of smog.
III. Intelligent use of open space can help to maintain a healthful climate.
  A. Open space dissipates islands of heat produced in urban areas.
    1. Covered surfaces, such as asphalt, absorb heat.
    2. Urban areas produce heat through combustion.
  B. Native vegetation of open space helps to reduce humidity built up in the cities and suburbs.
    1. Water needed for exotic plants in urban and suburban communities increases water evaporation.
IV. Invasion of open space by urban and suburban sprawl impairs its recreational use.
  A. Open space surrounding cities is often used by city-dwelling hikers and cyclists.
  B. Housing tracts and shopping centers occupy space that could be better used for public parks and campgrounds near densely populated cities.
V. Wildlife, essential to a healthful ecological system, is threatened by the elimination of open space.
VI. Empty beach land should be purchased by a state or the federal government and preserved for recreational use.
VII. The movement of population from rural to urban areas has increased urban congestion.

Some of the main headings of this outline are not logical divisions of the subject. Roman numeral II should be placed under I, VI should be worked into IV, and VII should be eliminated. Item III, B, 1 also needs to be absorbed into B. Revising the outline to correct these errors results in a more logical arrangement:

I. Open space plays a vital role in maintaining breathable air.
  A. Open space vegetation filters particles from the air.
  B. It produces oxygen through the process of photosynthesis.
  C. Automobiles and factories in urban areas produce smog.
II. Intelligent use of open space can help to maintain a healthful climate.
  A. Open space dissipates islands of heat produced in urban areas.
    1. Covered surfaces, such as asphalt, absorb heat.
    2. Urban areas produce heat through combustion.

    B. Native vegetation of open space helps to reduce humidity produced by evaporation of water used to irrigate exotic plants in cities and suburbs.
III. Invasion of open space by urban and suburban sprawl impairs its recreational use.
    A. Open space surrounding cities is often used by city-dwelling hikers and cyclists.
    B. Housing tracts and shopping centers occupy space that could be better used for public parks and campgrounds near densely populated cities.
    C. Empty beach land should be purchased by a state or the federal government and preserved for recreational use.
IV. Wildlife, essential to a healthful ecological system, is threatened by the elimination of open space.

The principle of parallelism, which requires that ideas of equal importance in a sentence be expressed in the same grammatical form, applies to the construction of outlines. An outline is parallel when the headings designated by the same kind of letter or numeral are phrased in parallel form. That is, if Roman numeral I is a prepositional phrase, the other Roman numerals should be prepositional phrases also. If A and B under I are nouns, so must be the other capital letters under II, III, and so on. A sentence outline is automatically parallel, for each entry is a sentence and hence parallel. The following outline is not parallel:

A Part-time Job for the College Student

I. Pays for college expenses
    A. Tuition
    B. Books
    C. For supplies
    D. Recreation
II. It provides a student with vocational training.
    A. He learns special skills.
    B. Work experience
III. Character development
    A. Self-reliance
    B. Responsibility
    C. Reliability
    D. Cooperation

None of the major headings of this outline are parallel: Roman numeral I is a verb phrase, II is a sentence, and III is a noun phrase. The capital letter entries illustrate the same flaw. Item C under I is a prepositional phrase, whereas the other items are nouns. Under II, A is a sentence, and B is a noun phrase. When these errors are corrected, the outline is more consistent. The ideas are presented more effectively.

A Part-time Job for the College Student

I. Helps to pay for college expenses
   A. Tuition
   B. Books
   C. Supplies
   D. Recreation
II. Provides student with vocational training
   A. Skills
   B. Experience
III. Develops student's character
   A. Self-reliance
   B. Responsibility
   C. Reliability
   D. Cooperation

The basis of outlining, as we have seen, is the division of larger topics into smaller ones. When you divide a topic into its parts, you must, logically, have at least two parts. In constructing an outline, therefore, avoid the single subdivision. If you divide a Roman numeral heading, you must have at least an A and a B under it. If you divide a capital letter heading, you must provide at least a 1 and a 2 under it, and so on through each successive stage of the outline. Consider the following outline:

The Benefits of Participation in Sports

I. Pleasure of competition
II. Value of exercise
III. Development of character
   A. Sportsmanship
IV. Interest and skill in a recreational activity

Item A under III represents only one division of a larger topic, development of character. If the writer wished to emphasize character development by analyzing it in greater detail than the other topics, he should have provided at least two subdivisions of this heading. If, however, he simply wanted to emphasize this one aspect of character development, he should have incorporated it in his main heading. These two possibilities are illustrated on page 192.

I. Pleasure of competition
II. Value of exercise
III. Development of character
   A. Sportsmanship
   B. Cooperation
   C. Self-discipline
IV. Development of interest and skill in a recreational activity

I. Pleasure of competition
II. Value of exercise
III. Development of good sportsmanship
IV. Development of interest and skill in a recreational activity

Finally, make certain that your outline headings convey specific, meaningful ideas. General headings such as "introduction," "body," "conclusion," or "examples," "functions," "types," and the like do not represent the subject matter of an outline very clearly and therefore provide little guidance when you translate the ideas from your outline to the composition.

After you have completed your outline, examine it carefully to see that its format is correct and that the organization of its ideas is logical and consistent. Be sure that you have included a title and a thesis statement and that you have used symbols correctly and consistently. As you check the body of the outline, make certain that you have avoided single subdivisions and vague, meaningless headings and that entries of the same rank are expressed in parallel structure. If your outline meets these tests, you are ready to begin your first draft.

EXERCISE 21

A. Compose a precise, accurate thesis statement for an outline based on the material concerning a good college teacher that was presented in section 4, "Gathering and Organizing Material" (pp. 175–79).

B. Use the detail in the following groups of sentences to phrase a concise, comprehensive thesis statement for an outline on the subject. Write your thesis statement in the blanks provided.

1. (1) College education demands that a student be able to express himself. (2) He must be able to read carefully and write clearly. (3) He must be able to speak his thoughts and listen attentively. (4) A college student must be able to handle language if he is to succeed in college.

THESIS STATEMENT _____

_____

2. (1) Cigarette commercials stress the soothing effects of smoking. (2) Medical reports reveal its dangers. (3) Cigarette smoking is unsightly – it stains the fingers of those who smoke. (4) Cigarette smoking is expensive also. (5) I do not plan to take up smoking.

THESIS STATEMENT _____

_____

3. (1) The foreign compact car is superior to the larger American car in handling ease. (2) One can park it easily and turn it sharply. (3) The foreign car is not as luxurious as the American car, but it costs less to operate. (4) It is also more convenient for urban living.

THESIS STATEMENT _____

_____

4. (1) Participation in sports is beneficial. (2) College students should participate in sports to learn a recreational activity. (3) Students who participate in sports learn good sportsmanship, persistence, and cooperation – all admirable personal qualities. (4) Participation in sports provides healthful exercise.

THESIS STATEMENT _____

_____

5. (1) The anxious extrovert has his hand continually in the air to answer questions. (2) He is never satisfied unless he can add his thoughts to the discussion. (3) The campus lover answers a question occasionally, but he is more interested in the cute little blonde on his right than in what goes on in class. (4) Some students never volunteer an opinion or an answer. (5) They sit there the whole semester, content to let others carry the discussion. (6) Classroom discussions evoke different reactions in students.

193

THESIS STATEMENT _____

_____

C. The outline below contains many of the defects explained and illustrated in the preceding pages. Study each entry carefully, and if it illustrates one of the following errors, write its number in the appropriate space.

1. item not placed under the logical heading _____

_____

2. item not parallel in form with other headings of equal rank _____

_____

3. heading vague and meaningless _____

_____

4. single subdivision of a heading _____

_____

Tips for New Students

THESIS STATEMENT   To make their adjustment to college as smooth as possible, new students should give a good deal of thought to their course of study, living quarters, orientation-week procedures, regular study routine, and reasonable social diversion.

   I. Selection of course of study (1)
      A. Consultation with counselor (2)
         1. Aptitude tests (3)
         2. Consider your high-school record. (4)
      B. Study of college catalog (5)
      C. Experts (6)
  II. Choice of living quarters (7)
      A. Residence on campus (8)
         1. Types (9)
         2. Advantages and disadvantages of types (10)
      B. Fun of living in campus fraternities or sororities (11)
      C. Residence off campus (12)
         1. Apartments in town (13)
      D. Rooms in private houses in town (14)
 III. Need for orientation and preparation (15)
      A. Tour the campus to discover the location of important buildings. (16)
      B. Familiarity with registration procedure (17)
      C. Familiarity with schedule (18)
      D. Purchase of books and supplies (19)
  IV. Importance of regular study routine (20)
      A. Necessity of established daily study hours (21)
      B. Completion of assignments on time (22)

   V. Value of social activities (23)
      A. Need for relaxation and recreation (24)
      B. Development of poise and self-confidence (25)
         1. School dances (26)
 VI. Conclusion (27)

D. Reconstruct the outline in C above to correct its format. Add whatever details are necessary.

E. Material for an outline on how to discover the theme (the author's main idea) of a short story is listed below. Organize the items into a topic or sentence outline, and write your headings in the appropriate blanks in the outline following this list. Construct a concise thesis statement as well as a title for your outline.

1. Read the story carefully at least twice.
2. Minor characters are easily identified also.
3. Minor characters receive less attention than major characters.
4. On the first reading examine character, plot, and setting.
5. Determine what happens to the protagonist (main character).
6. On the second reading examine character, plot, and setting more closely.
7. Identify major and minor characters on the first reading.
8. Major characters are easily identified.
9. Major characters receive the author's principal attention.
10. Identify the central problem that the protagonist faces.
11. To make certain you understand the theme, write it out.
12. State the theme in two or three declarative sentences.
13. Distinguish between favorably and unfavorably treated characters.
14. Identify the qualities of favorably and unfavorably treated characters.
15. Major characters are clearer in the reader's mind.
16. We know more about their general physical appearance.
17. We know more about their temperaments.
18. We know more about their motives.
19. Minor characters frequently serve as foils to the main characters.
20. Determine if the protagonist solves his problem.
21. Note the setting of the story—the time and place in which events occur.
22. Trace the sequence of important events that compose the plot.
23. Author approves of the qualities of favorably treated characters.
24. Author disapproves of the qualities of unfavorably treated characters.
25. Examine the effect of the setting on the fate of the protagonist.
26. If his fate is strongly affected by events of a particular time and place, the statement of theme must include this reference.
27. If his fate is not so strongly affected by setting, the theme will be more universal.
28. Express the theme as a general statement of human experience, but try to avoid such trite generalizations as "love conquers all," "crime doesn't pay," "as you sow, so shall you reap," and the like.
29. If the protagonist succeeds in solving his problem, the author must be implying that his qualities of character can achieve certain things in life.

30. If the protagonist fails to solve his problem, the author is probably implying that such qualities do not achieve certain things in life.

Title

THESIS STATEMENT _____

_____

I. _____

  A. _____

    1. _____

      a. _____

        (1) _____

        (2) _____

          (a) _____

          (b) _____

          (c) _____

      b. _____

        (1) _____

        (2) _____

    2. _____

      a. _____

      b. _____

    3. _____

  B. _____

    1. _____

    2. _____

      a. _____

      b. _____

    3. _____

      a. _____

      b. _____

    4. _____

      a. _____

    b. _____

II. _____

  A. _____

  B. _____

F. Compose a sentence outline on a subject listed in one of the following exercises: 18A, 18B, 19B, 20D.

6. WRITING THE FIRST DRAFT

Once you have completed the outline, you are ready to begin the first draft of your paper. Your outline provides the plan, the framework, of your paper. Now you must transform this plan into the finished structure.

The major headings of an outline will coincide with the main ideas of the composition, but there is not an exact correspondence between the main headings of the outline and the paragraphs of the composition. A Roman numeral heading may require one or more paragraphs for adequate development, depending on the amount of detail it encompasses. For example, the first main heading of the outline "The Advantages of Attending State University" (pp. 186–87).

> I. Setting
>   A. Pleasant valley
>   B. Low, rolling foothills

could easily be handled in one paragraph. Roman numeral II, "Social life," however, contains more detail and hence requires at least a paragraph or two for full development. Conversely, in a short composition, two Roman numeral headings might be included in one paragraph.

Plan your time so that you can revise your first draft carefully. Once you begin the first draft, move steadily forward. Do not worry about mechanics at this stage. The important thing is to get your ideas on paper. You can correct errors in spelling, punctuation, and grammar and make improvements in wording later, when you revise this draft. If you stop to check these items now, you may lose your train of thought.

EXERCISE 22

A. Write a first draft of a theme based on the outline you developed for Exercise 20C, 21E, or 21F.

B. Write a first draft of a theme based on the outline concerning the characteristics of a good college teacher that was presented in section 4, "Gathering and Organizing Material" (pp. 175–79).

7. REVISING THE FIRST DRAFT

Do not begin to revise your first draft immediately after you have completed it. Set it aside for several hours (overnight if possible) and think about something else. When you return to your paper, your mind will be clearer and fresher, and you will be able to view the first draft more objectively.

In your revision, concentrate first on the content and organization of your ideas. Read your paragraphs carefully to make certain that they are unified, well developed, and coherent. The following suggestions, which were discussed in the first four chapters, should be helpful.

Content and Organization

Unity The controlling idea of each paragraph should be clearly and concisely stated in a topic sentence. Each sentence of the paragraph should support this idea.

Development Each paragraph should contain enough detail— enough facts, illustrations, comparisons, and judgments—to explain the controlling idea adequately. The supporting detail should be concrete and specific. Every generalization should be supported by sufficient evidence to persuade a fair-minded reader.

Coherence The ideas in each paragraph should be arranged in a logical sequence. The sentences in each paragraph, as well as the paragraphs themselves, should flow smoothly together.

The last suggestion regarding coherence needs further comment. Our previous discussion of coherence concentrated on coherence *within* the paragraph. When you write a longer composition, you must make certain that the thought flows smoothly *between* paragraphs as well as between sentences. If you have organized your paper carefully, there should be a steady development of thought from paragraph to paragraph, but you can accentuate this continuity through judicious use of transitional expressions and through repetition of key words. In the following passage, for example, the writer uses both these devices to ensure continuity between paragraphs:

> Even the shift in the kind of curriculum is upsetting. The students are used to having the day arranged for them from, say, nine to three, high-school fashion. They now find themselves attending classes for only fifteen hours or so a week. The concentration in

depth on a few subjects is a new idea to them. The requisite self-discipline is often something they learn only after painful experience.

Furthermore, college is the students' first encounter with live intellectuals. They meet individual members of the faculty who have written important books or completed important pieces of research. The various intellectual fields become matters of personal experience. The students learn that work does not just happen to get done. They find that the productive intellectual is not a superman but an everyday figure. They will also make the discovery that there are those who consider intellectual pursuits reason enough for an entire life. Students are nearly always surprised to find such pursuits valued so highly.

Students are surprised, too, at their first meeting with really violent political opinion. . . . [From James K. Feibleman, "What Happens in College," *Saturday Review*, October 20, 1962.]

Furthermore, the first word of the second paragraph, informs us that the writer is adding another illustration of the idea he has been developing in the preceding paragraph. The transition between the second and third paragraphs is especially smooth.

. . . Students are nearly always surprised to find such pursuits valued so highly.

Students are surprised, too, at their first meeting . . .

The repetition of the word *students* in the latter sentence plus the use of the transitional *too*, which signals an additional illustration of the author's point in the preceding two paragraphs, provides an uninterrupted bridge of thought as we move from one paragraph to the next. The repetition of key words such as *students* and its pronoun *they* throughout the passage also ties the paragraphs together.

Emphasis

After you have tested your paper for unity, development, and coherence, examine it once more to make certain you have given your most important ideas the proper emphasis. To make your reader receptive to the effect you wish to create, you must communicate your thoughts clearly and forcefully. The most emphatic positions in a composition are the beginning and the end. Reread your opening and closing sentences. Now is the time to revise and polish these sentences. What you say in the opening sentence often determines the kind of reading your paper will receive. If your first sentence successfully arouses the interest and curiosity of a reader, he will probably give your paper a sympathetic reading. If it is rather dull and colorless, his reading will probably be more perfunctory. The first few sentences are especially important if the purpose of your paper is to argue a point. In this case you must establish yourself as a reasonable individual, not as a fanatic. If your introduction makes a reader suspicious or uneasy about your motives, it will be difficult to persuade him of anything.

What you say in the closing sentence is even more important. You can regain a reader's interest after an uninspiring introduction with lively material in the body of the paper, but you have no second chance after he has finished reading. What your reader reads last, he usually remembers best. If your last sentence is vague and inconclusive, his final impression is not apt to be favorable. Read over your first draft carefully, therefore, and revise your opening and closing sentences to make them as effective as possible. The following discussion will provide some specific suggestions for opening and closing sentences.

Beginning the Paper

A paper longer than 500 words may require an introductory paragraph to introduce its subject and explain its purpose, but for most short themes the first paragraph can both introduce the subject and develop the first main idea. Whether your introduction is a single sentence or a whole paragraph, however, begin with a sentence that is interesting and says something important about the subject.

There are a number of ways to begin a composition. Occasionally you may wish to shock your reader with a *startling statistic* or a *bold statement:*

> Two of every three people in the world today live on a starvation diet.

> In much of the so-called free world, democracy is a fraud.

Or you may attract his attention with an *appropriate quotation:*

> No one has bettered the New York *Times*' description of James Fisk, Jr.: "First in war, first in peace and first in the pockets of his countrymen." [From *Time*, February 23, 1959, p. 104.]

> "When I hear the word *culture* I reach for my revolver," said the late Marshal Goering. We all agree he was a barbarian; but,

confidentially, when you hear the word *poetry,* do you reach for a mystery story . . . ? [From Gilbert Highet, "Could It Be Verse?" *The Powers of Poetry,* Oxford University Press, 1960.]

A relevant *personal experience* can be effective in tempting a reader:

I shall never forget Friday, November 22, 1963. I was lounging in the Student Center chatting with a friend when someone suddenly announced over the loudspeaker that President Kennedy had been assassinated. I could not believe my ears. The girl on the sofa across from me started to cry. Later that day I wondered whether the President's death would bring a new awareness to the American people of the need to unite, to stand together as they faced an uncertain future.

Quite often a *simple, direct statement of the main idea or purpose* of your paper will be your best choice:

A good teacher is one who knows his subject, loves his subject, and is willing and able to share it.

In this paper I wish to consider Plato's view of an ideal society as he presented it in *The Republic.*

These suggestions do not exhaust the possibilities, of course. As you gain writing experience, you will discover other effective ways to introduce your subject and to elicit reader interest at the same time. As you experiment with different opening statements, keep these suggestions in mind.

First, limit your introduction to one or two sentences, and get directly to the point unless you are writing a long paper. Wandering, irrelevant introductions like the following are deadening:

Why I Want to Be a Doctor

I guess I've always wanted to be a doctor. My grandfather on my mother's side was a doctor, and I was very fond of Granddad. He used to take me with him on his house calls. . . .

Next, avoid apologizing. A theme that begins "I am not an expert on politics, but . . ." is not likely to arouse much interest.

Third, be wary of the broad generalization as an opener. Statements like "Americans have always envied the Europeans' cultural sophistication" are simply too comprehensive to be supportable. They will not impress an intelligent reader.

Finally, make certain that your first sentence is easily understood without reference to the title. For a theme entitled "Tobacco and the Teen-ager," the following beginning sentence would only confuse the reader: "I guess everybody has tried it by the time he is seventeen."

Ending the Paper

For the short theme of 300 to 500 words a special summarizing paragraph is not necessary. A sentence or two is usually sufficient. If your paper is well organized and coherent, your *final detail* will often provide a satisfactory conclusion:

> And, finally, boxing should be banned because of the severe physical damage inflicted on the fighter himself. This result is not surprising, however. In no other sport is it the primary purpose of one contestant to knock his opponent senseless, and it is a rare fighter who can absorb such punishment without suffering serious aftereffects. If it does not kill him — and the possibility is not remote — it may well leave him with the characteristic stumbling shuffle, the thick tongue, the battered face, and the impaired vision of the punch-drunk ex-fighter.

Sometimes, however, you may wish to emphasize your central idea with an apt *quotation:*

> Emerson wrote, "The search after the great man is the dream of youth and the most serious occupation of manhood." Only when people know the best in men will they learn to reject the least in men. The jerks have had their day; it is time now for heroes. [From Marya Mannes, "Let's Stop Exalting Punks," *The Saturday Evening Post,* October 6, 1962, pp. 10–14.]

Or you may refresh your reader's mind by *enumerating the main points* of your paper:

> To answer the usual essay question, then, (1) read the question carefully to determine exactly what is called for; (2) rephrase the question to serve as the central idea of your essay; (3) develop your central idea in one or more paragraphs, using appropriate illustrations, reasons, and factual detail; and (4) organize your paragraphs as you would for an expository or argumentative theme.

A concluding sentence that *repeats the main idea expressed in the opening sentence* can also provide a nice finishing touch:

> Television westerns may provide satisfying entertainment for millions of viewers, but their monotonous plots, stereotyped characters, and simplified themes leave me bored and dissatisfied.

Study the final paragraph of your first draft. If you think a special concluding sentence would add emphasis to your paper, add one. But do not tack on unneeded sentences after you have completed your thought, especially if they contain an apology. An apology at the end of your paper is just as ineffectual as one at the beginning. And do not inject a new idea into your final sentences. A paper that concludes,

> A good climate, expanding job opportunities, abundant recreational areas — all these make Florida a pleasant place to live. One wonders, however, how pleasant it will be as it becomes more crowded.

makes a reader wonder whether the writer has had second thoughts about the validity of his own conclusion.

Proportion

The preceding discussion has stressed the importance of *position* in achieving emphasis. Of equal importance is *proportion,* or balance. In a well-proportioned theme the more important points are given more space; they are developed at greater length. Minor ideas and illustrative detail are not allowed to overshadow or obscure the central thesis. Observe the application of this principle in the following theme:

Democracy on Campus

Perhaps no democratic society has put so much faith in the importance of education as the American. The premise that each individual has a right to the kind of education that will allow him to develop his potential for growth to the fullest is as firmly established in the American mind as the desire for political and religious freedoms. And in few countries of the world has the opportunity for obtaining an education, especially a university education, been made so available to such a large segment of the population. Yet in spite of an almost universal regard for higher education in the United States, recent suggestions calling for fundamental changes in the structure and operation of the American university reveal a basic misunderstanding of the nature of higher education and of the purposes it serves. Particularly misleading, and ultimately dangerous to the welfare of a democracy, is the notion that higher education would be improved if the university were transformed into a truly democratic institution with students and faculty allotted equal power in its governance.

Those who favor a much greater role for students in the administration of a university often argue that students should be treated as full educational partners, that they deserve a representative voice in the educational decisions that affect their lives. They should therefore, so runs the argument, have a say in the selection and retention of faculty, the expenditure of university funds, the determination of course content and grading practices, the kind of research undertaken by faculty, the selection of the president, and so on. Student demands for more power and influence are understandable. The increasing size and impersonality of modern American universities, the emphasis on research to the detriment of good teaching, the general exploitation of undergraduates to finance the more expensive graduate programs—all of these conditions surely indicate that all is not well on American campuses. Students have a right to complain; they do deserve a role in university affairs. But that role should be advisory, not equal to that of the faculty or administration. A university is not a political unit in which power is shared, with students electing their teachers and the administrative officers. It is an educational, a tutorial institution, the function of which is not to govern or rule but to communicate knowledge and cultivate the mind, to transmit the cultural heritage; and it is foolish to speak of democracy in connection with a university's function or operation. Moreover, if students were to be made full partners in the running of a university, they would have to devote much of their time to the process, time that would be taken from their studies, that is, from the work for which they entered the university in the first place.

The conception of the university as a political institution underlies two other demands frequently made in recent years. The first is that the university embark on a program of practical political action to help remedy pressing social problems, and the second, a corollary of the first, that the curriculum be modified or restructured to make courses more "relevant." The proposal that a university engage in political action to ease problems such as poverty, oppression of minorities, slum housing, and the high cost of health care has a certain appeal; for during the past fifty years or so the university has contributed much to improving the quality of life in this country through the work of distinguished university scholars and scientists. The preeminent position of American technology, for example, would have been impossible without the discoveries made by scientists working in university laboratories. The university has also provided many able scholars and experts to advise governmental committees studying the complexities of international trade and foreign policy, and of atomic energy and nuclear disarmament. Although it is legitimate to expect the university to involve itself in important national problems, its role is to study problems and propose solutions, not to engage in partisan politics in support of a cause. When it resorts to such action, it deserts its traditional moral commitment to objectivity, to the dispassionate consideration of conflicting points of view. Moreover, it invites retaliation from the public on whose support it depends; and when the public loses confidence in the neutrality of the university, it will strip it of its independence, to the detriment of both the university and the public.

The demand that course work be made more relevant to student interests may simply reflect a justifiable desire on the part of students for capable, energetic teachers who are vitally interested in their subject and eager to teach it. But this demand is also made by militant activists, who want to transform the university into a political agency, and by those reluctant to do the hard intellectual labor required of anyone serious about getting an education. The danger to the intellectual integrity of the university were activists' demands to be met has been alluded to above. For the unmotivated, indifferent student, the cry for relevance masks a desire to take up whatever is current, controversial, and popular. It reflects a parochial mind set of those who cannot or will not concentrate on concerns beyond their own immediate needs. Meeting the demands of such students is neither possible nor desirable. On the one hand, it is difficult to keep university courses geared to the latest student interests, since these interests change from one generation of students to another; and on the other hand, trying to keep courses relevant to a student's immediate needs overlooks needs that are not immediately obvious to him but which will be gradually revealed over the years. College study is hard, demanding work, but it is also rewarding to those who approach it with determination and patience. As Jacques Barzun, an eminent historian, reminds us, "What has been acquired with a will is always relevant."

From its beginning in the seventeenth century the American university has contributed immensely to the intellectual, cultural, and economic well-being of this country. In its 240-year history it has helped the American people and their government to meet difficult challenges in a changing world, and in the process it has itself been changed. But it has never abandoned its central concern for the use of and respect for intelligence, so vital to the democratic process. Those who would soften this insistence on intellectual achievement and distinction in hopes of making the university more democratic misunderstand the nature of education as well as the democratic process. Equal opportunity does not mean that all will excel; it means that all should have the chance to excel. If this distinction is blurred, the future of this country will be bleak indeed.

The writer's purpose in this essay is to persuade his reader that the desire to transform the American university into an agency for political action and to restructure its curriculum to keep it relevant to the current interests of its students is unsound. In the first paragraph he introduces his subject and in the last sentence presents his thesis. The second, third, and fourth paragraphs are the longest, for in these paragraphs the writer concentrates on what he judges to be the strongest arguments of the opposition. Surveying the theme as a whole, we can see how he has achieved emphasis through position and proportion. The opening paragraph leads into the subject. The more fully developed middle paragraphs carry the main burden of his case. And the final paragraph, reminding the reader of an important point implied in the beginning paragraph—that equal opportunity when applied to higher education does not guarantee intellectual achievement—concludes his essay forcefully.

Mechanics and Usage

When you are reasonably satisfied with the clarity and organization of your ideas, look over your paper once more to check its mechanics —grammar, punctuation, spelling—diction, and usage. Consult a dictionary or an English handbook whenever necessary as you consider the following questions:

1. Is the meaning of each sentence clear? Are there any dangling or misplaced modifiers, ambiguous pronoun references, or shifts in point of view that cloud the meaning?
2. Is each sentence complete? Are there any sentence fragments, run-together sentences, or sentences with comma splices?
3. Are the sentences correctly punctuated? Are paragraphs properly indented? Are quotation marks used when required?
4. Is each word correctly spelled? Are apostrophes properly placed?
5. Do subjects and verbs, pronouns and antecedents agree?
6. Do the words convey the meaning clearly and precisely? Are emotive terms used justifiably?

EXERCISE 23

A. The following paragraph communicates the writer's idea clearly and forcefully. Examine the opening and closing sentences in particular. What devices does he use to arouse reader interest and to stress his main idea?

Is the sport of hunting, simply as such, a man-worthy thing or isn't it? Let it be supposed that all hunters obey all regulations. Let it be supposed that no whiskey bottle is dropped to pollute any glen or dingle, no fence is broken, no fawn is shot, no forest is set afire, no robins are massacred in mistake for pheasants and no deer-hunters in mistake for porcupines (or possibly chipmunks), and no meditative philosopher, out to enjoy the loveliness of autumn, is ever plugged through the pericardium. The question persists: Is it a spectacle of manhood (which is to say of our distinctive humanness), when on a bracing morning we look out upon the autumn, draw an exhilarating breath, and cry "What a glorious day! How golden in the light of the sun, how merry the caperings of creatures; *Gloria in excelsis Deo!* I will go out and kill something"? [From Alan Devoe, "On Hunting," *American Mercury*, February, 1951. By permission of *The American Mercury*, P. O. Box 1306, Torrance, California 90505.]

B. The following article is a grimly interesting account of *apartheid* in the Union of South Africa. Read it twice. On the second reading observe the methods used to provide coherence and emphasis. In particular, note the devices used to tie the paragraphs together: (1) the use of transitional expressions in the opening sentence of one paragraph to link its thought with that of the preceding paragraph, (2) the repetition of key words, (3) pronoun reference, (4) parallelism, and (5) consistency of point of view. What techniques does the author use to elicit reader interest at the beginning and to emphasize his point at the end?

This Is Apartheid

Two years ago, a question was asked in all seriousness in South Africa's Parliament in Cape Town: Does *apartheid* on the beaches extend to the high-tide or low-tide mark? Aghast, M.P.s finally concluded that in either case Africans could wade across from black beaches into white water, spoiling it for white swimmers. The problem was finally solved by taking a precedent from international conventions; *apartheid* on the beaches was extended out to the three-mile limit.

Such debates take up much of the South African Parliament's time. Once a government minister declared that it was scandalous that so many whites shook hands with Africans, said that Africans would prefer to be greeted in the traditional native way—an upraised hand with no pressing of the flesh. Out went government directives ordering traditional greetings to replace handshakes. The orders were quickly countermanded, however, when an opposition M.P. gleefully announced, after boning up on traditionalist lore, that if the greeting were employed, a white woman meeting a black man would have to kneel down and kiss both his feet.

Equal Escalators.   *Apartheid* affects every aspect of South African life. Whites and nonwhites not only have separate park benches, public toilets, post office windows, but in many buildings, separate elevators. Africans often outsmart white starters by getting on or off white elevators on the second floor, where the starters cannot catch them. Escalators, however, are integrated; the only rule, and a humane one at that, requires passengers to wear shoes — in the past, too many barefoot blacks have lost their toes.

African men shopping for hats must first put on a skull cap provided by the store before trying any on; African women are not allowed to try on hats at all. Blacks' and whites' blood is kept separately in blood banks, although most doctors would not hesitate to use whatever blood is available in an emergency. Recently, however, a white ambulance driver in Johannesburg refused to pick up an African woman in labor on the sidewalk.

On the road, black Africans travel on separate buses and use separate bus stops. Only white bus stops have benches. Blacks also use separate railroad coaches. Nonwhites cannot eat in dining cars, but special nonwhite stewards serve meals to blacks in their coaches. Nonwhites on airplanes are usually confined to seats at the front or rear; if the plane is so crowded that the only free seats are next to whites, stewardesses first must ask permission from the white passengers to seat the blacks next to them; if permission is not granted, the blacks are usually shifted to other planes. They are served on plates and cups of a different color from white passengers', and their dishes are washed separately. When the nonwhite leaves the aircraft, his headrest is immediately tagged and its cover laundered separately from others on the plane.

Without a Prayer.   While whites can move about South Africa freely, Africans cannot move into an urban area for more than 72 hours without special permission. To qualify as a permanent resident of an urban area, an African must have either been born there or worked continuously for one employer for ten years. If he marries a woman from outside the area, she may not stay with him for more than 72 hours. Blacks in Johannesburg can own their own houses, but can only lease the land they stand on for 30 years. Whites in arrears with their rent are only evicted; Africans are criminally charged and can be imprisoned.

Under the Immorality Act, sexual relations between the races are forbidden. Many whites, fearful of being run in under the law, will not even drive a servant home in the evening without having wife or children along in the car. But sometimes it is difficult to tell what race is white. After a Chinese named Song had himself declared white because he "was generally accepted as white," the government changed the law to read that a person is now white "so long as he generally is accepted as white and is not obviously not white." The new interpretation takes white status away from the visiting Japanese, who gained it only last year when they concluded a trade agreement with the South African government. And poor Mr. Song, who neglected to get his wife declared white with him under the old law, violates the Immorality Act whenever he goes to bed with her.

Little Christian charity is extended toward blacks by South Africa's Dutch Reformed churches. Most refuse to admit blacks to their services. A current joke has a white policeman entering a church on a Sunday morning, where he finds a lone black on his knees. "What are you doing, Kaffir?" asks the cop. "Scrubbing the floor," answers the African. "O.K.," says the cop. "But God help you if I catch you praying." [Lee Griggs, "This Is *Apartheid*," *Time*, July 6, 1962, p. 19. Reprinted by permission from *Time, The Weekly Newsmagazine*. Copyright Time, Inc., 1962.]

C. Construct three effective opening sentences for each of the following topics. Use any of the methods illustrated on pages 202–4 or any of your own invention.

1. consumer protection in a world of industrial giants

   a. _____

   _____

   b. _____

   _____

   c. _____

   _____

2. the nuclear family — a fading relic?

   a. _____

   _____

   b. _____

   _____

   c. _____

   _____

3. the Women's Liberation movement

   a. _____

   _____

   b. _____

   _____

   c. _____

   _____

D. Find three examples of good concluding sentences in recent magazine or newspaper articles, and write them in the appropriate spaces below. Be prepared to tell why you think the conclusion is successful.

1. SUBJECT MATTER _____

   Concluding Sentence _____

   _____

   _____

2. SUBJECT MATTER _____

   Concluding Sentence _____

   _____

   _____

3. SUBJECT MATTER _____

   Concluding Sentence _____

   _____

   _____

E. Revise the draft of the paper you prepared for Exercise 22A or 22B.

8. PREPARING THE FINAL COPY

If you can type, type your final copy on 8½ x 11-inch unlined white paper. Double space so that your instructor can insert comments between the lines when necessary. Double spacing also makes for easier reading. If you must write your final copy, use ink and write on only one side of the paper. The other side may be required for later revisions when your theme is returned to you. Next, space the body of your composition evenly on the page with suitable margins on each side and at the top and bottom. Center your title and place it a few spaces above the first sentence of your text. Capitalize the first word and all other words in the title except articles and short prepositions. Number your pages and endorse your paper in the manner prescribed by your instructor. The endorsement usually includes your name, the title of your paper, and the date.

Before submitting your final copy, read it aloud to yourself (or to a friend) once more to catch any omission of words or punctuation errors. Examine your title in this reading also. Is it brief, accurate, and consistent with the tone of the paper? Will it catch a reader's attention, stimulate his interest? Remember that the title is not part of the composition itself. As mentioned earlier, the first sentence of the theme should not depend on the title for its meaning.

EXERCISE 24

A. Turn in a final copy of the theme you revised for Exercise 23E.

SUMMARY

Like the paragraph, the theme requires careful attention to unity, development, coherence, and emphasis. Because of its increased length and complexity, however, you must plan its construction in greater detail. To help you with this planning, we have suggested the following steps:

1. Decide on a subject. If you can choose the topic, select one from your own experience—one that will appeal to your reader.

2. Limit your topic in accordance with the length of your paper and the interests and background of your reader.

3. Think through your subject.

4. Gather and organize your material; group major and minor ideas, and arrange them in a logical sequence to effect your purpose.

5. Outline your theme. For a short paper, especially one written in class, a rough outline will suffice. For a longer paper the formal outline is almost essential.

6. Write your first draft as rapidly as possible, using your outline as a guide. Put the first draft aside for a few hours, and do not think about it.

7. After you have been away from your first draft for awhile, revise it, giving close scrutiny to content and organization as well as to mechanics. In particular, check opening and closing sentences and the continuity of thought between paragraphs.

8. Prepare a final copy, observing the conventions for preparing a manuscript prescribed by your instructor.

As we stressed at the beginning of this chapter, no simple rules will enable you to write clear, convincing, interesting themes. But careful planning and use of these suggestions in your writing and rewriting will do much to improve your skill and success.

PART TWO | **Reader**

ONE | The Aims of Education

JAMES THURBER
University Days

This essay is based on the author's experiences as a student at Ohio State University. Like most of Thurber's work, it reveals his capacity for converting seemingly commonplace and insignificant conflicts or problems into uncommon and significant humor. Although the situations and characterizations are undoubtedly exaggerated for humorous effect, they are never pushed quite beyond the point of credibility. Much of the success of Thurber's humor lies in his skillful use of this technique.

As you read, be aware of the author's use of topic sentences and of his paragraph development and ask yourself what purpose he has beyond that of humor as an end in itself.

(1) I passed all the other courses that I took at my University, but I could never pass botany. This was because all botany students had to spend several hours a week in a laboratory looking through a microscope at plant cells, and I could never see through a microscope. I never once saw a cell through a microscope. This used to enrage my instructor. He would wander around the laboratory pleased with the progress all the students were making in drawing the involved and, so I am told, interesting structure of flower cells, until he came to me. I would just be standing there. "I can't see anything," I would say. He would begin patiently enough, explaining how anybody can see through a microscope, but he would always end up in a fury, claiming

that I could *too* see through a microscope but just pretended that I couldn't. "It takes away from the beauty of flowers anyway," I used to tell him. "We are not concerned with beauty in this course," he would say. "We are concerned solely with what I may call the *mechanics* of flars." "Well," I'd say, "I can't see anything." "Try it just once again," he'd say, and I would put my eye to the microscope and see nothing at all, except now and again, a nebulous milky substance — a phenomenon of maladjustment. You were supposed to see a vivid, restless clockwork of sharply defined plant cells. "I see what looks like a lot of milk," I would tell him. This, he claimed, was the result of my not having adjusted the microscope properly; so he would readjust it for me, or rather, for himself. And I would look again and see milk.

(2) I finally took a deferred pass, as they called it, and waited a year and tried again. (You had to pass one of the biological sciences or you couldn't graduate.) The professor had come back from vacation brown as a berry, bright-eyed, and eager to explain cell-structure again to his classes. "Well," he said to me, cheerily, when we met in the first laboratory hour of the semester, "we're going to see cells this time, aren't we?" "Yes, sir," I said. Students to right of me and to left of me and in front of me were seeing cells; what's more, they were quietly drawing pictures of them in their notebooks. Of course, I didn't see anything.

(3) "We'll try it," the professor said to me, grimly, "with every adjustment of the microscope known to man. As God is my witness, I'll arrange this glass so that you see cells through it or I'll give up teaching. In twenty-two years of botany, I—" He cut off abruptly for he was beginning to quiver all over, like Lionel Barrymore, and he genuinely wished to hold onto his temper: his scenes with me had taken a great deal out of him.

(4) So we tried it with every adjustment of the microscope known to man. With only one of them did I see anything but blackness or the familiar lacteal opacity, and that time I saw, to my pleasure and amazement, a variegated constellation of flecks, specks, and dots. These I hastily drew. The instructor, noting my activity, came back from an adjoining desk, a smile on his lips and his eyebrows high in hope. He looked at my cell drawing. "What's that?" he demanded, with a hint of a squeal in his voice. "That's what I saw," I said. "You didn't, you didn't, you *didn't!*" he screamed, losing control of his temper instantly, and he bent over and squinted into the microscope. His head snapped up. "That's your eye!" he shouted. "You've fixed the lens so that it reflects! You've drawn your eye!"

(5) Another course that I didn't like, but somehow managed to pass, was economics. I went to that class straight from the botany class,

which didn't help me any in understanding either subject. I used to get them mixed up. But not as mixed up as another student in my economics class who came there direct from a physics laboratory. He was a tackle on the football team, named Bolenciecwcz. At that time Ohio State University had one of the best football teams in the country, and Bolenciecwcz was one of its outstanding stars. In order to be eligible to play it was necessary for him to keep up in his studies, a very difficult matter, for while he was not dumber than an ox he was not any smarter. Most of his professors were lenient and helped him along. None gave him more hints, in answering questions, or asked him simpler ones than the economics professor, a thin, timid man named Bassum. One day when we were on the subject of transportation and distribution, it came Bolenciecwcz's turn to answer a question. "Name one means of transportation," the professor said to him. No light came into the big tackle's eyes. "Just any means of transportation," said the professor. Bolenciecwcz sat staring at him. "That is," pursued the professor, "any medium, agency, or method of going from one place to another." Bolenciecwcz had the look of a man who is being led into a trap. "You may choose among steam, horse-drawn, or electrically propelled vehicles," said the instructor. "I might suggest the one which we commonly take in making long journeys across land." There was a profound silence in which everybody stirred uneasily, including Bolenciecwcz and Mr. Bassum. Mr. Bassum abruptly broke this silence in an amazing manner. "Choo-choo-choo," he said, in a low voice, and turned scarlet. He glanced appealingly around the room. All of us, of course, shared Mr. Bassum's desire that Bolenciecwcz should stay abreast of the class in economics, for the Illinois game, one of the hardest and most important of the season, was only a week off. "Toot, toot, too-tooooooot!" some student with a deep voice moaned; and we all looked encouragingly at Bolenciecwcz. Somebody else gave a fine imitation of a locomotive letting off steam. Mr. Bassum himself rounded off the little show. "Ding, dong, ding, dong," he said, hopefully. Bolenciecwcz was staring at the floor now, trying to think, his great brow furrowed, his huge hands rubbing together, his face red.

(6) "How did you come to college this year, Mr. Bolenciecwcz?" asked the professor. "*Chuffa* chuffa, *chuffa* chuffa."

(7) "M'father sent me," said the football player.

(8) "What on?" asked Bassum.

(9) "I git an 'lowance," said the tackle, in a low, husky voice, obviously embarrassed.

(10) "No, no," said Bassum. "Name a means of transportation. What did you *ride* here on?"

(11) "Train," said Bolenciecwcz.

(12) "Quite right," said the professor. "Now, Mr. Nugent, will you tell us—"

(13) If I went through anguish in botany and economics—for different reasons—gymnasium work was even worse. I don't even like to think about it. They wouldn't let you play games or join in the exercises with your glasses on and I couldn't see with mine off. I bumped into professors, horizontal bars, agricultural students, and swinging iron rings. Not being able to see, I could take it but I couldn't dish it out. Also, in order to pass gymnasium (and you had to pass it to graduate) you had to learn to swim if you didn't know how. I didn't like the swimming pool, I didn't like swimming, and I didn't like the swimming instructor, and after all these years I still don't. I never swam but I passed my gym work anyway, by having another student give my gymnasium number (978) and swim across the pool in my place. He was a quiet, amiable blonde youth, number 473, and he would have seen through a microscope for me if we could have got away with it, but we couldn't get away with it. Another thing I didn't like about gymnasium work was that they made you strip the day you registered. It is impossible for me to be happy when I am stripped and being asked a lot of questions. Still, I did better than a lanky agricultural student who was cross-examined just before I was. They asked each student what college he was in—that is, whether Arts, Engineering, Commerce, or Agriculture. "What college are you in?" the instructor snapped at the youth in front of me. "Ohio State University," he said promptly.

(14) It wasn't that agricultural student but it was another a whole lot like him who decided to take up journalism, possibly on the ground that when farming went to hell he could fall back on newspaper work. He didn't realize, of course, that that would be very much like falling back full-length on a kit of carpenter's tools. Haskins didn't seem cut out for journalism, being too embarrassed to talk to anybody and unable to use a typewriter, but the editor of the college paper assigned him to the cow barns, the sheep house, the horse pavilion, and the animal husbandry department generally. This was a genuinely big "beat," for it took up five times as much ground and got ten times as great a legislative appropriation as the College of Liberal Arts. The agricultural student knew animals, but nevertheless his stories were dull and colorlessly written. He took all afternoon on each of them, because he had to hunt for each letter on the typewriter. Once in a while he had to ask somebody to help him hunt. "C" and "L," in particular, were hard letters for him to find. His editor finally got pretty much annoyed at the farmer-journalist because his pieces were so uninteresting. "See here, Haskins," he snapped at him one day, "why is it we never have anything hot from

you on the horse pavilion? Here we have two hundred head of horses on this campus — more than any other university in the Western Conference except Purdue — and yet you never get any real low-down on them. Now shoot over to the horse barns and dig up something lively." Haskins shambled out and came back in about an hour; he said he had something. "Well, start it off snappily," said the editor. "Something people will read." Haskins set to work and in a couple of hours brought a sheet of typewritten paper to the desk; it was a two-hundred word story about some disease that had broken out among the horses. Its opening sentence was simple but arresting. It read: "Who has noticed the sores on the tops of the horses in the animal husbandry building?"

(15) Ohio State was a land grant university and therefore two years of military drill was compulsory. We drilled with old Springfield rifles and studied the tactics of the Civil War even though the World War was going on at the time. At 11 o'clock each morning thousands of freshmen and sophomores used to deploy over the campus, moodily creeping up on the old chemistry building. It was good training for the kind of warfare that was waged at Shiloh but it had no connection with what was going on in Europe. Some people used to think there was German money behind it, but they didn't dare say so or they would have been thrown in jail as German spies. It was a period of muddy thought and marked, I believe, the decline of higher education in the Middle West.

(16) As a soldier I was never any good at all. Most of the cadets were glumly indifferent soldiers, but I was no good at all. Once General Littlefield, who was commandant of the cadet corps, popped up in front of me during regimental drill and snapped, "You are the main trouble with this university!" I think he meant that my type was the main trouble with the university but he may have meant me individually. I was mediocre at drill, certainly — that is, until my senior year. By that time I had drilled longer than anybody else in the Western Conference, having failed at military at the end of each preceding year so that I had to do it all over again. I was the only senior still in uniform. The uniform which, when new, had made me look like an interurban railway conductor, now that it had become faded and too tight made me look like Bert Williams in his bell-boy act. This had a definitely bad effect on my morale. Even so, I had become by sheer practice little short of wonderful at squad manoeuvres.

(17) One day General Littlefield picked our company out of the whole regiment and tried to get it mixed up by putting it through one movement after another as fast as we could execute them: squads right, squads left, squads on right into line, squads right about, squads

left front into line, etc. In about three minutes one hundred and nine men were marching in one direction and I was marching away from them at an angle of forty degrees, all alone. "Company, halt!" shouted General Littlefield, "That man is the only man who has it right!" I was made a corporal for my achievement.

(18) The next day General Littlefield summoned me to his office. He was swatting flies when I went in. I was silent and he was silent too, for a long time. I don't think he remembered me or why he had sent for me, but he didn't want to admit it. He swatted some more flies, keeping his eyes on them narrowly before he let go with the swatter. "Button up your coat!" he snapped. Looking back on it now I can see that he meant me although he was looking at a fly, but I just stood there. Another fly came to rest on a paper in front of the general and began rubbing its hind legs together. The general lifted the swatter cautiously. I moved restlessly and the fly flew away. "You startled him!" barked General Littlefield, looking at me severely. I said I was sorry. "That won't help the situation!" snapped the General, with cold military logic. I didn't see what I could do except offer to chase some more flies toward his desk, but I didn't say anything. He stared out the window at the faraway figures of co-eds crossing the campus toward the library. Finally, he told me I could go. So I went. He either didn't know which cadet I was or else he forgot what he wanted to see me about. It may have been that he wished to apologize for having called me the main trouble with the university; or maybe he had decided to compliment me on my brilliant drilling of the day before and then at the last minute decided not to. I don't know. I don't think about it much any more.

QUESTIONS AND EXERCISES

VOCABULARY

1. nebulous (*paragraph* 1)
2. lacteal (4)
3. opacity (4)
4. variegated (4)
5. anguish (13)
6. amiable (13)
7. husbandry (14)
8. arresting (14)
9. mediocre (16)
10. interurban (16)

LANGUAGE AND RHETORIC

1. Why does the author begin new paragraphs at 2, 5, 13, 14, and 15?
2. A single topic sentence in paragraph 1 serves not only for that paragraph but for paragraphs 2, 3, and 4. Identify that sentence.
3. Locate the topic sentence that serves for paragraphs 5 through 11. Is there any controlling idea in this section?

4. Why are paragraphs 7 through 12 treated as separate paragraphs?
5. Why does paragraph 18 have no explicit controlling idea? What is the purpose of the paragraph?

DISCUSSION AND WRITING
1. What implicit comment about college athletics does the section portraying the economics class make? Do you agree or disagree with the author? Why?
2. What implicit comment about required courses do the sections dealing with the botany, gym, and ROTC classes make? Have you ever had similar attitudes toward a college regulation or requirement? If so, write a paper explaining your attitude and the reasons for it.
3. Describe an interesting or unusual instructor you have had, focusing on a single trait that makes him interesting or unusual.
4. Recount a particularly interesting or humorous incident from your own college experience, presenting the incident as concretely as you can.

LOUIE CREW

The Physical Miseducation of a Former Fat Boy

In the previous selection, James Thurber recalls in a humorous way some of his experiences as a college student, among them his brief and unfortunate brush with physical education. In this selection, Louie Crew takes a more sobering look at that particular phase of his own secondary school and college experience. Like Thurber, Crew suffered a handicap—being overweight—and we can readily understand from this account of his past and present experiences why he might consider his to have been a "physical miseducation."

Observe how the author draws upon a number of different personal experiences to develop a single thesis.

(1) When I was six, a next-door neighbor gave me my first candy bar, and I fattened immediately in a home where food was love. It is hardly surprising that when I first entered physical education courses

in the eighth grade my coaches were markedly unimpressed or that thereafter I compensated by working harder at books, where I was more successful. Although I did learn to take jokes about my size and experienced the "bigness" of being able to laugh at myself (the standard fat man's reward), at thirty-five I am furious to recall how readily and completely my instructors defaulted in their responsibilities to me. Some remedies I have learned in my thirties persuade me that it is not inevitable that the system will continue to fail other fat boys.

(2) My personal remedies for physical ineptitude have a firm base in ideas. Four years ago I weighed 265 pounds. Only my analyst needs to know how much I consequently hated myself. In six months I took off 105 pounds and initiated a regular jogging and exercising schedule that has gradually, very gradually, led to increased self-confidence. Yet my physical education teachers in secondary school and college never showed the least interest in my physical problems, never sat down and initiated the simplest diagnosis of my physical needs, never tempted me into the personal discoveries that I had to wait more than a decade to make for myself.

(3) Instead, my physical educators offered two alternatives. Either I could enter the fierce competitive sports that predominate in our culture and therein make and accept the highest mark I could achieve; or I could opt for the less-competitive intramurals, modeled after the big boys' games, and accept my role as a physically incompetent human being, sitting on the sidelines to cheer for a chosen team of professionals. These limited alternatives were repeatedly justified as teaching me how it is out in the "real world," in "the game of life," allegedly divided between the participators and the watchers.

(4) Now, as I jog in midwinter dawn, all muffled with socks over my hands, making tracks with the rabbits in Carolina dew, I am not competing with anyone, unless I whimsically imagine Father Time having to add another leaf to my book. I am celebrating me, *this* morning, *this* pair of worn-out tennis shoes, the tingle in my cheeks, the space being cleared in my stomach for my simple breakfast when I get back. . . . I was very articulate at fourteen — fat but articulate — and I believe that a sympathetic, interested coach could have shared this type of insight, this type of reality, with me, and perhaps thereby he could have teased me into the discoveries I had to make many years later. But the coach would have had to love kids like me more than he loved winning if he had hoped to participate in my physical education. I had no such coach.

(5) Perhaps an athletic friend could have shared insights into my physical needs and suggested alternative fulfillments. I certainly had many athletic friends, because I sought avidly to compensate for my physical failures by liking and being liked by athletes. Unfortunately,

these friends were all schooled in the competitive rules of keeping trade secrets and of enjoying and hoarding compliments. Human sharing had not been a part of their education.

(6) I recall how at thirty-two I tentatively jogged around a block for the first time, how the fierce hurt in my gut was less bothersome than the fear that I would not make it. I had to learn to love myself for making it, and for making it again the next day, rather than to participate in my hecklers' mockery of the sweating fat man. I remember jogging no faster at sixteen and being laughed at by the coach, who kept me that much longer a prisoner in my role as the jovial class clown.

(7) I became a water boy and trainer, winning the school's award for "most unselfish service." Is not the role familiar? I even served two summers as a camp counselor. I could not walk to first base without puffing, but I could call a kid "out" with a tongue of forked lightning. I had been taught well.

(8) My physical educators were signally unimaginative. We played only the few sports that had always been played in our area. Further, they maintained a rigid separation between "sports" and "play." Football, baseball, basketball, and track were "sports." Fishing, hiking, boating, and jogging were "play." Golf was "play" until you had a team that won five trophies; then you developed the cool rhetoric of "sport."

(9) I remember going on a boy-scout trip in the Talledega National Forest in Alabama for a week. My anticipation was immense. I liked the woods. I liked walking. I liked the sky, trees, rocks, ferns. . . . We were to walk only about five or ten miles a day through a wilderness, camping out around an authentic chuck wagon that would move in advance during the day. The trip itself, however, was a nightmare for me. The coach/scoutmaster led at a frantic pace, because he wanted to get each lap done with and, as he said, he wanted "to make men" out of us. The major activity was to race ahead so as to enjoy "breathers" while waiting to heckle us slower folk when we caught up. When we came to a clearing overlooking the vast chasms of blue-green shimmer, the biggest breach of the unwritten code would have been to stop to look for ten minutes. The trip was to get somewhere (nobody quite knew why or where), not to be somewhere.

(10) For a long time I treasured illusions that my experiences with physical miseducation resulted merely from my provincial isolation, that real professionals elsewhere had surely identified and rectified these ills. But as I have moved from south to west to east, even to England, I have found very few real physical educators. Almost no one is interested in educating individuals to discover their own physical resources and to integrate them with all other personal experiences. Almost everyone is interested in developing ever-better

professionals to provide vicarious entertainment for a physically inept society.

(11) Most of the professional literature describes the training of professional sportsmen and evaluates the machinery developed to serve this training. My favorite example of this perverse pedantry is my friend's M.A. thesis studying the effects of various calisthenics on sweat samples. One is scared to imagine what secretions he will measure for his doctoral dissertation. Yet it is fashionable to mock medieval scholars for disputing how many angels could stand on the head of a pin!

(12) Once while working out in a gymnasium at the University of Alabama, I jestingly asked some professionals how many pounds I would have to be able to lift to be a man. To my surprise, I received specific answers: one said 280 pounds (he could lift 285); another said, "one's own weight"; another. . . . But I was born a man! It is surely perverse for a man to trap himself by confusing *being* with *becoming*.

QUESTIONS AND EXERCISES

VOCABULARY
1. compensated (*paragraph* 1)   6. tentatively (6)
2. defaulted (1)   7. mockery (6)
3. inevitable (1)   8. provincial (10)
4. ineptitude (2)   9. rectified (10)
5. articulate (4)   10. vicarious (10)

LANGUAGE AND RHETORIC
1. What are the author's thesis and purpose in this essay, and where does he state them explicity?
2. By carefully choosing words or phrases from the article, describe the author's tone — his attitude toward his subject and audience. Point out the basis for your choices.
3. Does paragraph 9, the one about the Boy Scout trip, stray from the central subject of this essay? Support your answer.
4. What is the rhetorical function of paragraph 10?
5. How do the anecdote in the concluding paragraph and the author's comment on it relate to his thesis?

DISCUSSION AND WRITING
1. Do you know of any comparable educational experiences undergone by people who had physical problems other than being overweight? If so, write a paper about one or more of them. What conclusions about physical education — if any — do they suggest?
2. Do you agree or disagree with the author's views on physical education?

Write a paper based on personal experience supporting your view of the subject.

3. The author shows us what he thinks a physical educator should *not* be and by so doing suggests what a physical educator *should* be. What do you think a physical educator should be and do? (One way to approach this question would be to write a paper describing a physical educator you are familiar with.)

4. The author feels that one of the major problems with physical education is the emphasis on competition. How do you feel about competition in physical education? Explain your point of view.

5. Although this essay deals only with physical education, we can certainly draw parallels with other subjects and teachers. Write a personal experience essay comparable to this but about another subject.

SYLVESTER MONROE

Guest in a Strange House: A Black at Harvard

In response to the social pressures and racial conflicts faced by this country during the last half of the 1960s, our traditionally white-oriented colleges and universities began not only to admit but actively recruit blacks and members of other minority groups. But merely admitting a person to a college does not guarantee that the educational experience will be favorable for him, nor, if he is only one of a small number of students from a minority group, that it will be comfortable. In this essay written while he was an undergraduate, Sylvester Monroe recounts what he found college life like as a black at Harvard.

As you read, ask yourself what purpose the author seems to have in mind and how his use of first person narrative contributes to that purpose.

(1) I am part of a new and growing group of black students for whom Harvard is a new experience. In fact, until I was a sophomore in high school, I had never even heard of Harvard College. When I graduate from Harvard this June, I will be the first member of my family to receive a college degree. But, even after three-and-one-half years at Harvard, I still find it extremely difficult—even impossible—to think of myself as a "Harvard man." Instead, I feel more like a guest in a strange house where my welcome has all but run out. I am nearing the end of a four-year visit during which I have never felt at home.

(2) The problem is that the traditional Harvard just isn't my Harvard. The Harvard of my experience has been three years of a totally black experience—black roommates, black friends, black dining-hall tables, black dances, black student organizations, black building takeovers, black studies, and black ideology, all isolated within the confines of an otherwise white university.

(3) A recent black graduate of Harvard told me that although black students have studied here for more than a century, their experience really represented only a passing through in which they were always careful never to upset the status quo. "For more than one hundred years," he said, "black students have found themselves, in effect, in a revolving door that has momentarily offered access to Harvard and then quickly spun them out into the cold world again."

(4) After almost a century without change the 1960s created a new kind of black student, full of the awareness that black is beautiful and proud and powerful and often violently antiwhite. Responding to the militant stance of urban black people during the Sixties, Harvard and other prestigious white colleges started to recruit those students. The big push came in 1968, when for the first time there were almost 100 black students in Harvard's freshman class. (As late as 1965 there were less than two dozen black students in the entire college.) Each year since 1969, when I arrived, Harvard has admitted about 130 black freshmen, bringing the current black enrollment to more than 520 in a total undergraduate population of about 6,000 students.

(5) Wherever they could be found—in the graduating classes of inner-city high schools or on ghetto street corners—young black kids who had never even heard of the Ivy League were brought to Harvard "to make it" in the white world. Unquestionably, it was a bold and—in one sense—even admirable venture; yet it also was blind. For, in essence, Harvard was bringing black students to a swimming hole and telling them to swim.

(6) Consequently, a lot of black students were able to stay afloat only with the aid of summer enrichment programs like ABC (A Better Chance), Upward Bound, and others designed to help bridge the enormous gap between black inner-city schools and prestigious white ones. In my own case the jump from the 100 per cent black Wendell Phillips High School on Chicago's South Side was bridged by a year at the Duke University ABC program in 1966, and then three years at St. George's prep school in Newport, Rhode Island.

(7) But there were countless others who, without the benefits of such transition, were simply left to drown. Harvard did not recognize any responsibility to black students beyond the initial step of bringing them here.

(8) Beginning in the mid-Sixties, Harvard and a steadily growing

group of black students began feeling their way through a totally new experience—a kind of "great experiment" in which a handful of confused and frightened black youths found themselves charged with the mammoth task of developing better racial relations with a scared and uncertain white college community.

(9) Even as late as 1969 black students were coming to Harvard *expecting* to be accepted and absorbed into the mainstream of university life. Although filled with anxiety about a variety of concerns, including the fear of failing academically, very few came with any intention or desire to separate themselves from white people.

(10) In fact, in those years between 1965 and 1969 most blacks still had white roommates, and many of them even participated in white social activities. (They did so partly because the number of blacks hadn't grown sufficiently to form black organizations and partly because blacks were genuinely seeking to get along with the white community.)

(11) When I first came here, I had two white roommates—by choice. Although I got along well with them during my freshman year, relations with other whites often were not as pleasant, for it seemed at times that there was just too much that white Harvard students did not know.

(12) I remember vividly the questions they would ask: Someone would want to know whether my parents grew up on a plantation or whether my grandmother was a slave. Or someone else might ask whether my family's diet consisted mainly of soul food or whether anyone in my family had ever won a dance contest because of natural rhythm. I recall a friend's telling me once that a white girl even wanted to touch her (Afro-styled) hair.

(13) Although I had experienced much the same kind of ignorance and naïveté in prep school, somehow it all seemed a lot worse at Harvard. It was with increasing difficulty that I tried to ignore feelings that I was being used as a guinea pig, a black showpiece for the Harvard administration—which, in fact, was what most of us were.

(14) As it turned out, rather than suffer the tongue-in-cheek naïveté so evident in many of those questions, many of us began desperately seeking other black students while consciously avoiding any unnecessary contact with anyone white—student or faculty.

(15) It didn't take long to find a small group of blacks who felt pretty much as I did, and we began meeting for late evening bull sessions anywhere we could be assured of being alone. The main topic of discussion always centered on our daily experiences on a white campus or on the similarities of our past lives in inner-city ghettos. But, better than anything else about those meetings, I remember the deep sense of closeness and solidarity we felt. It was like a breath of

fresh air after we had put up all day with the patronizing attitudes of white students and professors. After several of these bull sessions I decided about midway through my freshman year that I would have black roommates for the rest of my stay at Harvard. For the past three years that is exactly how it has been.

(16) It was early in that first year also that I became influenced by the black ideology of the Association of Afro-American Students (Harvard Afro) — at that time a highly active and political black student organization that was partly responsible, during the student strike in the spring of 1969, for bringing about the establishment of an Afro-American Studies Department.

(17) Because everybody around me had been black on the South Side of Chicago, I wasn't confronted with my blackness until I had arrived at St. George's School. But even there I never really had to put it into any particular perspective. Instead, I always told myself that although I am black, I am first of all a human being, and that ultimately the latter fact would prove more important than the former in whatever I might do. But as a result of my associations with Harvard Afro, the emphasis gradually shifted, despite the many attempts I made to prevent it. For the first time in my life I realized that the facts of race and color do not change simply because one goes to a white prep school or college. Everything I have done since then has been guided by a conscious black perspective.

(18) To understand the profound effect this change of attitude had upon me is to understand how I suddenly felt about the classes I was taking, indeed, about almost every facet of my life at Harvard. For example, in the spring term of my freshman year, during a humanities lecture, I suddenly found myself wondering what possible connection there could be between *Beowulf* (the subject of the lecture) and any solution to the problems of black people in America. Quickly I decided there was none, walked out of the lecture hall, and stopped attending the course.

(19) In the same way I canceled my participation in many other black-white activities that seemed to me of no particular value in preparing to help better the plight of all the black people I'd left back home in Chicago. I stopped eating at mixed dining-hall tables in order to avoid going through the empty motions of talking to white students. I stopped taking courses that weren't taught entirely in lectures, because I didn't want to talk with white teaching fellows. Our desire to avoid any kind of exchange with whites was so intense that during the annual sophomore dinner in the Leverett House dining hall, after finishing a specially prepared dinner of steak and wine and apple pie, about ten of us — all sitting at the same table — walked out just as the house master began his welcoming address!

(20) In other words, for the past three years my stance—and that of the great majority of my contemporaries—has been that I simply have no time for those parts of the Harvard College curriculum and social life that seem to have nothing positive or relevant to offer to my experiences and goals.

(21) What has been most frustrating in my four years here is that I have found so very little in any aspect of the school that has not reflected a negative attitude toward black people and their worth as contributing members of the human race. It is that way in history courses. It is that way in English. It is that way in house activities. It is that way in sports (according to one of my roommates who is a leading member of the varsity basketball team).

(22) Intellectually, I still believe there is a great deal to be gained by staying here. Thus, I have remained, but not without suffering the painful experience of fulfilling academic requirements that adopted a negative posture toward black people. In my major, social studies—a combination of American history and economics—I was required to take one-and-a-half courses in history. One of these was an intellectual-history course covering the span of American history from the beginning to the present in sixty-seven lectures. Black peoples' contributions were mentioned in only two of those during the entire year: once with respect to the issue of slavery and once to explain black intellectuals' involvement with socialism and communism in the early twentieth century.

(23) Similarly, my other roommate, an economics major whose interest is economic development, had to take a course in which the professor would ask such questions as: "Why hasn't black Africa developed economically?"

(24) As the years have brought more black students to Harvard, more of them have found it easier to live and interact among themselves, developing cultural and educational programs that meet their own needs. Harvard is today confronted not only with more black students than ever before but with increasingly louder and more militant demands for "relevancy" in the college experience. The black challenge has become a demand for Harvard's acceptance of the full responsibility for bringing black students here, in the same way that the students have had to wrestle with the keen sense of guilt they feel being here while their families still struggle in black ghettos.

(25) I remember well the guilt my roommate and I felt as sophomores living in a plush, apartmentlike dormitory suite equipped with such luxuries as a refrigerator, private bath, private bedrooms, and a living room with a large plate-glass picture window looking out over the banks of the Charles River. To this day it still seems terribly in-

consistent that we are actually living better as students in a college dormitory than we have ever lived in our own homes in two of the many overcrowded, dirty housing projects of Chicago and New York City.

(26) The one sure way of easing such guilt was to demand "relevance" from Harvard, which means, in effect, instruction that can be directed toward improving the quality of life for blacks as a whole in this country. I recall my participation in the 1969 black student takeover of a Harvard administration building. The issue we demonstrated against was alleged hiring discrimination by the university against black painting contractors and construction workers. But when a university dean shouted through a bullhorn that unless we left the building immediately we'd all be suspended from school, I suddenly couldn't think of any good reason for being there in the first place, except that I felt if I hadn't gone in, I'd have been a traitor to the black cause. Much later in the summer I realized that I had occupied University Hall not so much for the sake of the painters but instead to convince myself and my peers that being at Harvard had not made me forget where I came from.

(27) By seeking to relieve their guilt via building takeovers, strikes, and other kinds of demonstrations and by exercising their desire for "privacy," black students have baffled and embittered the white Harvard community.

(28) To them black isolation is an ambivalent stance. As one white educator reflected, "It is like an incredible paradox in which black students who once objected to separatism in all-black colleges now shun the mainstream of college life at Harvard and develop isolated programs of their own."

(29) In 1969, when blacks demanded that the university make some changes in its curriculum, many white faculty were frightened by the students' implied threats of violence if their demands were not met. Consequently, motivated by fear more than reason, the faculty voted to support the students' demands for a separate black-studies program, which is today essentially a social science and humanities-oriented program of readings in the history of black culture.

(30) I think the faculty vote reflected also a conscious desire to "give the niggers anything they want so long as it will keep them quiet." It was also, I think, an easy way of washing their hands of the whole matter, leaving to the students themselves the responsibility of educating black students.

(31) The situation is similar with respect to the other aspects of black isolation. Even though whites at all levels of the university have complained about such things as being denied seats at all-black dining-hall tables, none of them, it seems, has been particularly dis-

turbed enough really to do anything about it. Neither does there seem to be much concern at all that more frequently black students are missing classes and subsequently not receiving the instruction they desperately need. Instead, under the pretense of "respecting their wishes" whites are simply ignoring black students altogether, leaving them to sink or swim on their own.

(32) But the blame does not belong only to the whites. Blacks have been equally complacent about their own responsibilities as students. More and more young blacks who come here are becoming much too comfortable behind a superficial shield of black solidarity. Somehow, they are blinded, it seems, by the small amount of effort it takes to isolate oneself from almost everything that isn't particularly appealing.

(33) In essence, too many blacks simply misuse the ideological strength of black solidarity as a kind of cover to dupe the white community into believing that behind their united front of blackness they are mature, self-confident, and functioning black individuals, who know exactly what they want and how they will get it. But what I see and hear instead are insecure and frightened young black men and women, who—in the words of a James Brown song—are constantly "talking loud and saying nothing" in an attempt to persuade themselves, more than anybody else, that they have the right answers.

(34) Eating lunch with a group of black freshmen and sophomores last spring, I overheard one of them say to another: "You know, I'm really glad I'm at Harvard and not Howard. I've heard they [the Howard faculty and administration] don't take no stuff down there." I realized that he was glad to be at Harvard because here, being black, he can get through without ever really applying himself. Yet maybe he should have preferred being at Howard, where the instructors would make certain he got the basic remedial skills that so many of us never mastered before coming to Harvard. Black students often do not get adequate remedial preparation before entering Harvard through no fault of their own. What is in part their fault is that in four years of college many never even attempt to acquire these skills.

(35) On the other hand, it is quite difficult to get that kind of extra help at Harvard without asking for it, which only compounds the problems of black students who are isolated from the white college community. "There are a number of black students now doing *B* work who could be doing *A* work," says Archie C. Epps, Harvard's black dean of students. "The reason they are not is that they have isolated themselves from the intellectual strength of the Harvard community."

(36) Martin A. Kilson, a professor of government who is one of the most powerfully influential black individuals at Harvard adds, "The

problem with black students at Harvard is that they are too caught up in ideology. Most people who deal in ideologies believe only ten per cent of it, at most. But blacks at Harvard want to believe ninety per cent of their own ideological bullshit."

(37) Meanwhile it is 1972, and increasingly I hear of blacks—just three or four or five years out of school, holding degrees from Harvard or Yale—who discovered that they could not handle the everyday demands of their jobs. The world, it seems, has suddenly caught up with many of them and pulled the covers from an empty four years in the Ivy League. One by one, they've thrown up their hands to the realization that there is no great demand for "showcase niggers" today.

(38) The first fifteen black students with degrees in Afro-American studies have already graduated from Harvard. While a couple of them have gone to law school or divinity school, the overwhelming majority are now teaching black history. I cannot help thinking that if the future holds nothing more for the graduates of black-studies departments than teaching jobs in the black community, then who will be the black doctors, the technicians, and the architects of the future black community? I cannot help thinking also that it might have been better for many of us to have gone to Tougaloo College in Mississippi or Fisk or Howard or anywhere other than a place like Harvard, where if one is black, he must necessarily shut himself off from the strength of the institution in order to affirm his self-identity.

(39) As for me personally, I am on the brink of being thrust out into that same complex and demanding white world, and, quite frankly, I feel very inadequate about my past three years at Harvard, which were lived in an almost totally isolated black vacuum. To be sure, I am thoroughly confused.

QUESTIONS AND EXERCISES

VOCABULARY

1. ideology (*paragraph* 2)
2. status quo (3)
3. prestigious (4)
4. anxiety (9)
5. naïveté (14)

6. ambivalent (28)
7. paradox (28)
8. complacent (32)
9. superficial (32)

LANGUAGE AND RHETORIC

1. What audience does the author seem to have in mind in writing this essay? What clues indicate the nature of that audience to you?
2. What do you believe to be the author's purpose in writing this essay, and what is the basis for your opinion?

3. In your own words, state the thesis of this essay. Where does the author make that thesis explicit?
4. What tone (or attitude) does the author seem to have toward his subject? Point out specific evidence of that tone.
5. Does the author's use of personal experience and the first person strengthen the essay, or would it have been stronger if he had used a more objective approach, depending largely on factual details and examples from other sources? What is the basis for your answer?

DISCUSSION AND WRITING
1. What is your reaction to the basic experience and situation recounted here? What seems to be the root of the problem? Who is responsible? What do you think should be done about it? (Wherever you have firsthand experiences to draw upon, use these in developing your answers.)
2. Have you ever been a "guest in a strange house"? That is, have you experienced a sense of alienation and isolation somewhat as this author has? If so, write a paper recalling one particular experience of this kind.
3. In paragraphs 18 through 20 the author raises the question of the relevance of traditional college studies and social life for most black students. Do his reactions strike you as justifiable? What alternatives were available to him? Have you ever found yourself raising such questions? What did you do? What were your alternatives?
4. The author is particularly disturbed because he has "found so very little in any aspect of the school that has not reflected a negative attitude toward black people and their worth as contributing members of the human race." Based on your own educational experience, are you aware of the existence of such an attitude? Write an essay illustrating your answer.
5. After reading this selection, you might like to go on to the personal experience essay "No One Has Ever Called Me a Nigger" by Gilbert Moore in Section Five. Moore's essay provides an excellent basis for comparison.

MIRIAM COX
The College Is for Everyone Cult

I can see him now, sprawling over a chair in my office in the 10,000-student California junior college where I teach English. He has just announced "But that's what you're paid to do!" Not insolently, not belligerently, just matter-of-factly.

"The College Is for Everyone Cult" by Miriam Cox. From *Junior College Journal*, September, 1966. By permission of *Junior College Journal* and the author.

He's a personable eighteen-year-old, reasonably well-groomed, facile of speech—and with an unbroken stretch of failing grades marching through the squares opposite his name in my record book. Clearly, to borrow from Sigrid Undset, this lad was not built to climb the tree of knowledge.

But something impels me to probe a bit into his problem. That he has a big one is evident to me but apparently not to him.

"Yes, I'm flunking in my other classes too," he admits cheerfully. "But I don't mind."

In a flash I re-live one of those moments of agony during my own college days when I quivered to look at a returned paper for fear my grade might have dropped ever so slightly. But the timbre of my voice is unchanged as I ask, "Then, why are you here?"

"It's no good hanging around the house all the time, getting into Mom's hair."

"Did you try to find a job?"

"Nope. Don't want to work yet. I've got the rest of my life to do that. Besides, everybody knows you must have a college education to get anywhere these days."

"But you aren't getting a college education if you fail all of your classes!"

"Oh, well, I'm in no hurry. College is free. Eventually, maybe I'll pick up enough to get by."

A slow sizzle begins to develop along the back of my neck. But I murmur only, "Do you know about our eligibility and probation rules?"

He shrugs, and grins engagingly.

I glance again at his row of F's and D's. Each one represents a sizable chunk of time that I expended over casually scrawled papers to pinpoint this particular student's English deficiencies and help him conquer them.

"Do you have any idea how much time and vitality it took to check these papers that you tossed off perfunctorily and without study because you 'don't mind flunking'?"

Then it comes—his complacent, "That's what you're paid to do!"

The sizzle becomes volcanic. "No! I'm paid to help young people get an education, not 'get by'! And you're mistaken about junior colleges being free: taxpayers underwrite them heavily every April. Are you comfortable about the part of that tax money you're using up?

To say that this young man is a typical junior college student would be ridiculous. It would be equally ridiculous to say that he's in any sense unique, though he's more candid than most. I believe that he and an appalling number like him, are natural products of the current college-is-for-everyone cult.

College isn't for everyone: it is only for everyone who can profit by it and is willing to work for it. I'm proud to be a part of the burgeoning junior college movement that flings wide the doors of higher education to even the most financially limited of our citizenry. That our evening classes are thronged with people well past the traditional school ages—people who do excellent academic work despite concurrent pressures of earning a living and conducting a home—is irrefutable testimony of the worth of a system that recognizes the right of every individual to reach for continued formal education as long as he wants it. Not for me a system, still prevailing in some parts of the world, that abruptly deflects or terminates a person's education on the basis of rigid examinations from whose sentence there is no reprieve! Enter the hero!

But enter the monster too, a hydra-headed one. For, at the very time that thousands of earnest students struggle for admission to increasingly selective private colleges, state colleges, and state universities, and then go right on struggling to maintain respectable academic standing in the face of fierce competition, other thousands are flocking to junior colleges. Large numbers of these, of course, are as capable as any who go directly to the four-year institutions—of this we have ample proof—and take their places with distinction in those institutions for the junior and senior years.

Yet with them comes another horde of less competent or less motivated people like the young man in my office. And they come garbed in exactly the same attitudes they wore through high school—that education is a free ride and they will be passed simply because they are there. The awakening comes, of course, but at a monetary expense that puts an increasingly shrill edge on the taxpayer's voice and at a teacher-morale expense that is incalculable.

A second hydra-head looms in a different form—that of the many academically inept young people who enter junior college in a state of near desperation because they have been indoctrinated to see it as the only open sesame to success in modern life. Toward these students the sensitive teacher can feel only compassion. For too often, instead of going into the excellent trade and technical classes offered by junior colleges, they feel impelled—again that indoctrination—to enter the more demanding academic program. Their entrance examinations having revealed crippling deficiencies, however, they are guided into remedial courses first, presumably—as many a teacher has ruefully observed—to accomplish in one or two college semesters what they failed to accomplish in the leisurely trek through twelve previous years of school. Fearful and tense, many of these students work hard and hopelessly, unable to function even in these classes designed specifically to succor the educationally handicapped. College for them becomes not an invitation to learning but an invitation to defeat.

Now, I applaud Carlyle's "The great law of culture is: Let each become all that he was created capable of being." I agree also with Kahlil Gibran's, "Even those who limp go not backward." And I am sympathetic with his further observation that "In your longing for your giant self lies your goodness; and that longing is in all of you." But the statement that echoes loudest in my ears, seasoned as they are with many years of teaching, is Gibran's, "Pity that the stag cannot teach swiftness to the turtles." Is it a pity, or an immorality—this dangling of a college diploma in front of thousands of young people in our society who might reasonably expect to fulfill the longing for their "giant selves" as turtles but will never make it as stags?

There are over seven hundred junior colleges in the United States, and the number is increasing rapidly. They perform an inestimable service by providing strong programs for thousands of bright students who transfer to four-year colleges and universities for upper division work, while at the same time equipping other capable students to step into business, nursing, and industrial positions after a two-year occupational course. We can look with pride at these accomplishments of the junior college, but we need to look with equal candor at the constant vitiation of their strength through the concurrent influx of scholastically inept young people who either *coast* in with that appalling it's-free-and-I-can-slide-by-again attitude or *grind* in with the pitiable I-must-get-a-college-diploma-or-else . . .

Insistent and persuasive voices are urging that the first two years of college be offered to—or even required of—all high school graduates in the United States. Admirable—on the surface. But if large segments of those high school graduates are lotus eaters, or are scholastically unfitted for the two years of free college that they and their parents will be conditioned to regard as inalienable rights, we're in for trouble that will make our present woes seem lilliputian. Witness again that young man in my office!

The magnitude of the problem is thrown into even sharper relief by the realization that soon a *majority* of the young people aspiring to baccalaureate degrees will spend their freshman and sophomore years at these open-for-everyone colleges. California's Coordinating Council for Higher Education has already pointed out, for example, that roughly 77 percent of the state's high school seniors are close to a junior college and should be urged to enroll there. Still stronger forces are operative in the form of announcements by various state universities throughout the nation that they have reached their upper enrollment limits and, thus, must turn away many eligible students.

That junior colleges are meeting their responsibilities as an integral part of the system of higher education is attested to, among other ways, by the fact that some have already inaugurated honor courses to capitalize on the talents of high-achievers. But always at the opposite end of the teeter-totter and extending far up its length is that heavy group of underachievers who cannot or will not function on the college level. Will they in time, by sheer weight of numbers, force colleges down to their level? We are painfully concerned with the dropout problem these days, and rightfully so; but perhaps some of that concern should spill over into the "drop-in" problem epitomized by the attitude of the college-is-free and that's-what-you're-paid-to-do young man in my office. Even more of that concern should focus on the other kind of young person — the one who is nudged uneasily into college by a phony, society-nurtured conviction that to be less than a college-trained man is to be something less than a first-class citizen.

As a teacher who has taught in three states and on several age levels, I find the dramatic new impetus of the junior college movement meritorious and tenable. But I believe that the hydra-headed monster lurking in it is too formidable to be ignored. It will take many a Hercules to vanquish him. The heroes who rise to do battle must whack at all the heads, the most dangerous one of which may well be the bland acceptance of a monstrous untruth — that college is for everybody.

TWO | # The Changing Times

KARL FLEMING
Tripping Down Hippie Highway

Among the more visible evidence of our changing times is the number of young people who live on the road, hitchhiking aimlessly along any highway that will support their ventures. For some who have dropped out of the conventional culture, following the road has become a way of life. It is these young people and the places they frequent that Karl Fleming attempts to record in the following essay.

Note how the author's use of description supports his purpose.

(1) Far out. Hundreds of hitchhiking freaks with beards, back packs, guitars, flutes, wild hair and dogs — the Panzer troops of the Age of Aquarius — in steady motion along California 1, the Hippie Highway.

(2) Where the Hippie Highway becomes a freeway between Ventura and San Luis Obispo, the freaks are jammed up at every on-ramp. In Santa Barbara, they are strung out 50 at a time near the State Street intersection, awaiting rides from fellow freaks who own vans. The straight people never pick them up. The straights pretend not to see them, or shout, "Go to work, you creeps."

(3) But the drug-age nomads don't work much. They exist by panhandling, signing up for food stamps or selling a little dope. They stay stoned all day on weed, hash, acid, mescaline, cocaine, and uppers and downers; they crash at night in ditches, woods, churchyards, empty buildings or on the beach. "I crash where I fall down,"

says a gap-toothed acid freak on Big Sur, where there are maybe 1,000 like people living year-round in more or less, sanctified "families" of two to 75 up creeks and canyons along a 50-mile stretch.

(4) The authentic year-round road freak typically is about 19. He dropped out of school—and life—after he finished high school, or maybe just before. Most of his kind come from middle-class backgrounds. Boys outnumber girls, two to one. Some pair off more or less monogamously; others take their sex as casually and as transiently as a puff of grass. Everybody shares everything: dope, food, pennies. When dope runs short, a family member will split to The City—San Francisco or Los Angeles—and work long enough to earn some bread and score a stash of drugs.

(5) And everybody keeps moving. The freaks, when they hitchhike, aren't headed anyplace in particular—just looking for a place to get it together. Some stand along the highway hitching south with the right hand, north with the left. Some wander off into Oregon or Washington. But generally, for the freaks the Pacific Coast Highway between Laguna and San Francisco is where it's at.

(6) There is a steady stream from the East. Many try to stop in New Mexico. But the pigs—police are always "pigs" to the freaks—are tough. And the ten communes around Taos, startled at reports that possibly 10,000 invading freaks were on the way, have posted "No Visitors" and "No Crashing" signs. One of them, the Reality Construction Co., guards its place with guns.

(7) Along U.S. 101, San Luis Obispo is a heavy scene, a hostile detour from the Hippie Highway. Word-of-mouth among the freaks is that the Middle America farm and ranch folk thereabouts delight in lassoing hippies, shaving their heads and dragging them on ropes behind their Jeeps. The townsfolk are said to be convinced that the hippies capture pet dogs, skin them and eat them.

(8) Isla Vista is heavy, too. The police, following student demonstrations that resulted in a bank burning and much violence, are repressive. And a general air of fright prevails because three youths were brutally attacked recently while in their sleeping bags on the beach. Two died and the third was badly hurt. So crashing on the beach is out. Downtown at "The Switchboard," where volunteer workers try to reason with desperately spaced-out dope users on the phone, freaks slouch on battered sofas, looking for a place to sleep before heading on. "We may sleep badly," says a fat chick headed north, "but we sleep together."

(9) At night around the "Campus Cue" near the university entrance, the freaks tackle pedestrians: Any spare change? Spare food? A joint? A lot of them have to crash on the concrete floor of a vacant fraternity house. Bad Karma.

(10) "Isla Vista is a bummer—the people there aren't together," says a braless chick riding past it in a gaily decorated surplus Navy van with her "old man," a shirtless dude with a red beard and a wild laugh, and their animals, a dog named Cannabis (after marijuana) and a cat named Sandoz (after the company that perfected LSD). Virtually every freak couple has a dog. Pets are surrogate children for the "family."

(11) The van's interior is green with a purple dashboard and curtains and rugs strung throughout. A set of copper bells jingles intermittently. The driver, Tom, is alternately munching sunflower seeds and currants, and smoking a joint. "I'm kind of a Communist," he says. "I get vehement about police. It's not the individual cop who's a pig. It's the whole concept. I talk about it a lot to this straight guy I know. He's getting better, but he's still a capitalist mother-------."

(12) He stops to let out one of his hitchhikers, a dumpy brunette in high-buttoned shoes, a T-shirt and jeans. No bra. As she exits she crawls over a purse. "Is that yours?" she asks Tom's old lady.

(13) "No, it's yours," Tom's old lady says.

(14) "Far out," says the girl. She takes the purse, a faraway look in her eyes.

(15) The highway is clogged with traffic. Tough-looking bikers on Easy Rider choppers, square tourists in VW's, fancy Detroit cars, campers and trailers with Dad and Mom in front grimacing at the freaks—and the kids in back, smilingly giving them the V peace sign.

(16) At the first big freak enclave, Salmon Creek, twenty crazies jump up and down beside the highway, some of them waving pasteboard signs at passers-by which read: "Spare food?" "Spare dope?" "Spare chicks?" Occasionally a passing van tosses a joint off or dumps a girl out, and she joins the Salmon Creek family, which camps 200 yards off the highway behind a waterfall.

(17) "We go wherever we smell dope," announces a wild-eyed shirtless dude tripping on acid. Occasionally he and his people move back into the hills and "rip off" (steal) a cow or sheep, butcher and cook it. "It's a groovy place," says a skinny, unwashed little teen-ager in an Army shirt and busted-out boots. "We all share with each other. I've lived here eight months with nothing but a sleeping bag and $2. You can panhandle and you can get purple microdots [the currently favored form of LSD] for $1. And on Friday nights when the weekend people come up, we have a party and they're free."

(18) At Big Sur, the sign says the population is 500, but there are at least that many freaks living along the cold, sparkling Big Sur River. One of the top freaks, Honest John, is missing—off in Mexico scoring 100 vials of laboratory cocaine. But 100 or so others loll around the Big Sur River Inn store, just off the highway, in varying stages of

stupor. A long-hair in a knee-length purple coat is rattling a tam-bourine over a knot of twenty people and chanting, "Peace be upon you." A freak named Fantasy is spreading word that "the vigilantes are going to move in and start shaving heads." White Hawk, a thirtyish toothless veteran of eight years on the road, rises, a snake skull dangling from a leather thong around his neck, a knife stuck in the top of one of his worn fringe boots. He is tripping on mescaline, and he has his dog, Shatunga, stoned too. White Hawk moves toward an approaching tourist, the dog staggering behind him, muttering, "Come on, tourist, I gotta make my bread for today."

(19) Near the store, hash is to be had for $5 a gram at one battered old car, acid from 50 cents a tab up, depending on quality, at another. Weed is the staple drug, the thing the freaks start the morning with, and punctuate the day with, the way straights use coffee. Between that they "do" acid, speed or mescaline.

(20) What food there is is shared. But the diet is sparse and un-healthy. Malnutrition is universal and hepatitis is widespread. It infects even the fish in the river, where the freaks skinny-dip in the sunshine (and charge tourists $5 a head to see "a nude hippie love-in"). Venereal disease is rampant.

(21) Along the river and the highway, freaked-out and paranoid acid heads hide in the bushes, their wild eyes darting right, then left. Other freaks know to watch for them, and give them rides.

(22) One night at Big Sur, around a fire where one of the families is encamped, a heavy-breasted girl of 19 named Jane sits dragging on grass and running down freak philosophy. "It's mellow in the woods," she says. "I hade one acid trip and it straightened my head out. Then I went to the city and started thinking about a job and the future and not living just for today and I got all screwed up again. That's getting into a competition thing. That's a bummer."

(23) "Do you ever wonder," a long-haired dude echoes, "about people who move to a town, get a job and stay there all their lives? If you make plans, man, it's a bummer. I just stay in a place until I know it's time to go."

(24) Suddenly feet crash through the forest and a long-hair appears in the firelight carrying wood in his arms. "I'm a wood nymph. I'm a wood nymph," he yells. He is wearing a pair of boots—and nothing more.

(25) Around the dying campfire, a half dozen freaks sway silently, staring vacantly into the darkness, as a joint of supergrass passes from hand to hand, its tip glowing red. A torch is passed to a new genera-tion.

QUESTIONS AND EXERCISES

VOCABULARY
1. Panzer (*paragraph* 1)
2. panhandling (3)
3. sanctified (3)
4. monogamously (4)
5. transiently (4)
6. Karma (9)
7. vehement (11)
8. grimacing (15)
9. enclave (16)
10. paranoid (21)

LANGUAGE AND RHETORIC
1. Basically, this essay is a description of people and places. What details or passages do you find to be particularly descriptive?
2. This is a rather loosely structured essay. Considering the author's apparent purpose, can you see why he has structured it in this way?
3. The author actually gathered much of his material through a brief period of personal experience; however, he has chosen to record the material in a more objective third person technique. Do you consider this to have been a good choice? Why or why not?
4. The author reveals his attitude toward the subjects of this essay in a number of ways. What is that attitude, and what are some of the ways he reveals it?

DISCUSSION AND WRITING
1. If you have hitchhiked over a substantial distance or period of time, write an essay recounting one such experience or describing some person or persons you met while on the road.
2. This selection is based on a particular stretch of highway along the California coast between Los Angeles and San Francisco. Write a paper describing some highway you are familiar with.
3. Note the author's attitude toward the hitchhikers described here. What is your own attitude toward such persons, and what is your basis for it? Draw as much as you can from personal experience to explain your attitude.
4. In his concluding sentence the author says, "A torch is passed to a new generation." Do you feel that this conclusion is justified? Try writing a paper in which you describe or characterize some aspects of the "new generation" as you know it.

EDWARD WITTEN

The Flower Children at Taos

That mecca of the hippie movement, Haight-Ashbury, may be dead, but the flower children still exist — many of them now living in rural communes around the country. One of the most popular centers of communal living has been Taos, New Mexico, the land of D. H. Lawrence, where thousands of young people have come together to establish a new life style in "families" of their own making such as the one described here. The author goes beyond that description and evaluates the new life style, suggesting — after some pointed criticism — that these young Americans may not only enrich us all but may show us the way to a new life.

Notice the author's effective use of parallel structure and his smooth transitions between paragraphs.

(1) The tourists still come: elderly couples or prospering families treating the teen-age children to a Western tour. They pause at the magnificent gorge carved by the Rio Grande, examine the Indian pueblo, stroll quietly around the central plaza that is ringed by curio shops, restaurants, gas stations and hotels (New Mexico's main visible industries). The native Spanish majority, and the substantial Indian and Anglo minorities try to carry on as usual. But Taos has become a legend; here a minor artists' and writers' colony once gathered; and the children of that legend now rise up to engulf the natives.

(2) Haight-Ashbury is dead, they tell you; the land echoes with tales of a wonderful new life where the desert climbs to the mountains that reach the sky. Madly, joyously the young stream to Taos, as if the streets were gold. They flock to Taos, as they flocked to California, because they hear that it's the scene. They do not know what they seek, or where to find it. Many have little money, nowhere to stay, no means of transportation but thumbing it. A confused Californian asked me, Where is the commune? He had heard that three thousand hippies lived together in the wilderness. Perhaps, finding only others as bewildered as himself, he spent the night in some lonely hollow. Or perhaps he found what he had come to seek.

(3) Taos has no single community, and many visitors only get lost. But tiny communities to suit a range of tastes do ring the town. They glorify drugs, or keep clean; they welcome transients, sharing what they have with whoever wants it, or try to fuse a stable, exclusive group; they pair off so rigidly as to suggest middle class marriage, or make a fetish of sharing their sex. The Taos Community Information Service (funded by a millionaire!) wages a hopeless battle to channel incomers to appropriate destinations, and to establish a sort of local youth solidarity. In an open message to the natives of Taos, it groped toward an ideology: "The future of America is coming to Taos . . . a generation earnestly seeking new values, an honest land on which to nurture tender shoots. . . . The purpose of the hippie in coming is NOT to inflict a culture on Taos. He has rejected his culture, his purpose is to *learn from your culture,* and to be a part of that culture if indeed it reflects the holiness that he sees here. . . . The hippie is dirty, we hear. He has come to be cleansed. Will you show him a clean soul?"

(4) The flower children thrilled to discover the American Indians, who preserve among us values they had thought belonged to Eastern mystics, as once they thrilled to uncover within themselves a world they had sought in external struggles. The exotic design of the pueblos (mimicked in white buildings throughout the Southwest) defiantly shows that the Indian survives. The Taos pueblo, at the base of New Mexico's highest mountains, has the most spectacular architecture and setting of surviving pueblos.

(5) As I wandered about, a middle-aged woman accosted me with the question: "Are you a hippie?" (My hair had just been massacred for a restaurant job.) I asked her if I looked like one, and she said: "If you're a hippie, get off our land." All year, she explained, these bothersome hippies have camped here and pretended they can live like Indians. Her husband, lieutenant-governor of the reservation, pointed out that New Mexico Indians are fighting to block tax proposals in the constitutional convention which could lead to seizure of their land. The Taos pueblo is struggling to reclaim title to its sacred Blue Lake region in the mountains, part of a national forest since FDR entrusted all the land he could reach to the National Park Service. These hippies, he said, meddle with our way of life and destroy all our work.

(6) Relations are scarcely better with the Spanish or Anglos. The newcomers gaily tell of a real estate agent who has helped them out. But they seem to exult in their disdain for the natives. In reality, the resolute minority cultures of Indians and Spanish are only convenient metaphors for the new settlers of Taos. The joy riders, whether they find their high time or leave in disgust, can only destroy goodwill;

they play Indian, but they will not teach or learn from the Indians. The serious ones belong solely to the immediate group, they want no real interaction with outsiders. "Life is holy," their poster reads, "Celebrate it." They believe that free men, unspoiled by external manipulation, have the strength to purify themselves; they come to Taos so that only the land, whose purity they trust, may control them.

(7) I came to Taos as an afterthought, with little money and no sleeping bag, so I was fairly lucky to be invited to spend the night with The Family. Isis and Ceres demurely refused to describe our destination as we rattled six gloomy miles south from Taos, down a dirt road to the old farm buildings of The Family. As we entered the crowded barracks, one of the guys triumphantly undressed, but nudity seemed a depressingly male trait, so I resigned myself to a rather dull bull session. A girl explained how she had found happiness by being mercilessly honest until she knew exactly who she was. Swiping an old argument from David Reisman, I suggested that this kind of frankness is coercive: it demands that the other party expose himself too (lots of nods and she exclaims, "That's why I do it").

(8) The conversation turned to Family squabbles. The other brothers and sisters resented Gretchen for attaching herself to one guy, so that no one else knew her. One of the youngest girls had suggested that, to get to know each other better, they draw names from a hat until everybody had slept with everybody. A sadder, wiser guy objected that he had "slept with a thousand chicks, and never known a one of them." Someone invited sad-but-wise into her bed for the night. The discussion died, and I dozed at the foot of a huge bed occupied by a tiny girl who, like the other children, had joined The Family with her mother but seemed to belong to no one in particular. An attractive but slightly plump girl entered, stripped, and sat beside me to explain how she had come here when another Family collapsed in Phoenix (a third survives in Des Moines). She was delightfully slow to disappear beneath the covers.

(9) Sad-but-wise, smiling broadly, led yoga early the next morning, to which nearly everyone came nude. The Family imposes strict discipline: strenuous yoga, punctual breakfast, no hard drugs. Some of the brothers say the old tyranny began with rules like these. The Family insists upon them, because it is serious about its long-range plans; only a hardy soul will survive here. Their membership fluctuates, but they do not particularly welcome visitors, and resolve to develop a solid, permanent group. Numbering perhaps two dozen, they overflow their rented farm buildings, which they must abandon in any case when the roads cease to be passable in winter. They hope to build a permanent dwelling somewhere in the mountains.

(10) Only by retreating to a place they make do they believe they

can escape a polluted civilization. As they fled the cities, now they flee even Taos. After yoga, one girl said they needed butter and eggs for breakfast. "No trips to town!" someone shouted. "But we have to go into town," she said, "we need breakfast." "If that's your attitude," he replied, "of course we have to go into town." They refuse to take normal jobs in town, Isis explained, "because if we can't do it ourselves, it's not worth doing." How do they subsist? One brother, she says, earns $100 a month from the Community Information Service; this pays the rent of $65 a month ($50 before the owner realized how numerous they were). Sometimes dinner is rice from the garden; sometimes they get money by selling the "community" newspaper in town. She agreed with me that until they raise their own food they are not really independent, and promised that one day they will not go to Taos even for food.

(11) They dream of a new world in the mountains where nothing will divide free men. They believe that when The Family knits itself tightly enough, it will not need to impose decisions—each member will make his own choices, the group will function automatically. But today many feel that a handful really run the group. They believe that human beings, free to guide themselves, will join in rich and easy relationships. But sexual relationships especially are rough among them today, and sensitive individuals are soon hurt.

(12) The Family's new world would implicitly be aesthetic in the fine sense of insisting that every tool (object) is a vital thing (subject). A shoddy and immature aesthetic taste, however, now pervades The Family. They expect someday to unleash man's natural creativity; but now they consider themselves writers, artists, and musicians merely because the mountains and the (truly wonderful) sunsets can entrance them. Isis said she likes Bob Dylan's latest record. "But it's so maudlin," I objected. "That's why I like it," she said, "no more of this against everything business, it's only—*music*." Only music? For most of these people, "only music" means something that lets them dream—something they can place between themselves and physical objects. They forswear drugs, they say, for contemplation (and to safeguard the unity of the group), but "contemplation" is still only a misty-eyed convention. They study mysticism of the East, the Indians, Immanuel Velikovsky; their mysticism, however, shields and dissolves, never transforms. If they really mean "artistic" and not "adolescent," they must learn to fortify their involvement with the world, not to cushion it in dreams.

(13) Youth is born the enemy of time. Already one can scarcely find an explanation of how The Family was born. Asked if they suppose a place like Taos has existed before, most of the brothers only shrug, although, since a few of them have apparently led this life for a

decade or two, their experience can hardly be unique. They magnify the distance between themselves and all other generations; they doubt that their battles echo any from the past, or that this battle may be merely another phase in their development. They seem to believe they elude the reach of time. These are children of myths, and someday, if they endure, they will tell of their genesis. Perhaps they will recount how Time's winged chariot drew near, the Phoenix rose to slay him, and together they plunged to a flaming death. From the ashes flowers grew.

(14) There is no honest compromise between passing a moment with The Family and settling permanently with them, so I did not linger. Surely, I felt, these flowers will soon perish—too much ugliness, dishonesty, and tension burden their "free" lives. And yet, the graceful, well-formed apes, Koestler speculated in *Darkness at Noon*, must have giggled at the first awkward, clumsy human. I am sure that The Family will splinter long before the legend of Taos dies, and Taos, like nearby ghost towns of the gold rush, declines to a quiet tourist attraction. But I invent myths and do not believe: have I the right to judge? Somewhere America has gone astray, or these children would not be here; America must not vent her contempt upon them. They have not taken an easy road, and I believe Isis when she says she has learned more in eight months here than in all her past life. If, like the Indians, they can live a foreign life among us, they will enrich us, and they may show us the way.

QUESTIONS AND EXERCISES

VOCABULARY
1. commune (*paragraph 2*)
2. transients (3)
3. fetish (3)
4. ideology (3)
5. accosted (5)
6. exult (6)
7. Isis (7)
8. Ceres (7)
9. maudlin (12)
10. genesis (13)

LANGUAGE AND RHETORIC
1. The author frequently uses parallel structure to ensure coherence. Point out instances of this technique in paragraphs 3, 11, 12, and 13.
2. What is the author's attitude toward the flower children of Taos? Is it favorable, unfavorable, or neutral? Locate the passages in which he reveals his attitude. What is the thesis of this essay, and where is that thesis clearly stated?
3. The last sentence of paragraph 6 and the first sentence of paragraph 7 provide an effective transition between these two paragraphs. What tech-

nique does the author use for this transition? Find similar instances of effective transition between other paragraphs.
4. Why is it significant that the girls who invite the author to spend the night with The Family are called Isis and Ceres?
5. The language of this selection reveals a variety of styles: the formal, precise, sophisticated; the informal, knockabout language of conversation; and the poetic. Find examples of each type. What does this versatility in the use of language tell us about the author? Does it help to achieve his purpose in this article? If so, how does it help?

DISCUSSION AND WRITING
1. Would you like to live in a communal family such as the one described in this essay? Give reasons for your answer. Write an essay describing or explaining what you consider to be an ideal living situation.
2. What are the advantages and disadvantages of communal living compared with the traditional family structure? Make a list of these, analyze the list, and then develop an essay on the subject.
3. Does communal or group marriage have more to offer than a traditional marital relationship? Support your answer.
4. Despite his criticism of The Family, the author concludes that if their plan succeeds, "they will enrich us, and they may show us the way." Do you agree or disagree? How might they enrich us? What way might they show us?
5. If you have had any experience in communal living or know someone who has, what do you feel its effect has been on you or on that person?

STEFAN KANFER
The Returned: A New Rip Van Winkle

You may recall Washington Irving's story of Rip Van Winkle, who slept for twenty years and awakened to a world that had changed so dramatically he had become a stranger in his own village. In this essay, Stefan Kanfer compares Rip's situation to that of American prisoners of war returning home after the Vietnam War. Noting how change has accelerated in our time, he shows how a contemporary Rip Van Winkle after an absence of only four years might find himself in as unfamiliar a land as that fictional character did almost two centuries ago.
Note the author's use of descriptive detail to develop his essay.

The very village was altered; it was larger and more populous.

"The Returned: A New Rip Van Winkle" by Stefan Kanfer. From *Time*, February 19, 1973. Reprinted by permission from *Time, The Weekly Newsmagazine.* Copyright Time Inc.

There were rows of houses which he had never seen before, and those which had been his familiar haunts had disappeared. Strange names were over the doors—strange faces at the windows—everything was strange . . . the very character of the people seemed changed. There was a busy, bustling disputatious tone about it . . . A fellow . . . was haranguing vehemently about rights of citizens—elections—members of Congress—liberty . . . and other words which were a perfect Babylonish jargon . . .

(1) WASHINGTON IRVING set his story in the late 18th century, when it took 20 years and an American Revolution to bring about such alterations. With contemporary efficiency and such time-saving devices as the Viet Nam War, change now occurs at quintuple speed. The returning P.O.W.s have been away an average of four years; it is long enough to make them a new breed of Van Winkle, blinking at a world that can hardly believe how profoundly it has changed. Nor will it really believe until it sees itself with the returning P.O.W.s' fresh, hungry eyes.

(2) The little things are what the ex-prisoner will notice first, phenomena that civilians have long since absorbed. That local double bill, for exqmple: *Suburban Wives* and *Tower of Screaming Virgins*. Four years ago, it would have been restricted to a few downtown grind-houses. Today, blue-movie palaces are as much a part of the suburbs as the wildly proliferating McDonald'ses. Shaking his head, the new Van Winkle heads for a newsstand. Here, there is still more catching up to do. A copy of *Look?* No way. *Life?* No more. How about a copy of *Crawdaddy, Screw, Money, Rolling Stone?* Rip has heard of none of them. He looks, dazed, at the roster of more undreamt of magazines: *Oui, Penthouse, World, Ms.* "Pronounced Miz," says the proprietor who starts to elucidate, then drops the subject and the magazine. Who, after all, could explain Gloria Steinem? Ah, but in this roiled world a few bedrocks remain. There it is—the good old *Saturday Evening Post.* No, it is the good old *new* old *Saturday Evening Post,* risen from the grave and swathed in thrift-shop clothing, an item of that rising phenomenon, nostalgia.

(3) Every age has enjoyed a peek in the rear-view mirror. But in the last few years, total recall has become almost a way of life. Rip examines magazines devoted to trivia, recalling the names of Tarzan's co-stars and the Lone Ranger's genealogy. He sees ads for Buster Keaton festivals and even for Ozymandian musicals like *Grease,* celebrating the vanished glories of '50s rock 'n' roll. The stranger pushes on; nostalgia—at preposterous prices—peers at him from shop windows. Fashion bends backward with shaped suits and long skirts, wide-brimmed hats, ubiquitous denims and saddle shoes. He has,

alas, missed miniskirts and hot pants. He is just in time to see almost all women in long pants. Well, why not? But men in high heels?

(4) He peers in the window of a unisex shop, and then, holding fast to the corner of a building to maintain his balance, he seeks stability at a furniture store. Surely this window will yield a glimpse of the familiar. After all, what is furniture but chairs, tables — and *waterbeds?* It is time, he feels, to cross the street.

(5) Jesus freaks are gathered at the corner, mixing freely with other louder groups. They carry the perennial banners of militancy, each inscribed with the device, Liberation. Over it are the words Gay, Black, Women's, Chicano and People's. These are the remnants of a great tidal wave of protest that broke in Rip's absence, still sporadically coursing through the streets and campuses. The year 1968 was at once its crest and ebb. Rip was gone when Martin Luther King was assassinated in Memphis and when 172 cities went up in smoke, when 3,500 were injured and 27,000 arrested. He was gone when Bobby Kennedy was murdered two months later, and when two months afterward, the city of Chicago seemed to become the epicenter for every disaffected demonstrator in America.

(6) Perhaps there was something in the global ionosphere that year, something that still clings like smoke in an empty room. Without benefit of an unpopular war to trigger protest, Paris also was torn by civil disturbances; so were Mexico City and Tokyo. Even in Prague, the people rose up — only to be pushed into submission by armored tanks. Today all protest seems, somehow, to be an echo of that hopeful dreadful time; but to the new listener there is no resonance, only the flat remnants of unassimilated rage.

(7) A striped pole catches Rip's eye. He settles into a chair — only to hear a fresh diatribe from the barber — who now calls himself a stylist. Once, long hair was the exclusive property of the hippies; they have gone but the hair has remained. Now all the straights sport it. The barber talks on about a world gone into reverse. Nixon has toured Communist China, which is now in the U.N. The Empire State Building is no longer the tallest building in the world. The World Trade Center is. Eighteen-year-olds can vote. The New York Giants will soon play in New Jersey. In the American League, pitchers will no longer bat.

(8) The stock market, Rip learns, has hit 1000, yet the go-go funds and glamour conglomerates are a sere and withered group. Unfamiliar newsworthies are summoned to his attention: Mary Jo Kopechine, Clifford Irving, Arthur Bremer, Vida Blue, Archie Bunker, Angela Davis, Daniel Ellsberg. There are new countries leaping up from the headlines, nations born while he was away: Bangladesh, Botswana and Qatar. There was another country, too, called Biafra. Like those

radioactive elements produced in a laboratory, it was destined for a brief, intense half-life before it vanished forever. But the eyes of its starving children still stare from old magazines—and in the memory.

(9) His hair cropped, or rather, styled—at absurd prices—Rip retires to a bar for refreshment and intelligence. The TV set is in color now, and there is something called Cable that makes the reception better—although for what purpose is not so clear. True, there are no more cigarette commercials, and some programs called *Sesame Street* and *The Electric Company* are brightening the day for children. But for adults, it is, as always, lame adventure series and innocuous sitcoms, the halt leading the bland. There are fewer talk shows and more movies made expressly for TV—all of them, it seems, starring James Farentino and George Peppard.

(10) Not all movies are made for the tube, announces a defensive film buff down at the other end of the bar. He tells of the emerging genres: black films with superheroes carpet bombing the inner cities; hetero-, homo- and bi-sexual hits; Andy Warhol spectaculars that may yet replace Seconal; and of course, the constantly refilled pornucopia.

(11) Yet films can still provide comfort for the weary and over-burdened. Rip learns that the stalwarts have not toppled. Gregory Peck, Paul Newman, John Wayne, Steve McQueen are impervious to criticism; throw a rock at them and it still produces sparks. As for the theater, that too has its enduring endearing qualities. There are laments for the passing grandeur of the now tacky Broadway; butter and egg musicals, and Neil Simon comedies still pull in the theater parties. Save for the new nudity, the visitor might never have been away.

(12) Rip wanders from the bar in search of nourishment. Next door is a restaurant; it is not until he examines the menu that he sees the words "health foods"—and by then it is a little late to run. On the shelves are strange labels: Granola, mung beans, Tiger's Milk, lecithin, all at nonsensical prices. Vitamin E, he learns, is expected to cure everything but the common cold; Vitamin C takes care of that. Adelle Davis has become the Brillat-Savarin of the counterculture. Her self-help books beckon from the paperback rack: *Let's Get Well, Let's Have Healthy Children, Let's Eat Right To Keep Fit.*

(13) Let's not, mutters the ex-prisoner. Abandoning his pep-up and soy derivative, he pushes onward to a record store. His favorites have quite literally passed on. Judy Garland, Janis Joplin, Jimi Hendrix—all killed by various ODs. The Beatles? Fragmented. The unheard of Woodstock? While he was gone it was born, matured, grew senile and became a comic epitaph on an old emotion. Some stalwarts remain here too: Streisand, Elvis Presley, Joan Baez, The Stones. But who

are the Partridge Family? Cheech and Chong? Dr. Hook and The Medicine Show?

(14) Fighting off a syncope, Rip flees to a bookstore. He is just in time for the revisionist historians. When Rip left the U.S. the faint afterglow of Kennedy magic was still warm to the touch. Then they called it charisma. Now they call it Shamelot. Such books as Henry Fairlie's *The Kennedy Years* and David Halberstam's *The Best and the Brightest* sound the knell of the '60s and its leaders. The returnee has missed the spate of Concerned Books: *Soul On Ice, Deschooling Society, The Whole Earth Catalog*—when Rip left, earth was only dirt—plus almost every float in Norman Mailer's Mr. America Pageant. Lose a few, win a few. He has also missed *Love Story, Myra Breckenridge, The Sensuous Woman*. He browses through the current paperbacks; words rise up and greet him like so much Urdu: ecology, software, encounter groups, moon rocks, body language, future shock, acupuncture, transcendental meditation, deep zone therapy. His trembling hands try the poetry shelf, but the words of Auden seem as odd as the day he has just lived:

> *In the deserts of the heart*
> *let the healing fountain start,*
> *In the prison of his days*
> *teach the free man how to praise.*

(15) According to the poet, then, we are all behind bars—locked inside the jail of mortality. No matter how bitter his past, the prisoner must find a way to leave the personal desert for the world of common humanity. But how can one enter that world when there are no doors? How can one "praise" what one cannot understand?

(16) "Surely I must be exaggerating," Rip thinks. "Why try to understand it all in one gulp? Why try to overtake history? Start slowly, read the leading fiction bestseller. Escape for a while." He picks up *Jonathan Livingston Seagull*. The story of a what? Of a goddam bird? His eye roves to the self-help books. Here's one: *Primal Scream*. He tries it . . .

(17) The air is cool in the police car, and the cops, although jittery, relax when they see that their passenger is unarmed. They have their own stories to tell, of new ambush attacks, and of strong desires for shotguns to repel something they call the Black Liberation Army. But after they listen to their passenger's story, there is a quiet in the car, and there is no further attempt to educate the new Rip Van Winkle. There is no attempt to go to the station. Rip is, suddenly, a free man all over again, and stuttering, he tries to find praise. Praise for his country, for an America that, despite all the staggering changes,

somehow is still America. There is, finally, only one way. "Where to?" asks the driver. Rip looks out the window for a long, lonely moment trying to remember something. "Home," he says.

QUESTIONS AND EXERCISES

VOCABULARY

1. proliferating (*paragraph* 2)
2. elucidate (2)
3. roiled (2)
4. preposterous (3)
5. unassimilated (6)
6. diatribe (7)
7. sere (8)
8. genres (10)
9. syncope (14)
10. charisma (14)

LANGUAGE AND RHETORIC

1. What is the author's purpose in this essay? Does he have a specific thesis? Support your answer.
2. The author depends heavily on the allusion or reference to Rip Van Winkle as a basis for this essay. Comment on the appropriateness and effectiveness of his use of that source.
3. Consider the author's use of description to develop his essay. Is there too much? Too little? What would you add or delete?
4. How has the author organized his essay, and how appropriate is that structure to his purpose?
5. Do you consider the conclusion of this essay to be effective? Why or why not?

DISCUSSION AND WRITING

1. If you have ever had the experience of returning home after having been away for quite some time, write a paper in which you note the changes that had taken place.
2. Write a letter to a friend or relative who used to live in your community but moved away several years ago, and describe how the community has changed since his or her departure.
3. Like everyone else, each writer sees things from his own unique point of view and therefore differently from anyone else. If you were attempting to show how life in the United States has changed over the past four or five years, what would you focus on?
4. Generally speaking, what is your reaction to the developments that are described in this essay? Do you approve or disapprove of the overall tendencies? Why do you feel as you do?
5. Does the picture of American life that is recorded in this essay seem to you to be a reasonably accurate one? Discuss your response to the essay, noting particularly any significant ways in which your view of the situation differs from the author's.

MARCIA SELIGSON
The New Wedding

There's a myth afoot in our land that the wedding is a dodo bird, extinct, or dying if not dead. Rumor to the contrary, in 1971 (figures are not yet available for 1972) there were 2,196,000 marriages in the United States, 648,000 more than in 1961. In addition, seven out of eight first-time couples were married in a church or synagogue, and 80 per cent of all first-time weddings were formal (an increase over previous years), 96 per cent of marrying couples held a reception (another increase), and over 84 per cent of first-time brides wore formal bridal gowns. The American wedding industry is a booming $7 billion-a-year business.

What concerns us here is a second myth about weddings in America. It has to do with youngsters of the new consciousness. It says that they have no sense of romantic love, that their relationships consist of leaping from bed to bed with the capricious speed of fleas hopping from one dog to another. "Doing your own thing," it is believed, implies living only for the moment, for the peak experience, eschewing concepts like "future" and "commitment" and "responsibility." Couples move in with each other easily, swiftly, and move out with the same ease, only to be replaced before the mattress has cooled. Musical sheets. Those few who stay together surely do not permit anything as mundane as a marriage ceremony.

But one Manhattan rabbi has performed more than 500 weddings, all of them of the "new" species, most often joining couples who have been living together but who still—to smash the mythology—opt for marriage. Says the Reverend William Glenesk, the clergyman who joined Tiny Tim and Miss Vicki: "The new wedding is a ceremony to confirm what a couple has found by living together, not to make promises about what they hope will happen." It is a celebration of what is already there, a public reaffirmation of the commitment and continuity, rather than a beginning. "We don't believe that our wedding is going to be the most important event in our life together," said a West Coast bride, "and we don't believe that a wedding makes you a married couple."

The key word in the New Wedding is "meaningful." "I had never been to a wedding that had any meaning at all until the past year or so," says one girl who was recently married on a beach in Virginia. "When Tom and I planned our wedding, we talked about all the formal church and hotel affairs we'd been to—those of friends and relatives—and realized how empty they were. Phony, with all that etiquette junk and everything done for the parents who just wanted to show off for their friends. You never knew what the couple was like, and you never cared. And there was no real joy at all. We knew we wanted to have something that would be more than just another drunken party—something uniquely ours."

What seems to be most "meaningful" to the new breed is the beauty of an outdoor setting. Beaches, hilltops, meadows, parks, caves, rocks. Free space. Serenity. The revelers in the movie *Goodbye, Columbus* spent thousands of dollars transforming a hotel ballroom into a forest; these kids simply use the forest. And the setting dictates the tone of the new fete, which is natural and informal. One cannot quite summon up visions of haughty, white-gloved waiters trooping through the sand dunes with silver trays of miniature quiche Lorraine. Or a trumpety band blasting out the strains of a bossa nova through the Grand Canyon. Or a bride in Priscilla of Boston lace and satin greeting her chiffoned guests in a receiving line—on top of a rock.

The New Wedding, like the counterculture it springs from, belongs mostly to children of the successful middle class, offspring of folks who have "made it" in traditional American terms. In theory the New Wedding opposes the old by being spontaneous, without artifice, and "personally relevant" (an expression used as often in this crowd as is "dearly beloved" in the black-tie set). Sometimes it is so even in practice.

The most graphic departure from the conventional American wedding scheme is that the new frontier has usurped control from their parents. Normally, the event is unquestionably in Mother's hands, and the bride bows out beneath the tidal pressures of money and minutiae. That's the unspoken bargain between Mama and daughter. The New Wedding, in spirit, is a statement about who the bride and groom are. Mother is but another guest.

The conventional middle-class American wedding serves as a reconciliation—at least for one day—of disparate elements within the family. The two brothers who have loathed each other for twenty years bury their hatchets in the veal parmesan; octogenarian greataunts are invited to waltz by young lads who can't remember the Korean War. Folks who in normal life have nothing much to say to one another somehow find a commonality on wedding days. But the New Wedding—does it need to be said?—stretches the generation gap into a continental divide.

Not long ago I attended a New Wedding in the woods of Malibu Canyon, just north of Los Angeles. The setting was lovely, utterly removed from any vestiges of city life, and the day was sunny, balmy. Virginia and Ken, the bride and groom, are in their early twenties and have lived together about a year; he is a film editor and she works in a plant store; both are from L.A., both are Jewish. Although Virginia's parents know that she has been living with Ken, they expected her to have a veritable Barnum and Bailey spectacular at one of the local hotels, and a great rift followed her declaration of wedding intentions. But tempers eased, and now both sets of parents are present, along with a dozen or so close relations and fifty of the couple's friends.

One has to park the car at the bottom of a rolling grassy hill and walk half a mile. Lining the path and sitting poised in trees are young friends playing soft rock tunes on flutes, guitars, and harmonicas. The scene is idyllically beautiful, and the aura of open friendliness and joy is pure, untrammeled by the robot presence of banquet managers or the rigor mortis of etiquette edicts. I saunter up the hill, feeling the magic of the day. But almost immediately I have my first confrontation of many with the generation chasm. Behind me, the bride's Aunt Florence, wearing a pink brocade Hadassah gown, has caught the heel of her pink shoe in a tree root, and now she wants to go home. I don't know whether to laugh or sympathize, so terror-stricken is she about this wedding, so incapable of bending to it, of flowing with it, of seeing how inescapably pretty and sweet it is.

But then nothing that occurs this day will bear any familiarity to Aunt Florence. The bride does not march down an aisle, enveloped in trick lighting; she is standing on the hill when we arrive; she is without shoes and wears a long peasant dress made of patchwork tablecloths; her coronet is of daffodils. Ken is splendid in orange-and-yellow striped bell-bottoms, a fringed Apache vest, and a matching daffodil headpiece. All the friends are dressed flamboyantly, exuberantly, as if for a fabulous costume revelry. Bare midriffs, leather shorts, gypsy wildnesses. The elders, of course, are in their spiffiest wedding finery—except for one or two chic matrons, in peasant frocks from Beverly Hills boutiques, who are urgently "With It."

People are talking and drinking wine. Joints are being passed with some discretion (nobody hands one to Aunt Florence). Both sets of parents are trying—they are really trying—desperately, with smiles as frozen as the masks of Comedy. Soon a rabbi appears—one of the "hippie rabbis," as they are known around L.A., not because they themselves are hippies, mind you, but because they do this kind of wedding. The joints are extinguished. (This cleric has insisted ahead of time that no pot smoking take place while he is on the premises; others prefer the presence of marijuana to cigarettes or alcohol.)

Everybody casually sits down on the grass—chairs have been provided for Aunt Florence and the like—in a circle around Ken, Virginia, and the rabbi. Easy rapping flows into the "ceremony." A young girl carrying an infant (which she periodically nurses in front of everybody during the day—another freakout for the relatives) hands the child away, picks up a guitar, and sings a Joni Mitchell ballad in a clear soprano. The rabbi then recites some familiar lines from *The Prophet*, beginning "Love one another but make not a bond of love. . . ."

Virginia speaks a Carl Sandburg poem, looking lovingly into Ken's eyes: "But leave me a little love/A voice to speak to me in the day's end/A hand to touch me in the dark room/Breaking the long long loneliness." So far everything is terribly romantic and touching; even the elders, poised stiffly in wooden chairs, their regal hairdos and garbs successfully defying the strong breeze, even they are moved. After all, Ali MacGraw and Ryan O'Neal in *Love Story* read Elizabeth Barrett Browning to each other in their nuptials; so it must be okay.

But then the recitation takes a turn, a bizarre turn with Ken and Virginia together reciting the Fritz Perls "Gestalt Prayer": "I do my thing, and you do your thing. I am not in this world to live up to your expectations/And you are not in this world to live up to mine./You are you and I am I and if by chance we find each other, it's beautiful." (The last line, "If not, it can't be helped," is tactfully omitted from the reading.) The families start to twitch nervously and glance around at each other over their shoulders with unspoken "You-see-I-knew-it" looks of anger.

Then something incredible happens, something awful, the coalescence of the parents' terror of how this all would turn out. Okay, maybe all these hippies aren't making love on the grass or going berserk on LSD, but suddenly this strange ceremony (not a word of Hebrew or a "for better or worse") . . . suddenly it gets *political*. Virginia stands up and reads from Emma Goldman on women's suffrage, about asserting herself "as a personality and not as a sex commodity" and "refusing the right to anyone over her body" and "refusing to bear children, unless she wants them" and "refusing to be a servant to God, the State, society, the husband, the family. . . ." And the kids shout "Right on, sister," and the family just drops dead.

In ancient Jewish lore, when a girl marries a Gentile, she is declared dead by the father and, in effect, is treated as such forever. Virginia—I see by the faces of the judges on the chairs, faces at once iced and terrified—has just been pronounced a corpse. When, at the end, the couple shatters the traditional glass, adding the hope that the noise will drive away such repressive forces in our society as Nixon and Agnew—well, hardly anybody even notices. They are all comatose.

The party following is jolly, with group singing and folk dancing and games like Spin the Bottle and Pin the Tail on the Donkey, and an organic feast, which includes fruit salad, homemade breads, and the inevitable honey-in-the-comb. The only incongruous note is the presence of a whole roast suckling pig, which reclines dead center in the mélange of food—like a gigantic middle finger pointed upward.

The pig is just one more stab to the older generation, which has not yet recovered from Emma Goldman. Their rage and confusion suffuse the otherwise joyful ambience. I am saddened by the real depths of the breach: they cannot step down off their chairs, and the kids cannot understand or lessen their pain. As a final event, Ken and Virginia open the gifts—a gesture meant hopefully to involve both planets— but even here barriers prevail. One present is a garish cut-crystal something—a bowl, or a decanter, or a lamp, it's hard to tell which— and the next is a membership in a Zero Population Growth organization.

Mother has tried hard throughout the day, but finally she falls apart, goes limp. I go over to her as she is sipping some rose-petal soup; it is as if she is in shock. "This has nothing to do with anything I've come to associate with a wedding," she mourns. "I don't know what to do here, and, to tell you the truth, I don't even believe they're really married."

Any wedding symbolizes the end of the child's childhood and dependence. Unconsciously parents prepare themselves for the inevitable, just as one unconsciously prepares for pain before an operation. But, traditionally, parents see the wedding as *their* day, the final chapter that *they* are the authors of. To disrupt these ingrained assumptions is to cause an earthquake of major proportions. The New Wedding is an earthquake.

In addition, the New Wedding, in its pure form, is a very real, though infant, metaphor of change. It speaks of a "greening of America," of a journey by certain young couples away from fraudulence and toward a new humanism. "Some of our ancient language simply doesn't express the meaning these kids want to express to each other when they take marriage vows," says the Reverend A. Myrvin DeLapp. "Their great concern is for the honesty of the human relationship; the sense of personhood is to be honored."

If the New Wedding truly defines the newlyweds' vision of marriage, then one thing becomes clear: these kids have expectations as lofty, and hope and optimism as widespread, as anybody who ever got married in America. But they also bear a new sense of adult reality, a sense that married life is not quite what the bridal magazines have been hawking. New vows frequently stress deep friendship and self-growth rather than roses and perfect union. And "foreverness" is dead: "Till death do us part" is replaced by such less permanent vows as "So long as I am able," or "As long as our love endures," or "For as long as we dig it."

What the New Wedding expresses — sometimes poignantly, sometimes stridently — is a claim for self, for dignity and autonomy, for alternatives and for change. Leaving aside its many laudable goals as well as the inevitable pain it introduces, the New Wedding nonetheless preserves our craving for the wedding ritual. As American life gets more fragmented, the drive to create new rituals — as well as to reaffirm the old — becomes stronger. We reach especially to the most primitive and important of all rituals — the rites of passage. Birth, marriage, and death, to be sure, are our most elemental and major steps. Since the wedding is the only one of these ritual commemorations at which we are fully and consciously present, it is our most essential rite. No matter the various forms it may take, it is anchored at the very core of civilization.

In such a rite, the ceremony itself is an outgrowth of the society for which the individual is being groomed. Traditional American weddings are ritual events of fierce, even gluttonous, consumption, orgies of intensified buying, probably never again to be repeated in the life of the wedded couple. The New Wedding has shelved the consumerism and all the rest it finds fraudulent in the traditional ceremony. Still, the New Wedding remains a wedding, and its changes should not mask the continuities it provides.

THREE | The Media and Their Messages

DANIEL J. BOORSTIN

*Television: More Deeply Than We Suspect
It Has Changed All Of Us*

Measured by almost any standard, it is obvious that the medium of television has an enormous impact on our society. In this essay, Daniel J. Boorstin examines what some of those effects have been. Considering the matter from a historical perspective, he writes that "the television set has democratized experience, but while our experience is now more equal than ever before, it is also more separate." He sees the ultimate effect of this "new segregation" as a loss of touch with reality and calls for ways in which we can use television itself to help break down the walls between us.

The essay is an excellent example of how several different methods can be combined to develop a thesis.

(1) Just as the printing press democratized learning, so the television set has democratized experience. But while our experience now is more equal than ever before, it is also more separate. And no Supreme Court ruling can correct this segregation, no federal commission can police it. It is built into our TV sets.

(2) When a colonial housewife went to the village well to draw water for her family, she saw friends, gathered gossip, shared the laughs and laments of her neighbors. When her great-great-granddaughter was blessed with running water, and no longer had to go to

the well, this made life easier, but also less interesting. Running electricity, mail delivery and the telephone removed more reasons for leaving the house. And now the climax of it all is Television.

(3) For television gives the American housewife in her kitchen her own private theater, her window on the world. Every room with a set becomes a private room with a view—a TV booth. Television brings in a supply of information, knowledge, news, romance, and advertisements—without her having to set foot outside her door. The range and variety and vividness of these experiences of course excel anything she gets outside, even while she spends hours driving around in her automobile. At home she now has her own private faucet of hot and cold running images.

(4) But always before, to see a performance was to share an experience with a visible audience. At a concert, or a ball game, or a political rally, the audience was half the fun. What and whom you saw in the audience was at least as interesting, and often humanly more important, than what you saw on the stage. While watching TV, the lonely American is thrust back on herself. She can, of course, exclaim or applaud or hiss, but nobody hears except the family in the living room. The other people at the performance take the invisible forms of "canned" laughter and applause.

(5) And while myriad island audiences gather nightly around their sets, much as cave-dwelling ancestors gathered around the fire, for warmth and safety and a feeling of togetherness, now, with more and more two-TV families, a member of the family can actually withdraw and watch in complete privacy.

(6) In the 1920s, in the early days of radio, "broadcast" entered the language with a new meaning. Before then it meant "to sow seeds over the whole surface, instead of in drills or rows," but now it meant to diffuse messages or images to unidentified people at unknown destinations. The mystery of the anonymous audience was what made sensible businessmen doubt whether radio would ever pay. They had seen the telegraph and the telephone prosper by delivering a message, composed by the sender, to a particular recipient. They thought the commercial future of radio might depend on devising ways to keep the radio message private so that it could be sent to only one specific person.

(7) The essential novelty of wireless communication—that those who received "broadcast" messages were no longer addressees, but a vast mysterious audience—was destined, in the long run, to create unforeseen new opportunities and new problems for Americans in the age of television, to create a new sense of isolation and confinement and frustration for those who saw the images. For television was a one-way window. Just as Americans were segregated from the

millions of other Americans who were watching the same program, so each of them was segregated in a fantastic new way from those who put on the program and who, presumably, aimed to please. The viewer could see whatever they offered, but nobody (except the family in the living room) could know for sure how he reacted to what he saw.

(8) While the American felt isolated from those who filled the TV screen, he also felt a new isolation from his government, from those who collected his taxes, who provided his public services, and who made the crucial decisions of peace or war. Of course, periodically he still had the traditional opportunity to express his preference on the ballot. But now there was a disturbing and frustrating new disproportion between how often and how vividly his government and his political leaders could get their message to him and often and how vividly he could get his to them. Even if elected representatives were no more inaccessible to him than they had ever been before, in a strange new way he surely felt more isolated from them. They could talk his ear off on TV and if he wanted to respond, all he could do was write them a letter. Except indirectly through the pollsters, Americans were offered no new modern avenue comparable to television by which to get their message back. They were left to rely on a venerable, almost obsolete 19th-century institution, the post office.

(9) Of all the forces which have tempted us to lose our sense of history, none has been more potent than television. While, of course, television levels distance—puts us closer and more vividly present in Washington than we are in our state capital and takes us all instantly to the moon—it has had a less noticeable but equally potent effect on our sense of time. Because television enables us to be there, anywhere, instantly, precisely because it fills the instant present moment with experience so engrossing and overwhelming, it dulls our sense of the past. If it had not been possible for us all to accompany Scott and Irwin on their voyage of exploration on the moon, we would have had to wait to be engrossed in retrospect by the vivid chronicle of some Francis Parkman or Samuel Eliot Morison, and there would then have been no possible doubt that the moon journey was part of the stream of our history. But with television we saw that historic event—as we now see more and more of whatever goes on in our country—as only another vivid item in the present.

(10) Almost everything about television tempts the medium to a time-myopia—to focus our interest on the here-and-now, the exciting, disturbing, inspiring, or catastrophic instantaneous now. Meanwhile, the high cost of network time and the need to offer something for everybody produce a discontinuity of programming, a constant shifting from one thing to another, an emphasis on the staccato and motley

character of experience—at the cost of our sense of unity with the past.

(11) But history is a flowing stream. We are held together by its continuities, by people willing to sit there and do their jobs, by the unspoken faiths of people who still believe much of what their fathers believed. That makes a dull program. So the American begins to think of the outside world as if there too the program changed every half hour.

(12) Of all the miracles of television none is more remarkable than its power to give to so many hours of our experience a new vagueness. Americans have become increasingly accustomed to see something-or-other, happening somewhere-or-other, at sometime-or-other. The common-sense hallmarks of authentic first-hand experience (the ordinary facts which a jury expects a witness to supply to prove he actually experienced what he says) now begin to be absent, or to be only ambiguously present, in our television-experience. For our TV-experience we don't need to go out to see anything in particular. We just turn the knob. Then we wonder while we watch. Is this program "live" or is it "taped"? Is it merely an animation or a "simulation"? Is this a rerun? Where does it originate? When (if ever) did it really occur? Is this happening to actors or to real people? Is this a commercial? A spoof of a commercial? A documentary? Or pure fiction?

(13) Almost never do we see a TV event from what used to be the individual human point of view. For TV is many-eyed, and alert to avoid the monotony of one person's limited vision. And each camera gives us a close-up that somehow dominates the screen. Dick Cavett or Zsa Zsa Gabor fill the screen just like Dave Scott or President Nixon. Everything becomes theater, any actor—or even a spectator—holds center stage. Our TV perspective makes us understandably reluctant to go back to the seats on the side and in the rear which are ours in real life.

(14) The experience flowing through our television channels is a miscellaneous mix of entertainment, instruction, news, uplift, exhortation, and guess what. Old compartments of experience which separated going to church, or to a lecture, from going to a play or a movie or to a ball game, from going to a political rally or stopping to hear a patent-medicine salesman's pitch—on television, such compartments are dissolved. Here at last is a supermarket of surrogate experience. Successful programming offers entertainment (under the guise of instruction), instruction (under the guise of entertainment), political persuasion (with the appeal of advertising) and advertising (with the appeal of drama).

(15) A new miasma—which no machine before could emit—enshrouds the world of TV. We begin to be so accustomed to this foggy

world, so at home and solaced and comforted within and by its blurry edges, that reality itself becomes slightly irritating.

(16) Here is a great, rich, literate, equalitarian nation suddenly fragmented into mysterious anonymous island-audiences, newly separated from one another, newly isolated from their entertainers and their educators and their political representatives, suddenly enshrouded in a fog of new ambiguities. Unlike other comparable changes in human experience, the new segregation came with rocket speed. Television conquered America in less than a generation. No wonder its powers are bewildering and hard to define. It took 500 years for the printing press to democratize learning. Then the people, who at last could know as much as their "betters," demanded the power to govern themselves. As late as 1671, the governor of colonial Virginia, Sir William Berkeley, thanked God that the printing press (breeder of heresy and disobedience) had not yet arrived in his colony, and prayed that printing would never come to Virginia. By the early 19th century, aristocrats and men of letters would record (with Thomas Carlyle) that movable type had disbanded hired armies and cashiered kings, and somehow created "a whole new democratic world."

(17) With dizzying speed television has democratized experience. Like the printing press, it threatens — and promises — a transformation. Is it any wonder that, like the printing press before it, television has met a cool reception from intellectuals and academics and the other custodians of traditional avenues of experience?

(18) Can TV-democratized experience carry us to a new society, beyond the traditional democracy of learning and politics? The great test is whether somehow we can find ways in and through television itself to break down the walls of the new segregation — the walls which separate us from one another, from the sources of knowledge and power, from the past, from the real world outside. We see clues to our frustrations in the rise of endless dreary talk-shows, as much as in the sudden increase in mass demonstrations. We must find ways outside TV to restore the sense of personal presence, the sense of neighborhood, of visible fellowship, of publicly shared enthusiasm and dismay. We must find ways within TV to allow the anonymous audience to express its views, not merely through sampling and statistical averages, but person-to-person. We must find ways to decentralize and define and separate TV audiences into smaller, more specific interest-groups, who have the competence to judge what they see, and then to give the audiences an opportunity to react and communicate their reactions. We must try every institutional and technological device — from more specialized stations to pay TV, to cable TV, and other devices still unimagined.

(19) Over a century ago, Thoreau warned that men were becoming "the tools of their tools." While this new-world nation has thrived on change and on novelty, our prosperity and our survival have depended on our ability to adapt strange new tools to wise old purposes. We cannot allow ourselves to drift in the channels of television. Many admirable features of American life today—the new poignance of our conscience, the wondrous universalizing of our experiences, the sharing of the exotic, the remote, the unexpected—come from television. But they will come to little unless we find ways to overcome the new provincialism, the new isolation, the new frustrations and the new confusion which come from our new segregation.

QUESTIONS AND EXERCISES

VOCABULARY

1. myriad (*paragraph* 5)   6. motley (10)
2. myopia (10)   7. exhortation (14)
3. catastrophic (10)   8. surrogate (14)
4. instantaneous (10)   9. miasma (15)
5. staccato (10)   10. provincialism (19)

LANGUAGE AND RHETORIC

1. What audience does the author seem to have in mind for his essay, and what clues lead you to that conclusion?
2. Early in the essay the author states his thesis. Identify that thesis. What is the author's purpose in the essay?
3. The author uses a number of methods of development, including analysis (division), cause and effect, and comparison and contrast. Identify one example of each of these methods, and comment on its appropriateness in relation to the author's purpose.
4. The body of this essay (that is, the portion exclusive of the introduction and conclusion) is divided into five parts. What paragraphs comprise each of these parts, and how does this organizational pattern suit the author's thesis and purpose?
5. The author is a historian. How has he utilized his knowledge of history in developing this essay?

DISCUSSION AND WRITING

1. Based on your own experience with television, do you agree with the author's idea that it tends to segregate people from one another? Support your answer.
2. According to the author, one of television's most dangerous effects is that it creates a sense of vagueness in the viewer and therefore a lessening of the ability to distinguish between fiction and reality. Do you think this is a valid criticism? Why or why not?

3. In paragraph 18 the author calls for us to "find ways in and through television itself to break down the walls of the new segregation. . . ." Reread
that paragraph, consider the problem, and see if you can think of one way
that this might be done.
4. The author argues that television separates people. Can you make a case in
support of the opposite idea—that television brings people together? Be
sure to support your position with specific examples, factual details, and
so forth.
5. Write a letter to a television station expressing your support of, or opposition to, a particular program or programming policy. Give specific reasons
to justify your opinion.

HOLLIS ALPERT

Indecent Exposures

Motion pictures frequently leave deep impressions on their audiences,
but domestic viewers seldom consider what the effects of those impressions might be when American-made films are viewed by foreign
audiences. In this selection, Hollis Alpert notes that Hollywood's image
of America has shifted from the glamorous to the sordid. His survey of
several American films distributed in the first two years of this decade
raises an interesting question about the effects of our changing times
and shifting values on our image abroad.
    The author uses specific references to, and details from, many films
to illustrate his thesis.

(1) In old and now nostalgic times Hollywood was habitually flog-
ged for perpetrating a false and tinselly view of America and its life-
styles. Bedrooms, you'll remember, were furnished with twin beds so
as to eliminate any impure audience imaginings of sex during the
night. Yet, on awakening, lovely women stretched out sleepy arms in
exquisitely filmy negligees; if they went into the kitchens—ah, what
spanking clean, marvelously equipped kitchens; and those living
rooms—sunken often, and usually bedecked with sprays of fresh-cut
flowers. Wherever the word glamour came from, it was surely re-
invented by Hollywood, and it sold here and abroad.
(2) When I came to New York, a late and still wet-behind-the-ears
teen-ager, it was a particular New York I was looking for, and it came

"Indecent Exposures" by Hollis Alpert. From *World Magazine*, November 7, 1972.
Reprinted by permission of *World Magazine*.

from scenes in certain movies, the names and plots of which have long faded from memory. There was this marvelously spacious apartment, which opened out onto a spacious terrace that overlooked the splendid skyline. On the terrace a white-coated servant served frosty glasses of orange juice to the late-rising inhabitants. It was many years before I realized that soot showering down on the terrace would have made the juice undrinkable.

(3) Rarely do we get that kind of movie anymore, yet I came across the same setting again in a recent movie called *Who Is Harry Kellerman and Why Is He Saying Those Terrible Things About Me?* This time it was Dustin Hoffman on that penthouse terrace, and about him were all the appurtenances of gracious (Hollywood, ca. 1949) living; but he was not happy. No indeed. Instead, he was obsessed with fantasies of suicide, and one showed him actually plunging down to Fifth Avenue below, directly across from Bergdorf Goodman's. Movie attitudes toward New York, toward urban living, toward the country at large have changed, and with a nearly literal vengeance, almost as though films are striking back at their own timeworn myths and shattered dreams.

(4) Comedies that were once madcap have turned sour. Take *The Out-of-Towners* (1970), which, as written by Neil Simon, detailed the luckless adventures of a couple from Ohio who pay New York a visit so that the husband can be interviewed for an executive job that would require moving to the metropolis. First off, their plane is stacked up over LaGuardia, then diverted to Boston. The train they are forced to take to New York carries no food. In the city there are taxi and transit strikes, so they must walk to their hotel through garbage-littered streets (there is also a sanitation strike) in drenching rain. Because of lateness they lose their hotel reservation. On the way to find other quarters they are mugged and robbed. In Central Park they are assaulted by weirdos and, reduced to near starvation, they battle with a dog for the remains of a child's box of Cracker Jacks. In spite of all this, the husband manages to keep his job appointment, but understandably he's had enough. He turns down the offer and thankfully heads back to Ohio.

(5) But does it end there? Hardly. Their homeward-bound plane is hijacked to Cuba. Surprisingly, few critics faulted the film for unreality. In the main they found it more depressing than funny. During the past year the film was shown widely abroad, even finding its way into the Communist bloc in Europe, where it must surely have strengthened adverse attitudes toward our decadent and apparently failing democracy.

(6) But by this time Europeans and Asians hardly need to be convinced of how badly off we are. Our movies are doing the job for us.

Last year *Desperate Characters,* another film about the problems of living in New York, walked off with three important prizes at the Berlin film festival, which chooses its prestigious jurors from several different countries. And what did this film show? I quote from a description in *Newsweek:*

> The world of [the two main characters] has grown increasingly familiar: buildings sold and standing empty, doorsteps littered with human excrement, streets blocked with sleeping bodies and busy with the pleas of panhandlers, mad phone calls piercing the armor of the home, rocks tossed through windows, wreckage without rhyme or reason. . . . When they seek to retreat, they find their country house sacked in a sick act of malice; nothing is stolen, merely smashed or spoiled.

(7) Is it any better in Chicago? Well, there's *T. R. Baskin,* a film about a small-town girl who opts for life in the big city and finds little but loneliness and despair until, finally, she is disillusioned enough to consider the life of a hooker. Before *T. R. Baskin* there was *Medium Cool,* hailed by a preponderance of critics. It blended fiction with documentary as it showed Chicago in the summer of 1968 (agreed, not one of the city's finest hours) beset with riots in the midst of our democratic lifeblood, the political convention. I quote from *The Washington Post's* review: "One long tracking shot of the heroine walking along seemingly endless rows of troops and military vehicles sums up the surrealist nightmare of the event with the kind of irony that makes certain film images unforgettable." During the course of the film we see the Illinois National Guard training for riot duty; and we see housewives in a marksmanship school, training, presumably, to defend themselves with loaded .38s.

(8) There's something to be faced here. Films such as *Medium Cool* were not made to demonstrate to the world outside our boundaries that we are in a parlous condition, nor were they made, on the other hand, to attract visitors to our shores. Neither patriotism nor tourism is the issue. When the attempts are serious, as they were with *Desperate Characters* and *Medium Cool,* it is to seek and define the essential nature of the American experience in our time. And one would surely wish our film artists to remain free and unfettered. But for those concerned with the exporting of an American image through films, the net effect, reinforced by one film after another, must be disconcerting. And, if it is a problem, it is one without apparent solution.

(9) It was about five or six years ago that American films veered into a course that while seeming to look outward, perhaps more accurately looked inward. Maybe it began with *The Graduate,* with Dustin Hoffman inchoately questioning all the values of his parental generation.

Or was it *Bonnie and Clyde,* with its relatively sympathetic portrayal of two benighted outlaws of our Depression years? If not those two, then certainly *Easy Rider,* a tale of two drugrunning cyclists in search of their souls. In any case, a new genre was born, one that film historians were quick to label "the road picture."

(10) There had been road pictures before, of course. One of the happiest and larkiest was *It Happened One Night* (1935), and there was an early version of the Bonnie and Clyde story. But what our newer road pictures see is a quite different America. The advertising for *Easy Rider* put it blatantly: "A man went looking for America. And couldn't find it anywhere." Thus, the message of the new American movie. The America that had been sold to us through films, television commercials, and the now defunct *Saturday Evening Post* wasn't there. So, what was? The scenery was still uncommonly attractive. Said *Newsweek:* "The dazzling photography reminds us of how ravishingly beautiful parts of the nation remain." The two cyclists encounter, however, a society that is corrupt, hateful, and intolerant, and eventually meet their deaths from human symbols of that intolerance. For a time they cohabit with a hippie commune, idle away hours in a New Orleans brothel, take a psychedelic trip to nowhere. Toward the end, culture hero Peter Fonda tells culture hero Dennis Hopper: "We blew it." There was much argumentation as to the meaning of the line, but it may well have referred to the nation as a whole.

(11) And did our nation rise up and reject that dismal message? Not at all. So successful was the film here and around the world that our film industry geared itself up to turn out dozens more of the same. Why not? Profits are profits. Combine the net totals of *The Graduate, Bonnie and Clyde,* and *Easy Rider,* and the takings come to well over $125 million dollars. That despairing view of America the ugly has paid off.

(12) And continues to. The film audience-attendance figures are still in decline, and the industry is scared, cautious, worried, but when the exceptions come along, the results can be dizzying. We're back to New York again with *The French Connection* (estimated worldwide gross: $50 million), and the city never seemed seamier, more violent, or more corrupt. Marvelously, dreadfully well-made, it shows a cop fully as ruthless as the criminals he tracks and madly chases. He and his partner invade a Brooklyn bar, patronized by blacks, each and every one of whom empties his pockets of hash, heroin, and cocaine. While the cop lives in lower-middle-class style, the criminals are shown dwelling and eating in high style. At the end we know that the drug problem will only worsen, that its concomitant crime can only increase.

(13) But should our violence-ridden society be shown in another way, as in *Dirty Harry?* Here the scene is San Francisco, and a sadistic, psychotic killer is on the loose. To catch him (and kill him) our hero (the tall, implacable Clint Eastwood) must operate against police-department rules. Andrew Sarris called the film "one of the most distrubing manifestations of police paranoia I have seen on the screen in a long time." Because of the film's commercial success, *Newsweek* wondered: "Is the modern audience's thirst for blood insatiable?" The answer was available when *The Godfather* came along — estimated worldwide gross, upwards of $150 million.

(14) Call it a family picture. It has a father, mother, sons and daughters, and relatives. They have a family business, to which all are loyal. But this version of *Cheaper by the Dozen* has to do not with children, but with bodies, dead ones. And if a message behind all the carnage emerges it is that the family that slays together stays together. All over the world, wherever it opens, crowds line up to see this admittedly fascinating portrayal of our latest myth heroes, the Mafia.

(15) I talked with an executive of a major film-producing company. I mentioned to him this strangely masochistic export of films showing us at our worst. If there was an ideological battle going on, weren't our films helping us lose it? "You must remember," he said, "that it is mostly the successes that the world-at-large sees. After all, doesn't a *Love Story* help to balance the scale?"

(16) Maybe it does, but that's one glossy, sentimental charmer against an imposing line-up to the contrary: *Easy Rider, Midnight Cowboy, Alice's Restaurant, The French Connection, The Godfather,* etc., etc. On the other hand, is there a change in the wind? As against the American film of despair, there is the latter-day emergence of the film of Americana, its best example being *The Last Picture Show.* Replete with nostalgia, with genuine characters rather than caricatures, the film managed — according to critic Vincent Canby — to "illuminate a good deal more of one segment of the American experience than any other American film in recent memory." Andrew Sarris felt "There is something in it for which a great many people have been waiting a long time. . . . I suspect that people have had their fill of self-hatred."

(17) *The Last Picture Show* was written by a young novelist, Larry McMurtry and directed by the thirty-one-year-old Peter Bogdanovich. He and other young and successful talents have been moving into a position of artistic power in our film industry. . . . (Bogdanovich, in fact, recently joined directors William Friedkin [*French Connection*] and Francis Coppola [*Godfather*] in the formation of their own company.) It is to them we must look for changes in what our films will show us and the world, but don't count on them to do the work of

tourist bureaus. They are an uncommonly intelligent film generation, and pious protestations about the image of America they are conveying won't cut much ice with them. On the other hand, there is one message that the best of our films, despairing, nostalgic, ugly, or whatever, are sending out to the world: that we are singularly unafraid to show ourselves as we think we see ourselves. For the more thoughtful foreigner, whatever image our films give him, this in itself may well strike him as admirable.

QUESTIONS AND EXERCISES

VOCABULARY
1. appurtenances (*paragraph* 3)
2. parlous (8)
3. inchoately (9)
4. benighted (9)
5. blatantly (10)
6. concomitant (12)
7. implacable (13)
8. manifestations (13)
9. carnage (14)
10. masochistic (15)

LANGUAGE AND RHETORIC
1. What is the significance of the title "Indecent Exposures"? How does it reinforce the thesis?
2. What is the rhetorical function of the first two paragraphs? How do they contribute to the author's thesis?
3. The author uses examples, factual details, and comparison and contrast to develop his essay. Examine his use of these methods, and comment on their appropriateness to his purposes.
4. The author employs the same transitional device to move from one paragraph to another in paragraphs 5, 7, 11, 13, and 16. What is that device?
5. What is the author's attitude toward his subject? Does he approve or disapprove of what is happening to American films? What is the basis for your answer?

DISCUSSION AND WRITING
1. Reflect on the American films you have seen recently. Do they tend to confirm or refute the author's impression about the image of America? Support your answer.
2. If you have seen one of the movies mentioned by the author and disagree with his response to it, write a paper showing the basis for that disagreement.
3. Using examples of, and details from, movies you have seen, write an essay in which you illustrate some unified impression these movies give about the image of American society.
4. Attend a movie of your choice (or view one on television), and write a paper discussing the image of America that movie might convey to a foreigner.

5. This essay, and in particular the last paragraph, raises an interesting question about the function of movies: should filmmakers be concerned about the effect that their films might have on America's image abroad? How would you answer this question and why?

NANCY HENRY

Women's Mags: The Chic Sell

During the past decade, readers have witnessed the death of a number of mass circulation magazines, including *Life, Look,* and the *Saturday Evening Post.* But while many magazines were fighting— and losing—a battle for survival, others known as "special interest" publications were flourishing, particularly that group known as women's magazines. In the following selection, Nancy Henry reports on the development of these magazines and examines some of the reasons behind their success.

In addition to her numerous examples and extensive use of factual details, the author makes effective use of reasons and appeal to authority (that is, references to, and quotations from, persons involved with the subject under discussion).

(1) It has been a cruel decade for the magazine business. Rising production costs, postal increases and soaring paper prices have made it much more difficult to turn a profit. Television has proved a tough competitor for advertising and audience, and many of the mass circulation giants, among them *Life, Look* and *The Saturday Evening Post,* have floundered or failed in the contest.

(2) While other publications have struggled to survive, women's magazines have demonstrated a remarkable resistance to malnutrition. Dynamic editors who understand their readers' interests have undoubtedly played an important role, but perhaps the essential element in the success formula of the women's magazines is a "soft" advertising-editorial policy. An unusual degree of cooperation exists betweeen the editorial staff and the advertising sales department.

(3) Loyal advertisers are crucial for most magazines, because subscriptions and newsstand sales rarely cover 40 per cent of production costs. Consequently, a degree of coziness exists between the editorial and advertising departments of many magazines. Even *Look* and *The Saturday Evening Post,* which generally followed a "hard" pol-

"Women's Mags: The Chic Sell" by Nancy Henry. From *The Nation,* June 5, 1972. By permission of *The Nation.*

icy, ran annual cover stories on new automobiles. Those issues were invariably jammed with car ads. In such cases, editors inevitably insist that the story was scheduled first, then the salesmen went out to beat the bushes. But that scarcely disposes of the problem of editorial integrity. And nowhere are the dangers more dramatically demonstrated than in the women's magazines, where ads and editorial copy abundantly intertwine.

(4) The editors of women's magazines are particularly susceptible to advertiser influence because they are *always* writing about the products of the companies that support them. The bulk of the service magazines (*Good Housekeeping, Family Circle, Woman's Day,* etc.) consists of features advising the homemaker how to spend her food, fashion and furnishings budget. Most of their advertising also falls into these categories. *Vogue* and *Harper's Bazaar* purport to be the definitive guide for upper-income women seeking beauty and fashion perfection. Their ads, mostly for cosmetics and clothes, tout the brands the articles publicize.

(5) As "special interest" publications, the women's magazines promise the advertiser a precise target for his sales pitch. However, these magazines can offer much more than space: if an advertiser's product is mentioned favorably in the editorial columns—the endorsement being presumably objective—the reader's confidence in the magazine rubs off on that product. These magazines speak with authority; that is one of their great advantages over spot ads on daytime television. Their publishers capitalized on that prestige in their trade paper ads, and in such trademarks as the *Ladies' Home Journal's* "The magazine women believe in," and *Good Housekeeping*'s description of itself as "The magazine America lives by." A recent *Family Circle* was almost embarrassingly explicit: after telling advertisers how its editorial encourages women's home creativity, the punch line read, "Her husband knows self-experession costs money . . . and she spends it."

(6) Most editors and publishers of magazines that offer themselves as impartial consumer guides are understandably reluctant to discuss the widespread practice of giving advertisers preferential treatment in the editorial pages. However, *Vogue* publisher, Richard Shortway, says bluntly, "The cold, hard facts of magazine publishing mean that those who advertise get editorial coverage." As an example, Shortway pointed out that for the past five years *Vogue*'s January 1st cover has featured the David Crystal firm's La Coste dress with the alligator emblem. "Now that is not the most dynamic dress in the world," said Shortway. "We zipped it low this year to give it a little pizazz. But from this cover, the firm will probably sell forty or fifty thousand of that one dress."

(7) Page trading, a one-for-one exchange of editorial pages for advertising pages, is another bait used by women's magazines to lure advertisers. With ad pages priced from around $6,800 in *Harper's Bazaar* to about $39,000 in the *Ladies' Home Journal,* the financial rewards can be substantial. It is often difficult for the casual reader to pinpoint such relationships, because the advertising payoff may appear in a different issue or be spread out over several issues. Occasionally, however, ads and their complementary features are run simultaneously, as in last October's *Good Housekeeping.* That issue carried an 8-page home decorating feature, "Fresh Ideas for More Livable Living," which describes the rooms shown as "Debut '72," and calls it an effort by the home furnishings industry "to bring you fresh ideas and inspiration." If the reader is still not persuaded to refurbish the house, the front of the magazine has yet another 8 pages headlined, "Debut '72" and consisting of brand-name advertisements. The layout of the two sections is so similar that it is difficult to distinguish the article from the $230,000 of paid promotion.

(8) The "Debut '72" article may well have been scheduled before the salesmen went out to corral the advertising, but that leaves unanswered the question of how long an editor can retain independent judgment if enjoined to choose stories according to their prospects for generating advertising, or to coordinate an article's phraseology with advertising copy.

(9) Some particularly obtrusive instances of stories developed especially to accommodate advertisers appeared late last fall during the great fake hair boom. Several of the women's magazines came forth simultaneously with articles, features and in two cases entire issues promoting wigs. The inspiration for all these stories is evident in a May 24, 1971 *Advertising Age* article headlined "Wig Makers Flip Over Prospects for Soaring Sales." *Ad Age,* the trade bible, reported that the Monsanto Chemical Company planned to spend $4 million to $5 million—"more money than was spent by the whole wig industry last year"—to advertise its new Elura wig fiber. *Ad Age* also reported that Dynel Wigs had set an ad budget of $2 million—"more money than we've ever spent"—and that the Kanegafuchi Chemical Company would spend a "healthy sum" to promote its Kanekalon II wig fiber.

(10) The November issues revealed the extremes to which some editors were willing to go to capture choice pieces of this advertising pie for their publication. Trying to outdo each other on behalf of the wig industry, *Vogue* and *Harper's Bazaar* devoted entire issues to the promotion of artificial tresses.

(11) Beginning with a bewigged Raquel Welch on the cover, *Bazaar* complemented 16 full-page wig ads with more than 35 edi-

torial pages plugging wigs. Beauty editor Shirley Lord's lead article, captioned, "Yes, She Is Wearing Her Wig in the Bath," set the tone for the issue with the declaration, "It isn't a question of whether one should own a wig. The question is how many." And almost every model in the issue was indeed wearing a wig.

(12) *Vogue* gave its wholehearted approval to wigs with a cover photograph, more than 34 pages of editorial plugs, and three articles by the beauty editors. One of the latter proclaimed, "the simple and wonderful fact that synthetic, store-bought hair is a vast improvement over the home-grown variety any way you look at it." The reward was 21 full-page wig ads, a take of roughly $142,000 for *Vogue*.

(13) The *Ladies' Home Journal* was apparently also pitching for a piece of the action. Its Novemeber beauty section featured an extensive article called "Wigs for Women on the Go," which detailed the differences in wig fibers and told how to wear and care for wigs. Full-page layouts picturing Barbara Walters and Pia Lindstrom wearing various Elura and Dynel wigs further embellished the wig theme. Yet, in spite of the solicitude for the industry, the *Journal* did not attract many wig ads, a failure explained by a Monsanto spokesman who noted that Elura wigs were generally priced to sell to women in a higher income bracket than that of the average *Journal* reader.

(14) Strangely enough, editor James Brady chose *Harper's Bazaar*'s November issue, the very issue that was a model of total cooperation between the editorial staff and the advertising sales staff, to announce a new era of editorial independence at the magazine. On the editor's page, Brady wrote that his first memo to the *Bazaar* staff "had broken with the old slick fashion magazine tradition that advertisers get preferential treatment on the editorial pages. I don't really care what the competition does to woo the advertiser," said Brady. "On this question *Bazaar* must be on the side of the angels. The editorial staff here will make all editorial decisions on the basis of news and fashion merit. This is the only way to put out an honest publication that the reader will believe in and trust. And in the long run, this is what advertisers want: a magazine that tells the truth and has reader confidence."

(15) Brady excuses the discrepancy between his remarks on the editorial page and the remainder of the issue as "something I inherited. I came in in August, and that issue was already blocked out. I felt the honorable thing to do would be to honor those commitments that my predecessor had made. I did that, and we worked off all of those commitments by the end of December."

(16) Contrasting the present regime with the past, Brady says, "The reader now knows that if we show something on the cover of *Bazaar* or we give it 4 pages or 8 pages inside, it's because we believe that

it's a great dress or, a great suit, or a great new fashion look — not because we've been paid to put it in there. Our fashion editor, China Machado, now has total authority in that area. She has 45 pages to feature clothes in an average issue. Now she's going to pick the best forty-five things she can find. In the past, advertiser pressure was such that perhaps she would have thirty-five things dictated to her and ten things that were really her own choice."

(17) However, Brady's housecleaning has left a few dusty corners, and only an insider can assess how extensive his reform truly is. One suspect practice that continues is the plugging of perfumes by brand name on the fashion pages. It is also questionable to provide superfluous information, such as lush descriptions of a clotheshorse's lipstick or eyeshadow brand and color, when the photograph appears in black and white. In the May issue, a full-page ad for Fabergé nail polish urges, "Look Lacquered" with the "Lacquered Look from Xanadu." A few pages later, a blurb written by the beauty editor reinforces the effect of the advertisement by employing phrases identical to the ad copy's slogans.

(18) John Mack Carter took over the ailing *Ladies' Home Journal* in 1965 and steered the magazine to a record 7 million circulation and $46 million annual advertising revenues. Like most editors, Carter insists that the advertising department has absolutely no influence over the editorial side of the magazine, but there are subtle indications of cooperation. For example, the *Journal* features a monthly section of patterns, and employs a full-time patterns editor with an assistant. Yet, for several years, the only brand of patterns chosen for display in this section has been Simplicity — which also happens to be the only pattern company that advertises in the magazine. (Similar arrangements exist at *Glamour* with Butterick patterns, and at *McCall's* with McCall's patterns.) Carter's lame defense for this situation: "The simple answer is, Simplicity is the largest pattern company in the world. By the time our pattern people get through with the available material in Simplicity . . . there really isn't any room or need to go to other companies. It's really for our own benefit — our own simplicity of operation that we go to a single pattern company to get it."

(19) For Mr. Carter, simplified editing is apparently more important than providing greater service to the reader by exposing her to some of the exclusive features of McCall's, such as their "pounds thinner" patterns, or to Vogue patterns' more intricate designs. A few years back, and under the guidance of the same patterns editor, the *Journal's* sewing section was almost exclusively the showcase for Vogue patterns. But at the time Vogue was the principal advertising client.

(20) Prepared foods, heavy advertisers in all the service magazines, also receive frequent editorial boosts. Most of the recipes in the

Journal, Good Housekeeping, Family Circle, etc., stipulate mixes, canned or frozen foods as basic ingredients. Although such processed foods are considerably more expensive, the editors seldom suggest that a cook start from scratch with raw ingredients.

(21) The *Journal* carries advertiser promotion even further in a monthly column called "Poppy Cannon's Meal-A-Day Menus." Miss Cannon's menus always contain a substantial sprinkling of brand-name recommendations, and she takes particular pains to point out advertisers' new products.

(22) Nurturing advertisers can take more insidious forms. The service magazines appear to exercise censorship in their treatment of subjects that concern women but could offend advertisers. Magazines that carry substantial food advertising have yet to publish a major story on research which indicates that some chemical additives in prepared foods may be dangerous. On the other hand, both the *Journal* and *Good Housekeeping* have recently published articles on health foods, and both were negative. The *Journal* story was entitled "The Zen Macrobiotic Diet That Is Killing Our Kids." *Good Housekeeping*'s story, called "The Facts About Those So-Called Health Foods," concludes, "The *Good Housekeeping* Institute believes that good nutrition can be maintained with good quality, simple every day food." The article then refers the reader to its story, "Great American Meals the *Good Housekeeping* Way," which relies heavily on convenience foods.

(23) The abuses of the women's magazines are significant because these publications function as the major source of consumer information for 50 million readers. And, as self-regulation has obvious lapses, the only likely cure is pressure from the better-educated, more sophisticated readers.

QUESTIONS AND EXERCISES

VOCABULARY

1. chic (title)
2. complementary (*paragraph* 7)
3. refurbish (7)
4. obtrusive (9)
5. solicitude (13)
6. preferential (14)
7. discrepancy (15)
8. superfluous (17)
9. nurturing (22)
10. insidious (22)

LANGUAGE AND RHETORIC

1. State in your own words the author's thesis in this essay. What is her purpose?
2. What is the meaning of the title of this selection? How does it support the author's thesis?

3. In addition to examples and factual details, the author uses reasons and appeals to authority as ways to develop her essay. Point out examples of each method and its appropriateness to her purpose.
4. The author shifts to a different aspect of her essay in paragraphs 3, 6, 9, 14, 18, 20, and 23. Examine each of these transitions and explain the relationship the parts have to each other and to the essay as a whole.
5. Reread the author's conclusion (paragraph 23) and comment on its relevance to the purpose of her essay.

DISCUSSION AND WRITING
1. If you are familiar with any women's magazines, select one and write a paper in which you evaluate the author's thesis in relation to that publication.
2. Examine a women's magazine to see if you can determine the editorial policy on advertising. Is there any relationship between the contents of the magazine and the advertising it carries? Does the advertising seem to influence the content and nature of the articles in any way? Write a report of your findings.
3. In paragraphs 4, 5, and 6 of "Is Everybody Happy?" (Section Eight of this text), John Ciardi makes some observations about women's magazines. Do they seem to be consistent with what the author of the present selection has to say about the subject?
4. Choose a special interest magazine that appeals to you and study it to see if you can determine the relationship between its editorial and advertising policies.
5. Write a letter to a magazine of your choice in which you express approval or disapproval of something that appears in the publication. Support your position with specific reasons, examples, details, and so forth.

JOSEPH MORGENSTERN
The New Violence

For the better part of two decades, evidence has been accumulating that violence in the mass media can breed aggressive behavior in the mass audience, especially among children. Supporting documents from last month's report to the Surgeon General on "Television and Growing Up: The Impact of Televised Violence" give us the strongest suggestions to date that violent TV programs can have harmful effects on large groups of normal kids. It's unlikely, though, that millions of outraged parents will lower the boom on the broadcasters.

Much of the adult audience is on a violence trip of its own at the movies.

Americans love to watch images of violence in the fun house of the mass media. Violence is the best epoxy for holding an audience together between commercials, the very deathblood of such shows as "Mannix," "Gunsmoke," "Cannon," "Hawaii Five-O," "Adam-12," "Cade's County" and "Mod Squad," not to mention all those dumb, undifferentiated Saturday morning cartoons. A recent study by the British Broadcasting Corp. found that American television programs shown in England have twice as many violent incidents as British productions do.

Occasionally an urban riot, campus confrontation or choice assassination will cause the public or Congress to wonder briefly if all this mayhem in the media is such a good thing for the country, after all. The last time the question arose was in 1969, when Sen. John Pastore (Democrat of Rhode Island) sponsored a $1 million study of media violence and its possible relationship to "antisocial behavior among young people." Historically, the networks' position has been that no such relationship has ever been proved. Just to make sure it wouldn't be proved this time, the broadcasters tried to rig the Surgeon General's study in their favor. To a considerable extent they succeeded.

All candidates for membership on the advisory committee that commissioned the research and later summarized it were subject to vetoes by the three commercial networks. CBS declined to exercise any such veto; NBC and ABC had fewer scruples and blackballed seven candidates. The fourth network of 219 noncommercial (and largely nonviolent) stations (PBS) was not consulted. Two of the twelve committee memberships went to incumbent directors of research at NBC and CBS. Three more went to scholars who had been or still were employed by the networks.

Once the surveys and laboratory experiments were completed, all research data and conclusions were compiled into five large volumes, then summarized by the advisory committee in a 279-page report to the Surgeon General. Whether by intent or ineptitude, the committee misrepresented some of the data, ignored some of it and buried all of it alive in prose that was obviously meant to be unreadable and unread. The five supporting volumes are still being withheld from the public. Thus far, the news media have accepted the committee's summary as the last word on the research. Beneath the misleading headline "TV Violence Held Unharmful to Youth," The New York Times story stressed contradictions in the Surgeon General's report and, with incomplete quotations, gave the impression that televised violence leads to increased aggressive behavior only in small groups of youngsters.

In fact, the summary says much more than this, and the supporting data says more than the summary. The summary dismisses as unsubstantiated the catharsis theory—that viewing filmed violence allows pent-up emotions to be released harmlessly. While the summary does say that the most direct effects of media violence may occur among children predisposed to violence, it stresses that this violence-prone subgroup may constitute a "small portion or a substantial portion of the total population of young viewers." And an overview of one of the five volumes of supporting research says, in an italicized conclusion, that *"the present entertainment offerings of the television medium may be contributing, in some measure, to the aggressive behavior of many normal children. Such an effect has not been shown in a wide variety of situations."*

The conclusion was written by Dr. Robert M. Liebert, a psychologist at the State University of New York at Stony Brook, Long Island. Liebert participated in two of the 23 research studies, has read all 23 and feels strongly that the summary draws inaccurate conclusions from them. "I believe," he says, "that the most reasonable conclusion is that there is a link between televised violence and aggressive behavior for the majority of normal children. The data show no evidence that only a minority is influenced. This is a factual error."

Not all the researchers feel their work was misrepresented, of course, and not all the committee members feel their summary was self-canceling. "Prior to this report," says one of them, Dr. Ithiel de Sola Pool of MIT, "you could not have said that there is a causal relationship between TV violence and aggressive behavior in children. Now we can see that there is a significant causal relationship."

Beyond the baleful light of the box, violence rages in the streets and it's the rage in the movies. Within the past few months a striking new consensus has emerged on movie violence—indeed, on ultra-violence, to borrow a term from the stylish sadists of "A Clockwork Orange." Moviemakers have found ultra-violence ultra-profitable, the mass audience has found it enjoyable—and an influential majority of reviewers has found it intellectually attractive and artistically valid.

In the highly prised "A Clockwork Orange," roving bands of dehumanized hoodlums deal out a cool, affectless violence that includes kicking, stomping, gang rape and beating a woman's brains out with a big phallic sculpture. "Straw Dogs" dispenses with the cool and comes to a devastatingly powerful climax of rape, knifing, mutilation, acid-tossing, shooting, beating and burning. Santa Claus tries to crush a fallen kid's rib cage in "The French Connection." A maniac "hippie" in "Dirty Harry" does unspeakable violence to his victims; what the detective hero does to the maniac hippie is no more speakable and equally visible. Roman Polanski's "Macbeth" dispatches its victims with a vividly slit throat, a broadax in the back, a dagger in the forehead, a sword in the groin. When Macbeth himself was beheaded the other day at the Playboy Theater in New York, a matinee audience of high-school students on a field trip screamed in horrified delight as the thane's hands groped for the head that had already split.

If there's any such thing as ultra-sex, it's still largely confined to peep shows, porno houses and X-rated movies that some violence-laden newspapers refuse to advertise out of deference to their readers' sensibilities. But only one movie has ever been rated X for violence — "I Drink Your Blood" — and that rating was changed to an R when cuts were made. All the James Bond pictures carry GP's — suitable for general audiences, with parental guidance advised — even though 007's witty swashbucklings have turned gross and squalid in the new "Diamonds Are Forever." A kiddie version of ultra-violence has even crashed the Radio City Music Hall, which caters mostly to families and young children. The Hall recently played "The Cowboys," a GP-rated Western in which John Wayne is slowly shot to death by rustlers, then avenged when a group of children torture one rustler and kill them all.

Does this mean the movie industry's rating system is in a state of collapse? Motion Picture Association of America president Jack Valenti maintains that the ratings are still doing what they're supposed to do, marking certain pictures off limits to children and warning parents that certain other pictures may be unsuitable for children. "I don't think it's the rating system that's in collapse," Valenti says. "It may be that parents just don't care any more." A NEWSWEEK survey of theater operators in cities across the nation reveals little or no public dissatisfaction with the ratings or the violence of new movies. "Mores and customs change and movies have become franker," says a manager in Detroit. "Violence is acceptable," says a showman in Chicago. "It's what the people want."

That's no news in itself, of course. Mass audiences have always wanted violence and always gotten it, whether in bear baiting, melodrama, comic books or pro football. Nor is it news that violence, even pornographic violence, is more socially acceptable than sex. In 1949, in a pamphlet called "Love and Death," Gershon Legman wrote: "There is *no* mundane substitute for sex except sadism."

Yet something new did come over media violence in the 1960s. It was the result of an interaction that's always in progress between entertainment and reality. On one side was a convergence of events without parallel in American history — racial strife, assassination, confrontation, the war in Vietnam. On the other side, entertainment stayed in step with the world beyond the studios and gave us the showerbath murder in "Psycho," and the James Bond extravaganzas, with a hero sophisticated enough to lead his audience down hitherto forbidden paths of sex, sadism and stylish decadence. "The Untouchables" flourished on TV, the spaghetti Westerns — made in Spain by Italians — treated American audiences to a level of violence that Hollywood had hardly dared dream of. Roger Corman's "The Wild Angels" rode in on the emerging motorcycle myth. Richard Brooks upped the violence ante in "The Professionals," and Robert Aldrich gave audiences a half-hour high of slaughter in "The Dirty Dozen."

These movies were long on action and short on philosophy, but new attitudes toward violence were beginning to trickle down from literary and scholarly speculations of the day, just as Epicurean and Stoic notions of nature that were popular in Shakespeare's time found dramatic expression in his Edmund and Edgar. This was the decade in which Eichmann was executed, "In Cold Blood" appeared and the English translation of "On Aggression" was published. In the entertainment world it was also the period in which "Bonnie and Clyde" forced a rethinking of the mythology of violence with its daring new notions of criminal behavior and the lyric horror of its climax, and "The Wild Bunch," with another quantum jump in physical intensity, tried to explore the nature of life with the esthetics of death.

Many critics and moviegoers welcome the new ultra-violence as an extension of such experiments. "A Clockwork Orange" is praised as prophecy, or as a dark parody of the present. The horrors of "Macbeth" are seen as historical truths: lords and ladies were close to savagery and killed as savages. Admirers of "Straw Dogs" feel it illuminates the human condition with its vision of violence as a rite of passage in which a man puts himself in touch with his primal emotions — to become, for better or worse, a man.

A few eloquent dissents from this attitude have been advanced in recent weeks. Andrew Sarris, writing in The Village Voice, found a facile anti-intellectualism in "A Clockwork Orange," and woeful inadequacies in Kubrick's widely hailed technique. Pauline Kael, in The New Yorker, drew analogies between the drug culture's appetite for intense, violent mystery and the mock profundities of "El Topo." Writing about "A Clockwork Orange," Miss Kael condemned the movie's "finally corrupt morality" which betrays Anthony Burgess's novel by making the mod-sadist hero much more human and likable than the contemptible straights he preys on. "How can people go on talking about the dazzling brilliance of movies," her review asked, "and not notice that the directors are sucking up to the thugs in the audience?"

One way they can do it is by following the lead of the old New Criticism in literature, confining themselves to matters of style and structure—cool technicians reviewing the techniques of other cool technicians. Ultimate meaning can be a horrible can of worms, and there's no ethical obligation to deal with it if you believe that violent entertainment has no ultimate effect, apart from instruction or healthy catharsis. There's the rub, though. If the effect of TV violence on children has finally been demonstrated, it's not unreasonable to assume that ultra-violence in the movies has some effect on adults. It's not necessarily the same effect, a heightening of aggressive behavior. But neither do these movies necessarily enlighten their audience in ways that they're supposed to.

A film like "Straw Dogs" may put us in touch with our primal emotions, but that's no great trick—the Nazis did it constantly. It also sets up human existence, on a shaky allegorical level, as a simplistic choice between fighting violence with violence or capitulating to it completely. Where's some provision for the uses of intelligence, or at least craftiness? The film puts us in touch with a machismo that's supposed to be unfashionable in sophisticated circles these days, yet persists in philosophical disguise. A man can only be a true male, according to the movie, when he's won his merit badges in rape, combat and murder. It's as if de Sade had rewritten the worst of Hemingway for a special Nasty Edition of Playboy. There's only one possible role for a woman in this machoviolent setting. She's there to be raped, she wants passionately to be raped, she deserves to be raped and raped she most certainly is in "Straw Dogs," "Macbeth" and, of course, in "A Clockwork Orange."

This kind of entertainment is seductive in more ways than one. With its obscurity, macho bravura or both, it puts you promptly on the defensive. You can't be much of a man if you don't dig it, or at least concede its underlying wisdom. Man is base (and woman is baser), say the pundit artists. How true, how true, respond the admiring critics, only too glad to get a secure ride on the hate-humanity bandwagon. "I don't mind saying that I myself was sickened by my own film," says Sam Peckinpah, co-writer and director of "Straw Dogs." "But somewhere in it there is a mirror for everyone." Maybe so, but the mirror is framed in right-wing gilt. It shows the stereotyped liberal intellectual—Dustin Hoffman in simpers and specs—as a cowardly, contemptible nerd who won't take a stand till the barbarians are inside his own house: Neville Chamberlain Meets the New Madmen. "I'm not a Fascist," Peckinpah has been quoted as saying, "but I am something of a totalitarian."

He's a lot more candid than some of his colleagues. Don Siegel likes to be thought of as a tough action director, but the thread of Fascism in his "Dirty Harry" is as strong as the suspension cables on the Golden Gate Bridge. The gallant, ruthless, San Francisco detective tries to take a crazed killer out of circulation by fair means or foul, but he's hamstrung by all those dumb rules on arrest that were handed down by a doddering Supreme Court. Polanski takes a simple-minded, totalitarian approach to "Macbeth." The language and poetry seem beyond him, so he uses violence to explain everything. Stanley Kubrick has become a totalitarian of the arts who crushes other people's intricate moral ideas into a pulp of mod decadence.

There's a joke about a fake guru who tells all his disciples that "life is a river." Gurus of the new violence do something of the sort with stylization. Their techniques — slow motion, surreal performances, elegant décor, brilliant editing, fish-eye lenses, repeat frames — seem to comment on the action without saying anything. They lend distance, but they also dehumanize victims in the way that high-fashion photography dehumanizes models, and they create a high-fashion horror that can turn an audience on higher than the real thing. The Vietnamese war could look lovely in slow motion — Skyraiders floating in for the kill like seagulls, fragmentation bombs opening like anemones. But the horror would still be horror, with nothing added but technique. Dancing on a face while singing "Singin' in the Rain" is still dancing on a face. It becomes clear that "Bonnie and Clyde" was both watershed and quicksand. It used technique within a humanistic design and shocked us awake to violence. Now anti-humanists are using the same technique to lull us into dulcet dreams of death.

Purveyors of the new violence can tell themselves and their critics that they're involved in a program of character building, public service and ethical culture, but a few visits to neighborhood theaters suggest that a large part of the mass audience simply loves the violence as violence. The givens are not always the takens. Kids in the balcony at a recent Times Square showing of "Dirty Harry" were stomping their feet with glee at each shooting or beating. One boy was coming on strong as a munitions expert, giving his girl a run-down on the range and impact of each weapon as it appeared. When the massacres ended and the house lights came up, he breathed a sigh of deep satisfaction and said quietly: "That was nice."

That's the part of the ultra-violence trip that many filmmakers and critics don't like to deal with. At least two sets of signals are operating here, and the confusion between them raises some anguishing questions that no one knows how to answer. Where does an artist's responsibility end? With the truthful depiction of his personal vision, or with its social effects? What are the effects of ultra-violent movies, on the cavemen as well as the sophisticates of the mass audience? Once again we don't know, but it's not enough to say that Shakespeare and Marlowe were violent and civilization still survived. Technology has brought a new amplification effect into play. Never before has so much violence been shown so graphically to so many.

There's a sense of imminent disaster when you're in an audience that's grooving on ultra-violence, and you're tempted to say that things can't go on this way too much longer. They can, of course, and probably will. Today's ultra-violent films will be tomorrow's "Wednesday Night at the Movies" on TV—with anything sexy cut out, of course. If holograms bring free-standing images into our living room, we may have to shampoo the carpet after each new award-winning blood bath. Violence may also crest, as it has before, and cyclically subside. Something of the sort has happened in the rock world, which lowered its amps and pulled back from the abyss that opened at Altamont.

Whether it crests or not, however, media violence demands to be taken more seriously than it has been in the past. We know now, thanks to the Surgeon General's research, that it helps incite children to aggressive behavior. While we don't know what it does to adults, there's an ominous clue in the public's tolerance of horror in the newscasts from Vietnam. The only way we can possibly tolerate it is by turning off a part of ourselves instead of the TV set. It's very possible that incitement to violent deeds is the false danger for adults, and desensitization the real one. "Dirty Harry" didn't necessarily incite that self-styled weapons expert to buy himself a .44 and cut someone down with it. There's no proof—yet—that such ritualized primitivism turns adults on; not even the poor, the uneducated, the violence-prone, the people who can never get themselves together. The more immediate possibility is that it turns us off, like any other drug, that it freaks us out on make-believe fury, keeps us from doing anything constructive with our aggressions, that it frustrates, demeans and diminishes us.

FOUR | Male and Female

ERICH FROMM
Is Love an Art?

According to Erich Fromm, love is the only satisfactory answer to the problem of human existence, and yet most people have very little understanding of the nature of love. The following selection, the first chapter from Dr. Fromm's book *The Art of Loving,* considers the premises underlying most popular attitudes about love and urges that love be approached in the same searching spirit and with the same effort of will that characterizes the pursuit of any art.

In terms of rhetorical techniques, the essay is noteworthy for its coherence, which is achieved in part by a careful enumeration of points and in part by effectively tying one paragraph to another.

(1) Is love an art? Then it requires knowledge and effort. Or is love a pleasant sensation, which to experience is a matter of chance, something one "falls into" if one is lucky? This little book is based on the former premise, while undoubtedly the majority of people today believe in the latter.

(2) Not that people think that love is not important. They are starved for it; they watch endless numbers of films about happy and unhappy love stories, they listen to hundreds of trashy songs about love — yet hardly anyone thinks that there is anything that needs to be learned about love.

(3) This peculiar attitude is based on several premises which either singly or combined tend to uphold it. Most people see the problem

of love primarily as that of *being loved,* rather than that of *loving,* of one's capacity to love. Hence the problem to them is how to be loved, how to be lovable. In pursuit of this aim they follow several paths. One, which is especially used by men, is to be successful, to be as powerful and rich as the social margin of one's position permits. Another, used especially by women, is to make oneself attractive, by cultivating one's body, dress, etc. Other ways of making oneself attractive, used both by men and women, are to develop pleasant manners, interesting conversation, to be helpful, modest, inoffensive. Many of the ways to make oneself lovable are the same as those used to make oneself successful, "to win friends and influence people." As a matter of fact, what most people in our culture mean by being lovable is essentially a mixture between being popular and having sex appeal.

(4) A second premise behind the attitude that there is nothing to be learned about love is the assumption that the problem of love is the problem of an *object,* not the problem of a *faculty.* People think that to *love* is simple, but that to find the right object to love — or to be loved — is difficult. This attitude has several reasons rooted in the development of modern society. One reason is the great change which occurred in the twentieth century with respect to the choice of a "love object." In the Victorian age, as in many traditional cultures, love was mostly not a spontaneous personal experience which then might lead to marriage. On the contrary, marriage was contracted by convention — either by the respective families, or by a marriage broker, or without the help of such intermediaries; it was concluded on the basis of social considerations, and love was supposed to develop once the marriage had been concluded. In the last few generations the concept of romantic love has become almost universal in the Western world. In the United States, while considerations of a conventional nature are not entirely absent, to a vast extent people are in search of "romantic love," of the personal experience of love which then should lead to marriage. This new concept of freedom in love must have greatly enhanced the importance of the *object* as against the importance of the *function.*

(5) Closely related to this factor is another feature characteristic of contemporary culture. Our whole culture is based on the appetite for buying, on the idea of a mutually favorable exchange. Modern man's happiness consists in the thrill of looking at the shop windows, and in buying all that he can afford to buy, either for cash or on installments. He (or she) looks at people in a similar way. For the man an attractive girl — and for the woman an attractive man — are the prizes they are after. "Attractive" usually means a nice package of qualities which are popular and sought after on the personality market. What

specifically makes a person attractive depends on the fashion of the time, physically as well as mentally. During the twenties, a drinking and smoking girl, tough and sexy, was attractive; today the fashion demands more domesticity and coyness. At the end of the nineteenth and the beginning of this century, a man had to be aggressive and ambitious — today he has to be social and tolerant — in order to be an attractive "package." At any rate, the sense of falling in love develops usually only with regard to such human commodities as are within reach of one's own possibilities for exchange. I am out for a bargain; the object should be desirable from the standpoint of its social value, and at the same time should want me, considering my overt and hidden assets and potentialities. Two persons thus fall in love when they feel they have found the best object available on the market, considering the limitations of their own exchange values. Often, as in buying real estate, the hidden potentialities which can be developed play a considerable role in this bargain. In a culture in which the marketing orientation prevails, and in which material success is the outstanding value, there is little reason to be surprised that human love relations follow the same pattern of exchange which governs the commodity and the labor market.

(6) The third error leading to the assumption that there is nothing to be learned about love lies in the confusion between the initial experience of *"falling"* in love, and the permanent state of *being* in love, or as we might better say, of "standing" in love. If two people who have been strangers, as all of us are, suddenly let the wall between them break down, and feel close, feel one, this moment of oneness is one of the most exhilarating, most exciting experiences in life. It is all the more wonderful and miraculous for persons who have been shut off, isolated, without love. This miracle of sudden intimacy is often facilitated if it is combined with, or initiated by, sexual attraction and consummation. However, this type of love is by its very nature not lasting. The two persons become well acquainted, their intimacy loses more and more its miraculous character, until their antagonism, their disappointments, their mutual boredom kill whatever is left of the initial excitement. Yet, in the beginning they do not know all this: in fact, they take the intensity of the infatuation, this being "crazy" about each other, for proof of the intensity of their love, while it may only prove the degree of their preceding loneliness.

(7) This attitude — that nothing is easier than to love — has continued to be the prevalent idea about love in spite of the overwhelming evidence to the contrary. There is hardly any activity, any enterprise, which is started with such tremendous hopes and expectations, and yet, which fails so regularly, as love. If this were the case with any other activity, people would be eager to know the reasons for the

failure, and to learn how one could do better — or they would give up the activity. Since the latter is impossible in the case of love, there seems to be only one adequate way to overcome the failure of love — to examine the reasons for this failure, and to proceed to study the meaning of love.

(8) The first step to take is to become aware that *love is an art,* just as living is an art; if we want to learn how to love we must proceed in the same way we have to proceed if we want to learn any other art, say music, painting, carpentry, or the art of medicine or engineering.

(9) What are the necessary steps in learning any art?

(10) The process of learning an art can be divided conveniently into two parts: one, the mastery of the theory; the other, the mastery of the practice. If I want to learn the art of medicine, I must first know the facts about the human body, and about various diseases. When I have all this theoretical knowledge, I am by no means competent in the art of medicine. I shall become a master in this art only after a great deal of practice, until eventually the results of my theoretical knowledge and the results of my practice are blended into one — my intuition, the essence of the mastery of any art. But, aside from learning the theory and practice, there is a third factor necessary to becoming a master in any art — the mastery of the art must be a matter of ultimate concern; there must be nothing else in the world more important than the art. This holds true for music, for medicine, for carpentry — and for love. And, maybe, here lies the answer to the question of why people in our culture try so rarely to learn this art, in spite of their obvious failures: in spite of the deep-seated craving for love, almost everything else is considered to bë more important than love: success, prestige, money, power — almost all our energy is used for the learning of how to achieve these aims, and almost none to learn the art of loving.

(11) Could it be that only those things are considered worthy of being learned with which one can earn money or prestige, and that love, which "only" profits the soul, but is profitless in the modern sense, is a luxury we have no right to spend much energy on?

QUESTIONS AND EXERCISES

VOCABULARY

1. premise (*paragraph* 1)
2. intermediaries (4)
3. mutually (5)
4. domesticity (5)
5. coyness (5)

6. facilitated (6)
7. consummation (6)
8. antagonism (6)
9. prevalent (7)
10. theoretical (10)

LANGUAGE AND RHETORIC
1. The coherence in this essay is derived in part from the author's constant attempts to clarify relationships by means of analysis and classification. Point out specific examples of this practice.
2. Coherence is also established by the manner in which one paragraph is tied to another. Examine the first sentence of each paragraph, and show how many of these sentences employ transitional devices.
3. This brief essay is developed by a combination of methods including definition, analysis, and reasons. Point out one example of each.
4. Could paragraphs 1 and 2 be combined? Why are they presented as separate paragraphs?
5. Analyze paragraphs 3, 4, and 5 in terms of the topic sentence and the controlling idea for each.

DISCUSSION AND WRITING
1. According to the author, how do most people define love? How does he define it? Write an essay in which you define love as you understand it.
2. The author enumerates some of the ways in which people seek to make themselves lovable. What are some of the ways that he does not mention?
3. Discuss the advantages and disadvantages of each of the two approaches to marital love mentioned in paragraph 4 — the traditional idea of the marriage contract that would hopefully give rise to love and the modern idea of romantic love as a motive for marriage.
4. If you are prepared to accept what the author suggests about "the art of loving," what specific things can you do to act in accord with his ideas? How, apart from reading Dr. Fromm's book, might you go about mastering the "art"?

HERBERT A. OTTO
Has Monogamy Failed?

In this essay Herbert A. Otto examines the institutions of marriage and the family in light of recent social and cultural developments. Starting from the observation that these institutions are undergoing unprecedented change today, he outlines the ways in which our traditional marriage and family relationships are giving way to more flexible roles and structures.

Of the several methods of development in evidence here, pay particular attention to the author's use of analysis.

(1) Never before in the history of Western civilization has the institution of marriage been under the searching scrutiny it is today. Never before have so many people questioned the cultural and theological heritage of monogamy — and set out in search of alternatives. The American family of the 1970s is entering an unprecedented era of change and transition, with a massive reappraisal of the family and its functioning in the offing.

(2) The U.S. statistic of one divorce per every four marriages is all too familiar. Other figures are even more disquieting. For example, a recent government study revealed that one-third of all first-born children in the United States from 1964 through 1966 were conceived out of wedlock, thereby forcing many hasty marriages that might not have occurred otherwise. Some marriage specialists estimate that anywhere from 40 to 60 per cent of all marriages are at any given time "subclinical." The couples involved could materially benefit from the help of a marriage counselor, but they never reach a clinic. Divorce is still the most widely accepted means of coping with a marriage beset by problems. Relatively few couples having marital difficulties are aware of available marriage counseling services or utilize them. Divorce today is very much a part of the social fabric, and some sociologists refer to a "divorce culture." It is safe to say that most men, women, and children in this country have been touched by the divorce experience — either in their own families, or among friends and close acquaintances.

(3) The other day a good friend, senior executive of a large company and in his early forties, dropped by for a visit. He told me he had been thinking of divorce after sixteen years of marriage. The couple have a boy, twelve, and two girls, one of whom is ten, the other eight. "We've grown apart over the years, and we have nothing in common left anymore other than the children. There are at least twenty years of enjoying life still ahead of me. I was worried about the children until we discussed it with them. So many of their schoolmates have had divorced parents or parents who had remarried, they are accustomed to the idea. It's part of life. Of course, if the older ones need help, I want them to see a good psychiatrist while we go through with this. My wife is still a good-looking woman, younger than I, and probably will remarry. I'm not thinking of it now, but I'll probably remarry someday." This situation illustrates an attitude and the climate of the times. Divorce has become as much an institution as marriage.

(4) Paradoxically, the high divorce rate can be viewed as both a symptom of the failure of monogamy and an indication of its success. A large majority of men and women remarry within four years after their divorce. As Dr. Bernard Steinzor points out in his latest book,

When Parents Divorce, "divorce has become an expression of the increasing personal freedom afforded the average citizen." It is a fact that the average citizen continues to pursue personal freedom within the framework of marriage. Serial monogamy or progressive monogamy is today so widespread that it has arrived as an alternative structure. According to one analyst, we are close to the day when 85 per cent of all men and women reaching the age of sixty-five will have been remarried at least once. I am reminded of a cartoon that appeared in *The New Yorker* some time ago: A young couple is shown leaving what is identified by a sign as the home of a justice of the peace. The bride, dressed in the latest mod fashion, turns brightly to her young man and says, "Darling! Our first marriage!"

(5) The full-scale emergence of serial monogamy has been accompanied by an explosive upswing of experimentation with other alternative structures. Begun by the under-thirty generation and hippie tribal families, the 1960s have seen the growth of a new commune movement. This movement has started to attract significant segments of the older, established population. For example, I recently conducted a weekend marathon in Chicago—under the auspices of the Oasis Center—that was open to the public. Seven out of thirty-six participants were members of communes. Three of the seven were successful professional men in their mid-forties. Another participant, a college professor in his early thirties, mentioned that he had been a member of a commune composed of several psychiatrists, an engineer, a teacher, and a chemist. When I visited New York following the Chicago weekend, a senior editor of a large publishing house casually mentioned that he and some friends were in the process of organizing a commune. They were looking for a large brownstone close to their offices.

(6) The commune movement even has its own journal, *Modern Utopian*. Issued by the Alternatives Foundation of Berkeley, California, it is in its fourth year of publication. In 1969, this journal published the first comprehensive directory of intentional or utopian communes in the United States and the world. The addresses of close to two hundred intentional communities in this country are given. (It has been estimated that there are four to six times this number of communes in the United States.) California leads the *Modern Utopian* directory with more than thirty listed. New York has twenty-eight and Pennsylvania thirteen, with communes listed from thirty-five other states. Half a dozen books that I know of are currently in preparation on the commune movement.

(7) Communes of various types exist, varying from agricultural subsistence to religious. To provide a base for economic survival, many of the communes furnish services or construct marketable products

such as hammocks or wooden toys for preschoolers. Others operate printing presses or schools. Most communes not located in cities raise some of their own food. Relatively rare is the commune that is self-supporting solely on the basis of its agricultural operation. Sizes vary with anywhere from twelve persons or fewer to a hundred persons or more as members of an intentional community. The educational and vocational backgrounds of members also vary widely. The young people and school dropouts are currently being joined by a growing number of "Establishment dropouts." Many of these are people who have made successful contributions in their chosen vocations or professions and have grown disillusioned, or who are seeking to explore new life-styles.

(8) Communes often have their beginnings when several persons who know each other well, like each other, and have similar values decide to live together. Sometimes a commune is formed around a common interest, craft, or unifying creative goal. Political views or convictions may also play a role in the formation of a commune. There are a number of peace-movement and radical communes; sometimes these are composed of political activists, and sometimes of people who see the commune movement as a "radical approach to revolution." Members of one such group, the Twin Oaks community in Virginia, think of themselves as a post-revolutionary society. As detailed in *Modern Utopian*, this "radical commune" was organized as the result of a university conference:

> Twin Oaks was started by a group of people who met while attending an "academic" conference during 1966 at Ann Arbor, Michigan, on the formation of a Walden II community. One of the Twin Oakers related how this conference resulted in a very elaborate, academic type plan on how to get a Walden II community going. But when the conference was over, the professors all returned to their teaching posts, and nobody had any idea where they could get the several million dollars that the plan called for to start the thing. So eight people decided to start right away with whatever resources they could get together. . . .
>
> For while Twin Oaks was designed to be a living experiment in community, it also aims to stimulate others to do the same. As one member said, "We generally hold to the opinion that people who *don't* start communities (or join them) are slightly immoral." It's all part of the revolution being over — they define revolution as a "radical restructuring" of society, both economic and, more important, cultural. (But maybe you can't really separate the two.) One member summed up a desirable post-revolutionary society as: "A society that creates people who are committed to non-aggression; a society of people concerned for one another; a society where one man's gain is not another man's loss; a society where disagreeable work is minimized and leisure is valued; a society in which people come first; an economic system of

equality; a society which is constantly trying to improve in its ability to create happy, productive, creative people."

(9) The personal property a member brings to a commune remains his, although he may be expected to share it when needed. Some purists object that since members do not donate personal property for the benefit of the group, the current social experiments should not be referred to as "communes." Obviously, the term has acquired a new meaning and definition. The emphasis today is on the exploration of alternate models for togetherness, the shaping of growing dynamic environments, the exploration of new life-styles, and the enjoyment of living together.

(10) A number of communes are deliberately organized for the purpose of group marriage. The concept of group marriage, however, differs widely. Some communes exclusively composed of couples have a living arrangement similar to the "big family" or group family that originated in Sweden in 1967. These married couples share the same home, expenses, household chores, and the upbringing of the children. Infidelity is not encouraged. Other group-marriage communes tolerate or encourage the sharing of husbands and wives. On the other end of the group-marriage continuum are communes such as The Family near Taos, New Mexico. This group of more than fifty members discourages pairing—"Everyone is married to everyone. The children are everyone's."

(11) The life-span of many communes is relatively short due to four major disintegrative pressures that fragment intentional communities. Disagreement over household chores or work to be performed is a major source of disruption. When members fail to fulfill their obligations, disillusionment and demoralization often set in. Closely related are interpersonal conflicts, frequently fueled by the exchange of sex partners and resultant jealousy. Drugs do not seem to create a major problem in most communes, as there is either a permissive attitude or drug use is discouraged or forbidden. A small number of religious/ mystical communes use drugs for sacramental purposes and as a means of communion.

(12) The problems associated with economic survival generate considerable pressure. A final strong force that contributes to the collapse of communes stems from the hostility of surrounding communities. There are innumerable instances of harassment by neighbors, strangers, civil authorities, and police. The persistent and violent nature of this persecution is probably traceable to deep-seated feelings of threat and outrage when the neighboring communities discover a group in their midst suspected of having unorthodox living arrangements. These pervasive feelings of resistance and anger

(which may be partially subconscious) are conceivably engendered in many persons by what they perceive to be a threat to the existing family structure.

(13) The weight of tradition and the strong imprinting of parental and familial models assure that for some time to come the overwhelming bulk of the population will opt for something close to the family structures they have known. In view of this strong thrust, it is all the more surprising that preventive programs (other than didactic approaches) that center on the strengthening of the family are almost unknown. Also sadly lacking is massive federal support for programs designed to help marriages and families beset by problems. A network of federally supported marriage-counseling clinics making marital and premarital counseling services available throughout every state in the Union could accomplish a great deal toward reducing marital unhappiness and divorce.

(14) Present-day medical science widely recommends that we have an annual physical check-up as a means of prevention. In a similar manner, annual assessment and evaluation should be available to couples interested in developing and improving their marriages. The goal would be to identify, strengthen, and develop family potential *before* crises arise, with the main focus on helping a family achieve an even more loving, enjoyable, creative, and satisfying marriage relationship. The plan of a marriage and family potential center was developed in 1967 and 1968 by a colleague, Dr. Lacey Hall, and myself during my stay in Chicago. The project was supported by the Stone Foundation, but, owing to a number of complex reasons, the program was never fully implemented. As a part of the work in Chicago, and also under the auspices of the National Center for the Exploration of Human Potential, a number of "More Joy in Your Marriage" groups and classes have been conducted and have shown considerable promise as a preventive approach.

(15) Another highly promising field of inquiry is the area of family strengths. Little or no research and conceptualization had been done in relation to this area until the work of the Human Potentialities Research Project at the University of Utah, from 1960 through 1967. Paradoxically, family counseling and treatment programs have been offered for decades without a clearly developed framework of what was meant by family strengths, or what constitutes a "healthy family." In spite of extensive efforts to obtain foundation or government support for this research, no financial support was forthcoming. Ours remains a pathology-oriented culture saddled with the bias that the study of disorganization, illness, and dysfunction is the surest road to understanding the forces that go into the making of health and optimum functioning.

(16) The emergence of alternative structures and the experimentation with new modes of married and family togetherness expresses a strong need to bring greater health and optimum functioning to a framework of interpersonal relationships formerly regarded as "frozen" and not amenable to change. There is no question that sex-role and parental-role rigidities are in the process of diminishing, and new dimensions of flexibility are making their appearance in marriage and the family. It is also evident that we are a pluralistic society with pluralistic needs. In this time of change and accelerated social evolution, we should encourage innovation and experimentation in the development of new forms of social and communal living. It is possible to invent and try out many models without hurting or destroying another person. Perhaps we need to recognize clearly that the objective of any model is to provide an atmosphere of sustenance, loving, caring, and adventuring. This makes growth and unfoldment possible.

(17) It is in this light that the attention of an increasing number of well-known humanistic psychologists has been drawn to the institution of marriage. A new recognition of the many dimensions and possibilities of monogamy is beginning to emerge. For example, Dr. Jack Gibb and Dr. Everett Shostrom have each been conducting a series of couples groups at Growth Centers designed to revitalize and deepen love in the marital relationship.

(18) Another eminent psychologist and author, Dr. Sidney Jourard, suggests that we "re-invent marriage" by engaging in "serial polygamy to the same person." He points out that many marriages pass through a cycle of gratifying the needs of both partners, and are experienced as fulfilling until an impasse is reached. One partner or the other finds continuation in that form intolerable, and the marriage is usually legally dissolved at that point. He believes it is possible for the couple at this juncture to struggle with the impasse and to evolve a new marriage with each other, one that includes change, yet preserves some of the old pattern that remains viable. This is the second marriage that, whatever form it takes, will also reach its end. There may then again be a time of estrangement, a period of experimentation, and a remarriage in a new way—and so on for as long as continued association with the same spouse remains meaningful for both partners.

(19) One of the originators of the group marathon technique, Dr. Frederick Stoller, has another interesting proposal to add new dimensions to marriage and family relationships. He suggests an "intimate network of families." His intimate network consists of a circle of three or four families who meet together regularly and frequently, share in reciprocal fashion any of their intimate secrets, and offer one

another a variety of services. The families do not hesitate to influence one another in terms of values and attitudes. Such an intimate family network would be neither stagnant nor polite, but would involve an extension of the boundaries of the immediate family.

(20) Another possibility to introduce new elements of growth and creativity to monogamy is contained in my own concept of the "new marriage," i.e., marriage as a framework for developing personal potential. This concept is based on the hypothesis that we are all functioning at a small fraction of our capacity to live fully in its total meaning of loving, caring, creating, and adventuring. Consequently, the actualizing of our potential can become the most exciting adventure of our lifetime. From this perspective, any marriage can be envisioned as a framework for actualizing personal potential. Thus, marriage offers us an opportunity to grow, and an opportunity to develop and deepen the capacity for loving and caring. Only in a continuing relationship is there a possibility for love to become deeper and fuller so that it envelops all of our life and extends into the community. However, growth, by its very nature, is not smooth and easy, for growth involves change and the emergence of the new. But growth and the actualization of personal potential are also a joyous and deeply satisfying process that can bring to marriage a *joie de vivre*, and excitement, and a new quality of zest for living.

(21) There are a number of characteristics that form a unique Gestalt and distinguish the new marriage from contemporary marriage patterns:

● There is a clear acknowledgment by both partners concerning the *personal relevance* of the human potentialities hypothesis: that the healthy individual is functioning at a fraction of his potential.

● Love and understanding become dynamic elements in the actualization of the marital partners' personal potential.

● Partners in the new marriage conceive of their union as an evolving, developing, flexible, loving relationship.

● In the new marriage there is planned action and commitment to achieve realization of marriage potential.

● The new marriage is here-and-now oriented and not bound to the past.

● There is clear awareness by husband and wife that their interpersonal or relationship environment, as well as their physical environment, directly affects the actualization of individual potential.

● There is clear recognition by spouses that personality and the actualization of human potential have much to do with the social institutions and structures within which man functions. The need for institutional and environmental regeneration is acknowledged by both partners as being personally relevant, leading to involvement in social action.

● Husband and wife have an interest in exploring the spiritual dimensions of the new marriage.

(22) Since it is often difficult for two people to actualize more of their marriage potential by themselves, participants in the new marriage will seek out group experiences designed to deepen their relationship and functioning as a couple. Such experiences are now being offered at Growth Centers that have sprung up in many parts of the United States. Extension divisions of institutions of higher learning and church organizations are also increasingly offering such group experiences. Based on my many years of practice as marriage counselor, it has long been my conclusion that every marriage needs periodic rejuvenation and revitalization. This is best accomplished in a couples group that focuses on the development of greater intimacy, joy, and affection.

(23) The challenge of marriage is the adventure of uncovering the depth of our love, the height of our humanity. It means risking ourselves physically and emotionally; leaving old habit patterns, and developing new ones; being able to express our desires fully, while sensitive to the needs of the other; being aware that each changes at his own rate, and unafraid to ask for help when needed.

(24) Has monogamy failed? My answer is "no." Monogamy is no longer a rigid institution, but instead an evolving one. There is a multiplicity of models and dimensions that we have not even begun to explore. It takes a certain amount of openness to become aware on not only an intellectual level but a feeling level that these possibilities face us with a choice. Then it takes courage to recognize that this choice in a measure represents our faith in monogamy. Finally, there is the fact that every marriage has a potential for greater commitment, enjoyment, and communication, for more love, understanding, and warmth. Actualizing this potential can offer new dimensions in living and new opportunities for personal growth, and can add new strength and affirmation to a marriage.

QUESTIONS AND EXERCISES

VOCABULARY

1. monogamy (title)
2. scrutiny (*paragraph* 1)
3. subsistence (7)
4. unorthodox (12)
5. didactic (13)

6. pathology (15)
7. dysfunction (15)
8. pluralistic (16)
9. actualizing (20)
10. *joie de vivre* (20)

LANGUAGE AND RHETORIC

1. This essay is one of four in the text that use a question for a title (see Table of Contents). How effective do you think this technique is?
2. What is the thesis of the essay? What seems to be the author's purpose? Justify each of your answers.
3. What audience does the author appear to be writing for, and on what do you base your opinion?
4. Several methods of development can be found here, but analysis is one of the more important ones. Point out some examples of the method and explain their appropriateness to the author's purpose.
5. Paragraphs 2, 5, 13, 16, 21, and 23 are transition points in this essay. Explain what contribution they make to its overall structure.

DISCUSSION AND WRITING

1. The author states that "serial monogamy"—that is, marriage, divorce, and remarriage—has become one alternative marital structure. What are some of the advantages and disadvantages of this arrangement? What is your own reaction to it, and why do you feel as you do?
2. A high percentage of divorces occurs among young people. According to one sociologist, many of these young people rush into marriage lacking a clear understanding of what it is all about, and such marriages are likely to end in divorce. Consider the young married couples you know and have known, and decide if you agree or disagree.
3. If you are or have been married, write a paper based on your personal experience in which you respond to "the challenge of marriage" that the author discusses in paragraph 23.
4. Communal living is discussed at some length in this selection. Consider the advantages and disadvantages of communal living compared with the traditional family structure, and write an essay explaining your preference for one of the two arrangements.
5. What do you consider to be an ideal marital structure and arrangement? Explain the reasons behind your choice.

ELLEN WILLIS
The New Racism: Sexism

"Whatever happened to women? Nothing—that's the trouble," says Ellen Willis. With the aid of some equally militant females, the author adds another pair of terms to the literature of prejudice: *sexism,* the pervasive discrimination against women in our society, and *feminism,* the women's revolt against that discrimination. This report on the new feminism reveals the image of inferiority to which females are subjected from childhood. The author then discusses the continuing discrimination women encounter in school, in business, and in sexual relations. The report culminates in an analysis of what the author sees as the ultimate bastion of sexism—marriage.

Note the skillful transitions from one point to the next in the essay. In addition, examine the author's argument for any instances of exaggeration or oversimplification.

(1) Feminism has revived. It began stirring in 1963, when Betty Friedan deflated the myth of the fulfilled suburban housewife. It got a push from a prankish Southern Senator who, to point up the absurdity of the proposed Civil Rights Act, added a sex-discrimination clause to the fair-employment provision. And it made its first public appearance when a number of professional women founded the National Organization for Women (NOW), a civil-rights group concerned mostly with bread-and-butter issues—discrimination in education, employment, and public accommodations; restrictive abortion laws; lack of day-care facilities. At the same time, younger women involved in the radical movement were discovering that they were second-class revolutionaries. Men who proclaimed the right of all people to control their own lives still expected women to make the coffee, lick the stamps, take typing jobs to support their men's movement work—to do anything, in fact, except help make political decisions on an equal basis. In the past two years, more and more radical women have formed separate groups to discuss their situation as radicals and as women. Out of this separation has come the Women's

Liberation Movement, which is growing so fast that some large cities have as many as 20 groups. Although Women's Liberation is also interested in concrete issues, its perspective is very different from NOW's. Radical feminists do not want equal privileges in the existing society; they want to restructure it, changing its definitions of masculine and feminine, of work and the family.

(2) Like the early feminist movement, which grew out of the campaign to end slavery, the present-day women's movement has been inspired and influenced by the black liberation struggle. The situation of women and blacks is similar in many ways. Just as blacks live in a world defined by whites, women live in a world defined by males. (The generic term for human being is "man"; "woman" means "wife of man.") To be female or black is to be peculiar; whiteness and maleness are the norm. Newspapers do not have "men's pages," nor would anyone think of discussing the "man problem." Racial and sexual stereotypes also resemble each other: women, like blacks, are said to be childish, incapable of abstract reasoning, innately submissive, biologically suited for menial tasks, emotional, close to nature.

(3) Most important, both women and blacks have a history of slavery—only female slavery goes back much further. From the beginnings of civilization until very recently, women in most societies were literally the property of their husbands and fathers. Even now, many vestiges of that chattel status persist in law and custom. Wives are still known by their husbands' names. In many states, a wife is legally required to perform domestic services, have sexual relations on demand if her health permits, and live with her husband wherever *he* chooses or be guilty of desertion. Restaurants, bars, and other public accommodations can legally refuse to admit a woman without a male escort or exclude her altogether. And vote or no vote, politics has remained a male preserve. Women make up more than half the population, but hold less than 1 per cent of elected offices. They also get few political appointments, except for the inevitable "adviser on consumer affairs" (women's place is in the supermarket).

(4) In any case, the "emancipated" woman, like the freed slaves, has merely substituted economic dependence for legal subjection. According to Government statistics, white women workers earn even less than black men. Most women, especially mothers, must depend on men to support them, and that fact alone gives men power over their lives.

(5) By now, almost everyone recognizes racism as an evil. But in spite of all the parallels, most people either defend sexism or deny its existence. "Yes, it's a man's world," some say, "and that's the way it should be. Normal women like the female role." As respected a figure as Dr. Spock recently wrote in a women's magazine, "Biologi-

cally and temperamentally, I believe, women were made to be concerned first and foremost with child care, husband care, and home care." Then he explains away the discontent of many women with these roles by saying that their education has confused them! Other antifeminists insist, "Women *are* free. They can vote, work, and have orgasms—what more do they want? In fact, women are too free. They're taking over and robbing men of their masculinity." In between these extremes is the argument that "women can liberate themselves individually; they don't need a movement."

(6) The usual response to any mention of feminism is laughter. "Feminists" are little old ladies brandishing umbrellas, square-jawed mannish freaks, or humorless puritans. This prejudice is so strong that even some activists in the women's movement have been reluctant to call themselves feminists or identify in any way with the original women's-rights movement. Because antifeminist sentiment comes from women as well as men, it can't be dismissed out of hand as male propaganda aimed at keeping us in our place. The questions must be taken seriously. Is male supremacy natural and desirable? Are we already as free as we want to be? Do we need a movement?

(7) To get an idea of why I'm convinced we *do* need a movement, let's analyze the situation of the most privileged woman in history—the young, educated female who is so often referred to as the "emancipated," or "new," or "modern" woman. This is the woman who wants to enjoy sex, share love and an equal companionship with a man or men, and do engaging work outside the home as well as having children. How likely is she to achieve these not unreasonable goals?

(8) In the typical American family, a girl is trained from babyhood to be what the culture defines as feminine. Everyone encourages her to act cute and charming and flirt with her father, her uncles, and little boys. When she announces that she wants to be a fireman, her mother laughs: girls can't be firemen; you'll be a mother, like me. Or a nurse. Or a teacher. When she roughhouses, parents brag, "She's as tough as a boy." Yet at the same time they warn, "Someday you'll have to stop acting like a boy and be a lady." Most likely her brothers are free to play while she helps with the dishes, and her parents are more tolerant of their noise, dirt, and disobedience—after all, boys will be boys.

(9) When she reaches adolescence, she finds that if she wants friendship and approval from other kids she must direct most of her energy toward pleasing boys. That means being preoccupied with clothes and makeup—with how she looks instead of what she does. It means absorbing all the advice about how to have a "good personality" and "build up a boy's ego." (No one worries about her ego.) And it means coming to understand that her status in the world and her

worth as a person depend not on what she accomplishes, but on whom she marries. An A in physics is fine, but unless she is also pretty and sought-after, people will pity her and consider her braininess a compensation. She also learns that initiative in social activities belongs to the boys; it is her place to wait by the phone. When she wants a boy's company she can't approach him directly, but must maneuver him into asking her. She steps out of this role at her peril—if she is very pretty and self-assured she may get away with it, but otherwise she faces humiliating snubs. After a while—if, like most girls, she can't measure up to the standards of attractiveness glorified by the mass media and exemplified by the "popular" few—she develops feelings of inferiority that may last a lifetime. Sometimes she rebels and withdraws from the game, but only at the price of loneliness.

(10) Then comes college. If a girl hasn't already lost her incentive to do anything but catch a husband, she is likely to run into new obstacles. Parents will go out of their way to send a boy to the college he prefers; with a girl, they are more reluctant. They may insist that she live at home and go to a public college because it's cheaper, and what difference can it make to a girl? Or put pressure on her to study "something practical that you can fall back on," like teaching. Or make it clear that in return for their investment, she had better snare a professional man.

(11) At school she will have to cope with paternalism, condescension, and sometimes outright hostility from male instructors, especially if she takes "masculine" subjects like math or science. If she is particularly bright she may win the highest of all accolades, "You think like a man." She will find that, except in traditionally female fields, professional and graduate schools discriminate in their admissions and financial-aid policies on the grounds that it is a risk to train women who are going to have children and drop out. This becomes a self-fulfilling prophecy. Because of the stubborn prejudice against part-time students and the virtual absence of facilities for communal child care, a woman who gets pregnant accidentally or doesn't want to wait until her childbearing years are half over is often forced to drop out. Theoretically, the husband could stay home instead, but this idea so offends our deepest male-supremacist taboos that few wives would dare even to imagine such an arrangement.

(12) If a woman does manage to finish graduate school, she faces blatant discrimination in almost every profession, from college teaching and newspaper reporting to medicine and law. In spite of the Civil Rights Act, she has a harder time finding a job and is paid less than a man for the same work. She has to endure nosy personal questions from interviewers who want to know if she's getting married soon; if she's planning to have children; how she'll take care of

them if she does. And because of the stigma against women having any authority, she has less freedom on the job. Often, she is afraid to assert herself—all her life she has heard that aggressive women are nasty, man-hating misfits. (Note, for example, a recent ad for a Speed-writing course. Under the caption IS THIS YOUR BOSS? OR IS THIS YOUR BOSS? are two pictures, one of a fat, frowning woman, the other of a clean-cut, smiling man. Guess which we're supposed to prefer?) Her male associates or subordinates are likely to resent her unless she acts "feminine"—i.e., pretends to defer to their superior judgment. (Dr. Mary Meade, a school administrator and recent appointee to the New York Board of Education, has remarked that her technique for getting her suggestions accepted is to convince one of the men she works with to transmit it to the rest.) And she will be inhibited because she knows that a woman has to be twice as good as a man—any mistake will be attributed to female incompetence.

(13) The college graduate with no specialized training is even worse off. She will probably end up as a secretary or "gal Friday" with little or no chance of promotion to a policy-making job. The secretary in America is not only a typing-shorthand-telephone-answering machine, but a glorified housewife and quasi geisha girl. She is expected to look pretty and fashionable, have a "good personality," make coffee for the boss, soothe his temper, flatter him, and make him think her ideas are his own. Even if she does, in fact, do original work and make decisions, it is her boss who gets the money and status.

(14) The sexual emancipation of the "new woman" is as illusory as the economic. True, the cruder aspects of the double standard are in disrepute. But real sexual freedom implies that each sex cares equally about the physical and emotional needs of the other. In our sexist society, this is far from the case. Women are brought up to be sensitive to a man's needs, to put him first. Men accept this sensitivity as their due and rarely reciprocate. Rather, they tend to see women as objects, as pretty or ugly, easy to get or a challenge, a good catch or a last resort. In general, women are sexually attracted to men whose whole personality interests them; a man's pursuit of nice legs or breasts or long blond hair may have nothing to do with whether he likes the person they belong to. This naturally makes women more hesitant than men to enter sexual relationships. And their hesitancy then impels men to play more elaborate seduction games, reinforcing the hesitancy.

(15) In a way, the relaxation of sexual mores just makes a woman's life more difficult. If she is not cautious about sex, she is likely to get hurt; if she is too cautious, she will lose her man to more obliging women. Either way, her decision is based at least partly on fear and cal-

culation, not on her spontaneous needs and desires. Another myth that needs debunking is that women have won the right to equal sexual enjoyment. Unfortunately, as men have become more sensitive and knowledgeable about female sexuality, they have also begun to *demand* passion from women as an index of their virility. Orgasmic capacity has become another criterion of a desirable object, like good looks. Under such pressure, a woman who cares about a man is increasingly tempted to let him think she is turned on whether she is or not. To refuse him if she's not in the mood or explain to him how to excite her or take the initiative herself is to risk "deflating his ego," provoking accusations of frigidity, and inducing him to look elsewhere for confirmation of his talents.

(16) Men want women to be available and responsive, but without making too many demands or challenging their sexual prerogatives. By now it has become a psychiatric cliché that many men have reacted to their wives' new sexual aggressiveness with loss of interest or even impotence. The implication is clear; go back to your passive role, or else. Nearly all the participants in a recent magazine survey of young men's attitudes toward the birth-control pill resented the pill because they felt it made women too independent. Even men who defend the sexual revolution the loudest often display contempt for a woman who has a lot of affairs — not because they really think she is "bad," but because her departure from the traditional role is an implicit threat to their power position.

(17) Finally, the sexual double standard can never disappear so long as women are denied contraceptives and abortion on demand. Birth control is not so easily available as is supposed, especially to young, unmarried girls. (Bill Baird, the director of a Long Island birth-control clinic, is currently appealing a three-month sentence for publicly breaking Massachusetts law by handing an unmarried woman a bottle of spermicidal foam.) And thousands of women die or are seriously injured each year as the result of messed-up abortions. Our "new woman" is probably white and middle class and thus unlikely to stick a coat hanger through her uterus or give herself over to a $10-a-job butcher, but even high-class illegal abortions can be dangerous and degrading. Yet, in most cases a woman's only other alternative is to bear a child she doesn't want or cannot afford, emotionally, physically, or financially. One of the ugliest florescences of sexism is the state's power to force a woman to use her body for reproduction. The Constitution prohibits involuntary servitude and guarantees every citizen equal protection of the laws; how can compulsory pregnancy be justified? Politicians and churchmen who moralize about killing the fetus care more about an unconscious clump of cells than about the suffering of living women. Those who say, "She's had

her fun, she should take the consequences," are denying women (even married women, who dominate the abortion statistics) the right to sexual happiness on the same basis as men.

(18) The institution that affects women's lives most is marriage. For most women, it is a central goal. If a woman wants children, she must marry or suffer social ostracism and economic hardship. Marriage also removes her from the social-sexual rat race and gives her status: she has succeeded as a woman. But does it give her what she wants most — genuine love and companionship? If so, it is only because human tenderness and concern sometimes manage to flourish in the worst of circumstances.

(19) Marriage, though disguised as a freely contracted bond between equals, is in fundamental respects a master-slave relationship. It is more necessary to women, but more beneficial to men. A woman's training in being supportive and ego-building is basically practice for the subordinate role in marriage, where she is expected to put her husband's work and interests above her own and provide him with a comfortable domestic environment. A working wife is nonetheless held responsible for the household, though her husband may "help out."

(20) The constant celebration of homemaking in the media cannot conceal the fact that most housework is dirty and boring. Most people would prefer just about any job to being a domestic servant; few single women would stand for a female roommate trying to stick them with all the cleaning. But to do the same dirty work for a husband is supposed to be a privilege. The rationalization is usually that women are inherently altruistic, which makes about as much sense as Senator George Murphy's remark that Mexicans are better suited to stoop labor because they are "built low to the ground."

(21) It is equally specious to imagine that because women are uniquely equipped to give birth and nurse infants, they also have a special talent for changing diapers and wiping noses. Much, perhaps most, of child rearing involves routine work that, however necessary for the child, is not particularly edifying for the parent. And Dr. Spock to the contrary, many women have no temperamental gift for relating to children; many men undoubtedly do, or would if they ever had a chance to develop it. Anyway, taking care of children, however rewarding, is not the equivalent of work in the outside world. Children need love, support, someone to stand behind them and put their welfare first — more of what a culturally approved wife is already providing for her husband. A mother cannot use her children as outlets for her creative energies without making them into things that exist for her benefit instead of their own. But if she decides that she needs a vocation of her own, even if she already has one, she comes up

against institutionalized sexism. Full-time motherhood is the norm, and the system discourages alternatives. The community refuses to take any responsibility for the children of working mothers. Since most part-time jobs are marginal—both spiritually and economically—it is almost impossible, even when the husband is willing, for most couples to break with the traditional division of labor and share outside work, domestic chores, and child rearing. The only option for career woman-mother is to hire a poorer woman with fewer choices to take her place in the home. And this is nothing but exploitation, just piling the load on another woman's back.

(22) That is the other side of the woman problem. For most women —the millions of file clerks, factory workers, welfare mothers, working-class housewives, daughters of rigid patriarchal families—are not "new women" and have never pretended to be liberated. Citing the pseudo-emancipation of an educated minority as proof that women are free has been one of the crueler sports of postwar sociology and journalism.

(23) Many women insist that they are happy with things as they are. But would they have chosen the same life if they really had a free choice in the matter or could conceive of an alternative? Male supremacy has existed for so long that it has come to seem an unalterable absolute. What is significant is not that most women are making the best of it, but that more and more women are beginning to rebel, to insist on their primacy as human beings. As for the argument that the emancipation of women has already gone too far, this is akin to the conviction of many whites that the blacks are taking over. When a group is used to mistaking certain privileges for natural rights, any encroachment on those privileges is regarded as persecution.

(24) But the most dangerous illusion is that women can liberate themselves as individuals. Male supremacy is not a problem of individual relationships, but a pervasive social force. No man or woman is unaffected by it. The bohemian and radical subcultures are no less sexist than straight society. In hippie communes, the women still do the cooking and cleaning; the chauvinism of radical men inspired Women's Liberation. A woman cannot hope to find a man who is free of sexist attitudes, nor can she make a man give up his privileges by arguing. He will just find another woman who accepts the *status quo*. We will only begin to solve the problem when women organize and back each other up. That is the immediate goal of Women's Liberation—to get women together, make them see each other as sisters and allies instead of competitors for male favors. As yet we have no clear vision of the new society. That will come later. But we do know that sexism, like racism, is incompatible with human dignity. And we are prepared to fight.

QUESTIONS AND EXERCISES

VOCABULARY
1. generic (*paragraph* 2)
2. innately (2)
3. vestiges (3)
4. chattel (3)
5. sexism (5)
6. paternalism (11)
7. condescension (11)
8. accolades (11)
9. blatant (12)
10. prerogatives (16)
11. florescences (17)
12. specious (21)

LANGUAGE AND RHETORIC
1. Describe the tone of this selection. Does the author's earnestness occasionally lead to exaggeration or to oversimplification? For example, examine paragraphs 14 and 19.
2. Where does the author first make explicit her thesis? Is the conclusion effective? Before you answer the question, reread the first paragraph, in which the author states the aims of women's liberation.
3. Analyze paragraph 3 in terms of its controlling idea and its primary and secondary supporting detail.
4. The paragraphs in this article are skillfully connected so that the thought flows smoothly from point to point. What technique does the author use in the opening sentence of one paragraph to link it with a preceding paragraph? Point out specific instances of this technique.
5. In her defense of the Women's Liberation movement, the author deals with several myths and illusions about the woman's role in American society. What are these illusions? Identify the sentences that act as transitions connecting the sections dealing with these illusions.
6. What is the controlling idea of paragraph 11? What method of development is used to support the controlling idea? What devices are used to provide coherence within this paragraph?

DISCUSSION AND WRITING
1. How much truth is there to the analogy between the plight of the female in America and the plight of the black in America? Are women the victims of prejudice and discrimination? Support or refute the author's thesis by giving examples from your own experience or knowledge.
2. Do "normal women like the female role" the way it is? Do you agree with Dr. Spock that "biologically and temperamentally . . . women were made to be concerned first and foremost with child care, husband care, and home care"? What is the basis for your opinion?
3. The author regards marriage as built essentially on a master-slave relationship "more necessary to women, but more beneficial to men." Do you agree? Can you defend marriage as contributing equally to the growth and development of both husband and wife?
4. Should a husband have the right to sexual relations with his wife whenever he desires? Should a wife have such a right? Support your answers.
5. The author obviously has little regard for the role of the housewife. Is housework as "dirty and boring" as she claims? Can a woman be com-

pletely fulfilled through the roles of housewife and mother? Talk with some housewives and write an essay reporting your findings.

JEAN S. MULLEN
Women Writers in Freshman Textbooks

The role of the woman as writer intimately concerns each of us, because she is one of the key figures in the process of consciousness-raising among the men and women and the girls and boys of our society. She is in a strategic position to promote awareness of prevalent sexual stereotyping and discrimination, and she *cares* about the problem.

What are her particular difficulties in a publishing industry dominated by men? How much is her voice heard among authors and poets, not only those read and studied as "greats," but also those presented to college students as stylists to be admired and imitated? And in those countless "freshman English" courses, where multitudes of young men and women delve into contemporary or recent ideas to stimulate their own writing and discussion, how many women's voices are coming through to them?

In a limited and rather casual survey of freshman English anthologies a year ago, I discovered that the ratio of women writers to men was fairly constant: about 7% to 93%. In this preliminary sample, which involved twenty-one recent essay collections (published between 1960 and 1971), I observed the following data:

1. The overall average representation of women was about 7% (.069) of the total number of writers. Five anthologies were above this average; four were about average; and twelve were below the 7%. Those above average tended to be well above it: 10½%, 12%, 15½%, 19%, and 21%, a range which happened also to be chronological, the last two texts having been published in 1971.
2. Women were more likely to be represented in narrative or descriptive material, less likely in expository prose or logical argument. Thus the percentage of women writers went up slightly where short stories and poems happened to be included among the essays.
3. Where *overall examples* of stylistic excellence were offered, male writers predominated to the extent of 98% (67 to 1), while women's

writing was more likely to be used for specific examples of diction, metaphor, allusion, order, and emphasis (up to 12%). Men were presented as *the writers to emulate,* while women writers could illustrate useful techniques.

4. The same type of discrepancy appeared in linguistic matters. For examples of the control of tone, levels of usage, audience awareness, and spoken vs. written language, women writers were cited 12 to 17% of the time. But when it came to *linguistic principles* — the changing language, linguistic theory and history, or authoritarianism vs. relativism in language usage — there were 29 essays by men, while women writers were not represented at all.

5. Even more interesting and significant were variations in the appearance of women writers by subject matter. The general subject areas examined had to do with personal identity, the individual in relation to society, social responsibility, and moral choices.

   a. Personal identity: Small representation of women on self-understanding and self-fulfillment (6% or less), more on love and marriage (around 20%), but totally lacking in the area of higher education (75 essays by men, not one by a woman).

   b. Women writers had almost no voice on matters relating to the individual and society (freedom vs. conformity) or to social criticism, either generally or specifically, with the one notable exception of sociology and anthropology, where they were represented up to 25%.

   c. Again, however, on moral principles such as their view of religion, philosophy, and ethics, as well as on specific aspects such as capital punishment and abortion, women writers never exceeded 4%, and often were unrepresented. In the 21 texts studied, there were 37 essays on American government, democracy, or capital punishment by men, none by a woman, and 69 essays by men on religious or philosophical subjects, with only 3 by women.

6. This low representation of women writers studied by college freshmen is significant when correlated with other facts:

   a. Women are 51% of the society these freshmen are preparing to enter within a few years. A large percentage — supposedly up to half — of freshman classes are themselves women.

   b. According to the 1970 Report of the MLA Commission on the Status of Women in the Profession, "about half the Instructors and Lecturers in our profession are women," and it is well known that freshman English classes are most often taught by Instructors — thus, very often, by women.

   c. Despite these facts, of all the reading and study material available for stylistic imitation, inspiration, and stimulation of ideas, *over 90% is prepared and written by men.*

These were the findings of my first survey, which was admittedly too inadequate to be considered conclusive. I therefore greatly expanded its scope, and also somewhat streamlined it, by gathering information directly from the catalogs of the more prominent publishing companies. I examined both the introductory material and the tables of contents of 112 textbooks, comprising from one to fifteen separate essay anthologies issued by each publisher between 1960 and 1971. Although this is not strictly a "random sample," the attempt was made to include and to study *all* recent and relevant data that were available.

In the 112 anthologies studied, there were 5,795 essays by men, 472 by women. The percentage of men writers was thus 92.47%, of women writers, 7.53%. This is very close to the original study of the 21 texts, where the percentage of women came out to be approximately 7%. Ten publishers' texts ran below this average: $1\frac{1}{2}$ to $6\frac{1}{2}$%. Eight publishers' texts were above the average: $8\frac{1}{2}$ to 23%. One short paperback of ten essays (*Modes of Argument*, Bobbs-Merrill) included three (33%) by women, but this was not a typical standard text. As a matter of fact, five of the others in that series contained no essays written by women.

When the year of publication was correlated with the percentages of women writers, the results varied erratically. One textbook each from 1960, 1961, and 1962 showed the percentage of women to be 4%, 0 (35 male writers), and 9% respectively. From that time through 1971 women writers were represented as follows: 1963, under 4%; 1964, under 6%; 1965, 7%; 1966, $7\frac{1}{2}$%; 1967, below 6%; 1968, 7%; 1969, a drop to $5\frac{1}{2}$%; 1970, back up to 8%; and in 1971, $8\frac{1}{2}$%.

Nearly half of the textbooks in the survey were published in 1970 and 1971, at which time the percentage of women contributors took a distinct jump of 3%. The low representation of women writers in 1969 had coincided with the sudden upsurge of concern for sexual equality, and, since there is a recognized gap of about two years between the initiation of new ideas and trends and the appearance of them in book form, it took that long for publishers to "hear" and begin to reflect what women's liberation was saying.

Thus these figures may represent an advance of a sort, but such "progress" is scarcely impressive. Of the 36 textbooks published in 1971, it was the one done by students (*Student Voices/One*, Random House) that contained the highest percentage of women writers (23%). But while nine of the group included 15% or more women contributors, twelve accepted only 6% or fewer, and *five of these 36 college textbooks, published in 1971, contained not one piece by a woman writer.*

Unfortunately, it was not possible to consider student writers as a category, since names were generally omitted from student essays, when used. However, the ratio of men to women as *editors* was determined, with a view to discovering what correlation there might be between the number of women writers appearing in texts where a woman was one of the editors.

The findings here were interesting, and often disquieting. The ratio of men to women editors was 157 to 35; 17½% were women. Where publishers put out texts in which at least one editor was a woman, the representation of women writers averaged 8.6%, only a little higher than those same publishers' *overall* average of 7.4%. Six of those with a woman editor ran slightly higher than their publishers' averages, while five ran *lower*—and four of these ran below 6%, or lower than the *general* average.

In this group, the earliest anthology having a woman editor was 1964 (3% women writers), while one in 1966 had fewer than 5% women writers. However, two Bobbs-Merrill texts of 1965 and 1966 featured, respectively, 10% and 13% women writers. The remaining texts partially or wholly edited by women have appeared from 1968 on, although their inclusion of women as writers has not significantly increased so far. All this may reflect the familiar paradox of heightened consciousness held in check by long-instilled timidity, along with hypersensitive care that established codes may not be "changed too fast."

Several observations, some positive and some negative, might be noted with respect to the policies manifested by some of the editors. It is disappointing to find one of Bobbs-Merrill's short paperbacks on *Autobiography* edited by a woman but comprising no women writers. Oddly enough, one of the *subjects* is a woman (Colette), but her "autobiography" is handled here by a man, Vladimir Nabokov (as though she were unable to speak for herself). We take note also of a Glencoe (now Macmillan) textbook, *Logic, Style, and Arrangement*, edited by the male Dean of Instruction at Mississippi State College for Women, with fewer than 5% of the authors themselves women.

Harcourt Brace Jovanovich covers a variety of extremes in their textbook representation of women writers, from the *Playboy College Reader* (with no women, either as editors or writers) to two noteworthy books dealing entirely with women: Elaine Showalter's *Women's Liberation and Literature* and Mary Ellman's *Thinking About Women*. It may be significant, however, that in their 1971 *Cosmos Reader*, containing 6 women writers and 103 men, the section where women are best represented (3 women, 9 men) is called "Outsiders."

Random House likewise went to disconcerting extremes. In 1971 appeared, along with *Student Voices/One* (23% women writers), a text edited by Ray Kytle, Jr., entitled *Confrontations: Issues of the 70's*. Although these "issues" deal with higher education, the "new ethics," racial problems, the inner city, crime in America, ecology, and the world community, the only one relating to women is an essay on abortion, whose writer is anonymous. The pouting, bare-breasted coed pictured on the cover indicates plainly enough the editor's concept of the status of women. Another Kytle production in 1971, described by the publisher as "witty and contemporary," features twenty pages of the boring and brainless conversations of a "pretty, blond-haired, sexy freshman" named Yvonne, whose incredible naivete is patronized by both her instructor and her boyfriend. (We understand now that this text has been earmarked for early revision.)

Little imaginative effort seems to have been exerted to search out and include a variety of women writers. Where textbooks contain no more than three or four women writers, or even as many as eight or nine, certain prominent names appear again and again: Margaret Mead, Rachel Carson, Marya Mannes, Susan Sontag, Virginia Woolf, Mary McCarthy, Gertrude Stein, Diana Trilling, Agnes Repplier, Susanne Langer, Ruth Benedict, and Elizabeth Hardwick.

A larger assortment, but still with many repeats, turns up wherever poetry and fiction are included among the essays: Eudora Welty, Flannery O'Connor, Katherine Mansfield, Sylvia Plath, Phyllis McGinley, Katherine Anne Porter, Emily Dickinson, Willa Cather, and Anne Sexton. However, it is refreshing to see occasionally such names as Ann Birstein, Gertrude Samuels, Marlene Dixon, Elizabeth Cady Stanton, Mary Wollstonecraft, Ayn Rand, Eleanor Roosevelt, Karen Horney, Shana Alexander, and Pauline Fredericks.

The discrepancies between what some publishers claim for their collections and what is actually offered can be shown by a few sample quotations culled at random from the catalogs' introductory material:

D. C. Heath's *Toward the New America* (1970) is called a collection of pieces that "depict America whirling toward the future." In this text, America whirls right past the women's liberation movement and includes seven essays on "eros" and two on women, *all by men.*

Holt, Rinehart and Winston calls *Toward Liberal Education* (5th edition, 1967) "one of the most successful collections ever published." The proportion of its writers: 93 men to 3 women, or 3%. "Liberal?" In *The Rhetoric of No* (1969) we are told that each article was carefully chosen to relate to issues "that students are involved in outside the classroom." No issues relative to women were mentioned, and although two of the three editors were women, over 95% of the writers were men.

The Harcourt Brace Jovanovich text, *Crisis: A Contemporary Reader* (1971), supposedly "presents a compelling and realistic portrait of an America confronted by conflict and dissent" — but there is no woman's voice among the 32 men writers to express either her conflicts or her dissent.

For Houghton Mifflin's duo of textbooks (1968), *The American Experience* and *The American Culture,* it is claimed that "taken together, the books provide a definitive insight into American civilization as interpreted through social, familial and religious trends." With a ratio of 66 to 2, or under 3% women writers, the insight into 51% of America's population is scarcely definitive.

Odyssey's *The Questing Mind* (1971) is called "an introduction to some of the major persons and ideas of Western Civilization." They are all determined for us by the 30 men writers—no women. Scott, Foresman's *Contemporary Issues* claims that "relevance, relation, and immediacy underlie the selection of readings"—only two of which are by women (Cecilia Holland and Joan Baez) to 48 men.

Prentice-Hall has put out *The Current Voice* in two editions. The earlier one's readings reflect the "most vital and mature voices of our generation" (45 men, 1 woman who is a co-author, or 2%). The 1971 edition's writings "all illustrate something of the mode of the most vital literature of this century" (39 to 2, under 5% women). Young college women with a talent for writing could hardly fail to get the message that there must be something *less* "vital" and "mature" about women's writing.

Worlds In the Making was designed "to challenge the student to take hold of his own life, to become aware of his own values, to find new meanings in the changing present." This recent anthology included 84 men and 3 women writers, or under 3½% who would be able to present *women's* values and "new meanings," or attempt to clarify their ambiguous role at a time when one of the major problems of college women is their search for identity.

There are many more such examples, but these are typical.

In summary: In this survey, 112 freshman English textbooks from 18 different publishers were studied to ascertain the percentage of women writers. Their publication dates ranged from 1960 to 1971, with nearly half from 1970 and 1971. It was found that, for the whole decade, 92.47% of the writers were men, while 7.53% were women. The percentage increased slightly in 1970 and 1971 to 8% and 8½% respectively. Where at least one of the editors was a woman, representation of women writers was slightly higher here than for their publishers as a group (8½% where women were editors, and under 7½% for their publishers' overall average).

It is evident that women, as writers, are being overshadowed and overlooked by men in the area of freshman English readings designed to stimulate college students to think, to discuss, to evaluate, and to write their open, honest views on the issues of our time. Those of us who are in a position to exert active pressure on publishers can try to place our book orders with those companies and select those texts that have revealed greater awareness in the matter, and let the publishers know the reason for our choices. Conversely, we can reduce or cancel orders where publishers' consciousness of women's issues is low. We can also prepare texts for college students ourselves that will truly represent our bi-sexual society and its manifold problems.

We *all* should take note of areas in which there has been less writing by women, and consider these as invitations and challenges to our own creativity. This survey of publishers has indicated some heightened sensitivity and interest on their part. We can therefore expect an increasingly favorable reception toward women as writers and editors in the immediate future.

College freshman textbooks are not only a prime factor in sharpening the awareness of young men and women of the problems of sexual stereotyping; they can promote the image of woman as writer and intellectual, and give her the techniques for making this image a reality.

FIVE | Pride and Prejudice

FRANKLIN DUCHENEAUX

The American Indian: Beyond the Stereotypes

For the greater portion of the white population in this country, the image of the American Indian has been tragically out of focus. Nineteenth-century distortions ranging from the "noble savage" to "dirty redskins" have assumed contemporary counterparts in the sophisticated, intellectual tribal leader on the one hand and the Red Power militant on the other. Missing from all these pictures is an accurate representation of the human beings beyond the stereotypes. In this selection, Franklin Ducheneaux attempts to offset these images and to enable the reader to see for himself the status and situation of descendants of the original native Americans.

Look for the author's use of the first person point of view to lay out explicitly the purpose and structure of his article.

(1) In the nineteenth century, the white man's image of the American Indian was either that of the noble savage or the bloodthirsty, dirty redskin. The Indian in the first image could not open his mouth without having gems of great wisdom and profound philosophy pouring out in the most poetical, oratorical style. The second Indian was not happy unless he was dripping with the blood of a white man and holding aloft a scalp of flowing blond hair. Neither of these two extreme images was accurate.

(2) In the twentieth century, two different images have developed in the minds of white Americans. In one — the movie/TV image — the Indian is still pictured as the mighty warrior in majestic headdress,

"The American Indian: Beyond the Stereotypes" by Franklin Ducheneaux. From *Today's Education*, May 1973. Reprinted by permission of the National Education Association and the author.

attacking the wagon train or making fervent love to a dusky young Indian maiden. In the other, he is the sullen, broken spirit who drinks cheap wine and lives on the handouts of a sometimes benign, sometimes malicious federal government. These images are also inaccurate.

(3) While the foregoing images still flavor white America's picture of the Indian to some extent, two new images have arisen in recent years. One is that of the sophisticated, intellectual tribal leader who wears tailor-made suits and carries an attaché case. The other is that of the militant Indian; the Red Power publicity seeker, burning buildings, taking hostages, and desperately seeking identification with Crazy Horse and Sitting Bull—the Wounded Knee image of 1973. While these new images have a basis in fact, neither truly represents most American Indians.

(4) This article will attempt to give the reader a more accurate picture of the Indian—the native American. Nevertheless, it will be necessarily inadequate, for Indians, like all other creatures on this earth, differ—in their physical appearance and spiritual outlook, in their ambitions and desires, in their prejudices and fears.

(5) I will not discuss the Indians living in the urban areas, who were either born there or who went there from the reservations — either voluntarily or because insensitive federal Indian policies forced them to. I do not exclude them because they are not Indian. They are. I do not exclude them because they do not suffer many of the same social and cultural problems of the reservation Indian. They do, often to a more severe degree. I exclude them here because their surrounding environment is primarily non-Indian, whereas the reservation Indian lives in an Indian environment that is foreign to the adjacent non-Indian community. So the following discussion must be taken in the context of the Indian living on the reservation or near enough to be routinely affected by the problems and programs of the reservation.

(6) Indians are citizens of the United States and of the states in which they reside. Stating this may seem unnecessary, but the contrary idea with all of its implications still lingers in many minds. Most Indians became citizens by some act of Congress, particularly a 1924 act that made citizens of all noncitizen Indians then residing within the United States.

(7) Most Indians alive today are considered citizens by birth. Except for certain specific exceptions, they are entitled to all the privileges and subject to all the duties of citizenship.

(8) The Indian is entitled to the same services and benefits of the federal government and of his state of residence as other citizens *because* of his status as a citizen. He is entitled to all the protection

of the laws of the United States and of the states. He is entitled to vote in all general and local elections, to serve on juries, and to avail himself of the judiciary machinery to secure his rights and redress of grievances. He is subject to military conscription. Indeed, in the wars of this nation, the voluntary enlistment of Indians and their bravery have been outstanding.

(9) Like other citizens, Indians are subject to all the federal, state, and local taxes — except that property held in trust for them by the United States, income derived from that property, and transactions taking place on that property are tax exempt.

(10) Indians living in a trust relationship (i.e., owning an interest in trust property) have certain restrictions placed upon their use of that property to which other citizens are not subject. Except in tribal relations and when they are on the reservation, Indians are subject to all the criminal and civil laws of the federal, state, and local governments. Other, less important exceptions will not be discussed here.

(11) A trustee relationship exists between the United States and those Indian tribes recognized by the United States. It has been likened to the relationship that exists between a guardian and ward. However, it is *not* a guardian/ward relationship, although it has elements of that relationship.

(12) The trust relationship is firmly based on the Constitution of the United States (implemented by a series of treaties and statutes), which gives Congress the power to regulate commerce with the Indian tribes.

(13) The trust is most evident with respect to the land tenure on the reservations and the implications of tenure. Most of the land and related resources on an Indian reservation are held in trust by the United States for the beneficial use of the Indian tribe or individual. The Indian cannot sell such land or resource without the consent of the United States, and to some extent, the United States restricts other beneficial uses, such as leasing. Imposed upon the United States is a duty to protect these resources against the improvidence of the Indian and against the encroachment or avarice of outside interests.

(14) Prior to the advent of the non-Indian on this continent, the Indian tribes were true sovereign nations. The European colonial powers, the colonies, and the United States recognized and dealt with them as such. However, primarily because of the superior force of arms implementing the so-called *manifest destiny* of the United States, there began a slow but increasing erosion and limitation of tribal sovereignty. To paraphrase the Supreme Court, the United States extended its dominion over this continent by the might of the

sword, and the right of conquest gives a title that the courts of the conqueror cannot deny.

(15) Implied in the foregoing paragraph is this basic tenet of Indian law: The right of might has given the United States power to limit or abolish tribal sovereignty and self-government; but except as so expressly limited or abolished, Indian tribes retain their inherent right to tribal sovereignty and self-government. The corollary of this tenet is that those sovereign rights of self-government are not grants of rights from the United States but a retention of rights inherent in the Indian tribes.

(16) Within the boundaries of the Indian reservations, tribal government exists today. In many respects, these governments resemble those found in the countries and municipalities of this nation. Most tribal governments have legislative, executive, and judicial machinery, many based on the Anglo-Saxon model. Members of the tribes elect representatives by secret ballot. Except as limited by the United States, Indian governments exercise criminal jurisdiction over the conduct of their members. They regulate the internal affairs of their members, and, except as limited by the United States, control the use and disposition of property within their jurisdiction.

(17) Tribal governments have the power to impose taxes and license activity. In most respects, their powers are independent of the states and surrounding local communities and governments. Such normal governmental services as road construction and maintenance, education, welfare and social services are carried on and funded by the federal government simply because the tribes lack funds and resources. In short, the tribes have all the sovereignty and rights of self-government that have not been expressly limited by the United States.

(18) Any discussion of the "average" Indian will have inconsistencies because there is no such individual. However, I will attempt to portray one.

(19) The many federal agencies involved in Indian affairs have already drawn a statistical profile of the average Indian. Among other things, the profile depicts a man or a woman who has a shorter-than-average life-span, a lower-than-average income level, a greater-than-average suicide level, a greater-than-average alcoholism rate, and so on, ad infinitum et ad nauseam.

(20) Statistically, this profile is accurate. But a better picture can be inferred from looking at what the Indian wants, which is not too different from what you want. He wants a decent house and a warm bed. He wants peace and quiet in his home and law and order in his neighborhood. He wants a good education and a healthy body. He

wants the opportunity to work and the opportunity to relax. He wants most of what the non-Indian wants and has. But he refuses to accept some of the things the outside world has attempted to impose on him and refuses to relinquish certain of his rights as an Indian that the outside world has attempted to wrest from him. Above all, he wants to remain Indian. He does not want to remain poor because he chooses to remain Indian, but he does not want to sacrifice the Indian life in order to secure the good life.

(21) There are those Indians who want to reject all that is non-Indian and seek to rediscover and return to the "old ways." This is a want born of frustration, hatred, and fear of the non-Indian world, feelings which most Indians are heir to with good cause. In them lies the germ of Indian militancy and violence.

(22) There are those who want to throw off all that is Indian and merge facelessly into the non-Indian society. This is a want born of prejudice and discrimination, which most Indians have experienced. But it is my judgment that the "average" Indian is proud of his heritage and cultural past and is unwilling to relinquish his rights and identity as an Indian. Neither, however, is he tied to the past and willing to permit the dead past to bury a secure, contented future for himself and his children in this world he never made.

(23) During the greater part of his everyday existence, the "average" Indian is little different from his non-Indian neighbor in the same locality. A severe drought will affect the Indian farmer or rancher at least as disastrously as the non-Indian. The prospect of a draft call has as much meaning to the Indian as to the non-Indian youth. Local roads that are impassable during the winter are as impassable to the Indian as to the non-Indian. The Indian, though he lives in a community apart—the reservation—cannot help but be affected by the conditions, environment, problems, and progress of the surrounding non-Indian community.

(24) Still, a substantial, firm core of the Indian's existence is almost foreign to his non-Indian neighbor. It is the source of part of his weaknesses as well as the greater part of his strength.

(25) Where rural poverty exists, it bears down harder on the reservations. There, the general ills that affect the larger society are magnified and amplified. The core of Indian existence is affected by forces and influences in a manner or degree unknown to the non-Indian.

(26) Because of the trust relationship, he is afforded protections and subjected to restrictions not current in the non-Indian world. His relationship with his tribe and tribal self-government give him a duality of citizenship which the Supreme Court has found to be not inconsistent with the Constitution and laws of the United States. He has a

unique claim upon the United States above that of other citizens. His cultural background, heritage, and value system in many cases, are at odds with the non-Indian, Anglo-Saxon society of America.

(27) This article is not meant to be a definitive, authoritative description of the American Indian, his status and problems. It is offered rather as an expression of opinion by an Indian who has had some contact with most aspects of Indian life. I hope it will erase from readers' minds the stereotyped images of the Indian that have grown up over the years and place in their minds a caveat against current public mass media images that are being offered.

(28) Finally, for those readers who are or who may become involved in some fashion in Indian affairs, it is hoped that this overview will encourage them to inform themselves further, in general and in particular, on Indian issues before making snap judgments based on surface knowledge.

QUESTIONS AND EXERCISES

VOCABULARY
1. sophisticated (*paragraph* 3)
2. tenure (13)
3. improvidence (13)
4. encroachment (13)
5. avarice (13)
6. sovereign (14)
7. *manifest destiny* (14)
8. ad infinitum (19)
9. ad nauseam (19)
10. caveat (27)

LANGUAGE AND RHETORIC
1. Does this selection gain or lose in effectiveness through its use of the first person? Does the author's reference to the fact that he is an Indian (paragraph 27) add greater authority to the article? Why or why not?
2. The author states his purposes and limitations quite explicitly in paragraphs 4, 5, 18, 27, and 28. Do these explicit statements strengthen or weaken the article? Support your answer.
3. The author uses various kinds of definition to develop his purpose. Point out several examples of the method, and comment on their function.
4. This article may be divided into four sections consisting of paragraphs 1–5, 6–17, 18–26, and 27–28. Examine each of these sections and explain how they relate to one another.
5. Do you feel that after reading this article you have a more accurate picture of the American Indian? If you were writing a comparable article, would you add or omit any material?

DISCUSSION AND WRITING
1. Does this article alter in any way your previous impression of the American Indian? Support your answer.

2. Should Indians join the "white community" if they have the opportunity, or should they attempt to preserve their native ways through tribal living?
3. If, in your recent reading or viewing experiences, you have encountered any of the stereotypes of the Indian depicted in the first three paragraphs of this article, explain how those stereotypes were used and what effect they had on you.
4. What means would you recommend to overcome or break down stereotypes such as those noted in the opening paragraphs? Develop an essay based on one of those means.
5. Write an essay in which you attempt to define what you believe an "average" or "typical" American to be.

ROY BONGARTZ
The Chicano Rebellion

The Frito bandito is dead—a victim of the Chicano rebellion, and the Mexican Americans who comprise this new movement gladly accept full responsibility for the end of the familiar Mexican stereotype, asleep beneath his sombrero. Stimulated by the black people's drive for equality and justice, the civil rights movement in this country has expanded to embrace other minority groups, among them Mexican Americans, who form a substantial segment of our population. As Roy Bongartz clearly shows, the Chicano rebellion is a notable example of how self-awareness, education, and organization can help the victims of prejudice to become proud citizens.

In examining the various aspects of the development of this rebellion, the author is, in effect, actually defining the Chicano movement itself.

(1) Now it's the Mexican Americans—Chicanos, they are called in California—who are appearing on the scene of protest, with a self-evaluation that breaks radically away from the old, degrading stereotype of fatalistic loafer asleep under a sombrero. These young Chicanos are wide-awake, and when something happens, they intend to be the ones who make it happen. Militant Chicano student organizations are active throughout California, not only in colleges but in high schools as well, and they are growing in the rest of the Southwest: the Mexican-American Student Association, United Mexican-American Students, Mexican-American Student Confederation. They all make a central demand for courses in Mexican-American studies,

"The Chicano Rebellion" by Roy Bongartz. From *The Nation,* March 13, 1969. By permission of *The Nation.*

such as are now available at San Francisco State College, Sacramento State College, California State College in Los Angeles, San Fernando Valley College and the University of California at Berkeley.

(2) Teaching the course at Berkeley is Octavio I. Romano, an anthropologist, born in Mexico and raised in California, who wants to destroy the myth of the passive Mexican. He points out that Mexican Americans have been the main figures in the labor movement in the Southwest, that they published the first Western underground newspapers, that they have pushed through bilingual education in two states, that they clinched the victory for John F. Kennedy, that they have a strong influence on the Spanish language that extends into Mexico itself, even that they originated driftwood sculpture.

(3) Romano's most energetic attacks are aimed at sociologists who are preserving stale anti-Mexican prejudices in the academic jargon of scholarly works. In place of "the Mexican is lazy," the academic (in this case Celia Heller) writes: "The combination of stress on work and rational use of time forms little or no part of the Mexican-American socialization process." Instead of saying that you can't tell them apart, she writes: "They exhibit a marked lack of internal differentiation." Referring to this and other writers of Chicano studies, including William Madsen, Ruth Tuck, Lyle Saunders, Florence Kluckhohn, Fred L. Strodbeck, Julian Samora and Richard Lamanna, Romano says: "Contemporary social scientists [are] busily perpetuating the Mexican-American War. These opinions were, and are, pernicious, vicious, misleading, degrading and brainwashing."

(4) Romano has some new ideas on how to give a college course. For one, students will think up a subject and assign it as a term paper to the instructor, then grade the paper and discuss it in class. Students' own papers must be presented in three versions—one in academic style, one in a "journal" style for possible publication in a Chicano review, and the last a newspaper version to be submitted to a local paper. Students writing the papers for publication will work directly with the editors. Members of the course may take a third of class time to address their colleagues on any relevant subject. It is Romano's hope that by using students' own ideas and writings the course may improve and grow in the future. Sacramento State is already planning a four-year program leading to a B.A. in Mexican-American studies.

(5) But the Mexican Americans at Berkeley have not confined themselves to the classroom. A number of Romano's students are among the hundred-odd members of a student group called Quinto Sol, some of whom two years ago marched in upon hearings of the U.S. Civil Rights Commission in San Francisco to protest the exclusion of Mexican Americans from a program designed to recruit college stu-

dents from minority groups. They also attacked the commission for
having but one Mexican American on its staff of 350, yelling "Practice
what you preach!" at commission members until police threw them
out. Quinto Sol members invaded and occupied the office of the
university president at Berkeley to protest the purchase of California
grapes by the university cafeteria — student groups all solidly support the nation-wide grape boycott led by César Chavez and the
United Farm Workers. The Chicanos were forcibly removed from the
office and eleven of them were jailed.

(6) Says one Quinto Sol leader, Nick Vaca, 24, a graduate student
and an editor of a sharp new quarterly review called *El Grito* (The
Cry): "The message our group wants to give is that the Mexican American is not docile. That idea of the 'sleeping giant' is an insult — it's
that same old peon taking his siesta under his hat. Mexican Americans
are not an *emerging* people. We're already here!" Bill Vega, 24, and
John Carrillo, 27, who, along with Professor Romano, also help edit the
review, agree that the Chicano is here: but they add ruefully that he
is here in very few numbers at Berkeley — some 200 out of an enrollment of 25,000. Though they do not want to deny the Negro *his*
chance, they have been forced to vie with him for benefits from the
Educational Opportunity Program, whereby colleges recruit a certain
number of minority students who cannot satisfy the regular academic
entrance requirements and lack the money for college. Even though
there are nearly twice as many Mexican Americans as Negroes in
California, blacks in the Berkeley Opportunity Program outnumber
Chicanos 9 to 1. The average Chicano has an 8th-grade education;
the average Negro has ten and a half years of school (Anglos, 12.1
years) in California. Chicanos earn less money than Negroes; that is,
less than anybody in the state.

(7) A little more than two years ago a conference was held in
Berkeley to enable Mexican-American high school students from the
Bay area who were interested in college to meet counselors from all
the colleges in the state; the idea was to help them pick a school and
find out how to go about getting admitted. Nearly 2,000 Chicanos
applied to attend the conference, which had to be limited to 600 from
lack of space. Two counselors showed up, only Mills College and
Contra Costa bothering to send anybody. "We're facing a monu-
mental indifference to the Mexican American," says Romano. "And
they blame the kid in the *barrio* for being 'non-goal-oriented.'"

(8) In the continuous political free-for-all at Sather Gate, Berkeley
students wearing great Walt Disney pig heads rush a group of sign
carriers in a noontime skit lampooning police attacks on militants
over at San Francisco State. But Chicanos and their problems are
invisible. *El Grito* is aware that Berkeley students are supposed to

be radicals, but notes that they give Chicanos very little support. They don't back the grape boycott; they don't demand increased Chicano student enrollment. The editors believe that the Anglos are moved by self-interest and that the Mexican-American cause doesn't fit the pattern.

(9) Chicanos have only a toehold at Berkeley, but they are more numerous at some other colleges. At San José City College, for example, the Mexican-American Student Confederation (MASC) recently organized a Mexican Week for both students and townspeople. It provided an art show, film festival, discussions, a show of regional Mexican clothing, a *charreado* (football match), and a horse show put on by Los Charros de la Plata Aspada (Silver Spurs). The climax was a talk by an old Mexican revolutionary who had fought with Pancho Villa and Zapata. Says one MASC member, Manuel Madrid, 23, "Our main goal is to orient the Chicano to *think* Chicano so as to achieve equal status with other groups, not to emulate the Anglo. A decade ago, the idea was that the Mexican American wanted to be totally assimilated into the American culture. But not now."

(10) A Mexican-American counselor named Angelo Atondo is on the scene at San José City College as a direct result of Chicano student agitation. "The attitudes of Mexican Americans toward themselves has completely changed since I graduated from college in 1956," he says. "We never spoke Spanish. We would have been stared at. There was a silent taboo against Spanish." He explains that San José is an "open door" college, with a two-year program that can lead to continued studies at one of the state colleges or can give a diploma in a wide variety of vocational fields, mostly technical. "A student can get in here even if he had straight Ds in high school," says Atondo. "We salvage many students that way."

(11) One student who dropped out of high school is Lee Polanco, now 31, a qualified electrician who bitterly recalls answering a help-wanted ad by telephone, being invited for an interview, and then, because he's a Chicano, being greeted with: "What do *you* want? Get out of here!" Polanco, director of campus activities in MASC, is studying social sciences. "We found that the colleges were paying attention to the blacks because they were militant, so we started to get as militant as the blacks," he says. His friend Manuel Madrid adds, "I hope we don't have to get as militant as the blacks. But if we have to, we will."

(12) Polanco points out that of the 12,000 students at San José, some 1,200 are Mexican American, while 200 are black. But four courses are offered in black studies, and only one in a Mexican-American subject. Naturally the Chicanos want to adjust that balance.

"We're being ignored," says Madrid, "but we want to work with the blacks."

(13) Besides getting a counselor assigned to the college, the Chicanos succeeded in having a committee from their group screen the professor who teaches the one Mexican culture course; they even got some money from the administration for their Mexican Week. In addition to demanding more Chicano-oriented courses, including one in Spanish for the Spanish-speaking, they want free buses to town and back. Going beyond their own issues, they have held a vigil of sympathy for students at Mexico City who were killed or injured there by troops last year.

(14) Manuel Madrid also dropped out of high school from discouragement. "The white kids knew you weren't like them. Talking Spanish was a 'no-no.' It gave us an inferiority complex." One of the most encouraging things about Madrid and other dropouts now in college is their concern for the young coming up behind them. They go out to the high schools to talk with Chicano students and encourage them to stay in school, and they intend to have MASC make this a part of its official program. Madrid, who may well realize that he's on his way, still says, "Let's get a little uncomfortable about our friends back there."

(15) But these days there is much less apathy among the friends back in high school. Thirteen East Los Angeles Chicanos were arrested last May for organizing a boycott of their schools to protest intolerable conditions. In Livingston, fifty-three Chicanos skipped their high school classes on Mexican Independence Day, demanding it be made an official holiday. They also wanted the schools to hire Mexican teachers and counselors, and to offer courses in Mexican and black history. They wanted the double lunch periods ended—white kids at the first sitting; black and brown at the second. Police picked up truants, although at harvest time, when the big local farms need extra help, the compulsory attendance law is ignored.

(16) At Fremont High School, in Oakland, students demonstrated for weeks to demand a Chicano student union, and Mexican-American entertainment and speakers at assemblies. A Chicano group called Los Carnales at Redwood High in Visalia made twenty-one demands on the principal, including Mexican food in the cafeteria, mandatory attendance by all teachers at classes in black and Mexican culture, and a rule to keep police, probation and parole officers off the school grounds.

(17) Though nothing enrages the young Chicanos more than to be called "emerging," the facts are not only that their political awareness (like that of all young people) has become greatly sharpened of late

but also that their presence as an intellectual force is for the first time establishing itself. *Bronze,* a new militant paper at San José, deals with problems that haunt Mexican Americans. Writes Luis Valdez: "This is a society largely hostile to our cultural values. There is no poetry about the United States. No depth, no faith, no allowance for human contrariness. No soul, no *mariachi,* no chili sauce, no *pulque,* no mysticism, no *chingaderas.*" Valdez sees a gloomy future for Mexican Americans who lose their identity in the cities: "They have solved their Mexican contradictions with a pungent dose of Americanism, and are more concerned with status, money and bad breath than with their ultimate destiny." But he does not despair altogether. "There will always be *raza* [the race, the people] in this country. There are millions more where we came from." Manuel Madrid says that the 50,000 immigrants who arrive every year from Mexico "give us all a shot in the arm."

(18) Another student describes the strains of holding to a clear identity: "Sometimes you have to go to a Mexican show or a Mexican bar and be by yourself, to remind yourself of what you are. And then you . . . begin to see that you are becoming something that you are not and you know it. I had to relearn how it is to be a Mexican and what it is like for so many Mexicans to be poor in San José. *Hijo,* I was so dumb that I used to be proud to have Mexicans die in the war. I used to be so dumb that I used to think in college how beautiful it would be to pick *fruta* again and watch *la raza* work against the rays of the sun, that is how stupid I used to be."

(19) A number of newspapers have formed the Chicano Press Association, which includes *El Malcriado* in Delano, *La Raza, Carta Editorial* and *Inside Eastside* in Los Angeles, *El Gallo* in Denver, *El Papel* in Albuquerque, *Inferno* in San Antonio and *Compass* in Houston. A note in *El Grito* says they are all "very relevant to Mexican Americans, Spanish Americans, Chicanos, Hispanos, Spanish-Speaking Latin Americans, Mexican-Latin Spanish Speakers, greasers, spics and bandits." (One of *El Grito's* favorite targets is the way some *Tío Tomás* Mexicans try to dissociate themselves from *la raza* by using fancy group names: "a vacuous ethnic taxonomy," *El Grito* calls it.

(20) By far the most impressive evidence of intellectual liveliness among Chicano students is to be found in the pages of *El Grito,* named for the famous "cry" of the Mexican Revolution. It grew out of publication by Quinto Sol, the Berkeley student group, of articles attacking social scientists; these were called The Mexican-American Liberation Papers, and were priced at $2 for students, $15 for federal agencies, $500 for governors of states and $15,000 for the President of the United States. *El Grito* first appeared in the fall of 1967, after the

editors had each contributed $50 to $100 to pay the printing bill; it has been solvent ever since. The journal threatens its readers: "Subscribe now, or La Llorona will get you" (she's the witch who grabs bad Mexican children). The journal has been much helped financially by the fact that several of the Mexican-American college courses use it—900 copies, for example, go to San José State. But at Berkeley itself enthusiasm remains low; a mailing of 300 fliers brought in but one subscription. "Publishing in Berkeley is a real hang-up," the editors say.

(21) The editors want to explore relationships between Chicanos and Mexico. They believe they can see philosophies of life that are very different here and in Mexico. They say the United States has a nationalistic ideology that develops "self-interest groups through a combination of political and religious affiliation." The Mexican idea, in their view, is much broader—people tackling moral problems as world-wide concerns, not just Mexican. The editors have published some work, and want to carry more, from the Mexican *nueva ola*—new wave—currently being produced by a café clique in Guadalajara.

(22) Chicanos accuse both Jews and Negroes of nationalism. Writes Nick Vaca, "After viewing the effects of the nationalistic fervor in Israel, it is not surprising to note that it has been the Jewish merchant who has exploited and continues to exploit Negroes in the ghettos. . . ." Vaca is no more friendly toward the black, who, he writes, "is systematically 'putting down' his 'brown brother.'" The Chicanos were especially angered by a black teacher's remark: "While blacks were out protesting, Mexican Americans were sitting at home before their television sets, eating beans," Chicanos have much warmer feelings toward the smaller ethnic groups—American Indians, Filipinos, Hawaiians, Samoans and Koreans—and include them in demands for a fair share of educational opportunity.

(23) A more encouraging aspect of *El Grito's* point of view is its concern about aspects of American society that affect everybody. For example, they would like to do away with commercials in television and radio news broadcasts: "When a people have to wait for news of the world, for news of their country, and even of their own community, while mascara is peddled, then that people have lost the right to be called civilized." The editors would also put an end to Congressional hearings on local social problems: "It seems absurd, as we do today, to elect a man to Washington only to have him return to find out what problems exist. . . . People are electing representatives who do not know what is going on, and who then, at taxpayers' expense, must return in order to find out." *El Grito* also favors having the length of military service determined by income, and in wartime would draft industry, so that workers and management receive soldiers' pay.

(24) The journal runs thoroughgoing pieces on the use of Mexican national workers in the border areas, which *El Grito* calls the Mexican-Dixon line, and one of its contributors has offered the pertinent suggestion that U.S. aid to Mexico should go mainly to raising Mexican income, along the border, and "not, as is happening now, to lowering the American to present Mexican levels." A joint border authority would take over the economies of these international communities. The journal prints some of its material in Spanish, and derides such continuing tenets as that of Theodore Roosevelt, who said: "We have room for but one language here, and that is the English language, for we intend to see that the crucible turns our people out as Americans, of American nationality, and not as dwellers in a polyglot boarding house." The editors point out that many people "speak English somewhat colorfully," and suggest Lyndon Johnson, Mae West, Zsa Zsa Gabor, Wernher von Braun, Lawrence Welk, Everett Dirksen and George Jessel.

(25) Excellent graphic work, both drawings and photographs, enliven the pages of *El Grito*. The clash-and-blend flavor of Mexican-American life is expressed in a renewed tradition of bilingual poetry in which lines of Spanish alternate with lines of English. They do not translate each other, but move the thought along in the two tongues.

(26) Mexican Americans everywhere in the Southwest are feeling their oats, not only in traditional labor-movement unity but now also as students, writers, artists, teachers—as thinkers. A bilingual poem by John J. Martinez, a mathematics major at Berkeley, sounds the note:

> *brown power!*
> *qué?*
> *Together we must . . .*
> *Si!*
> *The problem . . .*
> *qué?*
> *It's your fault . . .*
> *who?*
> *I mean . . .*
> *qué?*
> *brown power!*
> *testing, testing, testing*
> *uno, dos, tres . . .*

QUESTIONS AND EXERCISES

VOCABULARY
1. stereotype (*paragraph* 1)
2. jargon (3)
3. perpetuating (3)
4. pernicious (3)
5. ruefully (6)
6. *barrio* (7)
7. lampooning (8)
8. assimilated (9)
9. pungent (17)
10. vacuous ethnic taxonomy (19)
11. clique (21)

LANGUAGE AND RHETORIC
1. How are paragraphs 19 through 25 related to the subject of this article? Does the expanded treatment of *El Grito* in these final paragraphs weaken the unity of the article? Support your answer.
2. If paragraph 6 were restructured, one section added to paragraph 5 and the remainder to form a paragraph by itself, where would you make the break? Would this change be desirable? Explain your answer.
3. What devices does the author employ to provide coherence within paragraph 20?
4. What is the controlling idea of paragraph 14? How is this paragraph developed?
5. In paragraph 23 the author says that "a more encouraging aspect of *El Grito's* point of view is its concern about aspects of American society that affect everybody." Explain the author's meaning here.
6. Reread the first sentences of paragraphs 4, 5, 9, 12, 14, and 17, and point out the specific devices of coherence employed in each sentence.

DISCUSSION AND WRITING
1. Do you believe the Chicanos are overly sensitive about the stereotype of the Mexican? Are stereotypes always degrading?
2. Is bilingual education for Chicanos a step forward or a step backward? On what do you base your answer?
3. How do you feel about Mexican-American studies, black studies, and Asian studies? Is there a genuine need for such programs? Is there any danger that these programs might lead to further segregation and discrimination?
4. In your opinion, do blacks in this country receive more than their share of attention? Have other minorities, in addition to Chicanos, been aided or handicapped by the black movement? Support your answers.
5. According to one student quoted in this article, Chicanos have rejected the idea of total assimilation into the Anglo culture. Is this a favorable or an unfavorable development? Defend your opinion. Should Chicanos cultivate their ties with Mexico, or should they concentrate on becoming better established and accepted in this country?
6. The author states that "Chicanos accuse both Jews and Negroes of nationalism." What grounds are there for this accusation? Could it also apply to Chicanos?

GILBERT MOORE

No One Has Ever Called Me a Nigger

In the struggle for democracy in America, the shrill extremes of competing forces often drown out the voices of reason—people like Gilbert
Moore, who shows in this personal statement what it is to be a black
man living in a white man's world. "No one has ever called me a nigger,"
says the author. But the anger, fear, and frustration that are the price
of being black finally amount to an imprisonment of the mind. This
quiet, unsensational detailing of his early years and the painfully
frank revelation of their emotional cost to the author may touch many
readers far more deeply than the fiery rhetoric of extremism.

Unlike the two preceding articles, this essay concentrates on the
personal experiences of the author. As you read, ask yourself what
effect this autobiographical approach has on the emotional impact of
the writing.

(1) No one has ever called me a nigger. I have never been bitten by a
rat. My mother has never been raped—either by a blue-eyed white
devil or a brown-eyed black one. I have come no closer to peddling
dope than did David Copperfield. I have never been spat on or chased
by German shepherds for trying to vote or sip coffee in places I had
no "right" to be in. All I can show for police brutality is a pile of
parking tickets in the glove compartment of my car. I have never been
civilly disobedient, nor have I picketed or boycotted or sat-in or layed-
in or written-in. I would like to see Accra and Nairobi, but no more
than I would like to see Copenhagen and Caracas. I have not the
faintest idea how to start a riot or quell one, or how to prevent people
from throwing garbage out of their kitchen windows. I don't know
why Joe Louis served honorably in the service and Cassius Clay
refuses to serve at all. I am not—nor do I care to be—a spokesman for
a cause or a decade or for 23 million people.

(2) We didn't have any rats but we *did* have mice—lots and lots of
mice. And for every mouse we had 26 roaches. At night these two
forces trooped about the floor of our Harlem kitchen in arrogant
hordes. We sprayed them and powdered them and poisoned them,

but to no avail. Instead of killing them, the chemicals seemed only to enhance their fertility.

(3) It did not occur to my parents that roaches might be blamed on the President of the United States. They did not consider it the mayor's fault that their children played marbles in the gutter and stickball in the middle of the street because there were no nearby playgrounds. The children seemed to be having fun, even though their bats were fashioned from old brooms and second base was in the immediate path of garbage trucks and white Cadillacs. No one called a rent strike when the banging on radiators failed to produce heat on cold January nights. No one complained because the hallways downstairs were lined with people wasting money they didn't have on the numbers. My mother never demeaned the police commissioner because her son had to hop over the heads of junkies on the way to school. All of these things — like flat tires and the common cold — were dismissed as "life." They were nothing at all to get worked up about.

(4) I am not sure how much race was then a part of my parents' lives; certainly it had little to do with mine. I was too busy with roller skates and snowball fights and five-cent bags of potato chips and catching high pop flies with one hand.

(5) My school, P.S. 186, was integrated — not because anyone insisted on it, but because there were still white families living in the neighborhood. Billy Roth, my fat and generous white friend, fell in love with Judy Metzl, the white girl with the long hair who sat in front of him in the fourth grade. Liking me as much as he did, loving her as much as he did, Billy thought it only reasonable that I should love her too. I agreed completely. Accordingly, *I* fell in love with Judy Metzl. Together we cared for her more than we did for Joe DiMaggio. Together we cared for her almost enough to bear the horror of her finding out.

(6) I remember disliking Harvey Anderson, who was handsome and Negro and good in arithmetic and an incredible show-off. And there was Henry Marshall, who was tall and blond and a constant bully. As adults *will* do, I assign each of my friends and acquaintances a race today; I didn't then.

(7) Surrounding nearby Stitt Junior High School were gangs with swashbuckling names, the Royalistics and the Sabers and the Buccaneers. They roamed streets and hallways with homemade guns and obedient switch blades, and with almost complete freedom to terrorize and declare war on each other. We occupied hell without really being a part of it. The insulation came largely from being West Indian.

(8) My father was born in Guyana, my mother in Jamaica. For much the same reason that millions once streamed from Europe to America,

they had left the Caribbean. They brought with them a specific set of rules: children do not play marbles or skip rope on Sundays; they do not smoke or drink until they are well over 21; they do not leave home until they are married and, having married, they *stay* married; they do not drop out of school until they are finished. Having attended school, they must do brilliantly and go on to become doctors, lawyers and professors.

(9) As I was to realize later, being West Indian involved a special kind of blackness. The West Indians in Harlem always seemed to have precious things that others around them wanted but usually didn't have: a family that somehow didn't crumble under oppression, their very own butcher shop in the midst of absentee landlordships and, most important, a faraway "home" to retreat to when America balked on its promise. For these sins, West Indians earned the title "Black Jews." For the "strange" way they spoke and behaved, West Indians were held up to mild but continuous ridicule. The only black men more patently ridiculous than they were Africans.

(10) My parents insisted on my being indoors shortly after the sun went down. And since the more exciting evils were available only at night, I missed out on samples of dollar-a-gallon wine, heroin and block fights in the moonlit schoolyard. I contented myself with daylight puffs of Pall Malls on the roof and, anyway, I really didn't want to go outside at night because it would mean missing my favorite radio shows: *The Lone Ranger, Superman, The Green Hornet, The Shadow* and *Lux Radio Theater.*

(11) All of this notwithstanding, my parents were afraid that the Buccaneers would someday take my life along with my baloney sandwiches. Accordingly, they packed me off to Jamaica. I did not go to the gilded Jamaica of Playboy clubs and well-tended golf courses and old English maid service. I passed right by urban Kingston and splendid Montego Bay and went on to a remote, primitive village called Maryland, where the mail was delivered by donkey-back, where bathtubs were under waterfalls and the public schoolhouse was school on weekdays and church on Sundays and where there were no radiators to bang on because it was always summer.

(12) To a boy of 12 from the city, Maryland was a paradise without equal. Wasn't it wonderful that I could do my homework by the light of a kerosene lamp, that I could climb trees and feast on mangoes, guavas, star apples, rose apples, jackfruit, coconuts, oranges, tangerines, bananas, naseberries and so on and on! Wasn't it wonderful that the kids walked barefoot to school, that you could go swimming and fishing whenever you liked and that bats were made from dried coconut palms instead of broomsticks! The names of things seemed so much nicer than the ones I knew: *cricket* for baseball; *braces* for sus-

penders; *frock* instead of dress, *Cambridge Certificate* for high school diploma, *trousers* instead of pants, *porridge* instead of cereal and *motor cars* instead of just plain cars.

(13) In the same one-room, wooden schoolhouse where my mother had gone 35 years before, all the faces were very much the same color. During a brief honeymoon period I was a very special kind of human being because I was an American. They marveled at my strange English, my disrespect for teachers and the quaint American habit of permitting little boys to wear long trousers.

(14) Before very long, Paradise and I got used to each other. I became a Jamaican. Here the new bully was Claude Bigby; the big show-off in arithmetic was Vanley Beckwith, and with all the passion I could muster, I fell in love with Hyacinth Swanson.

(15) From tiny Maryland School I went on to a much larger one in Kingston where I earned a Cambridge Certificate. By the time I was ready to leave Jamaica, I had learned how very much Saul loved his son David and that "two singular subjects joined by the conjunction *and* require a plural verb." I knew the capital city of every nation on the globe and I knew that occupying these cities were people of differing skin colors, who for reasons no one seemed completely to understand, did not always get along well.

(16) I was 18 when I came back to New York. My passport still vouched for my American citizenship, but those who could see and hear knew clearly that I wasn't. On the flight home I wore a tie, three inches wide, proclaiming the coronation of Queen Elizabeth of England; I pronounced "party" and "water" as though they had *t*'s in them when every American knew that they had *d*'s instead.

(17) I had imagined that my father, like everyone else in America, was wealthy. But he still lived on 146th Street where junkies continued to doze on sidewalks and in doorways. Only now there were twice as many of them as six years ago. The building superintendent spent much of his time making wine and he had more customers to satisfy. The good places I knew for a stickball game had become playlands for vermin. Fearful for their white lives, Billy Roth and Judy Metzl had fled for refuge in suburbs, but Harvey Anderson remained — still showing-off incredibly but not quite so handsome in appearance, for his life had become infected by heroin. He had become hip while I had grown ridiculous and so there could now be no communication between us.

(18) The things that made me an absurdity on 146th Street made me distinguished in the world outside, the world I was taught to reach out for. I quickly realized how important it was to be distinguished: by education, by speech, by an over-proclaimed heritage. No device, no affectation was too shameful, so long as it saved me

from routine blackness. But God did not always hear me. The devices often failed, leaving me unwhite, undistinguished.

(19) *Please let me be special, God. Let me stand out from the unhuman horde. Please, God.*

(20) It was alarming to be confronted with this stark negation of much that I had been taught. Didn't the essential worth of man have to do with things that could not be seen? Was not a man's soul primary? Or was it? Apparently a handful of physical features were of greater moment than anything else. More than anything else, those who lived in and around 146th Street were Negro. According to *Webster's* this meant that they were members "of a people belonging to the African branch of the black race and marked typically by dark pigmentation and woolly hair and everted lips and broad flat noses." It also meant that they had a skin color which I had never really noticed before: "a black to dark grayish, yellowish brown."

(21) Amid my confusion only one thing was clear: being Negro was a tragic accident. I began to work tirelessly—and largely unsuccessfully—at reducing the visual impact of those unsightly things which conspired to make me Negro. As for the "broad, flat nose" and the "everted lips," very little could be done short of expensive surgery and mutilation. I had to content myself with what are now unconscious habits, such as pressing the nostrils together and pursing the lips halfway into the mouth in the silly hope that they would remain that way.

(22) Attempting to alter the "black to dark grayish, yellowish brown" also produced very few tangible results. There were—and still are—on the market any number of bleaching agents whose manufacturers held out the glorious promise of lighter, if not white, skin. But I discovered to my daily chagrin that I was condemned to blackness, and nothing short of a bath in acid was going to change it. My attempts to straighten the telling kinks in my hair were also despairingly unsuccessful.

(23) My parents borrowed and borrowed some more and finally inched their way out of hell. They left behind them the vermin and temperament which endured all, complaining only to God. They learned to perceive links between campaign promises and schools in ruin. On 146th Street, radiators are still too often cold in January, but when they are, the building commissioner is deluged with phone protests; rats are still biting babies, but forces inside and out of the misery have been mustered to so something about it.

(24) Different also is the Negro's view of his Negritude. A few years ago we noticed that Africans representing proud new nations were wearing their Negroness with no apparent self-deprecation. Why couldn't we "Afro-Americans" do the same? As in any struggle for

change, new absurdities replace old ones. Consider again, the hair. We've reached the stage where hair length is virtually an index to militancy. The longer a young Negro man's hair is, the more insistent he is likely to be in demanding immediate freedom. If his hair is unkempt as well as long, then speculation will have it that he is an "extremist." Rash judgments of this kind are ill-advised; one can find, lurking here and there, closely cropped extremists and long-haired Uncle Toms.

(25) My physical features, not so long ago, were matters of grave concern. Now they are much less important. In purely esthetic terms, I'm quite pleased with the color of my skin. As to the nostrils and lips, I don't think about them anymore, although the old subconscious habit of pressing and pursing them persists.

(26) It would seem that for me, today, all should be well. But it isn't. Not at all. Not a day — scarcely a moment — passes that my Negroness does not intrude on my existence. It causes a kaleidoscope of anger, fear, frustration. The grand intrusion amounts to an imprisonment of the mind. I calculate that out of 16 hours awake, I waste seven struggling with the invasion. The seven hours are not all lumped together but are the sum of five minutes here and 10 seconds there. The arithmetic is terrifying: seven hours a day is 49 hours a week. If I live to be 100 years old, 30 of those years will have been frittered away. The rest of my time will be crammed with thoughts that a good many people are free to devote *all* their time to thinking about: death and sex and city sales tax and disarmament and Bach and South African lobster tail.

(27) Countless times each day I am aware of myself. Countless times a day the image of a faceless shell flashes across my consciousness. This shell shakes a hand, selects a subway seat, enters a restaurant, oils an ashen elbow, elects to speak and is not heard.

(28) *I understand there is an apartment available here and I was wondering if you'd be willing to let me rent it for a couple of years or so. I know what you're thinking but there's really no need to worry. You can just look at me and tell that I'm respectable. I'm so respectable that it's going to kill me. Look at my clothing. My shoes are shined. I just got this suit out of the cleaners. I shaved all the hair off my face less than an hour ago. Smell me. I use deodorant. Look at what's in my hand — a briefcase. Maybe I should open it and show you — you illiterate bastard. It's full of books and respectable looking papers. See that pipe in my other hand. Sometimes I smoke it. Won't you please let me stay here for a few years. I promise not to make a mess. I didn't make a mess where I was living before. Call them up and find out for yourself, you illiterate bastard. Won't you please put me up for a couple of years? . . .*

(29) Unspoken dialogues are tiresome; so are my friends when they tell me what color to love. But I abhor facelessness; it is corrosive of the whole mind and spirit. It is quietly malignant and thus much unnoticed by victims and healers alike. It has carved a wound in me that only death will completely heal. I can't seize manhood by a show of force as one would gold or governments. If it were possible, I would already have done so. I don't ask that there be joy in what I am. I ask that there be nothing at all in what I am. I remain a black. I want to be a man who is black.

QUESTIONS AND EXERCISES

VOCABULARY
1. demeaned (*paragraph* 3)
2. patently (9)
3. vermin (17)
4. everted (21)
5. self-deprecation (24)
6. esthetic (25)
7. kaleidoscope (26)
8. corrosive (29)
9. malignant (29)

LANGUAGE AND RHETORIC
1. What tone does the author establish in the first paragraph? What does this paragraph tell us about the author? Is the introduction effective? How does it contribute to the purpose of this essay?
2. Paragraphs 21 and 22 form a unit. What is the topic sentence of this unit?
3. What device of coherence is used in paragraphs 1, 3, 5, 8, 12, and 29? Does this device contribute anything beside coherence to the writing? Explain your answer.
4. Why does paragraph 19 consist of only three short sentences? What is the function of this paragraph?
5. Where is the thesis first made explicit? Where is it reiterated and reinforced?
6. What is the reason for italicizing paragraph 28?
7. This essay could be divided into four parts. What are these parts? How do they relate to one another?
8. Unlike the preceding two articles, this essay concentrates on the personal experiences of one man. Does this autobiographical approach increase the emotional impact of the writing? If so, how is it increased?

DISCUSSION AND WRITING
1. Is the author correct in his belief that children are not concerned about the race of their playmates, that it is adults who designate friends and acquaintances by race? If you have the chance to observe a racially mixed group of children at play, write an essay in which you report your observations and try to draw some conclusions from them.
2. When and how did you first become aware of racial differences? What

effect did this awareness have on you? Write an essay about some aspect
of this experience.
3. Why does the author make a point of showing that he quickly "became a
Jamaican" and fell into patterns of relationships with his new friends that
were identical to those patterns he had experienced earlier in Harlem?
4. Do you approve of the Moores' decision to send the author to Jamaica
rather than rearing him in Harlem? If the author had stayed with them in
Harlem, would he have been more prepared to accept his condition, or
would he have been more motivated to overcome it?
5. Why would a black want to bleach his skin or straighten his hair? What
are the implications of these actions? What does this say about the relative
status of blacks and whites in America and the relationship between the
two races?
6. What is the difference between "a black" and "a man who is black"? Is the
distinction as important as the author feels it is? Explain why or why not.

IAN STEVENSON
People Aren't Born Prejudiced

What is prejudice? Its characteristics and origins have by now been
carefully studied by psychologists and sociologists so that today we
know a good deal about how it is transmitted from one person to
another.

Prejudice is a false generalization about a group of people — or
things — which is held onto despite all facts to the contrary. Some generalizations, of course, are true and useful — often needed to put
people and things into categories. The statement that Negroes have
darkly pigmented skin and nearly always curly hair isn't a prejudice
but a correct generalization about Negroes.

Ignorance isn't the same as prejudice, either. Many people believe
that Negroes are basically less intelligent than white people because
they've heard this and never have been told otherwise. These people
would be prejudiced only if they persisted in this belief after they
knew the facts! Well documented studies show that when Negroes
and whites are properly matched in comparable groups, they have
the same intelligence.

Prejudiced thinking is rarely, probably never, confined to any one
subject. Those prejudiced against one group of people are nearly
always prejudiced against others. Prejudice, then, could be said to be

"People Aren't Born Prejudiced" by Ian Stevenson. From *Parents' Magazine*, February,
1960. By permission of Parents' Magazine Enterprises, Inc.

a disorder of thinking: a prejudiced person makes faulty generalizations by applying to a whole group what he has learned from one or
a few of its members. Sometimes, he doesn't even draw on his own
experiences but bases his attitudes on what he has heard from others.
Then he behaves toward a whole group as if there were no individual
differences among its members. Few people would throw out a whole
box of strawberries because they found one or two bad berries at the
top — yet this is the way prejudiced people think and act.

There are different kinds of prejudice, and two of these deserve
separate consideration. First there is that loosely spoken, loosely
held opinion that can be called conforming prejudice: people make
prejudiced remarks about other races, nations, religions or groups
because they want to conform to what they think are the conventions
of their own group. Attacking or deriding members of another group
who "don't belong" gives them a sense of solidarity with their own
group. It's rather sad but also fortunate that most prejudice is probably
this conforming kind. Fortunate, because this type of prejudice is
easily given up when a new situation demands it.

A number of studies have shown that while people may protest
about some social change, when the change actually takes place most
will fall silently and willingly into line. It's the rare examples of change
being resisted with violence that unfortunately receive most publicity.
A psychologist interested in this phenomenon once made an amusing
study of the differences between what people say they'll do and what
they really do in a particular situation that evokes prejudice. Traveling across the country with a Chinese couple, he found that the three
of them were received in 250 hotels and restaurants with great hospitality — and only once were refused service. When the trip was over,
he wrote to each of the hotels and restaurants and asked if they would
serve Chinese people. Ninety-two percent of those who had actually
served them said they would not do so!

The second kind of prejudice is less easily relinquished than the
conforming type, for this second kind stems from a more deep-rooted
sense of personal insecurity. A prejudiced person of this kind usually
has a feeling of failure or guilt about his own accomplishments and,
to avoid the pain of blaming himself, he turns the blame on others.
Just as the Jews once symbolically piled all their guilt on a goat and
drove it into the wilderness, so these prejudiced people make scapegoats out of Negroes, Southerners, Jews, Russians or whoever else
fits their need. Moreover, insecure people like these are anxious, too,
and anxious people can't discriminate among the small but important
differences between people who seem alike. So, on the one hand they
often can't think clearly about other people; and on the other, they
need to blame scapegoats in order to feel more comfortable. Both

these mechanisms promote faulty generalizations; these people respond to others not as individuals but as Negroes, Russians, women, doctors — as if these groups were all alike.

The first important point about how children learn prejudice is that they do. They aren't born that way, though some people think prejudice is innate and like to quote the old saying, "You can't change human nature." But you can change it. We now know that very small children are free of prejudice. Studies of school children have shown that prejudice is slight or absent among children in the first and second grades. It increases thereafter, building to a peak usually among children in the fourth and fifth grades. After this, it may fall off again in adolescence. Other studies have shown that, on the average, young adults are much freer of prejudice than older ones.

In the early stages of picking up prejudice, children mix it with ignorance which, as I've said, should be distinguished from prejudice. A child, as he begins to study the world around him, tries to organize his experiences. Doing this, he begins to classify things and people and begins to form connections — or what psychologists call associations. He needs to do this because he saves time and effort by putting things and people into categories. But unless he classifies correctly, his categories will mislead rather than guide him. For example, if a child learns that "all fires are hot and dangerous," fires have been put firmly into the category of things to be watched carefully — and thus he can save himself from harm. But if he learns a category like "Negroes are lazy" or "foreigners are fools," he's learned generalizations that mislead because they're unreliable. The thing is that when we use categories, we need to remember the exceptions and differences, the individual variations that qualify the usefulness of all generalizations. Some fires, for example, are hotter and more dangerous than others. If people had avoided all fires as dangerous, we would never have had central heating.

More importantly, we can ill afford to treat people of any given group as generally alike — even when it's possible to make some accurate generalizations about them. So when a child first begins to group things together, it's advisable that he learn differences as well as similarities. For example, basic among the distinctions he draws is the division into "good" and "bad" — which he makes largely on the grounds of what his parents do and say about things and people. Thus, he may learn that dirt is "bad" because his mother washes him every time he gets dirty. By extension, seeing a Negro child, he might point to him and say, "Bad child," for the Negro child's face is brown, hence unwashed and dirty and so, "bad." We call this prelogical thinking, and all of us go through this phase before we learn to think more effectively.

But some people remain at this stage and never learn that things that seem alike, such as dirt and brown pigment, are really quite different. Whether a child graduates from this stage to correct thinking or to prejudicial thinking, depends to a great extent on his experiences with his parents and teachers.

Generally speaking, a child learns from his parents in two main ways. Each of these may contribute to his development either as a prejudiced personality or a tolerant one. First, a child learns a good deal by direct imitation of his parent. If parents reveal prejudiced attitudes, children will tend to imitate those attitudes. If a mother or father, for example, tells a child, "I don't want you playing with any colored children," they foster in their child's growing mind the connection between "colored" and "bad" — and thus promote the growth of prejudice. If instead of saying "colored children," a mother says "nigger" in a derogatory tone of voice, this makes another harmful connection in a child's mind. Even before he clearly knows to what the words Negro or "nigger" refer, he would know that these words mean something "bad" and hence indicate people for him to avoid. It may be that some colored children, like some white children, are unsuitable playmates. But the prohibition should be made on the grounds of the particular reasons for this unsuitability, not on the basis of skin pigment.

How parents actually behave toward members of other groups in the presence of their children influences children as much or more than what parents say about such people. Still, parents can and do communicate prejudices in subtle ways, by subtle remarks. For example, some parents take pride in belonging to a special group, lay stress on the child's membership in that group, and consequently lead him to believe that other people are inferior because they're outside this group. Sometimes parents are unaware that the pride they take in such membership in a special group can be an insidious form of prejudice against other groups. This isn't always so, because often pride in belonging can be related to the genuine accomplishments of a group. But just as often, pride stems simply from thinking of the group as special and superior because of its selectivity, not because of its accomplishments. However, this kind of direct transmission of prejudice from parents to children is the conforming type, and so can usually be modified by later experience if the child comes into contact with other unprejudiced people or if he has the opportunity to get to know members of the group toward which he has had prejudiced attitudes. For example, during the Second World War and the Korean War, many white soldiers of both North and South fought with Negro troops; knowing Negroes as people, they lost their old prejudices.

Unfortunately, however, parents tend to restrict their children's experiences with different kinds of people, for fear that the children might be harmfully influenced. This naturally prevents the children from unlearning prejudices. Unfortunately these children who most need broadening and correcting experiences are often deprived of them.

Parents promote prejudice in a second, more subtle and harmful way by their own treatment of their children. Studies of markedly prejudiced persons show that they usually come from families in which they were treated harshly, authoritatively and unfairly—in other words, they were themselves the objects of prejudice. This parental behavior promotes prejudice in the children—apart from their imitation of it—in two ways. First, if parents treat a child harshly and punish him unfairly, they are relating to the child in terms of power instead of love. Treated as if he were always bad, the child will respond to his parents as if they were always dangerous. Growing skilled in the quick detection of threats or possible injury, he becomes sensitive to danger not only from parents but from other people as well. He makes quick judgments in order not to be caught unaware. Quick judgments are a facet of prejudiced thinking. An insecure and easily frightened person makes sweeping judgments about groups, finding it safer to treat the whole group as if it might be harmful to him. He thinks, often unconsciously and always incorrectly, that then he can never be hurt.

Secondly, when parents relate to a child in terms of power, when they punish him, say, with equal severity for accidentally knocking over a dish or for biting his baby brother, he not only thinks of his parents as dangerous people but he thinks of himself as dangerous, too. He must be bad, otherwise why would he be punished so often? Given this low opinion of himself, he will often try to raise it by putting the blame on others—using the old unconscious scapegoat mechanism. Here again, psychological studies have shown that people who are able to blame themselves when they're responsible for things going wrong tend to be much less prejudiced than people who blame others when things go wrong. But a child can only learn to accept blame fairly if his parents attribute blame fairly to him. If he is blamed for everything, he may—in his own defense—grow up unable to accept the blame for anything. If he cannot blame himself he has to blame others—he has to see them as more deficient and blameworthy than they are—which means making prejudiced judgments about them.

School can help undo the damage. Actual personal experience with children of other groups can show a child directly, immediately and concretely that not all members of a group are blameworthy, stupid, dirty or dishonest. In addition, unprejudiced teachers can instruct children in the ways of clear thinking that underlie tolerance. There is definite evidence that education reduces prejudices. It's been found, for example, that college graduates are less prejudiced on the whole than people with less education. Direct instruction about different groups and cultures, another study shows, reduced prejudice in those who were taught.

Fortunately, we seem today to be making progress in the direction of less prejudiced belief and behavior. Today, parents treat children with greater respect for them as individuals — in short, with less prejudice. This will continue to exert a healthy influence on the next generation. In fact, one survey has shown that it already has! College students of our generation, it demonstrates, are less prejudiced than college students of the last generation.

But since prejudice against members of a minority group or the people of other countries is a luxury we can increasingly ill afford — no parent should relax his vigilance in guarding against sowing the seeds of intolerance.

SIX | # The Limits of Language

JUDITH KAPLAN
Catch Phrases Don't Communicate

It has often been argued that the so-called generation gap is really a linguistic gap; and many young people, like the man mentioned in the following essay, maintain they cannot communicate across that gap because of some fault in the older generation. Judith Kaplan (who was eighteen years old when this essay was first published) argues that much of the responsibility lies with the young themselves, whose "catch phrases" become so overworked that they lose their meaning and actually fail to communicate anything at all.

See if you can determine from the author's tone and language what audience her essay is expected to reach.

(1) Recently while gorging on ice cream sundaes with some friends, I overheard a boy saying to his girl, "Baby, there's really a generation gap at our house! My parents just don't dig the whole drug scene. You know, like I really turn them off!"

(2) What was this fellow actually trying to say? Roughly, I translated to myself what might be his situation at home: His dad's probably a businessman, wears his hair short and close-cropped and has always been conservative and traditional. Son has long hair, most likely enjoys rock concerts, has smoked marijuana and is active in the peace movement. He and his parents cannot talk to each other. Why? Because both sides end up shrugging their shoulders and sighing, "I just don't understand you."

(3) This boy persists in belaboring the "generation gap," convinced that he can't communicate with his parents because of some flaw of theirs. Yet his own conversation was so chock-full of catch phrases that it was relatively meaningless.

(4) When people rely on such phrases, real communication is doomed to failure. Words like "swinger," "up tight," "groovy," "super" are overused to such an extent that their meaning and emotional content have been lost. The deep, underlying feelings that may have inspired the thought are simply not reflected in such cursory expressions. True, it's easier to use one word or phrase to cover a complicated thought. But it's certainly less revealing—and aren't you cheating yourself as well as your listeners?

(5) Recently I told a friend that my article was to be published in SEVENTEEN. "That's super," she said. Although she sounded enthusiastic, what did she really mean? Did she feel that this was a lucky break for me, or that it was a great magazine, or even that she wished she could do the same? The point is that she didn't say exactly what she meant. Granted, I had a general idea of what she was trying to convey, but nothing definite came through.

(6) Being ambiguous, I think, is just slightly better than saying nothing. Once, I remember, I was wearing a new dress, and a boy I liked came over and told me that I looked "groovy." What a letdown! I know it was a favorable comment, but it would have meant so much more to me if he had said I looked as fresh as a newly cut flower or that the color suited my eyes. "Groovy" left me empty inside—the compliment was over so quickly and it seemed so superficial.

(7) And how many times does a young person insist she wants to "do her own thing" without bothering to explain what her "thing" is? Could it be that she hasn't taken the time to analyze herself carefully and truly determine what she does want to do? What about those who talk loftily about "commitment" to such obscure goals as peace, nonviolence, equality? It's not often that they can elaborate on what they would really do if they could. Usually, it's all talk—and relatively little action.

(8) In short, many people use glib catch phrases as an easy way out. But it's sheer laziness not to bother to put meaning and substance behind an utterance. Television watching may be partly responsible for some of this habit: "Sock it to me," after all, is easier to remember than the many phrases for which it is often substituted. ·

(9) Obviously, then, talking and communicating are not always synonymous. A person can utter a lot of meaningless words or she can communicate with a glance something words wouldn't say as well. Talking transmits only words, but communicating transports thoughts and true feelings between people. To share these emotions with

friends is to give part of yourself—as opposed to chatting about the weather with your hairdresser. There really should be a difference in how one speaks about something meaningful—if *we* don't make that distinction, we have no right to complain that adults don't communicate with us.

(10) I'm not saying that our language should not be breezily informal enough to suit our fast-moving culture, and certainly there are times when only a short exclamatory word will express one's genuine feelings. (Even those rendered "speechless" can usually manage to say "wow!") Generally when someone asks, "How are you?" they don't expect a long discourse on the general state of your health. But expressions that are overworked become totally meaningless, and our generation cannot afford not to be expressive. There are too many important ideas to be expressed well! Language should not be a shortcut to hide our feelings.

QUESTIONS AND EXERCISES

VOCABULARY
1. belaboring (*paragraph* 3)
2. cursory (4)
3. ambiguous (6)
4. superficial (6)
5. glib (8)

LANGUAGE AND RHETORIC
1. The thesis of this brief essay is announced in its title, but the author also states her thesis early in the body of the essay itself. Point out that thesis. What is the author's purpose?
2. What audience is this selection addressed to, and what clues inform you that this is so?
3. When this essay was first published the author was eighteen years old. Can you find any evidence in the language of the essay that might suggest it was written by an eighteen-year-old female?
4. The author uses the first person point of view and draws frequently from her personal experience. How do these techniques contribute to the overall effect of her essay?

DISCUSSION AND WRITING
1. Do you agree or disagree with the author's thesis? If you agree, use your own examples and your personal experience to support the thesis. If you disagree, write an essay in which you use examples and reasons to support your position.
2. During one day of your campus activities, pay particular attention to the use of "catch phrases," such as those mentioned by the author, and take

notes recording specific examples and situations. Study your findings and
write a paper reporting your conclusions.
3. The author charges that "those who talk loftily about 'commitment' to such
    obscure goals as peace, nonviolence, [and] equality" seldom act, or even
    elaborate, on what they would do in support of their goals. Does this strike
    you as a valid generalization? Support your answer.
4. The author says "expressions that are overworked become totally mean-
    ingless." Apart from any mentioned in this essay, can you think of ex-
    amples to illustrate this point? Try to trace an example from its original
    meaning, through its overuse, to its loss of meaning.

NORMAN COUSINS

The Environment of Language

Language "has as much to do with the philosophical and political
conditioning of a society as geography or climate" says Norman
Cousins. Basing his essay on a study of the role of language in human
affairs, he points out not only how translation can create problems, but
how references to skin color may cause people to view their own racial
group as superior while condemning other groups to inferiority.

In addition to his extensive use of examples, the author uses cause
and effect and appeal to authority to develop his thesis.

(1) The words men use, Julian Huxley once said, not only express
but shape their ideas. Language is an instrument; it is even more an
environment. It has as much to do with the philosophical and political conditioning of a society as geography or climate. The role of
language in contributing to men's problems and their prospects is the
subject of an imaginative and valuable study now getting under way
at Pro Deo University in Rome, which is winning recognition in
world university circles for putting advanced scholarship to work for
the concept of a world community.

(2) One aspect of the Pro Deo study, as might be expected, has to
do with the art of conveying precise meaning from one language to
another. Stuart Chase, one of America's leading semanticists, has
pointed out that when an English speaker at the United Nations uses
the expression "I assume," the French interpreter may say "I deduce"

and the Russian interpreter may say "I consider." When Pope Paul VI sent a cable to Prime Minister Alexei Kosygin and Party Chairman Leonid Brezhnev on their accession to office, he expressed the hope that the historic aspirations of the Russian people for a fuller life would be advanced under the new leadership. As translated into Russian by the Vatican's own interpreter, the Pope's expression of hope came out in a way that made it appear that the Pope was making known his endorsement of the new regime. The eventual clarification was inevitably awkward for all concerned.

(3) The Pro Deo study, however, will not be confined to problems of precise translation. The major emphasis has to do with something even more fundamental: the dangerous misconceptions and prejudices that take root in language and that undermine human values. The color of a man's skin, for example, is tied to plus-or-minus words that inevitably condition human attitudes. The words "black" and "white," as defined in Western culture, are heavily loaded. "Black" has all sorts of unfavorable connotations; "white" is almost all favorable. One of the more interesting papers being studied by the Pro Deo scholars is by Ossie Davis, the author and actor. Mr. Davis, a Negro, concluded on the basis of a detailed study of dictionaries and *Roget's Thesaurus* that the English language was his enemy. In *Roget's*, he counted 120 synonyms for "blackness," most of them with unpleasant connotations: blot, blotch, blight, smut, smudge, sully, begrime, soot, becloud, obscure, dingy, murky, threatening, frowning, foreboding, forbidden, sinister, baneful, dismal, evil, wicked, malignant, deadly, secretive, unclean, unwashed, foul, blacklist, black book, black-hearted, etc. Incorporated in the same listing were words such as Negro, nigger, and darky.

(4) In the same *Roget's*, Mr. Davis found 134 synonyms for the word "white," almost all of them with favorable connotations: purity, cleanness, bright, shining, fair, blonde, stainless, chaste, unblemished, unsullied, innocent, honorable, upright, just, straightforward, genuine, trustworthy, honesty, etc. "White" as a racial designation was, of course, included in this tally of desirable terms.

(5) No less invidious than black are some of the words associated with the color yellow: coward, conniver, baseness, fear, effeminacy, funk, soft, spiritless, poltroonery, pusillanimity, timidity, milksop, recreant, sneak, lilylivered, etc. Oriental people are included in the listing.

(6) As a matter of factual accuracy, white, black, and yellow as colors are not descriptive of races. The coloration range of so-called white people may run from pale olive to mottled pink. So-called colored people run from light beige to mahogany. Absolute color designations — white, black, red, yellow — are not merely inaccurate;

they have become symbolic rather than descriptive. It will be argued, of course, that definitions of color and the connotations that go with them are independent of sociological implications. There is no getting around the fact, it will be said, that whiteness means cleanliness and blackness means dirtiness. Are we to doctor the dictionary in order to achieve a social good? What this line of argument misses is that people in Western cultures do not realize the extent to which their racial attitudes have been conditioned since early childhood by the power of words to ennoble or condemn, augment or detract, glorify or demean. Negative language infects the subconscious of most Western people from the time they first learn to speak. Prejudice is not merely imparted or superimposed. It is metabolized in the bloodstream of society. What is needed is not so much a change in language as an awareness of the power of words to condition attitudes. If we can at least recognize the underpinnings of prejudice, we may be in a position to deal with the effects.

(7) To be sure, Western languages have no monopoly on words with connotations that affect judgment. In Chinese, whiteness means cleanliness, but it can also mean bloodlessness, coldness, frigidity, absence of feeling, weakness, insensitivity. Also in Chinese, yellowness is associated with sunshine, openness, beauty, flowering, etc. Similarly, the word black in many African tongues has connotations of strength, certainty, recognizability, integrity, while white is associated with paleness, anemia, unnaturalness, deviousness, untrustworthiness.

(8) The purpose of Pro Deo University in undertaking this study is not just to demonstrate that most cultures tend to be self-serving in their language. The purpose is to give educational substance to the belief that it will take all the adroitness and sensitivity of which the human species is capable if it is to be sustained. Earth-dwellers now have the choice of making their world into a neighborhood or a crematorium. Language is one of the factors in that option. The right words may not automatically produce the right actions but they are an essential part of the process.

QUESTIONS AND EXERCISES

VOCABULARY
1. semanticists (*paragraph* 2)
2. invidious (5)
3. metabolized (6)
4. adroitness (8)
5. crematorium (8)

LANGUAGE AND RHETORIC

1. What does the author mean by his title, and how does that title contribute to this thesis?
2. What seems to be the author's purpose in writing this essay? Point out how he uses cause and effect to develop his ideas.
3. Reread the first and last paragraphs, and comment on their effectiveness as an introduction and conclusion.
4. This essay may be divided into four parts. Identify those parts by paragraph number, and explain their relationship to one another.

DISCUSSION AND WRITING

1. Compile your own list of meanings and associations for the words *black* and *white* by writing down the first things that come to mind in connection with each. Then ask several other persons to do the same thing. Consider your lists in light of the author's thesis, and write a report of your findings. (You may wish to substitute *brown* or *yellow* for *black*.)
2. If, as the author says, all people are in fact "colored," what is the basis for the way the term is commonly used? Who uses it, and what seems to be their purpose?
3. According to this essay, language not only expresses but shapes our thoughts and, therefore, helps to create "the dangerous misconceptions and prejudices . . . that undermine human values." If you are familiar with a second language, discuss the validity of this idea by comparing how the two languages might shape different conceptions and values.
4. Write a paper in which you discuss some aspect of the language of youth and the language of the adult generation and how each group's use of language tends to condition its perception of, and response to, the other group. Some suggested aspects: slang, "catch phrases" such as those mentioned in the Kaplan essay, verbal obscenity, and the language of educators.

OLIVIA MELLAN
Black English

Historically, most American schoolchildren have been taught to consider "good English" as that spoken by the educated (white) majority, and to regard all other forms and varieties of English as either substandard or nonstandard. As a consequence, students whose language habits differ from those of the majority are taught to discard their usual patterns in order to meet socially acceptable standards outside their own communities. More recently, some critics have condemned such practices as racist. In this essay, Olivia Mellan examines the differing, and at times conflicting, opinions over the teaching of Black English.

Note how effectively the author uses reasons and appeal to authority in developing her subject.

(1) Our melting pot myth is being shattered as black separatism grows in favor and fact. Many blacks do still emulate the values of white society, but many don't, and they resent attempts to assimilate them into a "majority culture." While "black culture" cannot be neatly defined and isolated (nor can "white" or "American" culture), both blacks and whites are becoming increasingly aware of marked differences in styles of dress, behavior patterns, values and attitudes, and these are mirrored in speech as well as "culture." This new awareness is reflected in the charge of "cultural fascism" that is being levied at traditional English classes, where "Standard English" is taught to blacks and their nonstandard "Black English" is frowned upon.

(2) Those who object to our long-standing efforts to eradicate Black English, claim that it harms the black child, brands the speech he has used since childhood as defective and by inference slurs the black culture that speech expresses. The child often accepts these judgments, disparaging his own language and culture in the same way whites do. Or, the child turns his back on school, English class in particular, and all that goes with a white-oriented teaching system.

(3) Aside from its psychological effects, "eradicationism" is under attack for another reason: it doesn't seem to be working. At least that's the conclusion of many educators who have been trying to teach black children to read and to speak "white English," and of many linguists. One such is Joan C. Baratz, co-director of the Washington-based Education Study Center, who writes of "the nationwide failure of so many black children to learn to read." The remedy Dr. Baratz and co-director William Stewart prescribe is to teach the black child to read nonstandard Negro English first, "starting where the child is" instead of where he should be. They are convinced that if we ignore the specific language the black child speaks, we block the successful teaching of Standard English, either written or spoken.

(4) Wayne O'Neil, MIT linguistics professor and education lecturer at Harvard, has a similar objection to standard pedagogy. "Trationally, schools have understood that part of their task is to get students to speak and write properly, where 'properly' is defined by whatever it is that characterizes the language of the middle class," he writes. "They have not been successful in this endeavor. A few indi-

viduals assimilate proper speech ways, but most go on speaking, a bit nervously after their school experience, the way they would have had schools never been invented, just as they go on avoiding the plays and books and art that schools concern themselves with—a bit nervous about that, too."

(5) Linguists who have studied the vocabulary and syntax of Black English find it to be a "separate but equal"-ly valid language system, with a highly developed structure of its own. Among the list of syntactic (grammatical), phonological (pronunciation) and lexical (vocabulary) features which distinguish Black English from Standard, there are syntactic features which resemble creole, or African languages. One such is the distinction between "he working" (meaning he is working right now) and "he be working," (meaning he is working continuously). This distinction is not present either in white non-standard dialects or in Standard English. To skeptics who question whether Black English is a separate "language" or merely a substandard "dialect of English," linguists explain that "language" and "dialect" are two points on a continuum, moving from "dialects" (two speech systems which are relatively close in syntax, vocabulary and historical development) to "languages" (where the differences begin to outweigh the similarities). For most linguists, it is irrelevant whether Black English is "language" or "dialect." It functions as a communication system.

(6) The eradicationist school has many defenders, however, with Kenneth B. Clark, the black psychologist and educator one of the strongest among them. Clark maintains that Standard English is the only language that should be taught in school, and that no attempt should be made to preserve native dialects, except perhaps as "exotic primitives." He accuses those who would preserve Black English of consigning blacks to perpetual inferiority by implying that they cannot be absorbed into the mainstream of American society. And some black parents agree with him. That is what they mean when they say, "Teach my child good English. Don't tell me he can't learn it just like whites do."

(7) Those who see eradicationism as psychologically harmful and educationally inefficient are persuaded there are better alternatives. One of these comes from the Center for Applied Linguistics in Washington, and it's called "bidialectalism" or "biloquialism." It begins by assuming that the black child *should* be taught Standard English, since that is what he needs to function in present-day America. But the biloquialists insist that the child's Black English should be respected, and that it can and should be preserved for appropriate surroundings such as home and playground.

(8) The critics of biloquialism say that it is a disguised racist view,

no better than overt eradicationism, and that it would still perpetuate social inequalities, forcing blacks to become "abnormal whites" in order to get ahead. Thomas Kochman, a linguist at Northeastern Illinois State College, attacks the whole concept of social mobility, terming it an improper motivation rather than a sacred value. Even blacks who do learn Standard English, he contends, will not find, that their "improved" speech patterns make it any easier for them to win jobs, better salaries or social acceptance.

(9) Biloquialism has also come under attack from black militants and black parents, and for two contradictory reasons. Some are against it because they believe it less effective than the tried-and-true eradicationist approach in getting a child to speak "good English" all the time. Others attack it because they resent *any* attempt, however modified, to force the language of white society upon blacks. Ironically, critics at both poles have called the biloquial approach racist.

(10) Nevertheless, the professionals who advocate biloquialism are optimistic about its future, because it would work and because most blacks would want it to work. Teaching materials to make it a classroom reality are being developed. One recently completed set of materials and tapes, entitled "English Now," by Irwin Feigenbaum, has just been put out by New Century in New York. Contrasts between Black English and Standard are offered to help the black child master certain Standard English features which "interfere" linguistically with his native dialect. Drills juxtaposing "he work hard" and "he works hard," for instance, are used to reinforce Standard English patterns. The materials are being tested in a North Carolina school system, and will be used in Pontiac, Mich.

(11) In a different vein, a sizable group of white teachers in urban schools has for the past two years been learning black language and exploring black culture in a course called "American Negro Dialect," at Columbia Teachers College. According to William Stewart, the professor since the course's inception, demand for this kind of training is steadily rising.

(12) But biloquialism is not the only alternative to eradicationism. There are linguists who want to bridge the linguistic gap by focusing on the white rather than the black child. Instead of "enriching the lives of urban [black] children by plugging them into a 'second dialect' [Standard English]," Wayne O'Neil asks, "why don't we . . . enrich the suburban kid with an urban dialect?" Ideally, this might "eradicate the language prejudice, the language mythology that people grew into holding and believing."

(13) O'Neil's theory remains untested and is supported by relatively few linguists and sociologists. However, the experts do agree

that biloquialism and the O'Neil suggestion could complement one another. Roger Shuy, Sociolinguistics Director of the Center for Applied Linguistics and a special consultant to HEW, thinks that a combined program might not only help blacks learn Standard English, but "might be the best method to successfully reorient attitudes toward language so that eradication of nonstandard dialects will no longer be necessary."

(14) One place to start is in experimental English classes in progressive elementary or secondary schools. Through drills in the two dialects, supplemented by discussions of language contrasts, students would add to their knowledge of both language and cultural differences. A course of this kind is bound to be more interesting, in the beginning at least, than are most English classes today—less apt to turn blacks *and* whites off than "Standard English" pedagogy. Of course there would be problems. White parents would have to be convinced that their children should study Black English and culture. Critics like Kenneth Clark probably would dismiss it as a wasteful expenditure of time and money in pursuit of a dubious goal. But in a time of racial polarization, a dual approach to language would offer one advantage: an opportunity for continuing dialogue between blacks and whites who still want to talk to each other with mutual respect.

QUESTIONS AND EXERCISES

VOCABULARY

1. emulate (*paragraph* 1)
2. assimilate (1)
3. eradicate (2)
4. disparaging (2)
5. pedagogy (4)

6. skeptics (5)
7. "bidialectalism" or "biloquialism" (7)
8. juxtaposing (10)
9. complement (13)
10. polarization (14)

LANGUAGE AND RHETORIC

1. What do you believe the author's purpose to be in this article, and what is the basis for your opinion?
2. Where does the author stand on the issue under discussion? What evidence do you see of her position?
3. Two of the methods of development employed here are reasons and appeal to authority, at times in combination. Point out examples of each method, and comment on their appropriateness to the author's purpose.
4. Reread the last paragraph of the article and evaluate its effectiveness as a conclusion.

DISCUSSION AND WRITING
1. What do you believe "good" English to be, and what is the basis for your belief? Do you consider Standard English better than Black English? Support your answer.
2. Should black schoolchildren be taught to use Standard English, Black English, or both? What is the basis for your opinion?
3. Listen to some conversational uses of black or other dialect on your campus as well as some Standard English. Compare the two for effectiveness.
4. Some linguists are noted here as suggesting that the linguistic gap be bridged by focusing on whites rather than blacks — for example, by educating whites to appreciate black dialect. How do you feel about this suggestion and why?

CASEY MILLER and KATE SWIFT
Is Language Sexist? One Small Step for Genkind

A *riddle* is making the rounds that goes like this: A man and his young son were in an automobile accident. The father was killed and the son, who was critically injured, was rushed to a hospital. As attendants wheeled the unconscious boy into the emergency room, the doctor on duty looked down at him and said, "My God, it's my son!" What was the relationship of the doctor to the injured boy?

If the answer doesn't jump to your mind, another riddle that has been around a lot longer might help: The blind beggar had a brother. The blind beggar's brother died. The brother who died had no brother. What relation was the blind beggar to the blind beggar's brother?

As with all riddles, the answers are obvious once you see them: The doctor was the boy's mother and the beggar was her brother's sister. Then why doesn't everyone solve them immediately? Mainly because our language, like the culture it reflects, is male-oriented. To say that a woman in medicine is an exception is simply to confirm that statement. Thousands of doctors are women, but in order to be seen in the mind's eye, they must be called women doctors.

"Is Language Sexist? One Small Step for Genkind" by Casey Miller and Kate Swift. From the *New York Times Magazine,* April 16, 1972. © 1972 by The New York Times Company. Reprinted by permission.

Except for words that refer to females by definition (mother, actress, congresswoman), and words for occupations traditionally held by females (nurse, secretary, prostitute), the English language defines everyone as male. The hypothetical person ("If a man can walk ten miles in two hours . . ."), the average person ("the man in the street"), and the active person ("the man on the move") are male. The assumption is that unless otherwise identified, people in general – including doctors and beggars – are men. As the beetle-browed and mustachioed man in a Steig cartoon says to his two male drinking companions, "When I speak of mankind, one thing I don't mean is womankind."

Semantically speaking, woman is not one with the species of man, but a distinct subspecies. "Man," says the 1971 edition of the *Britannica Junior Encyclopaedia*, "is the highest form of life on earth. His superior intelligence, combined with certain physical characteristics, have enabled man to achieve things that are impossible for other animals." As though quoting the Steig character, still speaking to his friends in McSorley's, the *Junior Encyclopaedia* continues: "Man must invent most of his behavior, because he lacks the instincts of lower animals. . . . Most of the things he learns have been handed down from his ancestors by language and symbols rather than by biological inheritance."

Considering that for the last five thousand years society has been patriarchal, that statement explains a lot. It explains why Eve was made from Adam's rib instead of the other way around and who invented all those Adam-rib words like female and woman in the first place. This inheritance through language and other symbols begins in the home (also called a man's castle) where man and wife (not husband and wife, or man and woman) live for a while with their children. It is reinforced by religious training, the educational system, the press, Government, commerce, and the law.

Consider some of the examples of language and symbols in American history. When schoolchildren learn from their textbooks that the early colonists gained valuable experience in governing themselves, they are not told that the early colonists who were women were denied the privilege of self-government; when they learn that in the eighteenth century the average man had to manufacture many of the things he and his family needed, they are not told that this "average man" was often a woman who manufactured much of what she and her family needed. Young people learn that intrepid pioneers crossed the country in covered wagons with their wives, children, and cattle; they do not learn that women themselves were intrepid pioneers rather than part of the baggage.

Sexist language is any language that expresses such stereotyped attitudes and expectations or assumes the inherent superiority of one sex over the other. When a woman says of her husband, who has drawn up plans for a new bedroom wing and left out closets, "Just like a man," her language is as sexist as the man's who says, after his wife has changed her mind about needing the new wing after all, "Just like a woman."

Male and female are not sexist words, but masculine and feminine are as sexist as any words can be, since it is almost impossible to use them without invoking cultural stereotypes. When people construct lists of "masculine" and "feminine" traits they almost always end up making assumptions that have nothing to do with innate differences between the sexes. We have a friend who happens to be going through the process of pinning down this very phenomenon. He is seven years old and his question concerns why his coats and shirts button left over right while his sister's button the other way. He assumes it must have something to do with the differences between boys and girls, but he can't see how.

What our friend has yet to grasp is that the way you button your coat, like most sex-differentiated customs, has nothing to do with real differences but much to do with what society wants you to feel about yourself as a male or female person. Society decrees that it is appropriate for girls to dress differently from boys, to act differently, and to think differently. Boys must be masculine, whatever that means, and girls must be feminine.

Unabridged dictionaries are a good source for finding out what society decrees to be appropriate, though less by definition than by their choice of associations and illustrations. Words associated with males — "manly," "virile," and "masculine," for example — are defined through a broad range of positive attributes like strength, courage, directness, and independence, and they are illustrated through such examples of contemporary usage as "a manly determination to face what comes," "a virile literary style," "a masculine love of sports." Corresponding words associated with females are defined with fewer attributes (though weakness is often one of them), and the examples given are generally negative if not clearly pejorative: "feminine wiles," "womanish tears," "a woman-like lack of promptness," "convinced that drawing was a waste of time, if not downright womanly."

One dictionary, after defining the word "womanish" as "suitable to or resembling a woman," further defines it as "unsuitable to a man or to a strong character of either sex." Words derived from "sister" and "brother" provide another apt example, for whereas "sissy," applied either to a male or female, conveys the message that sisters are expected to be timid and cowardly, "buddy" makes clear that brothers are friends.

The subtle disparagement of females and corresponding approbation of males wrapped up in many English words is painfully illustrated by "tomboy." Here is an instance where a girl who likes sports and the out-of-doors, who is curious about how things work, who is adventurous and bold instead of passive, is defined in terms of something she is not—a boy. By denying that she can be the person she is and still be a girl, the word surreptitiously undermines her sense of identity: it says she is unnatural. A "tomboy," as defined by one dictionary, is a "girl, especially a young girl who behaves like a spirited boy." But who makes the judgment that she is acting like a spirited boy, not a spirited girl? Can it be a coincidence that in the case of the dictionary just quoted the editor, executive editor, managing editor, general manager, all six members of the Board of Linguists, the usage editor, science editor, all six general editors of definitions, and ninety-four out of the 104 distinguished experts consulted on usage— are men?

Possibly because of the negative images associated with womanish and woman-like, and with expressions like "woman driver" and "woman of the street," the word woman dropped out of fashion for a time. The women at the office and the women on the assembly line and the women one first knew in school all became ladies or girls or gals. Now a countermovement, supported by the very term Women's Liberation, is putting back into words like woman and sister and sisterhood the meaning they were losing by default. It is as though, in the nick of time, women had seen that the language itself could destroy them.

Some long-standing conventions of the news media add insult to injury. When a woman or girl makes news, her sex is identified at the beginning of a story, if possible in the headline or its equivalent. The assumption, apparently, is that whatever event or action is being reported, a woman's involvement is less common and therefore more newsworthy than a man's. If the story is about achievement, the implication is: "Pretty good for a woman." And because people are assumed to be male unless otherwise identified, the media have developed a special and extensive vocabulary to avoid the constant repetition of "woman." The results—"Grandmother Wins Nobel Prize," "Blond Hijacks Airliner," "Housewife to Run for Congress"— convey the kind of information that would be ludicrous in comparable headlines if the subjects were men. Why, if "Unsalaried Husband to Run for Congress" is unacceptable to editors, must women keep explaining that to describe them through external or superficial concerns reflects a sexist view of women as decorative objects, breeding machines, and extensions of men, not real people?

Members of the Chicago chapter of the National Organization for Women recently studied the newspapers in their area and drew up a set of guidelines for the press. These included cutting out descriptions of the "clothes, physical features, dating life, and marital status of women where such references would be considered inappropriate if about men"; using language in such a way as to include women in copy that refers to homeowners, scientists, and business people where "newspaper descriptions often convey the idea that all such persons are male"; and displaying the same discretion in printing generalizations about women as would be shown toward racial, religious, and ethnic groups. "Our concern with what we are called may seem trivial to some people," the women said, "but we regard the old usages as symbolic of women's position within this society."

Thoughtful writers and editors have begun to repudiate some of the old usages. "Divorcée," "grandmother," and "blonde," along with "vivacious," "pert," "dimpled," and "cute," were dumped by the Washington *Post* in the spring of 1970 by the executive editor, Benjamin Bradlee. In a memo to his staff, Bradlee wrote, "The meaningful equality and dignity of women is properly under scrutiny today . . . because this equality has been less than meaningful and the dignity not always free of stereotype and condescension."

What women have been called in the press — or at least the part that operates above ground — is only a fraction of the infinite variety of alternatives to "woman" used in the subcultures of the English-speaking world. Beyond "chicks," "dolls," "dames," "babes," "skirts," and "broads" are the words and phrases in which women are reduced to their sexuality and nothing more. It would be hard to think of another area of language in which the human mind has been so fertile in devising and borrowing abusive terms. In *The Female Eunuch,* Germaine Greer devotes four pages to anatomical terms and words for animals, vegetables, fruits, baked goods, implements, and receptacles, all of which are used to dehumanize the female person. Jean Faust, in an article aptly called "Words That Oppress," suggests that the effort to diminish women through language is rooted in a male fear of sexual inadequacy. "Woman is made to feel guilty for and akin to natural disasters," she writes. "Hurricanes and typhoons are named after her. Any negative or threatening force is given a feminine name. If a man runs into bad luck climbing up the ladder of success (a male-invented game), he refers to the 'bitch goddess' success."

The sexual overtones in the ancient and no doubt honorable custom of calling ships "she" have become more explicit and less honorable in an age of air travel: "I'm Karen. Fly me." Attitudes of ridicule, contempt, and disgust toward female sexuality have spawned a rich glossary of insults and epithets not found in dictionaries. And the usage in which four-letter words meaning copulate are interchange- able with cheat, attack, and destroy can scarcely be unrelated to the savagery of rape.

Influenced by sexist attitudes, the language of human reproduction lags several centuries behind scientific understanding. The male's contribution to procreation is still described as though it were the entire seed from which a new life grows: the initiative and genera- tive power involved in the process are thought of as masculine, recep- tivity and nurturance as feminine. "Seminal" remains a synonym for "highly original," and there is no comparable word to describe the female's equivalent contribution.

An entire mythology has grown from this biological misunder- standing and its semantic legacy; its embodiment in laws that for centuries made women nonpersons was a key target of the nineteenth- century feminist movement. Today, more than fifty years after women finally won the basic democratic right to vote, the word "liber- ation" itself, when applied to women, means something less than when used of other groups of people. An advertisement for the NBC news department listed Women's Liberation along with crime in the streets and the Vietnam war as "bad news." Asked for his views on Women's Liberation, a highly placed politician was quoted as saying, "Let me make one thing perfectly clear. I wouldn't want to wake up next to a lady pipe-fitter."

When language oppresses, it does so by any means that disparage and belittle. Until well into the twentieth century, one of the ways English was manipulated to disparage women was through the addi- tion of feminine endings to nonsexual words. Thus a woman who aspired to be a poet was excluded from the company of real poets by the label poetess, and a woman who piloted an airplane was denied full status as an aviator by being called an aviatrix. At about the time poetess, aviatrix, and similar Adam-ribbisms were dropping out of use, H. W. Fowler was urging that they be revived. "With the coming expansion of women's vocations," he wrote in the first edition (1926) of *Modern English Usage,* "feminines for vocation-words are a special need of the future." There can be no doubt he subconsciously recog- nized the downgrading status implied in the -ess designations. His criticism of a woman who wished to be known as an author rather than an authoress was that she had no need "to raise herself to the level of the male author by asserting her right to his name."

The demise of most -ess endings came about before the start of the new feminist movement. In the second edition of *Modern Eng-*

lish Usage, published in 1965, Sir Ernest Gowers frankly admitted what his predecessors had been up to. "Feminine designations," he wrote, "seem now to be falling into disuse. Perhaps the explanation of this paradox is that it symbolizes the victory of women in their struggle for equal rights."

If Sir Ernest's optimism can be justified, why is there now a movement back toward feminine gender endings in such words as chairwoman, councilwoman, and congresswoman? Betty Hudson of Madison, Connecticut, is campaigning for the adoption of "selectwoman" as the legal title for a female member of that town's executive body. To have to address a woman as "selectman," she maintains, "is not only bad grammar and bad biology, but it implies that politics is still, or should be, a man's business."

Some women, of course, have yet to learn they are invisible. An eight-year-old who visited the American Museum of Natural History with her Brownie scout troop went through the impressive exhibit on pollution and overpopulation called "Can Man Survive?" Asked, afterward, "Well, can he?" she answered, "I don't know about him, but we're working on it in Brownies."

Nowhere are women rendered more invisible by language than in politics. The United States Constitution, in describing the qualifications for Representative, Senator, and President, refers to each as "he." No wonder Shirley Chisholm, the second woman since 1888 to make a try for the Presidential nomination of a major party [Margaret Chase Smith entered Presidential primaries in 1964], has found it difficult to be taken seriously.

As much as any other factor in our language, the ambiguous meaning of *"man"* serves to deny women recognition as people. In a recent magazine article, we discussed the similar effect on women of the generic pronoun "he," which we proposed to replace by a new common-gender pronoun "tey." We were immediately told, by a number of authorities, that we were dabbling in the serious business of linguistics, and the message that reached us from these scholars was loud and clear: It - is - absolutely - impossible - for - anyone - to - introduce - a - new - word - into - the - language - just - because - there - is - a - need - for - it, so - stop - wasting - your - time.

When words are suggested like "herstory" (for history), "hissicane" (for hurricane), and "mistresspiece" (for the work of a Virginia Woolf) one suspects a not-too-subtle attempt to make the whole language problem look silly. But unless Alexander Pope, when he wrote "The proper study of mankind is man," meant that women should be relegated to the footnotes (or, as George Orwell might have put it, "All men are equal, but men are more equal than women"), viable new words will surely someday supersede the old.

Without apologies to Freud, the great majority of women do not wish in their hearts that they were men. If having grown up with a language that tells them they are at the same time men and not men raises psychic doubts for women, the doubts are not of their sexual identity but of their human identity. Perhaps the present unrest surfacing in the women's movement is part of an evolutionary change in our particular form of life—the one form of all in the animal and plant kingdoms that orders and interprets its reality by symbols. The achievements of the species called man have brought us to the brink of self-destruction. If the species survives into the next century with the expectation of going on, it may only be because we have become part of what science writer Harlow Shapley calls the psychozoic kingdom, where brain overshadows brawn and rationality has replaced superstition.

Searching the roots of Western civilization for a word to call this new species of man and woman, someone might come up with "gen," as in genesis and generic. With such a word, "man" could be used exclusively for males as "woman" is used for females, for gen would include both sexes. Like the words deer and bison, gen would be both plural and singular. Gen would express the warmth and generalized sexuality of generous, gentle, and genuine: the specific sexuality of genital and genetic. In the new family of gen, girls and boys would grow to genhood, and to speak of genkind would be to include all the people of the earth.

SEVEN | The Web of Life

A. B. C. WHIPPLE
An Ugly New Footprint in the Sand

As author Whipple says, "You have to try to get away from pollution to realize how bad it really is." From his home in the Bahamas, Whipple observes the closing of another escape route, as he describes the first steps in the pollution of his environment. The "ugly new footprint" is, of course, oil on the beach, and this essay not only describes the coming of such pollution but also considers its causes. In pointing to technology as the primary source of the problem, Whipple suggests that the machine may, after all, have its "ultimate, mindless, all-unintended triumph over man. . . ."

The author chooses his words and sentence patterns with unusual sensitivity. Watch for his vivid images and his varied and rhythmic sentence patterns.

(1) There were strangers on our beach yesterday, for the first time in a month. A new footprint on our sand is nearly as rare as in *Robinson Crusoe*. We are at the very edge of the Atlantic; half a mile out in front of us is a coral reef, and then nothing but 3,000 miles of ocean to West Africa. It is a wild and lonely beach, with the same surf beating on it as when Columbus came by. And yet the beach is polluted.

(2) Oil tankers over the horizon have fouled it more than legions of picnickers could. The oil comes ashore in floating patches that stain the coral black and gray. It has blighted the rock crabs and the crayfish and has coated the delicate whorls of the conch shells with black

goo. And it has congealed upon itself, littering the beach with globes of tar that resemble the cannonballs of a deserted battlefield. The islanders, as they go beachcombing for the treasures the sea has washed up for centuries, now wear old shoes to protect their feet from the oil that washes up too.

(3) You have to try to get away from pollution to realize how bad it really is. We have known for the last few years how bad our cities are. Now there is no longer an escape. If there is oil on this island far out in the Atlantic, there is oil on nearly every other island.

(4) It is still early here. The air is still clear over the island, but it won't be when they build the airstrip they are talking about. The water out over the reef is still blue and green, but it is dirtier than it was a few years ago. And if the land is not despoiled, it is only because there are not yet enough people here to despoil it. There will be. And so for the moment on this island we are witnesses to the beginning, as it were, of the pollution of our environment.

(5) When you watch a bird over the beach or a fish along the reef you realize how ill-adapted man is to this environment anyway. Physically there is nothing he can do that some other creature cannot do better. Only his neocortex, the "thinking cap" on top of his brain, has enabled him to invent and construct artificial aids to accomplish what he could not do by himself. He cannot fly, so he has developed airplanes that can go faster than birds. He is slower than the horse, so he invented the wheel and the internal combustion engine. Even in his ancestral element, the sea, he is clumsy and short of breath. Without his brain, his artificial aids, his technology, he would have been unable to cope with, even survive in, his environment. But only after so many centuries is his brain dimly realizing that while he has managed to control his environment, he has so far been unable to protect it.

(6) Perhaps he simply is not far enough up the evolutionary ladder to survive on this planet for very much longer. To take only two of his inefficient physical functions, he is so far unable to control either his body wastes or his population. Man is a natural polluter, and his invention of the bathroom and the incinerator has, it now becomes evident, only postponed the problem. On this island we burn our papers, bury our tin cans and dump our garbage in the bay. It is not very efficient and perhaps not even very civilized. Yet so long as there are only a few people here, it has no ill effects. But when the inevitable wave of population sweeps out from the mainland, the islanders will face the problem of their own pollution just as the New Yorker does today.

(7) Man's sexual construction is perhaps the biggest accident of his physical makeup: it is only now becoming obvious—when it may

well be too late—that it would have been better if he required artificial aid to *have* children, rather than to *avoid* having them.

(8) Until the pollution of our deserted beach, it seemed simple to
blame everything on the "population explosion." If the population
of this island, for example, could be stabilized at a couple of hundred,
there would be very little problem with the environment in this
secluded area. There would be no pollution of the environment if
there were not too many people using it. And so if we concentrate on
winning the war against overpopulation, we can save the earth for
mankind.

(9) But the oil on the beach belies this too-easy assumption. Those
tankers are not out there because too many Chinese and Indians are
being born every minute. They are not even out there because there
are too many Americans and Europeans. They are delivering their
oil, and cleaning their tanks at sea and sending the residue up onto
the beaches of the Atlantic and Pacific, in order to fuel the technology
of mankind—and the factories and the power plants, the vehicles and
the engines that have enabled mankind to survive on his planet are
now spoiling the planet for life.

(10) The fishermen on this island are perfectly right in preferring
the outboard motor to the sail. Their livelihood is involved, and the
motor, for all its fouling smell, has helped increase the fisherman's
catch so that he can now afford to dispense with the far more obnox-
ious outdoor privy. But the danger of technology is in its escalation,
and there has already been a small amount of escalation here. You can
see the motor oil slicks around the town dock. Electric generators can
be heard over the sound of the surf. And while there are only about
two dozen automobiles for the ten miles of road, already there is a
wrecked jeep rusting in the harbor waters where it was dumped and
abandoned. The escalation of technological pollution is coming here
just as surely as it came to the mainland cities that are now shrouded
by fly ash.

(11) If the oil is killing the life along the coral heads, what must
it not be doing to the phytoplankton at sea which provide 70% of
the oxygen we breathe? The lesson of our fouled beach is that we
may not even have realized how late it is already. Mankind, because
of his technology, may require far more space per person on this
globe than we had ever thought, but it is more than a matter of a certain number of square yards per person. There is instead a delicate
balance of nature in which many square miles of ocean and vegetation
and clean air are needed to sustain only a relatively few human
beings. We may find, as soon as the end of this century, that the final
despoliation of our environment has been signaled not by starvation
but by people choking to death. The technology—the machine—will

then indeed have had its ultimate, mindless, all-unintended triumph over man, by destroying the atmosphere he lives in just as surely as you can pinch off a diver's breathing tube.

(12) Sitting on a lonely but spoiled beach, it is hard to imagine but possible to believe.

QUESTIONS AND EXERCISES

VOCABULARY
1. escalation (*paragraph* 10)
2. phytoplankton (11)
3. despoliation (11)

LANGUAGE AND RHETORIC
1. Are the allusions to Robinson Crusoe and to Columbus effective for introducing the subject of this essay? How do they suggest the conflict that is central to the pollution problem?
2. Like a poet, the author chooses his words and sentence patterns carefully. Examine paragraphs 2 and 3, and point out examples of vivid images, varied and rhythmic sentences, and the skillful use of conjunctions. Read these paragraphs aloud and listen to the sound of the prose.
3. Parallel structure is frequently used for coherence and emphasis. Find instances of this technique in paragraphs 2, 4, 5, and 9.
4. In paragraph 4 the author uses four different devices of coherence to connect sentences. Identify each type. What method of development is used in this paragraph?
5. Why does the author limit the concluding paragraph to one sentence? Is this conclusion successful? Support your answer.
6. What is the topic sentence of paragraph 10? How is this topic sentence developed?
7. Paragraphs 6, 7, and 8 form a unit. What is the topic sentence of this unit?
8. Where does the author state his thesis? State that thesis in your own words.

DISCUSSION AND WRITING
1. Who should be considered responsible for the oil polluting the author's beach? The tanker crew? The company that owns the tanker? A government agency? Who should be held accountable for such a problem, and what steps might be taken to overcome it?
2. In paragraph 3 the author says, "You have to try to get away from pollution to realize how bad it really is." Based on your own experience, write an essay in which you explain how you came to realize "how bad it really is."
3. Is man as ill adapted to his environment as the author contends? Has he managed to control his environment without protecting it? Develop in detail one example that would either support or challenge the author's contention.
4. The author cites the problems of waste disposal and population growth as

examples of man's inefficient handling of his environment. Do you think these are crucial problems? If so, propose some specific ways of dealing with one of them. If not, name a problem that is more crucial and explain what might be done to help overcome it.

5. Do you agree with the author's conclusion that the primary source of our environmental problem is technology? If you do agree, what steps could be taken to enable us to live more comfortably with our technology? Try focusing on one kind of machine or industry.

WAYNE H. DAVIS
Overpopulated America

In this article Wayne H. Davis argues that the most seriously over-populated nation is not measured so much by numbers as it is by the decreasing ability of the land to support life. Measured by these standards, America has a population problem that surpasses that of India. For the average Indian's contribution to the destruction of his land is minimal, but the average American's way of life imposes an enormous burden on his environment. If Davis is correct, American affluence rests on a crumbling foundation; and unless we establish a new perspective on both the population and pollution problems, our nation is not likely to survive.

The structure of this article consists of two basic parts: problem and solution. See if you can locate the dividing point.

(1) I define as most seriously overpopulated that nation whose people by virtue of their numbers and activities are most rapidly decreasing the ability of the land to support human life. With our large population, our affluence and our technological monstrosities the United States wins first place by a substantial margin.

(2) Let's compare the U.S. to India, for example. We have 203 million people, whereas she has 540 million on much less land. But look at the impact of people on the land.

(3) The average Indian eats his daily few cups of rice (or perhaps wheat, whose production on American farms contributed to our one percent per year drain in quality of our active farmland), draws his bucket of water from the communal well and sleeps in a mud hut. In

his daily rounds to gather cow dung to burn to cook his rice and warm his feet, his footsteps, along with those of millions of his countrymen, help bring about a slow deterioration of the ability of the land to support people. His contribution to the destruction of the land is minimal.

(4) An American, on the other hand, can be expected to destroy a piece of land on which he builds a home, garage and driveway. He will contribute his share to the 142 million tons of smoke and fumes, seven million junked cars, 20 million tons of paper, 48 billion cans, and 26 billion bottles the overburdened environment must absorb each year. To run his air conditioner we will strip-mine a Kentucky hillside, push the dirt and slate down into the stream, and burn coal in a power generator, whose smokestack contributes to a plume of smoke massive enough to cause cloud seeding and premature precipitation from Gulf winds which should be irrigating the wheat farms of Minnesota.

(5) In his lifetime he will personally pollute three million gallons of water, and industry and agriculture will use ten times this much water in his behalf. To provide these needs the U.S. Army Corps of Engineers will build dams and flood farmland. He will also use 21,000 gallons of leaded gasoline containing boron, drink 28,000 pounds of milk and eat 10,000 pounds of meat. The latter is produced and squandered in a life pattern unknown to Asians. A steer on a Western range eats plants containing minerals necessary for plant life. Some of these are incorporated into the body of the steer which is later shipped for slaughter. After being eaten by man these nutrients are flushed down the toilet into the ocean or buried in the cemetery, the surface of which is cluttered with boulders called tombstones and has been removed from productivity. The result is a continual drain on the productivity of range land. Add to this the erosion of overgrazed lands, and the effects of the falling water table as we mine Pleistocene deposits of groundwater to irrigate to produce food for more people, and we can see why our land is dying far more rapidly than did the great civilizations of the Middle East, which experienced the same cycle. The average Indian citizen, whose fecal material goes back to the land, has but a minute fraction of the destructive effect on the land that the affluent American does.

(6) Thus I want to introduce a new term, which I suggest be used in future discussions of human population and ecology. We should speak of our numbers in "Indian equivalents." An Indian equivalent I define as the average number of Indian citizens required to have the same detrimental effect on the land's ability to support human life as would the average American. This value is difficult to determine,

but let's take an extremely conservative working figure of 25. To see how conservative this is, imagine the addition of 1000 citizens to your town and 25,000 to an Indian village. Not only would the Americans destroy much more land for homes, highways and a shopping center, but they would contribute far more to environmental deterioration in hundreds of other ways as well. For example, their demand for steel for new autos might increase the daily pollution equivalent of 130,000 junk autos which *Life* tells us that U.S. Steel Corp. dumps into Lake Michigan. Their demand for textiles would help the cotton industry destroy the life in the Black Warrior River in Alabama with endrin. And they would contribute to the massive industrial pollution of our oceans (we provide one third to one half the world's share) which has caused the precipitous downward trend in our commercial fisheries landings during the past seven years.

(7) The per capita gross national product of the United States is 38 times that of India. Most of our goods and services contribute to the decline in the ability of the environment to support life. Thus it is clear that a figure of 25 for an Indian equivalent is conservative. It has been suggested to me that a more realistic figure would be 500.

(8) In Indian equivalents, therefore, the population of the United States is at least four billion. And the rate of growth is even more alarming. We are growing at one percent per year, a rate which would double our numbers in 70 years. India is growing at 2.5 percent. Using the Indian equivalent of 25, our population growth becomes 10 times as serious as that of India. According to the Reinows in their recent book *Moment in the Sun*, just one year's crop of American babies can be expected to use up 25 billion pounds of beef, 200 million pounds of steel and 9.1 billion gallons of gasoline during their collective lifetime. And the demands on water and land for our growing population are expected to be far greater than the supply available in the year 2000. We are destroying our land at a rate of over a million acres a year. We now have only 2.6 agricultural acres per person. By 1975 this will be cut to 2.2, the critical point for the maintenance of what we consider a decent diet, and by the year 2000 we might expect to have 1.2.

(9) You might object that I am playing with statistics in using the Indian equivalent on the rate of growth. I am making the assumption that today's Indian child will live 35 years (the average Indian life span) at today's level of affluence. If he lives an American 70 years, our rate of population growth would be 20 times as serious as India's.

(10) But the assumption of continued affluence at today's level is unfounded. If our numbers continue to rise, our standard of living will fall so sharply that by the year 2000 any surviving Americans

might consider today's average Asian to be well off. Our children's destructive effects on their environment will decline as they sink ever lower into poverty.

(11) The United States is in serious economic trouble now. Nothing could be more misleading than today's affluence, which rests precariously on a crumbling foundation. Our productivity, which had been increasing steadily at about 3.2 percent a year since World War II, has been falling during 1969. Our export over import balance has been shrinking steadily from $7.1 billion in 1964 to $0.15 billion in the first half of 1969. Our balance of payments deficit for the second quarter was $3.7 billion, the largest in history. We are now importing iron ore, steel, oil, beef, textiles, cameras, radios and hundreds of other things.

(12) Our economy is based upon the Keynesian concept of a continued growth in population and productivity. It worked in an underpopulated nation with excess resources. It could continue to work only if the earth and its resources were expanding at an annual rate of 4 to 5 percent. Yet neither the number of cars, the economy, the human population, nor anything else can expand indefinitely at an exponential rate in a finite world. We must face this fact *now*. The crisis is here. When Walter Heller says that our economy will expand by 4 percent annually through the latter 1970s he is dreaming. He is in a theoretical world totally unaware of the realities of human ecology. If the economists do not wake up and devise a new system for us now somebody else will have to do it for them.

(13) A civilization is comparable to a living organism. Its longevity is a function of its metabolism. The higher the metabolism (affluence), the shorter the life. Keynesian economics has allowed us an affluent but shortened life span. We have now run our course.

(14) The tragedy facing the United States is even greater and more imminent than that descending upon the hungry nations. The Paddock brothers in their book, *Famine 1975!*, say that India "cannot be saved" no matter how much food we ship her. But India will be here after the United States is gone. Many millions will die in the most colossal famines India has ever known, but the land will survive and she will come back as she always has before. The United States, on the other hand, will be a desolate tangle of concrete and ticky-tacky, of strip-mined moonscape and silt-choked reservoirs. The land and water will be so contaminated with pesticides, herbicides, mercury fungicides, lead, boron, nickel, arsenic and hundreds of other toxic substances, which have been approaching critical levels of concentration in our environment as a result of our numbers and affluence, that it may be unable to sustain human life.

(15) Thus as the curtain gets ready to fall on man's civilization let it

come as no surprise that it shall first fall on the United States. And let no one make the mistake of thinking we can save ourselves by "cleaning up the environment." Banning DDT is the equivalent of the physician's treating syphilis by putting a bandaid over the first chancre to appear. In either case you can be sure that more serious and widespread trouble will soon appear unless the disease itself is treated. We cannot survive by planning to treat the symptoms such as air pollution, water pollution, soil erosion, etc.

(16) What can we do to slow the rate of destruction of the United States as a land capable of supporting human life? There are two approaches. First, we must reverse the population growth. We have far more people now than we can continue to support at anything near today's level of affluence. American women average slightly over three children each. According to the *Population Bulletin* if we reduced this number to 2.5 there would still be 330 million people in the nation at the end of the century. And even if we reduced this to 1.5 we would have 57 million more people in the year 2000 than we have now. With our present longevity patterns it would take more than 30 years for the population to peak even when reproducing at this rate, which would eventually give us a net decrease in numbers.

(17) Do not make the mistake of thinking that technology will solve our population problem by producing a better contraceptive. Our problem now is that people want too many children. Surveys show the average number of children wanted by the American family is 3.3. There is little difference between the poor and the wealthy, black and white, Catholic and Protestant. Production of children at this rate during the next 30 years would be so catastrophic in effect on our resources and the viability of the nation as to be beyond my ability to contemplate. To prevent this trend we must not only make contraceptives and abortion readily available to everyone, but we must establish a system to put severe economic pressure on those who produce children and reward those who do not. This can be done within our system of taxes and welfare.

(18) The other thing we must do is to pare down our Indian equivalents. Individuals in American society vary tremendously in Indian equivalents. If we plot Indian equivalents versus their reciprocal, the percentage of land surviving a generation, we obtain a linear regression. We can then place individuals and occupation types on this graph. At one end would be the starving blacks of Mississippi; they would approach unity in Indian equivalents, and would have the least destructive effect on the land. At the other end of the graph would be the politicians slicing pork for the barrel, the highway contractors, strip-mine operators, real estate developers, and public enemy number one — the U.S. Army Corps of Engineers.

(19) We must halt land destruction. We must abandon the view of land and minerals as private property to be exploited in any way economically feasible for private financial gain. Land and minerals are resources upon which the very survival of the nation depends, and their use must be planned in the best interests of the people.

(20) Rising expectations for the poor is a cruel joke foisted upon them by the Establishment. As our new economy of use-it-once-and-throw-it-away produces more and more products for the affluent, the share of our resources available for the poor declines. Blessed be the starving blacks of Mississippi with their outdoor privies, for they are ecologically sound, and they shall inherit a nation. Although I hope that we will help these unfortunate people attain a decent standard of living by diverting war efforts to fertility control and job training, our most urgent task to assure this nation's survival during the next decade is to stop the affluent destroyers.

QUESTIONS AND EXERCISES

VOCABULARY
1. affluence (*paragraph* 1)
2. ecology (6)
3. detrimental (6)
4. endrin (6)
5. precipitous (6)
6. Keynesian (12)
7. exponential (12)
8. finite (12)
9. metabolism (13)
10. imminent (14)
11. feasible (19)

LANGUAGE AND RHETORIC
1. How does the tone of this article compare or contrast with the tone of "An Ugly New Footprint in the Sand"? Find words and passages that reveal Davis' tone.
2. What is the primary method of paragraph development in paragraphs 4, 5, 8, and 11?
3. Why is paragraph 2 so short? Could it be combined with paragraph 3? Paragraphs 2, 3, 4, and 5 form a unit. What topic sentence introduces this unit?
4. What is the function of paragraphs 16 through 20 in relation to the preceding paragraphs?
5. Which paragraphs open with transition markers in their first sentences?
6. This article consists of two parts: problem and solution. Where is the dividing point?
7. How does the author vary the length of his sentences in paragraph 12 to provide emphasis?

DISCUSSION AND WRITING
1. According to the author, cleaning up the environment will not solve our pollution problems. Explain why. Do you agree with Davis?

2. If the population problem is as serious as the author says, should people still be free to have whatever number of children they wish, or should they be limited by law to a certain number of children? How do you react to the author's recommendation that "we must establish a system to put severe economic pressure on those who produce children and reward those who do not"? Give specific reasons to support your answer.
3. The author states that we must make contraceptives and abortion readily available to everyone. Should contraceptives be made available to teen-agers? Should abortion be accessible to all who desire it? What limits, if any, should be placed on these proposals, and who should determine them?
4. Why does the author say that "rising expectations for the poor is a cruel joke foisted upon them by the Establishment"? What does he want us to do for the poor? Do you agree or disagree with his suggestions?
5. Compare and contrast Davis' ideas on the environmental problem with those of the author of the previous article. Consider especially the causes of the problem.

JEANE WESTIN

Planned Pethood

The preceding essay deals with what has become a widely recognized contemporary problem — overpopulation. This article deals with a less familiar but equally flagrant problem — the seemingly limitless expansion of our pet population. Author Jeane Westin describes the situation and examines some of the possible causes of, and solutions to, the problem.

This article is a good example of the use of factual details.

(1) There's a new population bomb ticking. While Americans have reduced their own birthrate to below replacement level, their pets are breeding potential disaster in the backyard. Maybe man won't overrun this planet, but his furry pet poodles, pointers and Siamese cats might.

(2) Nobody knows the exact number of surplus pets, but the Humane Society of the United States estimates that today there are at least 50 million homeless cats and dogs in this country — double the 1968 figure.

"Planned Pethood" by Jeane Westin. From *Parade*, June 3, 1973. By permission of the author.

(3) Many of those wind up in animal shelters, where most are eventually put to death. Others are dumped in a rural area in the belief that the animal will have a better chance to live. Not so, says the Humane Society. Domestic pets are generally unable to survive without man and most don't last long. The ones who do live form wild packs, menacing people as well as livestock and game. Many more strays are destroyed on the highway by autos.

(4) The Animal Protection Institute of America says over 500 million dollars were spent for animal control last year—most of it to catch, keep and kill 12 million dogs and 7 million cats. "All this killing is such a tragic waste," says API president Belton P. Mouras. "Irresponsible pet owners have turned our animal pounds and shelters into so many slaughterhouses. This has caused us an identity problem: We started out as kind people who want to rescue poor, lost animals. But we've been forced to become pet executioners."

(5) The pet population could be considerably reduced, experts say, if Americans were willing to have their animals de-sexed. But many owners are not willing to have their animals sterilized. To begin with, the operation can cost as much as $40 for cats and $100 for dogs. In some areas humane societies have pitched in to underwrite part of the cost, and in Los Angeles a low-cost, tax-supported clinic has been established, charging a flat rate of $17.50 for females, $11.50 for males. In a little more than a year that program has reduced the city's stray population by 6000 animals.

(6) But many owners reject sterilizing their pets on other grounds. Most frequently quoted is the notion that breeding a dog is an excellent way to teach sex education to children. Phyllis Wright, director of the National Humane Education Center at Waterford, Va., finds that idea appalling. In the past several years she has overseen the grim business of destroying 70,000 unwanted animals. "When people tell me they're going to breed a dog so their kids can watch 'the miracle of life,'" she says bitterly, "I invite them over here to watch the miracle of death."

(7) Other owners argue that a female dog or cat needs to have at least one litter to fulfill some maternal instinct; and that altered animals grow fat and lazy. Not so on both counts, say many veterinarians. Animal motherhood never experienced goes unmissed. And overweight is most often caused by overfeeding—in many cases a guilt offering by the owner for taking the pet's sex away.

(8) Another reason for not acting has to do with the humanization of the American family pet. "The typical owner won't sterilize Fido," says Belton Mouras, "because he doesn't want to sterilize himself. Owners confuse their own sexual feelings with their animals'."

(9) Whatever the reason for not practicing pet birth control, the resulting surplus has created some extra environmental burdens. Street and park pollution in some large cities is already a health hazard.

(10) Clearly a dramatic decrease in the pet birthrate is called for, a kind of planned pethood. But how? Mouras says pet owners should be held accountable for indiscriminate breeding. "Allowing a pet to breed unwanted litters should bring a substantial fine."

(11) Still, even a national sterilization drive won't totally solve the problem. It's impossible, say veterinary spokesmen, to alter millions of fertile cats and dogs, even if every vet operated night and day. "Surgery is ineffective," states Dr. Jack Morse, president of the California Veterinary Medical Association, who believes research should focus on cheaper, non-surgical methods.

(12) Along these lines, several new types of animal birth control are being explored. Syntex, a California pharmaceutical company, has developed a hormonal pellet which can be implanted under the skin, preventing both the estrus (the heat period) and conception. However, the pellet—if approved by the Federal Drug Administration—will not be on the market for three to five years.

(13) Meanwhile, immunologists are experimenting with an injection which, when given at puberty, immunizes the animal to its own sex hormones.

(14) And theoretically at least, laser beams and controlled radiation are in the future. Someday it may even be possible for pets to be rendered sexless via a painless pill put into their food. At present, surgery is the only expedient.

QUESTIONS AND EXERCISES

VOCABULARY
1. humane (*paragraph* 2)
2. underwrite (5)
3. indiscriminate (10)
4. hormonal (12)
5. expedient (14)

LANGUAGE AND RHETORIC
1. What seems to be the author's purpose in writing this article, and how has she used factual details to fulfill that purpose?
2. The author handles her material quite objectively. What does she gain and what does she lose by avoiding personal involvement with her subject?
3. What are the sources of information for this article?
4. Does the author convince you of the validity of her case? Why or why not?

DISCUSSION AND WRITING

1. What is your reaction to the situation recounted here? Are you moved to do anything about it? Why or why not?
2. Visit an animal shelter in your community, and write a paper based on the experience.
3. If you have pets of your own, how do you feel about having them sterilized, and what is the basis for your feeling?
4. One source quoted here says that pet owners should be held accountable for indiscriminate breeding and suggests that "allowing a pet to breed unwanted litters should bring a substantial fine." What is your reaction to this position and why?
5. If you have had to undergo the experience of having an animal put to death, write a paper about that experience and its effect on you.

RICHARD RHODES

Watching the Animals

The loves of flint and iron are naturally a little rougher than those of the nightingale and the rose.   —*Ralph Waldo Emerson*

I remembered today about this country lake in Kansas where I live: that it is artificial, built at the turn of the century, when Upton Sinclair was writing *The Jungle,* as an ice lake. The trains with their loads of fresh meat from the Kansas City stockyards would stop by the Kaw River, across the road, and ice the cars. "You have just dined," Emerson once told what must have been a shocked Victorian audience, "and however scrupulously the slaughterhouse is concealed in the graceful distance of miles, there is complicity, expensive races— race living at the expense of race. . . ."

The I-D Packing Company of Des Moines, Iowa: a small outfit which subcontracts from Armour the production of fresh pork. It can handle about 450 pigs an hour on its lines. No beef or mutton. No smoked hams or hot dogs. Plain fresh pork. A well-run outfit, with federal inspectors alert on all the lines.

The kind of slaughterhouse Upton Sinclair was talking about doesn't exist around here any more. The vast buildings still stand in Des Moines and Omaha and Kansas City, but the operations are gone.

The big outfits used to operate on a profit margin of 1.5 per cent, which didn't give them much leeway, did it. Now they are defunct, and their buildings, which look like monolithic enlargements of concentration-camp barracks, sit empty, the hundreds of windows broken, dusty, jagged pieces of glass sticking out of the frames as if the animals heard the good news one day and leaped out the nearest exit. Even the stockyards, miles and miles of rotting, weathered board pens, floors paved fifty years ago by hand with brick, look empty, though I am told cattle receipts are up compared to what they were a few years back. The new thing is small, specialized, efficient houses out where the cattle are, in Denver, in Phoenix, in Des Moines, especially in Texas, where the weather is more favorable to fattening cattle. In Iowa the cattle waste half their feed just keeping warm in the wintertime. But in Iowa or in Texas, the point of meat-packing today is refrigeration. It's cheaper to ship cold meat than live animals. So the packing plants have gone out to the farms and ranches. They are even beginning to buy up the ranches themselves so that they won't have to depend on the irregularities of farmers and cattlemen who bring their animals in only when the price is up or the ground too wet for plowing. Farmhouses stand empty all over America. Did you know that? The city has already won, never mind how many of our television shows still depict the hardy bucolic rural. I may regret the victory, but that's my lookout. We are an urban race now, and meat is something you buy shrink-wrapped at the supermarket.

There are no stockyards outside the I-D Packing Company. The pigs arrive by trailer truck from Sioux City and other places. Sometimes a farmer brings in two or three in the back of his pickup. He unloads them into the holding pens, where they are weighed and inspected, goes into the office and picks up his check. The men, except on the killing floor, are working on the cooled carcasses of yesterday's kill anyway, so there is time to even out the line. Almost everything in a packinghouse operates on a chain line, and for maximum profit that line must be full, 450 carcasses an hour at the I-D Packing Company, perhaps 300 heavies if today is heavies day — sows, overgrown hogs. Boars presumably escape the general fate. Their flesh is flavored with rut and tastes like an unventilated gymnasium locker room.

Down goes the tail gate and out come the pigs, enthusiastic after their drive. Pigs are the most intelligent of all farm animals, by actual laboratory test. Learn the fastest, for example, to push a plunger with their foot to earn a reward of pelletized food. And not as reliable in their instincts. You don't have to call cattle to dinner. They are waiting outside the fence at 4:30 sharp, having arrived as silently as the Vietcong. But perhaps that is pig intelligence too: let you do the work, laze around until the last minute, and then charge over and knock you down before you can slop the garbage into the trough. Cattle will stroll one by one into a row of stalls and usually fill them in serial order. Not pigs. They squeal and nip and shove. Each one wants the entire meal for himself. They won't stick together in a herd, either. Shoot out all over the place, and you'd damned better have every gate closed or they'll be in your garden and on your lawn and even in your living room, nodding by the fire.

They talk a lot to each other, to you if you care to listen. I am not romanticizing pigs. They always scared me a little on the farm, which is probably why I watched them more closely than the other animals. They do talk: low grunts, quick squeals, a kind of hum sometimes, angry shrieks, high screams of fear.

I have great respect for the I-D Packing Company. They do a dirty job and do it as cleanly and humanely as possible, and do it well. They were nice enough to let me in the door, which is more than I can say for the Wilson people in Omaha, where I first tried to arrange a tour. What are you hiding, Wilson people?

Once into the holding pen, the pigs mill around getting to know each other. The I-D holding pens are among the most modern in the nation, my spokesman told me. Tubular steel painted tinner's red to keep it from rusting. Smooth concrete floors with drains so that the floors can be washed down hygienically after each lot of pigs is run through.

The pigs come out of the first holding pen through a gate that allows only one to pass at a time. Just beside the gate is a wooden door, and behind the door is the first worker the pigs encounter. He has a wooden box beside him filled with metal numbers, the shape of each number picked out with sharp needles. For each lot of pigs he selects a set of numbers — 2473, say — and slots them into a device like a hammer and dips it in nontoxic purple dye. As a pig shoots out of the gate he hits the pig in the side with the numbers, making a tattoo. The pig gives a grunt — it doesn't especially hurt, pigskin is thick, as you know — and moves on to one of several smaller pens where each lot is held until curtain time. The tattoo, my spokesman told me, will stay on the animal through all the killing and cleaning and cutting operations, to the very end. Its purpose is to identify any animal or lot of animals which might be diseased, so that the seller can be informed and the carcasses destroyed. Rather too proud of his tattooing process, I thought, but then, you know the tattoos I am thinking about.

It would be more dramatic, make a better story, if the killing came last, but it comes first. We crossed a driveway with more red steel fencing. Lined up behind it, pressing into it because they sensed by now that all was not well with them, were perhaps a hundred pigs.

But still curious, watching us go by in our long white canvas coats. Everyone wore those, and hard plastic helmets, white helmets for the workers, yellow helmets for the foremen. I got to be a foreman.

Before they reach their end, the pigs get a shower, a real one. Water sprays from every angle to wash the farm off of them. Then they begin to feel crowded. The pen narrows like a funnel; the drivers behind urge the pigs forward, until one at a time they climb onto a moving ramp. The ramp's sides move as well as its floor. The floor is cleated to give the pigs footing. The sides are made of blocks of wood so that they will not bruise, and they slant inward to wedge the pigs along. Now they scream, never having been on such a ramp, smelling the smells they smell ahead. I do not want to overdramatize, because you have read all this before. But it was a frightening experience, seeing their fear, seeing so many of them go by. It had to remind me of things no one wants to be reminded of anymore, all mobs, all death marches, all mass murders and extinctions, the slaughter of the buffalo, the slaughter of the Indian, the Inferno, Judgment Day, complicity, expensive races, race living at the expense of race. That so gentle a religion as Christianity could end up in Judgment Day. That we are the most expensive of races, able in our affluence to hire others of our kind to do this terrible necessary work of killing another race of creatures so that we may feed our oxygen-rich brains. Feed our children, for that matter.

At the top of the ramp, one man. With rubber gloves on, holding two electrodes that looked like enlarged curling irons except that they sported more of those needles. As a pig reached the top, this man jabbed the electrodes into the pig's butt and shoulder, and that was it. No more pain, no more fear, no more mudholes, no more sun in the lazy afternoon. Kocked instantly unconscious, the pig shuddered in a long spasm and fell onto a stainless steel table a foot below the end of the ramp. Up came another pig, and the same result. And another, and another, 450 an hour, 3,600 a day, the belts returning below to coax another ride.

The pigs are not dead, merely unconscious. The electrodes are humane, my spokesman said, and, relatively speaking, that is true. They used to gas the pigs—put them on a conveyor belt that ran through a room filled with anesthetic gas. That was humane too. The electrodes are more efficient. Anesthesia relaxes the body and loosens the bowels. The gassed pigs must have been a mess. More efficient, then, to put their bodies in spasm.

They drop to the table, and here the endless chain begins. A worker takes the nearest dangling chain by its handle as it passes. The chain is attached at the top to a belt of links, like a large bicycle chain. At the bottom the dangling chain has a metal handle like the handle on a bike. The chain runs through the handle and then attaches to the end of the handle, so that by sliding the handle the worker forms a loop. Into the loop he hooks one of the pig's hind feet. Another worker does the same with the other foot. Each has his own special foot to grab, or the pig would go down the line backwards, which would not be convenient. Once hooked into the line, the pig will stay in place by the force of its own weight.

Now the line ascends, lifting the unconscious animal into the air. The pig proceeds a distance of ten feet, where a worker standing on a platform deftly inserts a butcher knife into its throat. They call it "sticking," which it is. Then all hell breaks loose, if blood merely is hell. It gushes out, at about a 45-degree angle downward, thick as a ship's hawser, pouring directly onto the floor. Nothing is so red as blood, an incandescent red and most beautiful. It is the brightest color we drab creatures possess. Down on the floor below, with a wide squeegee on a long handle, a worker spends his eight hours a day squeegeeing that blood, some of it clotted, jellied, now, into an open drain. It is cycled through a series of pipes into a dryer, later to be made into blood meal for animal feed.

The line swings around a corner, high above the man with the squeegee, around the drain floor, turns again left at the next corner, and begins to ascend to the floor above. This interval—thirteen seconds, I think my spokesman said, or was it thirty?—so that the carcass may drain completely before further processing. Below the carcass on the ascent is a trough like those lowered from the rear of cement trucks, there to catch the last drainings of blood.

Pigs are not skinned, as cattle are, unless you are after the leather, and we are after the meat. But the hair must be taken off, and it must first be scalded loose. Courteously, the line lowers the carcass into a long trough filled with water heated to 180 degrees. The carcass will float if given a chance, fat being lighter than water, so wooden pushers on crankshafts spaced equally along the scalding tank immerse and roll the carcasses. Near the end of the trough, my spokesman easily pulls out a tuft of hair. The line ascends again, up and away, and the carcass goes into a chamber where revolving brushes as tall as a man whisk away the hair. We pass to the other side of the chamber and find two workers with wide knives scraping off the few patches of hair that remain. The carcasses then pass through great hellish jets of yellowish-blue gas flame to singe the skin and harden it. The last step is polishing: more brushes. Our pig has turned pink and clean as a baby.

One of the small mercies of a slaughterhouse: what begins as a live animal loses all similarity as the processing goes on, until you can actually face the packaged meat at the exit door and admire its obvious flavor.

The polished carcasses swing through a door closed with rubber flaps, and there, dear friends, the action begins. Saws. Long knives. Butcher knives. Drawknives. Boning knives. Wails from the saws, large and small, that are driven by air like a dentist's drill. Shouts back and forth from the men, jokes, announcements, challenges. The temperature down to 50 degrees, everyone keen. Men start slicing off little pieces of the head right inside the door, each man his special slice, throwing them onto one of several lines that will depart for special bins. A carcass passes me and I see a bare eyeball staring, stripped of its lids. Deft knives drop the head from the neck leaving it dangling by a two-inch strip of skin. Around a corner, up to a platform, and three men gut the carcasses, great tubs of guts, each man taking the third carcass as it goes by. One of them sees me with my tape recorder and begins shouting at us something like "I am the greatest!" A crazy man, grinning and roaring at us, turning around and slipping in the knife, and out comes everything in one great load flopped onto a stainless-steel trough. And here things divide, and so must our attention.

My spokesman is proud of his chitterling machine. "I call them chitlins, but they're really chitterlings." It is the newest addition to his line. A worker separates the intestines from the other internal organs and shoves them down a slide, gray and shiny. Another worker finds one end and feeds it onto a steel tube flushed with water. Others trim off connective tissue, webbings, fat. The intestines shimmer along the tube into a washing vat, skinny up to the top of the machine where they are cooled, skinny back down where they are cooled further, and come up the other side ready for the supermarket. A worker drops them into wax buckets, pops on a lid, and packs them into shipping boxes. That is today's chitlin machine. They used to have to cool the chitlins overnight before they could be packaged. Now five men do the work of sixteen, in less time.

The remaining organs proceed down a waist-high conveyor; on the other side of the same walkway, the emptied carcasses pass; on a line next to the organ line the heads pass. By now all the meat has been trimmed off each head. A worker sockets them one at a time into a support like a footrest in a shoehine parlor and a wedge neatly splits them in half. Out come the tongues, out come the brains, and at the end of the line, out come the pituitaries, each tiny gland being passed to a government inspector in white pants, white shirt, and a yellow hard hat, who looks it over and drops it into a wax bucket. All these pieces, the brain, the tongue, the oddments of sidemeat off the head and carcass, will become "by-products": hot dogs, baloney, sausage. You are what you eat.

The loudest noise in the room comes from the big air-saw used to split the carcass in half down the backbone, leaving, again, connections at the butt end and between the shoulders. Other workers trim away interior fat, and then the carcasses proceed down their chain at 50 miles an hour to the blast freezer, 25 below zero and no place for mere mortals, to be chilled overnight.

Coming out of the freezer in another part of the room is yesterday's kill, cold and solid and smooth. A worker splits apart the two sides; the hams come off and go onto their own line; the shoulders come off and go onto theirs, to be made into picnics, shoulder roasts, trotters. Away goes the valuable loin, trimmed out deftly by a worker with a drawknife. Away goes the bacon. Chunks and strips of fat go off from everywhere in buckets carried on overhead hooks to a grinder that spins out worms of fat and blows them through a tube directly to the lard-rendering vats. Who uses lard anymore, I asked by spokesman. I don't know, he says, I think we export most of it.

At the end of all these lines men package the component parts of pig into wax-paper-lined cartons, load the cartons onto pallets, fork-lift the pallets into spotless aluminum trailers socketed right into the walls of the building so that I do not even realize I am inside a truck until my spokesman tells me, and off they go to Armour.

Processing an animal is exactly the opposite of processing a machine: the machine starts out with components and ends up put together; the animal starts out put together and ends up components. No clearer illustration of the law of entropy has ever been devised.

And that is a tour of a slaughterhouse, as cheerful as I could make it.

But the men there. Half of them blacks, some Mexicans, the rest whites. It gets harder and harder to hire men for this work, even though the pay is good. The production line keeps them hopping; they take their breaks when there is a break in the line, so that the killing floor breaks first, and their break leaves an empty space ten minutes long in the endless chain, which, arriving at the gutting operation, allows the men there to break, and so on. Monday morning absenteeism is a problem, I was told. Keeping the men under control can be a problem, too, I sensed: when the line broke down briefly during my tour, the men cheered as convicts might at a state license-plate factory when the stamping machine breaks down. It cannot be heartening to kill animals all day.

There is a difference, too, between the men who work with the live animals and hot carcasses and those who cut up the cold meat, a difference I remember from my days of butchering on the farm: the killing unsettles, while the cold cutting is a craft like carpentry or plumbing and offers the satisfactions of craftsmanship. The worker with the electrodes jammed them into the animal with anger and perverse satisfaction, as if he were knocking off the enemy. The worker at the guts acted as if he were wrestling bears. The hot workers talked to themselves, yelled at each other, or else lapsed into that strained silence you meet in deeply angry men; the cold workers said little but worked with deftness and something like pride. They knew they were good, and they showed off a little, zip zip, as we toured by. They used their hands as if they knew how to handle tools, and they did.

The technology at the I-D Packing Company is humane by present standards, at least so far as the animals are concerned. Where the workers are concerned, I'm not so sure. They looked to be in need of lulling.

Beyond technology is the larger question of attitude. Butchering on the farm when I was a boy had the quality of a ceremony. We would select, say, a steer, and pen it separately overnight. The next morning several of us boys—this was a boys' home as well as a farm—would walk the steer to a large compound and leave it standing, trusting as hell, near the concrete-floored area where we did the skinning and gutting. Then the farm mamager, a man of great kindness and reserve, would take aim with a .22 rifle at the crosspoint of two imaginary lines drawn from the horns to the opposite eyes. And hold his bead until the steer was entirely calm, looking at him, a certain shot, because this man did not want to miss, did not want to hurt the animal he was about to kill. And we would stand in a spread-out circle, at a respectful distance, tense with the drama of it, because we didn't want him to miss either.

The shot cracked out, the bullet entered the brain, and the animal instantly collapsed. Then the farm manager handed back the rifle, took a knife, ran forward, and cut into the throat. Then we dragged the steer onto the concrete, hooked its back legs through the Achilles tendons to a crosstree, and laboriously winched it into the air with a differential pulley. Four boys usually did the work, two older, two younger. The younger boys were supposed to be learning this skill, and you held your stomach together as best you could at first while the older boys played little tricks like, when they got there in the skinning, cutting off the pizzle and whipping it around your neck, But even these crudities had their place: they accustomed you to contact with flesh and blood.

And while the older boys did their work of splitting the halves with a hacksaw, you got to take the guts, which on the farm we did not save except for the liver, the heart, and the sweetbreads, in a wheelbarrow down to the back lane where you built, with wood you had probably cut yourself, a most funeral pyre. Then we doused the guts with gasoline, tossed in a match, and Whoosh! off they went. And back on the concrete, the sawing done, the older boys left the sides hanging overnight in the winter cold to firm the meat for cutting.

By now it was noon, time for lunch, and you went in with a sort of pride that you had done this important work, and there on the table was meat some other boys had killed on some other ceremonial day. It was bloody work, of course, and sometimes I have wondered how adults could ask children to do such work, but it was part of a coherent way of life, as important as plowing or seeding or mowing or baling hay. It had a context, and I was literary enough even then to understand that burning the guts had a sacrificial significance. We could always have limed them and dumped them into a ditch. Lord knows they didn't burn easily.

I never saw our farm manager more upset than the day we were getting ready to butcher five pigs. He shot one through the nose rather than through the brain. It ran screaming around the pen, and he almost cried. It took two more bullets to finish the animal off, and this good man was shaking when he had finished. "I hate that," he said to me. "I hate to have them in pain. Pigs are so damned hard to kill clean."

But we don't farm anymore. The coherence is gone. Our loves are no longer the loves of flint and iron, but of the nightingale and the rose, and so we delegate our killing. Our farm manager used to sleep in the sheep barn for nights on end to be sure he was there to help the ewes deliver their lambs, ewes being so absentminded they sometimes stop labor with the lamb only halfway out. You saw the beginning and the end on the farm, not merely the prepackaged middle. Flint and iron, friends, flint and iron. And humility, and sorrow that this act of killing must be done, which is why in those days good men bowed their heads before they picked up their forks.

| # In Quest of Value

NORMAN COUSINS
A Game of Cards

Several years ago Norman Cousins contributed the essay reprinted below to a series of brief personal credos by important public figures. These were later published in a book entitled *This I Believe*. That title clarifies the subject and the purpose of Cousins' essay—a terse declaration of his views on the nature and the destiny of man.

The analogy that gives this essay its title is one of the most effective uses of that rhetorical technique to be found in this textbook.

(1) Ever since I was old enough to read books on philosophy I have been intrigued by the discussions on the nature of man. The philosophers have been debating for years about whether man is primarily good or primarily evil, whether he is primarily altruistic or selfish, cooperative or competitive, gregarious or self-centered, whether he enjoys free will or whether everything is predetermined.

(2) As far back as the Socratic dialogues in Plato, and even before that, man has been baffled about himself. He knows he is capable of great and noble deeds, but then he is oppressed with the evidence of great wrongdoing.

(3) And so he wonders. I don't presume to be able to resolve the contradictions. In fact, I don't think we have to. It seems to me that the debate over good and evil in man, over free will and determinism, and over all the other contradictions — that this debate is a futile one.

For man is a creature of dualism. He is both good and evil, both altruistic and selfish. He enjoys free will to the extent that he can make decisions in life, but he can't change his chemistry or his relatives or his physical endowments — all of which were determined for him at birth. And rather than speculate over which side of him is dominant, he might do well to consider what the contradictions and circumstances are that tend to bring out the good or evil, that enable him to be nobler and a responsible member of the human race. And so far as free will and determinism are concerned, something I heard in India on a recent visit to the subcontinent may be worth passing along. Free will and determinism, I was told, are like a game of cards. The hand that is dealt you represents determinism. The way you play your hand represents free will.

(4) Now where does all this leave us? It seems to me that we ought to attempt to bring about and safeguard those conditions that tend to develop the best in man. We know, for example, that the existence of fear and man's inability to cope with fear bring about the worst in him. We know that what is true of man on a small scale can be true of society on a large scale. And today the conditions of fear in the world are, I'm afraid, affecting men everywhere. More than twenty-three hundred years ago, the Greek world, which had attained tremendous heights of creative intelligence and achievement, disintegrated under the pressure of fear. Today, too, if I have read the signs correctly in traveling around the world, there is great fear. There is fear that the human race has exhausted its margin for error and that we are sliding into another great conflict that will cancel out thousands of years of human progress. And people are fearful because they don't want to lose the things that are more important than peace itself — moral, democratic, and spiritual values.

(5) The problem confronting us today is far more serious than the destiny of any political system or even of any nation. The problem is the destiny of man: first, whether we can make this planet safe for man; second, whether we can make it fit for him. This I believe — that man today has all the resources to shatter his fears and go on to the greatest golden age in history, an age which will provide the conditions for human growth and for the development of the good that resides within man, whether in his individual or his collective being. And he has only to mobilize his rational intelligence and his conscience to put these resources to work.

QUESTIONS AND EXERCISES

VOCABULARY
1. altruistic (*paragraph* 1)
2. gregarious (1)
3. determinism (3)
4. disintegrated (4)
5. mobilize (5)

LANGUAGE AND RHETORIC
1. Does this essay have a specific thesis? If so, what is it? If not, why is there no thesis?
2. Aside from their introductory purpose, what is the function of the first two sentences, and what is the relationship between them?
3. Comment on the effectiveness of the card-game analogy. Is it valid? Is it really enlightening? Explain why or why not.
4. Does the use of *only* in the last sentence tend to make that statement an oversimplification? Support your answer.
5. This essay is composed of two parts. What paragraphs comprise each of the parts, what sentence links the two, and what is the relationship between them.

DISCUSSION AND WRITING
1. What is your reaction to the author's view of man's nature? That is, on what points do you agree with him, and on what points do you disagree? Explain your reasons for both.
2. In paragraph 3 the author refers to "circumstances . . . that enable him [man] to be nobler and a responsible member of the human race." In paragraph 4 he says, "we ought to attempt to bring about and safeguard those conditions that tend to develop the best in man." Does Cousins suggest what any of these circumstances or conditions are? What might he have in mind?
3. Do you agree with the statement in paragraph 4 that "the existence of fear and man's inability to cope with fear bring about the worst in him"? Explain why or why not. If you do agree, give examples or reasons to support your position. If you do not agree, explain what you believe brings about the worst in man.
4. Support or refute the contention in paragraph 4 that there is great fear affecting men everywhere in the world today. What specific fears do you feel, and what do you think might be done to overcome them?
5. Write an essay comparable in scope and plan to this one, in which you explain your beliefs about the nature and destiny of man.

H. L. MENCKEN
On the Meaning of Life

Like Norman Cousins in the preceding selection, H. L. Mencken is responding here to a request for an expression of his personal beliefs on the meaning of life. He opens with a statement that reflects his assignment and indicates his purpose in writing; he then considers the satisfactions that life offers him, and in doing so he touches on the importance of work, on man's relationship to man and to God, and on man's fate.

In considering the rhetorical aspects of this essay, note the author's broad purpose and then observe what effect this has in terms of thesis and structure.

(1) You ask me, in brief, what satisfaction I get out of life, and why I go on working. I go on working for the same reason that a hen goes on laying eggs. There is in every living creature an obscure but powerful impulse to active functioning. Life demands to be lived. Inaction, save as a measure of recuperation between bursts of activity, is painful and dangerous to the healthy organism — in fact, it is almost impossible. Only the dying can be really idle.

(2) The precise form of an individual's activity is determined, of course, by the equipment with which he came into the world. In other words, it is determined by his heredity. I do not lay eggs, as a hen does, because I was born without any equipment for it. For the same reason I do not get myself elected to Congress, or play the violoncello, or teach metaphysics in a college, or work in a steel mill. What I do is simply what lies easiest to my hand. It happens that I was born with an intense and insatiable interest in ideas, and thus like to play with them. It happens also that I was born with rather more than the average facility for putting them into words. In consequence, I am a writer and editor, which is to say, a dealer in them and concocter of them.

(3) There is very little conscious volition in all this. What I do was ordained by the inscrutable fates, not chosen by me. In my boyhood, yielding to a powerful but still subordinate interest in exact facts, I

wanted to be a chemist, and at the same time my poor father tried to make me a business man. At other times, like any other relatively poor man, I have longed to make a lot of money by some easy swindle. But I became a writer all the same, and shall remain one until the end of the chapter, just as a cow goes on giving milk all her life, even though what appears to be her self-interest urges her to give gin.

(4) I am far luckier than most men, for I have been able since boyhood to make a good living doing precisely what I have wanted to do — what I would have done for nothing, and very gladly, if there had been no reward for it. Not many men, I believe, are so fortunate. Millions of them have to make their livings at tasks which really do not interest them. As for me, I have had an extraordinarily pleasant life, despite the fact that I have had the usual share of woes. For in the midst of those woes I still enjoyed the immense satisfaction which goes with free activity. I have done, in the main, exactly what I wanted to do. Its possible effects upon other people have interested me very little. I have not written and published to please other people, but to satisfy myself, just as a cow gives milk, not to profit the dairyman, but to satisfy herself. I like to think that most of my ideas have been sound ones, but I really don't care. The world may take them or leave them. I have had my fun hatching them.

(5) Next to agreeable work as a means of attaining happiness I put what Huxley called the domestic affections — the day to day intercourse with family and friends. My home has seen bitter sorrow, but it has never seen any serious disputes, and it has never seen poverty. I was completely happy with my mother and sister, and I am completely happy with my wife. Most of the men I commonly associate with are friends of very old standing. I have known some of them for more than thirty years. I seldom see anyone, intimately, whom I have known for less than ten years. These friends delight me. I turn to them when work is done with unfailing eagerness. We have the same general tastes, and see the world much alike. Most of them are interested in music, as I am. It has given me more pleasure in this life than any other external thing. I love it more every year.

(6) As for religion, I am quite devoid of it. Never in my adult life have I experienced anything that could be plausibly called a religious impulse. My father and grandfather were agnostics before me, and though I was sent to Sunday-school as a boy and exposed to the Christian theology I was never taught to believe it. My father thought that I should learn what it was, but it apparently never occurred to him that I would accept it. He was a good psychologist. What I got in Sunday-school — beside a wide acquaintance with Christian hymnology — was simply a firm conviction that the Christian faith was full of palpable absurdities, and the Christian God preposterous. Since

that time I have read a great deal in theology—perhaps much more than the average clergyman—but I have never discovered any reason to change my mind.

(7) The act of worship, as carried on by Christians, seems to me to be debasing rather than ennobling. It involves grovelling before a Being who, if He really exists, deserves to be denounced instead of respected. I see little evidence in this world of the so-called goodness of God. On the contrary, it seems to me that, on the strength of His daily acts, He must be set down a most stupid, cruel and villainous fellow. I can say this with a clear conscience, for He has treated me very well—in fact, with vast politeness. But I can't help thinking of his barbaric torture of most of the rest of humanity. I simply can't imagine revering the God of war and politics, theology and cancer.

(8) I do not believe in immortality, and have no desire for it. The belief in it issues from the puerile egos of inferior men. In its Christian form it is little more than a device for getting revenge upon those who are having a better time on this earth. What the meaning of human life may be I don't know: I incline to suspect that it has none. All I know about it is that, to me at least, it is very amusing while it lasts. Even its troubles, indeed, can be amusing. Moreover, they tend to foster the human qualities that I admire most—courage and its analogues. The noblest man, I think, is that one who fights God, and triumphs over Him. I have had little of this to do. When I die I shall be content to vanish into nothingness. No show, however good, could conceivably be good forever.

QUESTIONS AND EXERCISES

VOCABULARY

1. metaphysics (*paragraph* 2)
2. insatiable (2)
3. volition (3)
4. inscrutable (3)
5. devoid (6)
6. agnostics (6)
7. palpable (6)
8. debasing (7)
9. puerile (8)
10. analogues (8)

LANGUAGE AND RHETORIC

1. Why does this selection have no specific thesis? How would you characterize its structure? Is it tightly or loosely organized? What is the relationship between thesis and structure in this article?
2. Two brief analogies are employed here: the comparison with the hen in paragraphs 1, 2, and 4; and the comparison with the cow in paragraphs 3 and 4. Comment on their effectiveness.
3. What is Mencken's dominant means of paragraph development?

4. How many paragraphs in this essay have their topic sentences in either the first or a combination of the first and second sentences?
5. What method of attaining coherence dominates paragraph 8?
6. What tone characterizes this selection? Point out words and passages that reflect it.

DISCUSSION AND WRITING
1. Do you believe "the precise form of an individual's activity is determined . . . by his heredity"? Support or refute this idea.
2. Do you agree or disagree with the statement in paragraph 4 that not many men make their livings at tasks that interest them? Give examples to support your position.
3. What do you think of a person who, like the author, does what he wants to do with little or no interest in his effect on other people? What are your reasons for feeling as you do?
4. The author finds his greatest means of attaining happiness in work and in relationships with family and friends. What is yours?
5. In paragraph 7 the author says that he finds little evidence of the "so-called goodness of God." Do you? If so, what is it?
6. Write a short essay like this one in which you explain what one thing gives you the most satisfaction from life.

JOHN CIARDI

Is Everybody Happy?

The "pursuit of happiness" is, according to our Constitution, an in-alienable right of every American. But how do we go about that pursuit, and how do we know when we are happy, if we do not really know what happiness is? In this essay John Ciardi examines three different con-cepts of happiness, charging that the ideas of happiness either as a matter of possession or as a matter of spiritual being are equally misleading. He then proposes an idea of happiness that avoids the two extremes without ignoring them, that defines happiness as neither a thing nor a state but a process.

Notice how the author employs definition and comparison as his primary methods of development.

(1) The right to pursue happiness is issued to Americans with their birth certificates, but no one seems quite sure which way it ran. It

may be we are issued a hunting license but offered no game. Jonathan Swift seemed to think so when he attacked the idea of happiness as "the possession of being well-deceived," the felicity of being "a fool among knaves." For Swift saw society as Vanity Fair, the land of false goals.

(2) It is, of course, un-American to think in terms of fools and knaves. We do, however, seem to be dedicated to the idea of buying our way to happiness. We shall all have made it to Heaven when we possess enough.

(3) And at the same time the forces of American commercialism are hugely dedicated to making us deliberately unhappy. Advertising is one of our major industries, and advertising exists not to satisfy desires but to create them — and to create them faster than any man's budget can satisfy them. For that matter, our whole economy is based on a dedicated insatiability. We are taught that to possess is to be happy, and then we are made to want. We are even told it is our duty to want. It was only a few years ago, to cite a single example, that car dealers across the country were flying banners that read "You Auto Buy Now." They were calling upon Americans, as an act approaching patriotism, to buy at once, with money they did not have, automobiles they did not really need, and which they would be required to grow tired of by the time the next year's models were released.

(4) Or look at any of the women's magazines. There, as Bernard DeVoto once pointed out, advertising begins as poetry in the front pages and ends as pharmacopoeia and therapy in the back pages. The poetry of the front matter is the dream of perfect beauty. This is the baby skin that must be hers. These, the flawless teeth. This, the perfumed breath she must exhale. This, the sixteen-year-old figure she must display at forty, at fifty, at sixty, and forever.

(5) Once past the vaguely uplifting fiction and feature articles, the reader finds the other face of the dream in the back matter. This is the harness into which Mother must strap herself in order to display that perfect figure. These, the chin straps she must sleep in. This is the salve that restores all, this is her laxative, these are the tablets that melt away fat, these are the hormones of perpetual youth, these are the stockings that hide varicose veins.

(6) Obviously no half-sane person can be completely persuaded either by such poetry or by such pharmacopoeia and orthopedics. Yet someone is obviously trying to buy the dream as offered and spending billions every year in the attempt. Clearly the happiness-market is not running out of customers, but what is it trying to buy?

(7) The idea "happiness," to be sure, will not sit still for easy definition: the best one can do is to try to set some extremes to the idea and then work in toward the middle. To think of happiness as

acquisitive and competitive will do to set the materialistic extreme. To think of it as the idea one senses in, say, a holy man of India will do to set the spiritual extreme. That holy man's idea of happiness is in needing nothing from outside himself. In wanting nothing, he lacks nothing. He sits immobile, rapt in contemplation, free even of his own body. Or nearly free of it. If devout admirers bring him food he eats it; if not, he starves indifferently. Why be concerned? What is physical is an illusion to him. Contemplation is his joy and he achieves it through a fantastically demanding discipline, the accomplishment of which is itself a joy within him.

(8) Is he a happy man? Perhaps his happiness is only another sort of illusion. But who can take it from him? And who will dare say it is more illusory than happiness on the installment plan?

(9) But, perhaps because I am Western, I doubt such catatonic happiness, as I doubt the dreams of the happiness-market. What is certain is that his way of happiness would be torture to almost any Western man. Yet these extremes will still serve to frame the area within which all of us must find some sort of balance. Thoreau—a creature of both Eastern and Western thought—had his own firm sense of that balance. His aim was to save on the low levels in order to spend on the high.

(10) Possession for its own sake or in competition with the rest of the neighborhood would have been Thoreau's idea of the low levels. The active discipline of heightening one's perception of what is enduring in nature would have been his idea of the high. What he saved from the low was time and effort he could spend on the high. Thoreau certainly disapproved of starvation, but he would put into feeding himself only as much effort as would keep him functioning for more important efforts.

(11) Effort is the gist of it. There is no happiness except as we take on life-engaging difficulties. Short of the impossible, as Yeats put it, the satisfactions we get from a lifetime depend on how high we choose our difficulties. Robert Frost was thinking in something like the same terms when he spoke of "The pleasure of taking pains." The mortal flaw in the advertised version of happiness is in the fact that it purports to be effortless.

(12) We demand difficulty even in our games. We demand it because without difficulty there can be no game. A game is a way of making something hard for the fun of it. The rules of the game are an arbitrary imposition of difficulty. When the spoilsport ruins the fun, he always does so by refusing to play by the rules. It is easier to win at chess if you are free, at your pleasure, to change the wholly arbitrary rules, but the fun is in winning within the rules. No difficulty, no fun.

(13) The buyers and sellers at the happiness-market seem too often

to have lost their sense of the pleasure of difficulty. Heaven knows what they are playing, but it seems a dull game. And the Indian holy man seems dull to us, I suppose, because he seems to be refusing to play anything at all. The Western weakness may be in the illusion that happiness can be bought. Perhaps the Eastern weakness is in the idea that there is such a thing as perfect (and therefore static) happiness.

(14) Happiness is never more than partial. There are no pure states of mankind. Whatever else happiness may be, it is neither in having nor in being, but in becoming. What the Founding Fathers declared for us as an inherent right, we should do well to remember, was not happiness but the *pursuit* of happiness. What they might have underlined, could they have foreseen the happiness-market, is the cardinal fact that happiness is in the pursuit itself, in the meaningful pursuit of what is life-engaging and life-revealing, which is to say, in the idea of *becoming*. A nation is not measured by what it possesses or wants to possess, but by what it wants to become.

(15) By all means let the happiness-market sell us minor satisfactions and even minor follies so long as we keep them in scale and buy them out of spiritual change. I am no customer for either puritanism or asceticism. But drop any real spiritual capital at those bazaars, and what you come home to will be your own poorhouse.

QUESTIONS AND EXERCISES

VOCABULARY
1. felicity (*paragraph* 1)
2. insatiability (3)
3. pharmacopoeia (4)
4. orthopedics (6)
5. catatonic (9)
6. perception (10)
7. purports (11)
8. static (13)
9. inherent (14)
10. cardinal (14)

LANGUAGE AND RHETORIC
1. Explain the reference to "Vanity Fair" in the first paragraph.
2. What is the meaning of the first sentence in paragraph 15? How does the author connect the concluding paragraph with the opening paragraph?
3. In paragraph 7 the author defines happiness from the points of view of a materialist and an Indian holy man. In paragraph 10 he presents Thoreau's idea of happiness. Reread the section of Chapter Two dealing with definition (pp. 63–69), and then fashion each of these three definitions of happiness into a minimum, formal definition.
4. What is the relationship of paragraph 11 to 10 and of paragraph 12 to 11?
5. Paragraph 9 provides an excellent example of a skillfully constructed, coherent paragraph. Explain how each sentence points backward and forward to the sentences preceding and succeeding it.

6. What is the thesis of this essay? Locate the paragraphs that explicitly reveal the author's views on happiness.
7. The author's tone is serious but not solemn, instructive but not dogmatic. Indicate how the thesis and the diction of this essay reveal this tone. Examine in particular paragraphs 2, 7, 9, and 13.
8. Find examples of the effective use of parallel structure.

DISCUSSION AND WRITING
1. What *is* happiness? How do *you* define it? Write an essay in which you attempt to define happiness, using specific examples rather than abstract language.
2. The author states that we Americans "seem to be dedicated to the idea of buying our way to happiness." What basis does he have for this conclusion? Do you agree with him? Explain why or why not.
3. Does advertising exist "not to satisfy desires but to create them"? Select some popular and effective advertisements, and examine them in the light of this statement. Write an essay about your conclusions.
4. Do you feel that the happiness of the contemplative man as described in paragraphs 7 and 8 is as illusory as "happiness on the installment plan"? What are the reasons for your answer?
5. Do you agree with the author that happiness depends on effort, that "there is no happiness except as we take on life-engaging difficulties"? Explain why or why not.
6. How does the author distinguish among "having," "being," and "becoming"? What does he mean by these terms? He argues that happiness is exclusively tied to becoming. Can you make a case for happiness as having or happiness as being?

CARL ROGERS
On No Longer Being Ashamed of America

I have never been a joiner or a supporter of *causes*. All my professional life I have preferred to work in the areas in which I have competence. I have been a revolutionary with a narrow focus.

Now, however, I believe that our culture is facing a life-and-death crisis on many fronts and that I have an obligation as a citizen to speak out. I am frightened about our destiny as a people, as a nation. I will

"On No Longer Being Ashamed of America" by Carl Rogers. From *Journal of Humanistic Psychology,* Fall 1972. Reprinted from *Intellectual Digest,* March 1973. Reprinted by permission of the author and the publishers.

discuss only those issues for which we have much of the know-how, or technology or funds to solve. These are issues that we could move toward solving if we had the individual and collective *will*.

Cities

Our large urban centers are seemingly ungovernable, choking on their own traffic, becoming insufferable garbage-littered ghettos, and rapidly becoming financially as well as psychologically bankrupt. Yet, according to the British economist Barbara Ward, by the year 2000 some 80 percent of us will be living in such cities.

In this incredible influx into the cities, it might be well to consider some lessons learned from a study of rats. John Calhoun designed an experiment in which one dominant male rat could keep any others from entering some sections of the experimental area. But no rat could dominate the central section. All the rats in every area had sufficient food and water and could breed as they wished.

The rats multiplied, of course, but in the areas controlled by a dominant male, overcrowding was not excessive. In the central un-controlled area, there was serious overcrowding accompanied by poor mothering, poor nest building, high infant mortality, bizarre sexual behavior, cannibalism and often complete alienation. More ominous still, the central area, with all its bad conditions, had a certain magnetic pull. The rats crowded together in it. Females in heat would leave the protected areas and head for the central area; many never returned.

The resemblance to human behavior is frightening. In humans we see poor family relationships, lack of caring, complete alienation, magnetic attraction of overcrowding and lack of involvement so great that it permits people to watch a long drawn-our murder without so much as calling the police.

We have not availed ourselves of the alternatives. We need to turn loose some of our city planners or, better yet, to unleash creative innovators like Buckminster Fuller, scrap our obsolete building codes and instruct these people to build small urban centers, designing them for human beings and human life. We could build smaller cities with great park and garden areas, with neighborhoods of all races and all economic levels. The human planning—both before and during the building of such a community—would be fully as important and as well financed as the architectural planning.

We know how to carry out every aspect of this. The only element lacking is the passionate determination that says, "Our cities are inhuman. They are ruining lives and mental and physical health at a devastating rate. We are going to change this, even if it costs us money!"

Marriage

It seems clear to me that conventional long-term marriage is either on its way out or will be greatly modified. I am not very concerned about this because I believe that the partners often find that the dissolution of the marriage constitutes a step toward their own growth. Then, too, the path is open for a wide variety of experimentation in styles of marriage. The one thing that is clear is that we are seeking man-woman relationships that will have permanence only to the degree to which they satisfy the emotional, psychological, intellectual and physical needs of the partners.

There are two issues that do concern me about marriage. The first is the incredible lack of education in interpersonal relationships. A young couple I interviewed recently had lived together for three years. After quarreling all of one evening—a rather common occurrence—they suddenly decided to get married. There was a rationale of sorts behind this bizarre decision. The man believed that marriage would resolve all their difficulties. He was surprised that it did not, and only during the interview did it seem to dawn on him that perhaps achieving a satisfactory marriage might take time and effort! It angers me that neither of these young people had received the slightest education in man-woman relationships. Here again we have all the necessary know-how, but we define education so narrowly that it excludes everything about living.

The other issue troubling me is that we have been both unimaginative and irresponsible regarding children, particularly children of divorced parents. First the child is torn by the stresses between his mother and father. Then he finds that we usually label one parent guilty. Next we shuttle the child back and forth between the two warring adults. Yet we know, quite accurately, what children need—continuing love and caring, a sense of stability, several sources of support and care and a feeling of being trusted. We have just never decided to *act* on behalf of the welfare of our children.

Race

Running like a fever through our culture are the attitudes we hold, mostly at the unconscious level, toward blacks, Chicanos, Indians and women. Dr. Norman Chambers, a black, and Dr. Lawrence Carlin, a blond Nordic, have worked with many black-white groups and with some Chicano-Anglo groups. They have invented a game called "Pleasantville." Pleasantville is the home of a new industry that employs many black workers new to the town. It's just a game, but the whites are astonished at the ease with which they can express the most bitter anger toward the blacks. Meanwhile, the blacks can voice their rage, and the polarization is out in the open for all to see.

The outcomes are an experiential, gut-level learning of racist attitudes on the part of the whites and a rare opportunity for honest confrontation on the part of the blacks. The surprising result is that they tend to become persons to each other and can talk openly and freely without reference to stereotypes or color.

Schools

There is just a slim chance that our schools and colleges may change rapidly enough to escape total irrelevance and total death. The most dramatic proof that we know how to bring education not only into the twentieth century but even into the twenty-first is the rapid change taking place in the public schools of Louisville Kentucky. This is an inner-city school system in which two years ago 83 percent of the pupils were below the national norm in achievement. Fourteen schools were made a special pilot project. Principals and teachers agreed to communicate fully and freely regardless of rank, to rely on consensus rather than coercion, to make decisions on the basis of competence rather than personal power, and to create a classroom atmosphere in which feelings had as much of a place as task-oriented behavior.

It is too early to know the final outcome, but the ferment is tremendous. The 14 schools are facing many problems, but the problems now are how to bring about change, how to live as a process, not how to prevent change.

Violence

I am very frightened by what seems to me a steady drift toward an authoritarian state. Imagine that in 1962 I told you about a country in which these events were taking place: students, both rebellious and completely innocent, have been teargassed, beaten and killed by police and militia. Members of a militant dissident party have been shot in their beds by police. Major trials are not for acts committed but for conspiracy to commit such acts — in other words, one can be found guilty of an intention. The military, as well as the espionage agency, is spying on thousands of citizens who are breaking no law. Young men by the thousands are refusing to serve in the armed forces. Every major city and state is training police and soldiers to suppress citizen riots. Brilliant and dedicated student and religious leaders and leading members of minority groups are serving prison terms for defying the government. Persons are harassed and arrested by the police for no other reason than wearing unusual clothing or having long hair.

If I had told you about such a nation in 1962, you would have asked what nation could be so ugly. It is humiliating beyond words to realize that we are that nation in 1972.

What can we do? A small number of young people are turning to violence. I can understand how an individual could become so bitter, so desperate to bring about change, that violence would seem like a possible channel of action. But the most obvious result of violence would be to bring in a totalitarian regime, which could take generations to undermine.

Face

Our courts have wrestled unsuccessfully to define obscenity. I would like to suggest a simple definition: the Southeast Asian war. It offended common decency; it was repulsive; it had no redeeming social value.

For 12 years we fought a war in Vietnam in which we changed our purposes several times, indicating that as a nation we did not know why we fought there.

We wrought enormous havoc in North Vietnam, doing our best to destroy its economy, its military and its people. Why did it take us so long to stop that incredible slaughter and waste and destruction, that sordid, interminable war? I believe it was because we were unable to admit that we had made a horrible, massive *mistake*. We could not bear to lose face.

The one thing we might gain from this incredible tragedy is a clear view of the enemy. If we peer closely through the blood and death and awful ruin, we can see the enemy clearly. He is *us*.

The New Person

What can we do about the creeping police state and our insensate warring? My answer is a version of Charles Reich's thesis. When enough people think through and believe and *live* a set of convictions based on a new value system, present institutions must change or fall.

In 1969 I spelled out some of the characteristics of the new, powerful person emerging in our culture and the vital, different set of values he both maintains and lives. I stressed his hatred of phoniness, his opposition to all rigidly structured institutions, his desire for intimacy, closeness and community, his willingness to live by new and relative moral and ethical standards, his searching quality, his openness to his own and others' feelings, his spontaneity, his activism and his determination to translate his ideals into reality. I am talking about a relatively small number of people. But I believe that these people constitute the change agents of the future. When some part of a culture is decayed at the core, a small group with new views, new convictions and a willingness to live in new ways is a ferment that cannot be stopped.

We are going to have a new America, in my judgment, an America of change and flow, of people rather than objects. We have the know-how to bring about this new America. And now, in an increasing number of significant persons, we have the determination and the will to create it. I think it is not unrealistic to believe that there will come into being a portion of the global community, residing on this North American continent, of which we will no longer be ashamed but in which we will feel a quiet, peaceful pride.

Indexes

INDEX TO READING SELECTIONS BY BASIC RHETORICAL TYPE

(Most selections are listed under more than one method.)

408

INDEX TO QUESTIONS ON LANGUAGE
AND RHETORIC

B   4
C   5
D   6
E   7
F   8
G   9
H   0
I   1
J   2